TELEVISION AND
RADIO ANNOUNCING

TELEVISION AND RADIO ANNOUNCING

Fifth Edition

Stuart W. Hyde

San Francisco State University

HOUGHTON MIFFLIN COMPANY   BOSTON
Dallas   Geneva, Illinois   Lawrenceville, New Jersey
Palo Alto

Once again,
to my wife, Allie, and to our children,
Stuart, Jr.,
John Christian, and
Allison Elizabeth Ann

Cover Credit

Norm Stelfox/Image Finders, Vancouver, Canada

Text Credits

Definitions adapted and reprinted by permission from the *American Heritage Dictionary, Second College Edition.* Copyright © 1982 by Houghton Mifflin Company.

From *The Complete Plays and Poems of William Shakespeare,* edited by William Allan Neilson and Charles Jarvis Hill. Copyright © 1942 renewed 1969 by Caroline Steiner and Margaret N. Helburn. Used by permission of Houghton Mifflin Company.

Printed in the U.S.A.

Library of Congress Catalog Card Number: 86–81341

ISBN: 0–395–35939–2

CONTENTS

Chapter 7   **FOREIGN PRONUNCIATION**   **175**

PREFACE

Television and Radio Announcing is designed to help you become a more effective communicator, and it emphasizes the communication and performance skills that are essential for a successful announcer. Like its predecessors, this Fifth Edition is a comprehensive and practical introduction to the diverse field of broadcast performance, and it covers many topics: careers; ad-libbing; working with equipment; pronunciation, voice, and usage; and specialized announcing techniques, from news reporting and interviewing to delivering commercials and play-by-play sports announcing.

New practice material includes several award-winning radio and television commercials. More copy with suggestions for interpretation appears in this edition. Practice material for foreign pronunciation now includes several news stories featuring names and words in Spanish, German, French, and Italian. Other languages are also represented, and foreign names and other words in those languages are given pronouncers. The Pinyin system for the pronunciation of Chinese words is included for the first time.

In this edition, radio news and television news have been given expanded coverage in separate chapters. New material there and elsewhere explains how the jobs of announcers have been affected by changes in broadcast technology, including compact discs, satellite uplinks, direct-drive turntables, and improved microphones, audio consoles, and portable cameras and recorders.

Individuals familiar with earlier editions of this text are aware that it advocates no single approach to the teaching of announcing. Rather, the text offers a wealth of useful material on both the mechanics and communicative value of announcing that permits instructors and students to evaluate and select the material most applicable to their needs. Although it may be said that the text provides too much information to be covered easily in a single semester, it is also true that the text provides ample material for subsequent years of study, practice, and reference.

Finally, a bit of advice for students who are using this book for a required course. Though you may not intend to become an announcer, a study of announcing will be of great benefit to you for other reasons. Everyone talks, not just announcers. In fact, most of our contact with other persons involves spoken communication. Consequently, an effort to improve your voice quality, diction, vocabulary, and ability to express yourself will pay high dividends.

For students who are interested in other aspects of broadcasting, a course in announcing will benefit you in several ways. In addition to improving your ability to express yourself with confidence, you will profit from this study whether you intend to become a writer, a producer, a director, or an executive. In short, a course in announcing deserves your best efforts, for in a certain sense, broadcasting centers on the performer.

S. W. H.

ACKNOWLEDGMENTS

In preparing the fifth edition of *Television and Radio Announcing*, I consulted with several dozen professional broadcasters, colleagues, instructors, equipment manufacturers, and advertising agency personnel. To all who helped, I extend sincere thanks for your cooperation and suggestions and your interest in the project.

Among my colleagues who provided special help are Dr. Stanley T. Donner, Professor Emeritus of the University of Texas at Austin; Ernie Kreiling, Professor of Telecommunications and syndicated television columnist; and Professors Herbert L. Zettl, Rick Houlberg, Herbert Kaplan, and John Hewitt, all of San Francisco State University. Special thanks go to Arthur Asa Berger, who drew the cartoons showing radio and television hand signals and to Professor Paul C. Smith, audio coordinator for the Broadcast Communication Arts Department at San Francisco State University. Paul is responsible for most of what I know about audio.

I am grateful to the following individuals who read the manuscript and made helpful suggestions for improvement: Dan Baker, California State University at Long Beach; Theodore Clevenger, Florida State University; Elbert Coalwell, KCUR Radio in Kansas City, Missouri; John S. Gibson, University of Texas at Arlington; Ann Harper, Butler University, Indianapolis, Indiana; Ralph E. Hillman, Middle Tennessee State University; Bruce Klopfenstein, Bowling Green University, Ohio; William Torrey, American University, Washington, D.C.; David Tucker, Wilkes College, Wilkes-Barre, Pennsylvania.

I am grateful also to Chet Casselman, who once again allowed me to use his excellent suggestions for writing news copy. Peter Cleaveland of ABC Radio News and Wayne Freedman of KRON-TV shared with me their techniques for producing both radio and television news packages.

Sports directors and announcers who were generous with their help include Don Klein, voice of the San Francisco 49ers; Art Popham, independent sports producer, Tacoma, Washington; and Walt Brown, former play-by-play announcer for the University of Arizona.

Broadcast personnel from KRON-TV who helped include Mike Ferring, news director; Darryl Compton, associate news director for operations; Todd Hanks, engineer; Mark Thompson, meteorologist; Bob McCarthy, traffic reporter; news anchors Bob Jiminez and Evan White; urban affairs specialist Belva Davis; and political analyst Rollin Post.

At KGO-TV, I was helped by co-hosts Terry Lowry and Fred LaCosse of "AM San Francisco" and by Jan Landis, Senior Producer of that show. Also at KGO-TV, help was extended by meteorologist Pete Giddings, news anchor Janet Zappala, floor director Joey Smith, and medical specialist Dr. Dean Edell.

At WBZ-TV, I received assistance from Andrew Radin, television news publicist; news anchor Jack Williams; talk show host Buzz Luttrell; and floor director Patsy Wheeler.

Radio station KFRC personnel were generous in updating my knowledge of popular music broadcasting. My appreciation is extended to Dave Sholin, program and music director; chief engineer Philip Lerza; production director Albert Lord; and disc jockey Bobby Ocean.

KTIM personnel who helped include Phyllis Gordon, Susan Bice, Lori Rose, Michael Fox, Bill Monihan, and Jeffrey Schaub. Thanks also to newscaster Leslie Lang of KTOB.

Jim Eason of KGO Radio assisted in the preparation of the material on radio talk shows, and James M. Staudenraus of United Press International provided information about the services of UPI.

Disc jockeys Pete Kelly of KZST, Santa Rosa; Fred Wayne of KFTY, Santa Rosa; Sherry Mouser of KSRO, Santa Rosa; and Rob Taylor of KTOB, Petaluma are thanked for posing for photos.

News reporters Randy Shandobil and Jay Sondheim of KTVU, Nancy Fleming and Jack Hansen of KGO-TV, Valerie Mihanovich of KCBS, and Mary Ward of KRON-TV are thanked for their help.

Advertising agencies that supplied copy for the book include Ammirati & Puris, Inc.; Ketchum Communications; Cunningham & Walsh, Inc.; Grey Advertising, Inc.; McDonald & Little Advertising; and Ingalls Associates, Inc.

Special assistance was provided by the following persons and their advertising agencies: Jim Deasy and Cindy Mills of Allen & Dorward; Gerry Sher of KABL; Mia Detrick of Peaches & Cream; and Paul C.

Mesches of Backer & Spielvogel Advertising. Chuck Blore of Chuck Blore & Don Richman, Incorporated, provided some of the most creative copy in the book.

Additional thanks go to Del Gundlach, creator of *Cheep Laffs*, freelance announcer Peter Scott, and Troy Alders of TLA Productions.

Equipment manufacturers who supplied photos include RCA; Beyer Dynamic, Inc.; Shure Brothers, Inc.; Electro-Voice, Inc.; Sony Corporation of America; Sennheiser Elec. Corp.; Swintek Enterprises, Inc.; Crown International, Inc.; Gotham Audio Corporation; AKG Acoustics, Inc.; Pacific Recorders & Engineering Corporation; Autogram Corporation; Studer Revox America, Inc.; Auditronics, Inc.; and Automated Processes, Inc.

TELEVISION AND
RADIO ANNOUNCING

1
BROADCAST ANNOUNCING

This book is about human communication, with a focus on the electronic media of radio and television. Its purpose is to help you improve your communication skills. Studying this subject can be of lasting benefit whether or not you intend to become a broadcast performer. Confident, effective expression has always been an invaluable tool. Today, with the ever-increasing significance of electronic media, competence in their use may become nearly as important as literacy was a century ago. This book is an aid toward developing media literacy.

In one sense, then, this book is about television and radio announcing. It discusses announcing as a profession, treats both the technical and the performance aspects of the field, covers correct usage of American and Canadian English, contains chapters on the major areas of specialization within the field, and provides broadcast copy for practicing performance skills.

In a broader sense, this book is about communication. If you apply yourself to the task, you can look forward to noticeable improvements in your abilities to (1) make pleasant speech sounds, (2) clearly articulate the speech sounds of the English language, (3) vary pitch and volume effectively, (4) pronounce words according to accepted standards, (5) select and use words, phrases, similes, and metaphors effectively, (6) express yourself confidently, (7) interpret copy, (8) speak ad lib, and (9) communicate ideas lucidly, both orally and through nonverbal communication.

The regular use of audio and videotape recorders can be of immense help in your development as a broadcast performer. After hearing and seeing yourself perform over a period of several weeks, you should begin to note and correct annoying mannerisms, speech malpractices, voice deficiencies, and personal idiosyncrasies that displease you. As

FIGURE 1.1
Disc jockey Sherry Mouser delivers a commercial live. Her microphone is a Sennheiser MD421U. (Courtesy KSRO, Santa Rosa, California)

you make adjustments and improve, you will gain confidence, and this, in turn, should guarantee further improvement. Although you may have to rely on a department of broadcasting for regular practice with a videotape recorder, an audio recorder of adequate quality can be obtained for a very small investment. If you are serious about becoming an effective communicator, you should purchase and use an audio recorder.

THE BROADCAST ANNOUNCER

The announcer is a product of the electronic age, but several related professions preceded that of the broadcast announcer by centuries or even by millennia. Preliterate storytellers, troubadours, the singers of psalms, town criers, and newspaper journalists of a later age all performed roles similar to those of modern announcers, for each was charged with providing a service to a public. With some, the emphasis was on the delivery of information; with others, the emphasis was on entertainment. Announcers are related to storytellers in that they speak directly to their audiences. Radio announcers also resemble writers of the print medium in that they often describe events not personally seen by their audiences. Television reporters and news anchors, on the other hand, frequently describe events while viewers are seeing live or on tape the event being described. In this, television reporters

FIGURE 1.2
News anchor Jack Williams works with both a hand-held script and a prompting device. (Courtesy WBZ-TV, Boston. Photo by Sarah Hood.)

and news anchors can be compared only with the narrators of news-reels of pretelevision days.

Despite the similarities that announcers share with people of earlier professions, there are some important differences. Both radio and television reach vast audiences, scattered over thousands of miles. In addition, radio and television possess instantaneousness. It was one thing for an oral historian to describe for the people of Macedonia the triumph of Alexander over the Persians; it was quite another thing for millions of Americans to hear H. V. Kaltenborn give a live report of a battle during the Spanish civil war. Radio made it possible for the first time in history to describe to millions of people events happening at that very moment. It was because of the opportunities radio presented for instantaneous communication over great distances, together with the fact that radio is a ''blind'' medium, that announcers became indispensable. Radio could not function without the services of people who provided direct oral communication and who described events, introduced entertainers, or read the news.

On radio, the announcer is the clarifying link between the audience and otherwise incomprehensible sound, noise, or silence. On television, the announcer is the presenter, the communicator, and the interpreter. The announcer is, thus, as important to the broadcast media as any person can be. Without such performers, both radio and televi-

FIGURE 1.3
Talk show host Buzz Lut-
trell interviews guests
during a live talk show,
"People Are Talking."
(Courtesy WBZ-TV, Bos-
ton. Photo by Sarah
Hood.)

sion as we know them would be impossible. Because announcers usually make direct presentations to their audiences, they represent economy as well. No other means of disseminating information is so swift
or need be so brief as the word spoken directly to the listener. Small
wonder, then, that radio and television announcers must be equipped
with native talent, undergo intensive training, possess broad educa-
tional backgrounds, and work diligently at practicing the skill. Their
function is important and the responsibility is considerable.

We use a variety of terms to describe announcers, among them *personalities, disc jockeys, hosts, narrators,* and *reporters.* Some people in
several categories of broadcast performance do not like to be called
announcers. Among them are news anchors, reporters, commentators,
sportscasters, and narrators. Specialization and codification have certainly made more precise nomenclature possible; when clarity demands it, it should be used. The term *announcer* will be used throughout this book for economy whenever the profession is being discussed
in general terms.

An announcer is anyone who speaks to an audience over radio or
television, through cable or other closed-circuit audio or video distribution, or electronic amplification, as in an auditorium or theater. Singers, actors, and actresses are considered announcers only when they
perform that specific function, as in commercial presentations. Announcing specializations are many and include the following:

FIGURE 1.4
News reporter Aleta Carpenter records a field report for a newscast. (Courtesy KDIA, Oakland, California)

Broadcast journalism:

reporters—field, special assignment, general assignment
anchors, or news readers
analysts
commentators
weather reporters
consumer affairs reporters
environmental reporters
entertainment reporters
farm news reporters
business news reporters
sports reporters

Sports:

play-by-play announcers
play and game analysts

Music:

disc jockeys
classical music announcers

Public affairs:

interviewers
panel moderators

Commercials:
voice-over announcers (television)
demonstration-commercial announcers (television)
straight oral presentation announcers (radio)

Narration:
readers of film and video documentaries

Acting as host or hostess on special programs:
talk shows (television)
phone-in talk shows (radio)
"magazine" shows ("Evening Magazine," "Entertainment Tonight"—
    television)
dance, popular music shows (television)
ballet, modern dance shows (television)
featured films
children's programs
game shows

Staff announcing:
readers of station breaks (radio and television)
readers of *trouble copy* (such as "please stand by"—television)
introducers of featured films (when title is not seen on screen)

There are also single-subject specialists who contribute to talk shows
or newscasts on subjects such as gardening, cooking, exercise, consumerism, science, art, and health. Other announcers record books
and newspapers for the blind. During parades shown on television,
announcing teams identify the participants, explain float construction,
and provide "color." Corporate and industrial audio and video productions often require the services of narrators. As you can see, there
are many announcing specializations, any one of which may be well
suited to your speech personality.

**EMPLOYMENT AS
AN ANNOUNCER**

According to the U.S. Department of Labor, approximately fifty-five
thousand men and women are currently employed as broadcast announcers. Most of these are full-time employees of radio and television
stations and networks. Many others are full- or part-time free-lance

FIGURE 1.5
Dr. Dean Edell produces
his daily program on
health and medicine from
his small office-studio.
(Courtesy Dr. Dean Edell
and KGO-TV, San
Francisco)

announcers, performing as narrators for both broadcast and nonbroadcast documentaries and instructional tapes. Because many free-lance
announcers work only sporadically, we may assume that not more
than sixty thousand persons earn their full income as radio and television announcers. The rapid expansion of cable television services, including all-news and all-sports cable operations, has created additional
opportunities for announcers, but the field remains highly competitive. The announcer who can offer a station more than announcing skills has a better chance for initial employment and career ad-
vancement than does a narrowly trained specialist. It should also be
observed that between 80 and 85 percent of all broadcast announcers
work for radio stations and radio networks. Your chances for success
as an announcer, then, will be enhanced if you prepare chiefly for
radio and if you bring to your job the ability to sell time, write and
produce local commercials, prepare weather reports, write or rewrite
the news, or program the computer at an automated station.

A growing number of men and women work not in broadcast stations but in industrial media. Audiotapes, video cassettes, and slide-
tape presentations are made for a variety of purposes, including em-

FIGURE 1.6
Urban affairs specialist
Belva Davis researches a
report, using a computer
terminal connected to a
data bank. (Courtesy
KRON-TV, San Francisco)

ployee training, introduction of new products, dissemination of information to distant branches, and similar in-house communications. The term *industrial media* is a loose one, for it applies to the media operations of hospitals, government agencies, schools, prisons, and the military, as well as those of industries. Few training or media departments can afford the services of a full-time announcer or narrator, so, if such work appeals to you, you should prepare for media writing and producing as well as announcing. One or more courses in message design and testing would serve you well.

The following chapters indicate the working conditions and the kinds of abilities you will need to succeed in each of the major announcing specializations. If you are a typical student of announcing, you probably are interested in one of three attractive job possibilities: news reporting, sports announcing, or music announcing. Few students show much enthusiasm for commercial delivery or for interviewing. This may be understandable, but you should resist the temptation to concentrate on one kind of announcing. It is true that most radio stations follow a single format—all music, all talk, all news—but the chances are that you will not find your first job at a station that features the format of your choice. You should, therefore, work on every facet of announcing, even while you emphasize the area of announcing in which you ultimately hope to specialize.

Television stations provide multiprogram service, but aside from the news and public affairs departments, they employ relatively few announcers. There are far more employees working in sales, traffic, and engineering than there are in announcing. Local television stations *do* produce commercials, and they also run commercials produced by local and regional production companies. This means that even the smallest community with a commercial television station may offer some work for announcers. If this field interests you, you can get specific information about how announcers are hired by calling the production unit of the sales or promotion department of the station. If a talent agency is involved in local production, you can find "Agencies, Theatrical" in your local telephone directory. A call to such an agency will provide you with information about how to present yourself for possible employment.

EDUCATION AND TRAINING

The subject matter of radio is not radio, nor is the content of television television. Both these influential media devote their hours of broadcast to nonbroadcast disciplines such as news, weather, music, sports, and drama. Though you should learn performance techniques and the history and theory of mass communication, you should not limit your study to these areas. The ability to talk knowledgeably about broadcasting, to manipulate consoles, turntables, and tape cartridge units, and to interpret skillfully a script prepared by someone else is necessary for employment, but you must offer more to the station and the public. Radio and television have little room for empty-headed announcers. For one thing, the broadcast announcer is being evaluated by increasingly sophisticated listeners. Americans are better informed today than they used to be. Informational media are reaching more people with more messages than ever before. A television generation has grown up to be quick to spot clichés and gimmicks.

Moreover, as radio stations have moved away from the policy of offering something for everyone toward special-appeal formats, they have attracted more homogeneous audiences that know and care about the program material being offered. Hence the majority of listeners to a single-format radio station are quick to detect and resent an announcer's lack of knowledge.

The dramatic explosion of knowledge in the past several years will make announcers who do not grow with the times inadequate for the 1980s and 1990s. The makers of dictionaries have been adding new

FIGURE 1.7
Bessie Moses translates
the news into the Inupiaq
Eskimo language. (Cour-
tesy KICY, Nome, Alaska)

words to their editions at an unprecedented pace; each represents to an announcer not only a new word to pronounce but a new concept, a new technological breakthrough, a newly perceived human condition, or a new phenomenon to know about.

Finally, both radio and television have increased considerably the number of broadcast hours devoted to unscripted presentations. Television program hosts and hostesses, radio disc jockeys, interviewers, announcers covering sports and special events, and talk show personalities use written material only occasionally; most of the time they are on their own. With such independence comes the need to have much information at hand to share with the audience.

What should you study if you intend to become an announcer? There are three general areas to consider. First, you should pursue subjects that will prepare you for your first announcing job; second, you should select courses that will enable you to offer one or more specializations beyond straight announcing; third, you must obtain a broad background in the liberal arts and sciences. The following lists of courses are arranged under the three categories, respectively. You may not be able to study all suggested areas, but you should at least discuss them with an advisor. If you are serious about an announcing career, your education must have breadth.

Announcing Training

Look for courses teaching the following skills:

Radio and television announcing, including interpretation, articulation, phonation, microphone use, camera presence, pronunciation, ad-libbing, script reading, and adapting the individual personality to the broadcast media

The International Phonetic Alphabet (IPA) (If your broadcasting department does not teach this, look to the speech department.)

Foreign language pronunciation (Most departments of music offer a course in "lyric diction," teaching principles of pronunciation of French, German, Italian, and occasionally Russian or Spanish.)

Skills of control room operations, including practice in manipulating audio consoles, tape cartridge machines, compact disc players, reel-to-reel tape recorders, and turntables

Small-format video production and editing (Some television stations expect field reporters to be able to tape and edit news stories.)

Writing for radio and television (Many stations expect announcers to write commercial copy, news, public-service announcements, and station promotional pieces.)

Education for Specialized Duties

Look for courses to prepare you for jobs in the following areas:

Broadcast journalism—courses in journalism, international relations, political science, economics, history, and geography.

Broadcast sales and advertising—courses in business, marketing, accounting, sales technique, sales promotion, and audience research.

Sports and play-by-play announcing—courses in history of sports, sports officiating, and the sociology of sport.

Weather reporting—meteorology, weather analysis, weather forecasting, and geography.

General Education

Look for courses that examine the following topics:

Social, ethical, aesthetic, and historical perspectives of broadcast communication

One or more of the nonelectronic arts—music, theater, literature, or art

Social and behavioral sciences—courses in psychology, sociology, political science, urban studies, and ethnic studies

Quantitative reasoning—essentially, mathematics and computational methods

One area of preparation is so important that it requires separate mention and explanation. Broadcast stations rely heavily on the use of computerized information systems. For years computers have been used at automated stations; now there are few areas of broadcast operations that do not make some use of computers. Among other applications, computers are central to most videotape editing systems, character generators, word processors, some graphics systems, scheduling and billing systems, and data-retrieval systems. In most of these applications, a specialized language—such as FORTRAN or COBOL—is not required. Some familiarity with information systems is highly desirable, and an ability to type well is mandatory. A course in information science should be selected with care, for most are not geared toward applications common in the broadcasting industry.

Certainly you must evaluate these suggestions in the light of your own aptitude, interests, and career plans. Any college counselor can

FIGURE 1.8
News anchor Bob Jiminez discusses last-minute script changes during a newscast. (Courtesy KRON-TV, San Francisco)

help you determine the appropriateness of these and other subjects. The important point is that only you can apply your growing knowledge to your announcing practice.

The typical community college requires 60 semester hours for the associate in arts or the associate in science degree; the typical four-year college or university requires about 125 semester hours for a bachelor's degree. Modern departments of broadcasting invariably require courses in history of broadcasting, writing for the electronic media, broadcast research, and communication theory. Whether you are enrolled in a two- or a four-year program, it is unlikely that you will be offered more than six semester hours of performance courses. You should, therefore, seek performance opportunities wherever they present themselves—on a campus radio station, in television directing and producing classes, or on public access cable stations. Remember, though, that the majority of your class hours will be spent in nonperformance courses.

If your goal is only to get your personality on the air or if you feel that you have a good liberal arts education, perhaps you should go to the most efficient and economical source of skills training: a good and reputable trade school. A strong word of caution is warranted. Some trade schools are neither reputable nor economical. Beware of broadcasting schools that try to convince you that scores of stations will want your services, that announcing is all glamour and little work, that "anyone can make it as an announcer," that all announcers earn huge sums of money, or that "age is no barrier to employment." Before enrolling in any broadcasting school, seek the advice of practicing broadcasters or professors of broadcasting. Ethical trade schools will welcome your caution and may even refer you to responsible people for advice.

As you have seen, announcing encompasses a wide range of activities. Most modern liberal arts colleges and their broadcasting departments are well equipped to help you begin the process of becoming a competent and versatile communicator, for that is what you must be if you expect to be able to face challenges such as these:

1. You are a staff announcer, and you are to read a commercial for a local restaurant featuring international cuisine. You must pronounce correctly *vichysoisse, coq au vin, paella, saltimbocca alla Romana,* and *Hasenpfeffer.*
2. You are a staff announcer, and you must read news headlines

including the place names Sault Sainte Marie, Schleswig-Holstein, Santa Rosa de Copán, São Paulo, and Leicester.

3. You are the announcer on a classical music program, and you need to know the meanings and correct pronunciation of *scherzo, andante cantabile, Die Götterdämmerung,* and *L'Après-midi d'un faune.*

4. You are a commercial announcer, and the copy for a pharmaceutical company demands that you correctly pronounce *hexachlorophene, prophylaxis,* and *epidermis.*

5. You are a play analyst on a sports broadcast, and you need to obtain extensive historical and statistical information on football in order to fill inevitable moments of inactivity.

6. You are the play-by-play announcer for a semipro baseball game, and you must pronounce the following American names: Martineau, Buchignani, Yturri, Sockolow, Watanabe, Engebrecht, and MacLeod.

7. You have been sent to interview a Nobel Prize winner in astrophysics, and you need to obtain basic information about the subject as well as biographical data.

8. You are narrating a documentary, and you must analyze the intent and content of the program to determine the mood, rhythm, structure, and interrelationship of sound, picture, and script.

9. You are covering a riot, and you are expected to assess responsibly the human dynamics of the incident.
10. You are a radio disc jockey, and you are on duty when word is received of the unexpected death of a great American (a politician, an entertainer, or a scientist). Until the news department can take over, you must ad-lib appropriately.

Obviously, no one type of course will completely educate you as an announcer.

THE ANNOUNCER'S RESPONSIBILITY

Before committing yourself to a career as a broadcast announcer, you should ponder the fact that, along with the undeniable privileges and rewards that accrue to people working in this field, there are several areas of responsibility as well. First of all, and most obvious, there is the obligation any performer owes to the audience: that of being informative, objective, fair, accurate, and entertaining. Not everyone who goes before an audience deserves respect. Announcers who are sloppy, unprepared, given to poor American English usage, or just plain boring may get what they deserve—a two-week notice. But there

FIGURE 1.10
Close-up of Kay Rogers reading the time on a specially adapted clock. For closer timing, she uses a darkroom timer with Braille markings. (Courtesy KEAR, San Francisco)

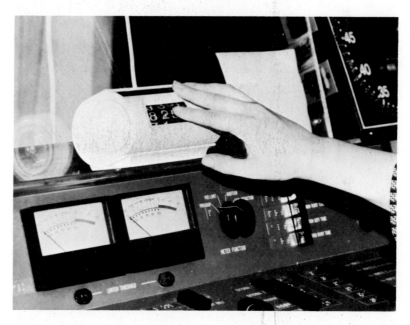

are others who work hard, possess outstanding skill, and never want for work but who, at the same time, pollute the public air. These are the announcers who sensationalize or slant the news, who seriously misrepresent shoddy products, who circulate unfounded rumors, or who fan the flames of prejudice by displaying misguided fervor. In a free society, such announcers are protected by the First Amendment to the Constitution; the only protection the audience has resides in the integrity of each individual announcer.

Another area of responsibility is that of emergency notification. During times of floods, hurricanes, tornadoes, and other natural disasters, broadcast announcers are frequently in a position to save lives through early warnings. The U.S. government has established an emergency

FIGURE 1.11
Television talk show hostess Terry Lowry elicits a question from the audience. (Courtesy "AM San Francisco," KGO-TV, San Francisco)

broadcast system that relies on broadcast licensees to disseminate disaster information. It is imperative that all broadcast announcers study the disaster manual (it is found at all stations) and be prepared to act swiftly and appropriately in an emergency.

Finally, there is the area of social responsibility. This goes beyond the normal responsibility of performer to audience. Nearly all announcers, whether they like it or not, influence society by their visibility and prestige. Years ago, Paul F. Lazarsfeld and Robert K. Merton perceived and described the "status-conferral function" of the mass media. In essence, they said, the general public attaches prestige to people who appear on the mass media and are more readily influenced by prestigious people than by equals. The public's reasoning is circular: "If you really matter, you will be at the focus of attention; and, if you *are* at the focus of mass attention, then you must really matter." A newscaster, then, is not simply an efficient conveyor of information; as a radio or television "star," the newscaster is trusted and believed in as a qualified authority. Even the entertainment show announcer or the disc jockey has automatic, though sometimes unwarranted, prestige.

FIGURE 1.12
Traffic reporter Bob McCarthy reports live during newscasts from a helicopter. (Courtesy Bob McCarthy and KRON-TV, San Francisco)

As an announcer in any of the broadcast media, you should be aware of your status and measure up to it.

Not all announcers have a sense of social commitment, and not all who do are in a position to accomplish very much. Still, you should be aware of the opportunities you may have to enlighten or confuse the public. As a nation, we have been slow to perceive and attack serious problems of urban deterioration; increasing crime; pollution of land, air, and water; racial inequities; poverty; the rise of antidemocratic action groups; and increased use of drugs. If you are committed to using the mass media to make a better society, you are already responsible and potentially important as the kind of communicator demanded by our times.

2
THE ANNOUNCER
AS COMMUNICATOR

Your goal as a radio or television announcer is to *communicate ideas or feelings effectively to other human beings*. This brief and rather obvious statement is the key to success in announcing. Understanding that effective communication ought to be your goal is by no means the same thing as achieving it. For some, the ability to communicate comes easily and is readily adapted to radio or television performance. For most, however, the difficulties in being effective, economical, and accurate even in daily conversation are constant reminders that much work lies ahead. This chapter discusses the communicative process and offers specific advice on interpreting copy. At the end of the chapter, ad-lib announcing is briefly considered.[1]

Unfortunately, some announcing students feel that they have succeeded when they have developed the ability to "sound like an announcer." American broadcasting has been served by several generations of announcers, and during that time a particular style of delivery has evolved. Despite the fact that top announcers in any part of the country reflect unique speech personalities, they are far outnumbered by announcers who strive for the voice quality, phrasing, and pronunciation of the stereotyped announcer. Good announcing is not imitation; it is *communication*. Top announcers retain their individuality as they concentrate on getting their messages across. True communication as an announcer begins when you *learn who you are, reflect yourself in your delivery, and know that you are speaking to individuals, not to a crowd*. Merely developing your vocal apparatus or expanding your vocabulary cannot guarantee that you will become an effective com-

---

[1] To ad-lib is to improvise and deliver one's remarks spontaneously. It is an abbreviation of the Latin *ad libitum* (literally "to the desire"), but it means "to be performed with freedom."

municator. Try always to be aware of two other aspects of effective oral communication: reflecting your personality and communicating the ideas or feelings inherent in the words you are uttering.

Announcers must be effective in each of several modes: ad-libbing, ad-libbing from notes, script reading with preparation, and script reading from *cold copy*—copy not seen by the announcer until the very moment of delivery. Typical of ad-lib announcers are radio and television field reporters, weather reporters, sports play-by-play announcers, radio disc jockeys, television talk show hosts and hostesses, and radio phone-in talk show hosts and hostesses. News anchors often see some of their copy for the first time as it appears on a prompting device. At the other extreme are documentary narrators and readers of recorded commercials; hours—sometimes days—are required for them to achieve the results demanded by a producer. You should practice all these modes until you feel comfortable with each of them.

One of your most challenging tasks as an announcer is to read in an effective manner copy written by someone else. You are the middle link in a chain that begins with a writer and ends with a listener or viewer. It is your responsibility to bridge the two in such a way that the writer's ideas are faithfully represented in the minds of your listeners.

PRINCIPLES OF EFFECTIVE COMMUNICATION

Copy begins not as a script but as ideas in the mind of a writer: an advertising agency copywriter, a news writer, a documentary scriptwriter, a station sales representative, or some other specialist in broadcast writing. Having conceived the idea, the writer's next step is to cast it into words (and in television, into pictures) that will best communicate the thoughts. The ability to select fresh, effective words and arrange them well is the art of broadcast writing; the ability to communicate these words effectively is the art of announcing.

Radio and television are media of oral communication. As a professional announcer, you can make messages more effective than they would be if communicated directly via the written word. On a basic level, you will not misread or mispronounce words; on another level, you will convey an emotion appropriate to your copy—enthusiasm, seriousness, jocularity—and will thereby provide variety and interpretation for your listeners; on yet another level, you will show the relative importance of the various parts of your message, thus enhancing its meaning. In short, you will present the material in its most persuasive and readily understood form.

Oral communication, however, can be ineffective when radio or television announcers fail to present their material clearly and convincingly. Too many professional announcers merely read words and consider themselves successful if they avoid stumbling over them. A word is a symbol of an idea; if the idea is not clear in your mind, or if you lack the ability to transmit it effectively through your spoken words, you reduce your chances of communicating the idea to your listener. Of course, reading words with little or poor interpretation conveys some of the ideas from writer to listener, but this is not good announcing, and no amount of rationalizing can justify it. Announcers are paid to be effective, and this means that they must develop far more than adequate oral reading skills.

Make it a point to listen to as many news reporters and commercial announcers as you can and study their deliveries. Listen especially to those you have come to avoid. Decide for yourself who among them are mere readers of words and who are true communicators. In all probability you will discover that you have unconsciously formed the habit of tuning in the announcers who communicate best and tuning out those who communicate least. Lay persons may not think in terms of the communicative ability of a given announcer, but they are nonetheless affected by it. They find themselves unconsciously listening to those who are best able to help them receive and assimilate ideas. They are being swayed to causes, concepts, and products at the same time, however subtly.

Many television announcers do a consistently better job of communicating than do their counterparts on radio because the visual medium demands that they give some physical interpretation to the words they speak. Eyes and facial expression, and sometimes hands and arms, convey meaning to the viewer.

Radio announcers who believe that only their voices are important may attempt to project vitality without body motion. Such playacting is unlikely to be convincing. Energy is easy to simulate, but unless the speaker is genuinely motivated by the content of the message, it usually seems phony. Uncalled-for enthusiasm hinders communication. To avoid it, you should announce for radio as though your listener were in the booth with you. You should use your face, hands, and body as you speak, as you do in ordinary conversation. Integrating all the tools of communication should help clarify and intensify your message, despite the fact that your listener cannot see you. Good physical gesturing for both radio and television is marked by two considerations: (1) honest motivation and (2) harmony with the size and moods of the ideas being expressed. Oversized grins, frowns, and grimaces and sweeping arm movements taught to generations of declaimers are seldom appropriate in radio and television.

If merely reading words constitutes a low level of oral communication, what is good oral communication? *Good communication occurs when the listener or viewer receives an undistorted and effective impression of the ideas of the writer or of the ad-lib speaker, with proper emphasis on each of the parts that make up the whole.* Basic to good interpretation is a thorough understanding of the material to be presented. Just as a musician or conductor must understand the intentions of the composer, so the announcer must understand the intentions of the writer. With the exceptions of the ad-lib announcer, the disc jockey, and people who write their own copy, the announcer is an interpretive rather than a creative artist. Announcers, like musicians, often create their own material, but most serve as a link between creator and audience.

Furthermore, the art of the musician is not just manufacturing beautiful tones or demonstrating great technical skill; it is also faithfully interpreting and executing the intention of the composer. However beautiful your voice may be and however rapidly and unfalteringly you may be able to read copy, you are not truly a good announcer unless you use your ability to communicate the ideas and the values of the writer as the writer originally conceived them.

INTERPRETING COPY

Understanding the intention of the writer is more difficult and demanding than is commonly thought. Many specific considerations must be discussed at length. Stanley T. Donner, Professor Emeritus of the University of Texas at Austin, has prepared an excellent approach to analyzing copy. He suggests that you work very seriously with the following points, using them as a check list when approaching new copy. Newscasters and disc jockeys very often read their copy without preparation, because the pressures of their work do not allow for it. But it is no exaggeration to say that their effectiveness in interpreting copy quickly is possible only because, at some time in their careers, they undertook deliberate and methodical practice. Using the suggested check list for serious analysis of various types of copy, you will become able to size up new copy almost unconsciously. While you still have the luxury of time, establish a solid foundation for the analysis of copy.

1. Read the copy twice to get the general meaning.
2. State the specific purpose of the copy in one brief sentence.
3. What is the general mood of the copy?
4. Where does the mood change?
5. What are the parts of the copy? What is the structure of the copy?
6. What help is the punctuation in reading the copy?
7. Are there any words or allusions you do not fully understand or cannot pronounce?
8. Read the copy aloud.
9. Do you have any genuine interest in the subject matter of the copy? Do you reveal this interest?
10. Who is your listener? Can you visualize him or her? Are you able to establish rapport? Are you actually talking to him or her?
11. If the copy is literary, who is the author?
12. Should you know anything about the origin and background of this copy?
13. Do you need to do any characterization?

This list of considerations suggests much more than might seem obvious at first reading. Let us elaborate on Donner's points.

1. *Read the copy twice to get the general meaning.* One problem confronting anyone who spends time and effort preparing copy for oral delivery is that too much concentration on pronunciation or timing may obscure the overall meaning and purpose. You should form an impression of the whole piece by silently reading through it at least twice before undertaking any of the more detailed work of preparation.

2. *State the specific purpose of the copy in one brief sentence.* This is the most important decision you will make. You must discern the major objectives of the copy. Just as it is pointless to begin a trip to some undetermined destination only to wonder why you did not arrive at a satisfactory place, so it is foolish to begin interpreting copy without first knowing its goal. Your job as an oral interpreter is choosing appropriate means; it is first necessary to determine appropriate ends. The interpretations of two identical sentences will differ if the sentences are used in different contexts or for different purposes; similarly, pieces of broadcast copy that seem superficially to call for the same delivery may actually require quite different interpretations. Raising questions about the purpose of the copy will help determine this.

Read this commercial and determine its specific purpose:

ANNCR: See the all—new Jaguar, on display tomorrow at the Foreign

Motorcar Centre, 16th and Grand. You'll love the Jaguar's

styling and appointments. If you love automobiles, come

see the new Jaguar tomorrow!

If you decided that the purpose of this copy is to awaken curiosity and interest in the new Jaguar, you analyzed the copy correctly. If you decided that its purpose is to promote the name and address of the sponsor, you were incorrect. The phrase "at the Foreign Motorcar Centre, 16th and Grand" is subordinate to the idea of the "all-new Jaguar." Though it is somewhat unusual to subordinate the name and address of the sponsor, the copy clearly indicates that it should be done in this instance. Perhaps the sponsor has the only foreign car agency in town, or perhaps sponsor identification has been built up over a long time by more conventional commercials. The moral here is that it is unsafe to decide automatically that the name and address of the sponsor is the phrase to be stressed in all copy.

Now read another commercial for the same sponsor:

ANNCR: See the fabulous Jaguar at the Foreign Motorcar Centre, at

16th and Grand. Serving you since 1933, it's the Foreign

Motorcar Centre, 16th and Grand in downtown River City!

Here phrases from the other commercial have been used, but it is obvious that in this version the name of the automobile is subordinate to the name and address of the sponsor. If you decided in analyzing this copy that its chief purpose was to impress on the audience the dealer's name, address, and reliability, you analyzed it correctly.

3. *What is the general mood of the copy?* Having determined the purpose of the copy, you may now determine its mood. To some extent the number of words in the copy limits the degree to which you can control the mood, especially in commercial copy. In the commercials for the Foreign Motorcar Centre, you must read 30 words in 10 seconds, or 180 words a minute, which is just about as rapidly as one should read aloud. In much radio and television work, excluding commercial announcements written with inflexible time limits in mind, the copy may be shortened or lengthened to allow for a rate of delivery geared to

a particular mood. The length of time taken for still other kinds of announcements—the introduction to a musical composition, for example—is not a particularly important consideration, although split-second timing frequently is (as we will see in Chapter 13 on the disc jockey). In sportscasting, the determinants of mood are set by the action of the game.

The mood of a piece of copy can be described as being ironic, jocular, serious, somber, urgent, sad, light, gloomy, sarcastic—or any of a number of other adjectives. Some copy is to be read in a straightforward manner with no apparent attempt to communicate a mood. Read the following news items, and jot down in the margin the dominant mood of each, including those that call for a straightforward delivery. Following these items, adjectives describing the mood of each are listed. The mood of each item, except the tornado reports, is to be revealed via only a hint of the emotion mentioned.

```
      1. (CHICAGO)  THE NATIONAL WEATHER SERVICE HAS

ISSUED TORNADO WARNINGS FOR THE ENTIRE UPPER MIDWEST. OF-

FICIALS SAY THAT CONDITIONS ARE SIMILAR TO THOSE THAT AC-

COMPANIED THE DEVASTATING STORMS OF MAY FIFTEENTH, IN

WHICH SEVENTY-ONE PERSONS WERE KILLED. SMALL-CRAFT WARN-

INGS HAVE BEEN RAISED FOR LAKE MICHIGAN, AND BOAT OWNERS

ARE URGED TO SECURE THEIR CRAFTS AGAINST THE EXPECTED

HEAVY WEATHER.

      2. (CLEVELAND)  AUTHORITIES HAVE CALLED OFF THE

SEARCH FOR A MISSING EIGHT-YEAR-OLD GIRL, SAYING THAT SHE

MAY HAVE BECOME THE THIRD VICTIM OF CLEVELAND'S PARKSIDE

KILLER. THE BODIES OF TWO GRADE-SCHOOL GIRLS WERE FOUND IN

THE WATERFRONT PARK LAST MONTH. THE MISSING GIRL, LYNN

JAMESON, DID NOT RETURN FROM SCHOOL LAST FRIDAY. HER LUNCH

PAIL AND SCHOOL BOOKS WERE FOUND IN THE PARK.

      3. (MIAMI)  A COAST GUARD OFFICIAL REPORT SAYS
```

THAT A CIVILIAN PILOT HAS REPORTED SIGHTING TWO MORE OIL
SLICKS OFF THE COAST OF FLORIDA NEAR FORT LAUDERDALE AND
WEST PALM BEACH. CLEAN-UP CREWS ARE STILL AT WORK ON A
MASSIVE OIL SLICK THAT SPREAD ONE WEEK AGO.

4. (WASHINGTON) THE FEDERAL ELECTION COMMISSION
HAS VOTED TO HALT SECRET CONGRESSIONAL "SLUSH FUNDS," A
PRACTICE IN WHICH LAWMAKERS USE PRIVATE DONATIONS TO PAY
PERSONAL AND OFFICE EXPENSES. THE COMMISSION UNANIMOUSLY
VOTED TO REQUIRE THAT ALL SUCH FUNDS BE PUBLICLY REPORTED.
THE DECISION REQUIRES THAT THE FUNDS COUNT TOWARD LAWMAK-
ERS' CAMPAIGN SPENDING LIMIT.

5. A BULLETIN HAS JUST BEEN HANDED ME THAT SAYS A
TORNADO HAS BEEN SPOTTED ABOUT TWENTY MILES FROM DULUTH.
THERE ARE NO ADDITIONAL DETAILS AT THIS TIME.

6. (WASHINGTON) THE GOVERNMENT SAID YESTERDAY
THAT PEOPLE ARE TAKING BETTER CARE OF THEMSELVES NOW THAN
EVER BEFORE, AND THAT THE PROBLEM NOW IS TO FIND WAYS TO
CARE FOR THE LARGE NUMBER OF PEOPLE WHO LIVE LONGER AS A
RESULT. THE REPORT SAID THAT SOCIETY'S SUCCESS IN KEEPING
PEOPLE HEALTHY AND HELPING THEM TO LIVE LONGER IS PLACING
GREAT STRESS ON THE NATION'S HEALTH CARE RESOURCES.

7. (QUEBEC) A CANADIAN RESEARCHER SAYS A SOLAR
DISTILLATION UNIT IS PROVIDING CLEAN WATER ON A DROUGHT-
STRICKEN ISLAND. RESEARCHER RON ALWARD OF QUEBEC SAYS HIS
WORK DEALS WITH THE USE OF SOLAR ENERGY ON THE ISLAND OF
LA GONAVE, OFF THE COAST OF HAITI. ALWARD SAYS RESIDENTS
OF THE SMALL FISHING AND FARMING COMMUNITY FORMED A

```
COOPERATIVE TO BUILD A SOLAR DISTILLATION SYSTEM TO PRO-

VIDE CLEAN WATER AFTER YEARS OF DROUGHT HAD DEPLETED THE

NATURAL SUPPLY.

        8.  (HUGO, OKLAHOMA)  IT TOOK EIGHTEEN DAYS, BUT

SEARCHERS HAVE FINALLY TRANQUILIZED ONE OF THE BABY

ELEPHANTS LOST IN THE DENSE SOUTHEASTERN OKLAHOMA BRUSH.

THE MANAGER OF THE CARSON AND BARNES CIRCUS SAYS THE

ELEPHANT WILL BE TIED TO A TREE IN AN EFFORT TO LURE THE

OTHER OUT OF HIDING.
```

Here are adjectives for these stories: (1) urgent, (2) somber, (3) angry, (4) slight note of victory—winning one for the public, (5) urgent, (6) light, (7) straightforward, (8) light, slightly humorous.

4. *Where does the mood change?* A long piece of copy may contain several moods, though the dominant one may remain constant. In commercial copy, one common construction calls for a change from gloom to joy as the announcer first describes a common problem (halitosis, loose dentures, irregularity) and then tells the listener how Product X can solve it. Spot such changes as you give your commercial a preliminary reading, and indicate them on your script. Unless the script calls for mock-serious delivery, be careful not to exaggerate the moods.

In narrating an extended television or film documentary or present-ing a five-minute or thirty-minute newscast, changes of mood are more numerous and more apparent. The next time you watch a newscast, make it a point to notice those changes; note too the devices the speaker uses to reflect the shifting moods. In carefully working out such changes in mood, the narrator or announcer contributes to the flow, unity, and overall meaning of the presentation.

In newscasting, as we have seen, changes in mood usually coincide with changes in news items. But many newscasts begin with brief headlines that call for several changes within a short span of time. Read these headlines, and determine the mood of each:

HERE IS THE LATEST NEWS:

OVER EIGHT INCHES OF RAIN HAS FALLEN ON SOUTHEAST

TEXAS IN THE LAST TWENTY-FOUR HOURS, AND THERE ARE REPORTS

OF WIDESPREAD DAMAGE AND SOME DEATHS.

A CHICAGO WOMAN WHO CLAIMED SHE KILLED HER HUS-

BAND IN SELF-DEFENSE AFTER TEN YEARS OF BEATINGS HAS BEEN

ACQUITTED BY AN ALL-MALE JURY.

A FOURTEEN-YEAR-OLD BOY HAS BEEN AWARDED THE

CITY'S HEROISM MEDAL FOR RESCUING AN INFANT FROM A SWIM-

MING POOL.

ON THE INTERNATIONAL SCENE, THERE IS RENEWED

FIGHTING IN EL SALVADOR BETWEEN GOVERNMENT TROOPS AND

GUERRILLAS, WITH HEAVY CASUALTIES REPORTED ON BOTH SIDES.

A THREATENED STRIKE OF MUSICIANS AND STAGE HANDS

AT THE CITY OPERA HAS BEEN AVERTED, AND THE SEASON WILL

TAKE PLACE AS SCHEDULED.

AND, THERE'S JOY AT THE ZOO TONIGHT BECAUSE OF

THE BIRTH OF A LITTER OF LIGERS--OR IS IT TIGONS?--ANYWAY,

THE FATHER IS A LION, AND THE MOTHER IS A TIGER.

I'LL HAVE DETAILS OF THESE AND OTHER STORIES AF-

TER THESE MESSAGES.

The mood implicit in each of these headlines requires flexibility in delivery with rapid changes of mood—a challenge facing newscasters daily.

5. *What are the parts of the copy? What is the structure of the copy?* Almost any example of well-written copy shows rather clearly differentiated parts. On the most basic level, copy may be broken down into its beginning, middle, and end. The beginning is the introduction and

customarily is used to gain attention. The middle, or body, contains most of the information. In commercials, the middle tells us the advantages of this product over all others. The end is generally used for summing up the most important points. It frequently urges action or repeats the name, address, and telephone number of the sponsor.

In most copy these three parts may be further subdivided. Commercial copy frequently follows this organization:

a. getting the attention of the listener or viewer
b. giving some concrete reason for further interest and attention
c. explaining step by step why this product or service is superior
d. mentioning or implying a price lower than the listener has been led to expect
e. repeating some of the selling points
f. repeating the name and address of the sponsor

This is the structure of a typical commercial. With practice, you will become able to size up the structure of such commercials in a matter of moments.

Here is an example of a commercial written according to this formula. Look for the parts of this commercial, and notice how they conform to the preceding six-part outline.

AGENCY: Deming Advertising, Inc.

CLIENT: Mertel Coffee Mills

LENGTH: 60 seconds

ANNCR: Are you a coffee lover? Most Americans are. Would you like to enter the world of gourmet coffees? Mertel's can help.

SFX: SOUND OF COFFEE BEING POURED INTO CUP

ANNCR: Gourmet coffee begins with whole beans, carefully selected, and freshly roasted.

SFX: SOUND OF COFFEE BEANS BEING GROUND

ANNCR: Gourmet coffee is ground at home, just before brewing. Choose your coffee according to your taste, and the time of day. A rich, but mild Mocha—Java for breakfast. A

hearty light French Roast for that mid-day pick-up. A
nutty Arabian with dinner. And a Colombian de-caf before
bed. Sound inviting? You bet. Sound expensive? Not so.
Mertel's Coffee Mills feature forty types of coffee beans
from around the world, and some are only pennies more per
pound than canned coffees. And, there's always a weekly
special. This week, it's Celebes Kalossi, at just $3.99 a
pound! Remember--if you want gourmet coffee, you <u>must</u>
begin with whole beans, and grind them just before
brewing. So, come to Mertel's Coffee Mills, and move into
the world of gourmet coffee! We're located at the Eastside
Mall, and on Fifth Street in downtown Russell. Mertel
Coffee Mills.

Outstanding commercials are both subtle and complex. Special consideration of the analysis of superior commercials will be found in Chapter 9.

6. *What help is the punctuation in reading the copy?* In addition to the symbols of ideas that we call words, writers have at their disposal a number of other marks that we call punctuation. They are of great potential help to the announcer, for they show the author's intentions regarding mood and meaning. They are equivalent to the marks indicating volume, tempo, and mood used by composers; no musician or conductor would consider disregarding these signs.

A famous example of disregarded punctuation occurs in Shakespeare's *A Midsummer Night's Dream.* Quince, one of the clowns, enters before the nobles of the realm and reads his prologue to the play *Pyramus and Thisbe* as though it were punctuated as follows:

> If we offend, it is with our good will.
> That you should think, we come not to offend,
> But with good will. To show our simple skill,
> That is the true beginning of our end.

Consider then we come but in despite.
    We do not come as minding to content you,
Our true intent is. All for your delight,
    We are not here. That you should here repent you,
The actors are at hand; and, by their show,
You shall know all that you are like to know.

You may have a good grasp of punctuation, but the section that follows is intended to relate that knowledge to *broadcast copy*. It asks for consistency and accuracy in the use of ellipses; it suggests an unusual use of question and exclamation marks; it states how certain marks, including quotation marks and dashes, should be vocally interpreted; and it lists several marks that you may use to mark your copy. Punctuation marks, like diacritical marks used to indicate pronunciation, are so small and differ so subtly that they cause occasional difficulties for an announcer—especially when the sight-reading of copy is required. Announcers working with written material must always maintain near-perfect eyesight; some announcers wear reading glasses during their air shifts although they need glasses at no other time. Wherever possible, you should review your copy prior to air time and, if you find it helpful or necessary, add to and enlarge punctuation marks. Some suggestions for the use of emphatic punctuation marks may be found on page 36. The section that follows reviews the chief marks and suggests their pertinence to announcers.

a. The *period* is used to mark the end of a sentence or to show that a word has been abbreviated. In copy written for broadcast, abbreviations such as FBI, NATO, and AFL–CIO are written without periods. Abbreviations such as Ms. and Mr. may appear with or without concluding periods. News writers often use ellipses to mark the ends of sentences and as a substitute for commas, dashes, semicolons, and colons—for example, "The Mayor was late to his swearing-in ceremony today. . . . He told those who had gathered for the ceremony . . . some two hundred supporters . . . that he had been held up in traffic." This practice is regrettable, but it is so widespread that you can expect, at some time, to be asked to work from copy so punctuated. And, should you become a news writer, chances are you will be expected to write copy in this style. Obviously, such punctuation is workable; the problem is that ellipses cannot indicate the shades of meaning conveyed by six other punctuation marks.

b. The *question mark* appears at the end of a sentence that asks a question. In marking copy it is helpful to follow the Spanish practice of placing an upside-down question mark (¿) at the beginning of a question, so that you will know it is interrogatory as you begin to read it.

c. The *exclamation mark* is used at the end of a sentence that demands some stress or emphasis. As with question marks, it is helpful to place an upside-down exclamation mark (¡) at the beginning of a sentence.

d. *Quotation marks* are used in broadcast copy for two different purposes: to indicate that the words between the marks are a word-for-word quotation and to substitute for italics. The first use is found extensively in news copy:

```
            . . . HE SAID AN ANONYMOUS MALE CALLER TOLD HIM TO

"GET OUT OF THE CASE OR YOU WILL GET BUMPED OFF."
```

In reading this sentence, you can indicate the quotation by the inflection of your voice, or you can add words of your own to make it clear that it is a direct quotation:

```
            . . . HE SAID AN ANONYMOUS MALE CALLER TOLD HIM TO

QUOTE, "GET OUT OF THE CASE OR YOU WILL GET BUMPED OFF."

END OF QUOTE.
```

In any event, do not say "unquote," since you cannot cancel out the quotation you have given.

Quotation marks are often used in news copy in place of italics:

```
            . . . HIS NEW BOOK, "READING FOR FUN," HAS BEEN ON

THE TIMES BEST SELLER LIST FOR THREE MONTHS.
```

e. The *semicolon* is used between main clauses that are not joined by *and, or, for, nor,* or *but.*

> ANNCR: The little boy dashed away through the night; his feet
>   made no sound on the dry pavement.

In reading a sentence that contains a semicolon, you should pause between the two clauses separated by the mark, but you should also indicate by inflection (in the example, on the words "night" and "his") that the two thoughts are related.

f. The *colon* is frequently used to introduce a long quotation such as the following:

> ANNCR: Senator Marble's reply was as follows: "I cannot conceive of any period in our nation's history when we were more in need of determined leadership than at present. We stand, today, at a crossroads."

A colon is also used before a list of several items, as in the following example:

```
EARTHQUAKES ARE COMMON TO CENTRAL AMERICAN NA-
TIONS: GUATEMALA, HONDURAS, NICARAGUA, EL SALVADOR, COSTA
RICA, PANAMA, AND BELIZE.
```

In reading a sentence that uses a colon, you should pause between the two words separated by the colon, but, as with the semicolon (to which the colon is related), you must indicate by inflection that the two phrases or clauses are related.

g. The *dash* (—) is a straight line, longer than but in the same position as the hyphen. In typewritten copy, the dash is customarily represented by two hyphens as --. It indicates hesitancy, an omission of letters or a name, or a sudden breaking of thought. Examples follow:

> ANNCR: We—we need to know.
> ANNCR: He looked around the room, but he couldn't seem to— wait a moment. Wasn't that a figure in the corner?

The dash is also used to summarize a preceding statement:

> ANNCR: Senator Marble has never lost sight of one very important fact of life—national defense.

In reading copy that uses a dash, you should first determine which of the rather different meanings just given is intended. If the purpose is to show hesitation or a break in the thought pattern, then the words preceding the dash should be read as though they are going to continue beyond the dash. When the break comes, it should come abruptly, as though you had no idea until you did so that you were going to stop. An exception to this occurs when the dash is combined with a mood of slowness and deliberation.

In using the dash to summarize a preceding statement, you should read the first part of the sentence as a build-up to the final statement, and the final statement should be read, after a pause, as though it is a summation and a crystallization of the entire idea expressed before the dash.

Dashes used in pairs may also set off a thought that interrupts or needs emphasis within a sentence. In this usage, the dashes could be replaced by commas, but emphasis would be lost.

> ANNCR: Senator Marble hoped that nothing—partisan politics, foreign pressures, or economic stresses—would cause a reduction in our armed forces.

When you are reading such a sentence, the phrase set off by dashes should be set apart by pauses, before and after. And, because the author set it apart for reasons of emphasis, it should be stressed by manipulating pace, volume, and voice quality.

h. Although parenthetical remarks (remarks that are important but not necessary to the remainder of the sentence) are used occasionally in radio and television copy, the same result is usually achieved with pairs of dashes. *Parentheses* are used in radio and television work to set apart the instructions to the audio operator, to indicate music cues, and to contain instructions or interpretations for the announcer, the actor, or the television camera director.

Parenthetical remarks are sometimes added to *newspaper copy,* usually for purposes of clarification, as in this example:

> Senator Johnson said that he called the widow and demanded that she "return my (love) letters immediately."

In this example a reader can see that (love) has been added by a reporter or editor. Identical copy used on the air could seriously misrepresent the senator's statement.

i. An *ellipsis* is an omission of words in a sentence. The mark that indicates such an omission is a sequence of three or four periods, as in the following example:

> ANNCR: Senator Marble stated yesterday, "I do not care what the opposition may think, I . . . want only what is best for my country."

In this example (which is rare in broadcast copy) ellipsis marks have been used to indicate that one or several words have been omitted from the original quotation. As mentioned before, some broadcast copywriters use a series of periods to indicate not an omission but a number of other things more properly accomplished by dashes, periods, commas, or colons:

> ANNCR: We hear next on the Sunday Symphony . . . Beethoven's "Eroica." Written in 1803–4, the work gives promise of the power which Beethoven . . . already 33 years of age . . . was just beginning to develop. Tremendous strength is the keynote of this composition . . . strength which flowed from a profound belief in his own ability.

To work with copy written with a series of periods taking the place of proper punctuation, you may want to repunctuate the copy, using appropriate marks.

j. The *comma* has several specific purposes but, generally speaking, it indicates a separation of words, phrases, or clauses from others to which they may be related but with which they are not necessarily closely connected in the structure of the sentence. Commas may link main clauses, separate a number of items in a series, separate a nonrestrictive modifier from the remainder of the sentence, indicate the name of a person being addressed or referred to ("I want you, John, to leave"), set apart an interjection ("I want you, let's see, at about five o'clock"), or set apart items in dates or addresses (Fresno, California; July 16, 1892).

The comma usually marks a pause in broadcast speech. Although the number of variations in the use of the comma prevents our making an exhaustive list of the ways in which it should be regarded, the comma frequently gives you an opportunity to pause briefly for breathing.

Because punctuation marks are quite small, most announcers have worked out systems of marking their copy that make use of marks that are much larger and, therefore, more readily seen. These are far from standard, but a few of the more commonly used marks follow.

a. A slanted line (/), called a *virgule,* is placed between words to approximate the comma.

b. Two virgules (//) are placed between sentences, or between words, to indicate a longer pause.

c. Words to be stressed are underlined.

d. Question marks and exclamation marks are enlarged.

e. Crescendo (∧) and decrescendo (∨) marks indicate that a passage is to receive an increase or a decrease in stress.

7. *Are there any words or allusions you do not fully understand or cannot pronounce?* To interpret someone else's copy, you must understand the meanings of the words. You should cultivate the habit of looking up all unfamiliar words in an authoritative dictionary. This means developing a healthy skepticism about your own vocabulary; through years of silent reading, you have probably learned to settle for approximate meanings of many words. For a quick test, how many of these words can you define and use correctly?

peer	impassible
burlesque	ordnance
fulsome	immerge
mendicant	apposite
catholic	ascetic

Check the definitions of these words in any standard dictionary. Some of these words are seen and heard frequently, whereas others only sound or look familiar. If you have correctly defined more than four of these words, you have an unusually large vocabulary.

Correct pronunciation of words is as important as accurate understanding. You should, therefore, be skeptical about your ability to pronounce words correctly. Check your familiarity with these words by writing them out phonetically:

drought	accessories
forehead	quay
toward	pestle
diphtheria	worsted

These words are correctly pronounced as follows:

WORD	INTERNATIONAL PHONETIC ALPHABET	DIACRITICS	WIRE-SERVICE
drought	[draʊt]	drout	(DRAWHT)
forehead	['fɔrɪd]	fôr'ĭd	(FOR'-IHD)
toward	[tɔrd]	tôrd	(TAWRD)
diphtheria	[dɪf'θɪriə]	dĭf-thîr'ē-ə	(DIFF-THIR'-EE-UH)
accessories	[æk'sɛsəriz]	ăk-sĕs'ər-ēz	(AK-SESS'-UH-REEZ)
quay	[ki]	kē	(KEE)
pestle	['pɛs,l̩]	pĕs'əl	(PES'-UHL)
worsted	['wʊstɪd]	wo͞os'tĭd	(WUHSS'-TIHD)

Appendix B is a pronunciation guide for about three hundred often mispronounced words. Use it to strengthen your ability to pronounce words according to accepted principles.

In addition to using and pronouncing words correctly, you must understand allusions in your copy. An allusion is an indirect, but pointed or meaningful, reference. A few common allusions are given in the following list. If you do not know their origin, search them out. The Bible, Shakespeare, and classical works are common sources; dictionaries of word origins, encyclopedias, and guides to mythology are also useful.

"He was hoist with his own petard."
"He found himself between Scylla and Charybdis."
"He was considered a quisling."
"She has a Shavian wit."
"She was given to spoonerisms."
"She was false as Cressida."
"He had the temper of Hotspur."
"He suffered as mightily as Prometheus."

You cannot expect to be familiar with all allusions in every piece of copy. During your career you may read copy written by hundreds or even thousands of people, each drawing on a separate fund of knowledge. You can, however, cultivate the habit of finding out about allusions not known to you. Self-discipline is required, because it is easy to convince yourself that context will make an allusion clear to an audience even if you do not understand it.

8. *Read the copy aloud.* Because you will perform aloud, you should practice aloud. Copy written for radio or television differs from copy written for newspapers, magazines, and books. Good broadcast copy usually makes poor silent reading. Short, incomplete, or ungrammatical sentences are often found in perfectly acceptable radio and television scripts:

> ANNCR: Been extra tired lately? You know, sort of logy and dull? Tired and weary—maybe a little cranky, too? Common enough, this time of year. The time of year when colds are going around. And when we have to be especially careful of what we eat. Vitamin deficiency can be the cause of that "down-and-out" feeling. And Supertabs, the multiple vitamin, can be the answer . . .

This is quite different from the copy an agency would write to advertise the same product in a newspaper. Reading it correctly requires a kind of skill developed most rapidly by practicing aloud.

Reading a long script can be difficult. You cannot afford to make even the minor errors the silent reader may make, such as skipping over words or sentences, passing over difficult material or unfamiliar words, and resting your eyes when they become tired. As an announcer, you must read constantly, read everything before you, read it accurately and with appropriate expression, and do all this with little opportunity to rest your eyes. As your eyes tire, you are more and more likely to make reading mistakes. One way of giving your eyes the rest they need is by reading ahead: When your voice is at about *this* point, your eyes should be about *here.* When your eyes have reached the end of the sentence, you should be able to glance away from your script while you finish speaking the words. Practice this, and you should be able to read even lengthy newscasts without excessive eyestrain. But as you practice, make certain you do not fall into an irritating habit of many announcers who read ahead: going into a monoto-nous, decelerating speech pattern at the end of every sentence. Unless you guard against it, you may be unconsciously relaxing your interpre-tation as you rest your eyes.

9. *Do you have any genuine interest in the subject matter of the copy? Do you reveal this interest?* Whatever the purpose or nature of the copy to be read, you must show interest in it if you are to communicate it effec-tively. In many instances you will have a genuine interest in the sub-ject—as in delivering the news or narrating a documentary script. At other times, such as when reading a commercial for a product you do not use or perhaps even dislike, it may be difficult for you to show genuine interest. As a professional you cannot afford to show disinter-est in, or disrespect for, the copy you are paid to read. You must try to put your biases aside. You are an intermediary between people who supply information and people who receive it. You act as a magnifying glass: it is your job to enhance perceptions with the least possible distortion.

The problem of showing interest when reading commercial copy can be acute for the disc jockey, who must read commercials for literally dozens of products or services during a typical work week. Even when you are provided with good copy for reputable advertisers, it is im-possible to develop a belief in each commercial cause. The following guidelines, therefore, may be helpful. (1) When you must read a great many commercials for dozens of different products and when it is impossible to develop honest enthusiasm for all of them, the best you can do is read each one with as much effectiveness and interpretive skill as possible. (2) When you are the exclusive speaker for a product or have had a long personal relationship with a sponsor, try to gain firsthand knowledge of the product and communicate your honest belief in it. (3) When you find yourself reading copy that is offensive, work to have the copy changed.

Assuming that your announcing copy deserves genuine interest, how can you reflect it in your interpretation? Certainly not by ranting, raving, table-thumping, or fender-pounding. Honest enthusiasm is seldom noisy or obtrusive. It manifests itself in inner vitality and quiet conviction. As a radio or television commercial announcer, you will seldom be dealing with life-or-death matters—advertisers to the con-trary notwithstanding—and you will be speaking to small groups of people who are, in effect, only a few feet away. In a sense, you are their guest. Your conviction is revealed through a steady focus on your listeners, your earnestness, and your personality. This does not rule out the possibility of a humorous commercial or introduction. Being sincere does not necessarily mean being somber!

10. *Who is your listener? Can you visualize him or her? Are you able to establish rapport? Are you actually talking to him or her?* Several aspects of this problem of communication have already been mentioned, but one more point should be made. Most of this chapter has emphasized the problems of reading scripts. It might be better if you considered your job to be one of *talking* scripts. Even though you work from a script and your listeners know it, they appreciate it when you sound as though you are not merely reading aloud. The best way to achieve a conversational style is to visualize the person to whom you are speaking and "talk" your message to him or her. Of course, some commercials lend themselves to intimate delivery and others do not.

The following two scripts may be used for practice in talking your scripts. The Blue Cross script should be delivered in a very straightforward, matter-of-fact manner. The Six Flags commercial is a marvelous exercise for practicing changes in rate of delivery, pitch, and volume, as well as for practicing conversational delivery. Both commercials defy conventional "rules" of structure, and both benefit from their originality. Music and sound effects will enhance both commercials.

```
AGENCY:  Allen and Dorward

CLIENT:  Blue Cross of Northern California

LENGTH:  60 seconds


 MUSIC:  LOUD ROCK AND ROLL MUSIC

   MOM:  Annie . . . would you turn that down, please?

 MUSIC:  R & R DOWN AND UNDER

   MOM:  Thank you dear. I'm a working mother with two teenage

         girls. Sometimes, it seems that they're at that difficult

         age. Sometimes, it seems they've been there for years.

         I've got my own business and we're all healthy. When I

         opened my shop, I signed up for Blue Cross protection. I
```

looked at other health plans, but it was obvious that the

Blue Cross Concept One Hundred Plan had everything we

needed . . . and, I can afford it! Last spring, Cindy was

in the hospital for a few days. Nothing serious . . . but

I know how much it would have cost me. Believe me. Plenty!

START FADE   I just couldn't handle a bill like that alone.

ANNCR: There's no reason for you to handle it alone. Our Blue

Cross Concept One Hundred Plan offers a full range of

benefits for your growing family. See our ad in this

Sunday's Magazine Section or TV Guide or call eight

hundred . . . six, four, eight . . . forty-eight hundred.

Blue Cross of Northern California.

MOM: As a single parent, Blue Cross was one of the best deci-

sions I've ever made.

AGENCY: McDonald & Little Advertising

CLIENT: Six Flags

CAMPAIGN: New season

LENGTH: 60 seconds

TITLE: IT STARTS OFF SLOWLY

ANNCR: It starts off slowly at first, climbing upward at maybe

two miles an hour. Then it hits the crest, picks up speed

and before you know it, it happens. The ground is gone.

The world is a blur far below; look down if you dare. And

don't think about the fact that you're moving at almost a

mile a minute and headed straight down into a lake. Or

that you're screaming and laughing at the same time. It's

all in good fun. Here on the biggest, fastest, highest
roller coaster in the world. The Great American Scream
Machine. Just one of the many many new experiences now at
the new Six Flags Over Georgia. There's a whole lot of new
to do this year at Six Flags. Things you'll never forget.
Because good times here are not forgotten.

11. *If the copy is literary, who is the author?* As an announcer you may
some day be engaged to read the words of a famous author. Aside
from the normal considerations of script analysis, timing, phrasing,
and mood determination, you should make a brief study of the author
and his or her works. If, for example, you were hired to narrate a
filmed documentary on the life of William Faulkner, you would do a
better job if you could take to the script some information about his life,
his strong ties to Oxford, Mississippi, his feelings about the South, the
Snopes and Sartoris families, the forces they symbolically represent,
and the criticism of his work. And this means research.

12. *Should you know anything about the origin and background of this copy?*
Unlike brief commercials, which tend to be self-explanatory, some
longer and more complex pieces are better interpreted if you know
the author and understand the author's intentions. Consider what
you should find out before attempting the following announcing
assignments:

   a. narrating a miniseries of television programs on urban transit
   b. narrating a program on migratory farm workers
   c. narrating a program on the works of a great painter
   d. narrating an instructional tape on the use of a new computer

Each of these topics requires specialized knowledge and an understanding of the author's motivations. Commercials are quite obviously
designed to sell products or services, but what are the purposes of
these programs? One good way to find out is by talking to authors,
producers, and directors. On a basic level, you will learn whether the
program is intended to be objective and factual or a position statement.
You may also discover the mood the author wants conveyed. You can
question passages that puzzle you, suggest improvements, and ultimately do a better job of interpretation.

13. *Do you need to do any characterization?* You may be asked at times to read copy calling for characterization. Commercials and documentaries are often written for actors, but both free-lance and staff announcers may find themselves with such assignments. The following commercial calls for both characterization and a regional dialect. In reading it, soften speech sounds such as "ers" and "ings." The personal pronoun *I* should be sounded more like "Ah," and *thing* should be "thang." Be careful, though, to avoid turning this reading into a demeaning stereotype. It is representative of a southern dialect, but there is no reason to assume that the person you play is a caricature. Certainly, the advertiser would want listeners to enjoy the performance and would want them to feel that the speaker is a pleasant person. The purpose of this commercial is to sell, and a part of selling is making listeners feel good about the sponsor and the product.

AGENCY:	McDonald & Little Advertising
CLIENT:	McDonald's
PRODUCT:	Egg McMuffin
LENGTH:	60 seconds
TITLE:	BREAKFAST IS A BIG THING

ANNCR: You know, down in Willacoochee where I hail from breakfast is a big thing with grits and fried steak of lean and all, but the other day I had a different kind of breakfast. I went to a McDonald's store. It was right after 7 in the morning, and they were cooking breakfast like I never saw. They take this muffin, it's not like biscuits, I suppose it's what people over in England sop syrup with, cause it's called an English muffin. But they take this foreign muffin and heat it up, and flat dab on it they put a yard egg, and this bacon that's more like ham, but they call it Canadian bacon. And right there on top of all of it they

put a piece of cheese. And I'm telling you that it sure is
mighty delicious. I never did have a breakfast before that
you could hold in your hand. But that would get kinda
messy with grits.

Courses in acting and participation in plays, including radio and
television plays, will help you learn character interpretation. At times
commercials call for no real characterization but demand a foreign
accent or a regional dialect. Commercials are commonly written for
Scandinavian, English, Irish, Scottish, German, Russian, and "Tran-
sylvanian" (or middle European) accents and dialects of the South,
New England, and rustic West. The dialects of some ethnic minorities
in America are seldom heard today because they are considered harm-
ful stereotypes. If you practice both characterization and dialects, your
job opportunities will expand considerably.

These, then, are some points to be considered in preparing your
copy. You cannot, of course, apply every point each time you pick up a
piece of copy. In time, however, you should develop a conditioned
reflex that allows you to size up a script and interpret it effectively
without relying on a checklist. In the meantime, the suggestions here
may help you spot your weaknesses and measure your progress.

AD-LIB ANNOUNCING

At some point, you are sure to find yourself working without a script,
when all your acquired skills of phonation, articulation, and interpretation cannot guarantee effective communication. When you are on your
own as an ad-lib announcer, only your ability as a compelling conver-
sationalist will earn you listeners. Much of the broadcast day consists
of unscripted shows. Disc jockeys, telephone-talk hosts and hostesses
(*communicasters*), interviewers, children's show personalities, game
show hosts and hostesses, and panel moderators are among those who
seldom see a script and must conduct their programs spontaneously.
Field reporters may work from notes, but they never see a script.

Ad-lib announcing can be practiced, but it probably cannot be
taught. The formula for success is easy to state but difficult to achieve:
*know what you are talking about, be interested in what you are saying, be eager
to communicate with your listener, and try to develop an attractive personality.*
In ad-lib interviews, *show a genuine interest in your guests and their views.*
The ad-lib announcer has a greater opportunity to show spontaneity

than does a script reader; at the same time, the ad-lib announcer runs a greater risk of boring the listener. Scripts are usually tightly written, whereas an ad-lib announcer can wander from point to point. Scripts have specific objectives, but the ad-lib announcer is free to ramble without a clear objective. Scripts often are polished and tightened during recording sessions, but the ad-lib comments of an announcer cannot be modified once they have been uttered. Scripts call for interruptions only when they are motivated, but some ad-lib interviewers throw in a question just as their guest is about to make an important point in response to the *last* question. Despite all potential pitfalls, ad-lib announcing must be practiced and perfected by anyone who wants to become a professional announcer. Keeping the formula in mind, practice ad-lib announcing at every opportunity, using a tape recorder for self-evaluation.

1. *Know what you are talking about.* Ordinarily we take this for granted. We expect a sportscaster to have a thorough knowledge of sports and a disc jockey to know music. The problem arises when an announcer must ad-lib on an unfamiliar topic. As a staff announcer, you may be asked to interview a person about whom you know little and about whose special interests you know nothing at all. Suppose, for example, you are to interview an astrophysicist about an important discovery. How would you prepare for this interview? Most radio and television stations maintain both a library and a morgue, or collections of newspaper and magazine clippings, news releases, and other published biographical material. You might well begin your research there. Many stations maintain a computer that is tied into an information bank. Inquiries typed into the computer's keyboard will, in less than a minute, provide you with reams of information on almost any topic or famous person.

As a talk show host or hostess you would, of course, not rely on a station library or morgue. To be competent, you would have to be a voracious reader of newspapers, news magazines, current fiction and nonfiction best sellers, and a number of general interest periodicals and journals. At a large station, you also would have the help of a research assistant when specific information was needed about a particular guest or topic. Chapter 10 discusses the role of radio and television talk show hosts and hostesses.

2. *Be interested in what you are saying.* To raise this point may seem superfluous, yet anyone who listens attentively to radio or television ad-lib announcers will detect some who seem to have no interest in

what they are saying. Especially guilty are some weather, traffic, and business reporters on radio who make frequent reports throughout the day. It is easy to fall into a routine delivery pattern, to speak too rapidly, and to show no interest in what one is saying.

3. *Be eager to communicate with your listener.* Only if you really want to communicate should you consider radio or television announcing in the first place. If you want to speak merely for and to yourself, buy a tape recorder and have fun "doing your own thing."

4. *Develop an attractive personality.* Very little can be offered on this point. Most people who are attractive to others have found out how to be truly themselves, are able to show their interest in others, and have wide intellectual curiosity. Wit, wisdom, and charm are easily detected and warmly appreciated but hard to come by.

Practice: Ad-lib Announcing

The exercises that follow rely on the use of an audiotape recorder. Most can be adapted to television performance, but the advantages of being able to practice extensively without requiring studio, cameras, and crew make audiotaped performances more practical for most students.

Twenty topics for practice in ad-lib announcing follow, but do not look at them until you are fully prepared to begin practicing. To prepare, find an isolated area that is free from distractions. Cue up a tape on an audio recorder. Have a stop watch or a clock or watch with a sweep-second hand available to you. Then, choose a number from 1 to 20. Without looking at any of the other topics, read the list item corresponding to the number you have chosen. Start your stop watch. Give yourself exactly 1 minute to formulate your thoughts. Make notes, if desired. When the minute is up, reset the stop watch, and start it and the tape recorder simultaneously. Begin your ad-lib performance, and try to speak fluently on your topic for a predetermined time—1 minute for your first few efforts and 2 minutes after you have become more experienced.

As you form your thoughts, try to think of (1) an appropriate opening; (2) material for the body of your remarks; and (3) a closing statement. Do *not* stop your commentary because of stumbles, hesitancies, or any other problems you experience. Do *not* put your recorder in "pause" while collecting your thoughts. This exercise is valueless unless you work your way through your ad-libs in "real time." In order to improve, you must have firsthand knowledge of your shortcomings;

the only way to gather this knowledge is to follow these instructions to the letter, regardless of initial failures. You should also heed a further suggestion: keep all your taped performances so that you can review them and measure your progress.

The twenty ad-lib topics that follow are in random order. Some are rather trivial, and some are of immense importance; some should be approached with humor, and others demand a more sober delivery. Keep note of the number of each topic as you perform it so that you will have a fresh challenge each time you practice. Remember—you must decide on the length of your performance *before* you look at the topic you have selected.

Ad-lib Topics

1. Describe the most important person in your life and give reasons for your choice.
2. Describe the environment in which you live.
3. Discuss the most influential book you have ever read.
4. What do you hope to be doing in ten years?
5. Tell about the most embarrassing experience you have ever had.
6. Tell about your earliest memories of school.
7. Describe the most enjoyable (or otherwise memorable) pet you have ever had.
8. Express your feelings about nuclear power plants.
9. If you could enact or change one law, what would it be, and why would you take the action you propose?
10. Discuss your favorite type of music.
11. Tell about your first date.
12. Tell about the most influential teacher you've ever had.
13. Discuss an important—and recent—news item.
14. Describe your childhood memories of some important holiday.
15. Talk about your strengths and weaknesses.
16. Express your feelings about universal military training.
17. What qualities do you find in your friends that attract you to them?
18. Express your feelings about capital punishment.
19. Discuss the most memorable motion picture you've ever seen.
20. Describe your home town.

This chapter opened with the observation that the key to successful radio and television announcing is the ability to communicate ideas or feelings effectively to other human beings. All the ensuing suggestions were offered as various means to that end. In the last analysis, though, your success as an announcer will be determined by something that cannot be taught, studied, or purchased: talent. With talent, careful attention to the suggestions in this book can help you grow toward true professionalism; without it, hard work will develop your abilities to a level of adequacy, but further growth may be difficult. Before committing yourself to an announcing career, you should make a serious appraisal of your talent. First, assume that you are talented (mental outlook is very important for any performer; if you think you are untalented, you will almost certainly measure down to that level). Second, set yourself a target date for your evaluation and establish a work regimen. Allow yourself at least six months of practice before attempting to appraise the results. Third, practice, practice, practice! Finally, evaluate yourself as honestly and objectively as you can. If you have any doubts, ask qualified people to help you. Do not compare yourself to an established professional with a headstart of twenty or thirty years. Your purpose is to measure your growth and your potential. If you discover that you simply do not have enough ability to satisfy your aspirations, face up to this. If, on the other hand, the evidence indicates a promising future, intensify your practice. If nothing more comes of your hard work, you will at least benefit from extensive practice in oral communication.

3
PERFORMANCE

All your preparation for announcing culminates in performance, and it is on the basis of your performing ability that you will be judged by audience and employer alike. Of course, you must develop other skills—such as operating an audio console for radio work and editing videotape for television news operations—but your before-camera or on-air work will ultimately determine your success. This chapter concentrates on several performance skills that you must develop. Additional information on performance may be found in Chapter 1, "Broadcast Announcing"; Chapter 6, "Voice and Diction"; Chapter 9, "Commercials and Public-Service Announcements"; Chapter 10, "Interview and Talk Programs"; Chapter 13, "Music Announcing"; and Chapter 14, "Sports Announcing."

This chapter addresses the topics of microphone and camera fright, microphone and camera consciousness, clothing and makeup for television, the use of prompters and cue cards, and miscellaneous tips for performers. Before turning to these topics, let us briefly consider a different aspect of performance that can be defined and discussed but cannot be taught: audience rapport.

Rick Houlberg made this pertinent comment after concluding a study of viewer preferences of newscasters:

After all the preparation, clothing, hard work, and luck, something more is needed for the on-air broadcaster to be successful. We know what that something is although we haven't been able to fully describe or study it. This something made us believe Walter Cronkite and send birthday presents to soap opera characters, this something makes us choose one television newscaster over another, this something keeps us listening to one rock radio DJ despite a play list which is almost exactly the same as the four other available rock stations. This something is a connection made between the on-air performer and the audience.[1]

In his research, Houlberg found that most respondents chose the television newscaster they watched because of these factors: "he or she made their problems seem easier," "would like to know more about the newscaster off the air," "the newscaster is almost like their everyday friends," and "made them feel contented." "The newscasters' professional characteristics—items such as objectivity, reliability, honesty, being qualified, and knowing the local market—are second in importance . . . when choosing which local newscaster to watch," Houlberg concludes.

The message here is clear: it is up to the broadcast performer to project an attractive, warm, and friendly personality to the audience. *Attractive* in this sense does not refer to physical appearance, for Houlberg found that neither physical appearance nor sex was significantly important to his respondents. Synonyms for *attractive* are *appealing*, *engaging*, and *charming*. These qualities can be used by a sensitive performer to build audience rapport—a relationship of mutual trust or emotional affinity. It is not likely that a student can be taught these qualities, for they come from within, but being aware of them can help you channel your inner feelings of respect for your audience, concern for people, and dedication to your profession into more effective communication. With this brief discussion of an extremely important topic, we turn to those skills and practices that can be taught in the classroom.

OVERCOMING MICROPHONE AND CAMERA FRIGHT

An irrational fear of performing before a microphone or camera is a common reaction for an inexperienced performer. Occasionally, a student will relish every opportunity to perform and will delight in performance playbacks. For most of us, though, it is normal to have "butterflies" before and during a performance and to feel disappointment on seeing and hearing the results during taped playbacks.

---

[1] From an unpublished presentation of research into "para-social interaction," conducted by Dr. Rick Houlberg of San Francisco State University.

Some tension is not only to be expected, but also can actually help your performance. Mic fright,[2] as this phenomenon is traditionally called, results in the release of adrenalin into the bloodstream, which causes one to become more alert and more energetic. Within bounds, mic fright can be an asset to a performer. A person who is keyed up generates more positive energy than a performer who is routinely working through a piece of copy in an unfeeling manner.

Excessive nervousness, however, can seriously impair a performance. You are suffering from extreme mic fright when any combination of these symptoms is present: physical tension, shallow breathing, constricted throat, dry mouth, and (at an extreme) upset stomach and shaking knees and hands. In terms of your performance, these conditions cause you to go up in pitch, to run out of breath in the middle of sentences, to have your voice "break," to lose concentration, to read or speak at an excessive rate of speed, or to adopt a subdued attitude. At its greatest extreme, mic fright can make you entirely unable to communicate. Generally speaking, mic fright is caused by the following conditions.

Lack of Experience   Nothing but time and regular performances will help. Performances do not have to occur on the air or in a class session. Perform a variety of written and ad-libbed assignments, and record them on an audio recorder. Even television performances will benefit from being recorded and played back for evaluation on an audio recorder.

Lack of Preparation   It is not possible to prepare for ad-lib announcing (a news report live from the field or the badinage that is expected of you as a talk show host), but it *is* possible to *practice* ad-lib announcing. To gain confidence and to develop a smooth ad-lib delivery, practice by talking aloud to yourself. Walk through your living quarters and describe what you see; when driving, talk about what you drive past. Sharpen your ability to hold your friends' attention as you relate anecdotes or discuss matters of mutual interest. Remember, you must practice ad-lib announcing by speaking *aloud*. With written scripts, of

---

[2]*Mic* is an abbreviation for *microphone*. Equipment manufacturers are about equally divided in their literature between *mic* and *mike,* but nearly all tape recorders and audio consoles are labeled *mic.*

course, it is possible to practice. Though time pressures may make it impossible for professional announcers to "rehearse," you are under no such strictures. If you want to improve your performances, you must prepare thoroughly.

Fear of Failure   Most of us are more afraid of failing—of making fools of ourselves—than we are of physical dangers. It is supremely important for you to conquer this fear and to realize that you can progress only by daring to try a variety of approaches in your announcing work. To remain safely within a comfortable shell and perform in a laid-back, low-key manner is to forgo any chance of major improvement. If you are a member of a class in broadcast announcing, keep in mind that you and your classmates are all in the pressure cooker together. Mature students will applaud and encourage the efforts you make to explore your potential.

Almost any performance will benefit from conviction on your part. That is, if you believe in your message and if you sincerely want to communicate it to others, your fear of failure may simply be pushed aside by your conviction. Professional announcers do not always have the luxury of believing in what they are paid to say, but, as a student, you usually are free to choose messages that are of interest or importance to you.

As you perform, try to concentrate on your message. Forget about self and forget about audience, whether that audience is made up of listeners/viewers or classmates. Assume that you are speaking to one or two people whom you respect and with whom you want to communicate. If you truly have a desire to get your message across, you can overcome your concern about failure.

Lack of Self-Esteem   Some of us simply feel that we are not important enough to take up the time and attention of others. This is an incredibly debilitating attitude, and there is nothing to recommend it. Modesty may be a virtue, but self-effacement is not.

Each of us is a unique creation. You are the only "you" who lives or who has ever lived. Because you are unique, you have something unique to offer. If you respect yourself, you will perform at an acceptable level; if you respect your listeners, you will find something worthwhile to say to them; if you respect your subject matter, you will find ways to get it across. Self, listeners, and topic are interrelated variables that must mesh if you are to communicate successfully. Successful communication will inevitably increase your self-confidence and boost your self-esteem. Enhanced esteem will bring about ever-better performances. Better performances will raise esteem. And so it goes. Daring to tell yourself that what you have to say is worthy of the interest and time of others is the start of a new and healthier attitude toward yourself.

But let's face it: if you are presenting dull material in a lackadaisical manner, you have no right to expect the rapt attention of your listeners. If you conduct a boring interview with a boring guest, there is no reason to try to tell yourself that what you are doing is important. We return now to *conviction*—the belief that what you have to offer is important and valid. To raise your self-esteem, be certain that what you offer your listeners is worthy of their attention.

Lack of Time (or Effort) to Prepare Mentally for Performance During the minutes before a performance, you should remove yourself (physically if possible, mentally if not) from the confusion of a typical production situation. Find a way to relax, to gather your thoughts, to concentrate on the upcoming performance. Think over what it is you have to say or read. Think about mood; about appropriate pace; about the importance of the message; about the problems of diction, pronunciation, or whatever you are working on. Perform physical relaxation exercises. If possible, sit in a comfortable chair. Begin to physically relax—starting with your head, then your neck, your shoulders, and so on. After you have attempted to relax your entire body, imagine that tension or stress is being discharged from the ends of your fingers. If you try, you can actually feel the tension leaving your body. At this point, think again about your assignment, and keep your message and your objectives clearly in mind as you prepare to perform.

Dislike of One's Voice or Appearance It is common for students of announcing to dislike their reflections on audiotape or videotape. This is not surprising, because we neither see nor hear ourselves as others do. Most people do not believe that they sound like the voice that comes back to them from an audio recorder. The reason is simple: all our lives we hear ourselves speak through both air and bone conduction. The sound waves that emanate from our mouths are what others hear; the physical vibrations that go through the bones of the head to the tympanic apparatus of the ear are heard by us (the speaker) alone. The combination of air- and bone-conducted sounds is what we *think* we sound like to others. Only when we hear ourselves through air conduction alone, as from an audiotape player, do we truly hear ourselves as others hear us.

Appearance is another matter. We are used to seeing ourselves head on, as in a mirror. Even when posing for photographs, we typically look straight into the camera lens. We are not nearly as accustomed to seeing ourselves in profile or in one-quarter or three-quarter shots. Television spares us nothing; replays show us how we look to others but, because we are not accustomed to these views, we tend to like them less. Television can also distort our appearance to some extent. Most of us look heavier on television than in real life.

If we truly understand that audio and video recordings are surprises only to ourselves, and that others accept our sound and our appearance on tape just as they accept us in person, we are well on our way toward overcoming mic or camera fright.

The vocal folds, which are central to good vocal tones, tighten up during times of moderate to extreme nervousness. The tighter the folds, the less they vibrate, and this results in higher pitch and a strident-sounding voice. Hot liquids can help relax the vocal folds. Hot tea, bouillon, coffee, or even hot water can help you achieve a better speaking voice (this is true even after nervousness has been conquered).

In summary, you can keep your nervousness within bounds if you prepare thoroughly, practice at every opportunity, believe in what you are saying, concentrate on your message, stop analyzing your feelings and emotions, think of your listener, perform relaxation exercises, accept yourself as you are, believe that you can and will succeed, and understand that nearly all of your colleagues are fighting the same battle.

Microphone Consciousness

Microphones are marvelous instruments, but they can do their job only when they are properly used. Improper use sometimes results from inexperience or ignorance, but more often than not, the problem is caused by a lack of *microphone consciousness*. Typical examples of faulty microphone consciousness include the following:

1. Failing to clip on a lavaliere microphone before beginning a performance

2. Walking away from the set after a performance without remembering to unclip the lavaliere mic
3. Making unwanted noises near an open mic, such as drumming fingers on a table near a desk mic
4. Moving away from a mounted microphone or moving out of range of a boom mic
5. Failing to properly move a hand-held mic between you and a guest you are interviewing
6. Positioning yourself and the guest improperly in relation to a desk microphone
7. Making sudden, unplanned changes of an extreme degree in volume
8. Moving in and out in relation to a mounted mic
9. Failing to understand, and properly relate to, the pickup patterns of microphones
10. Attaching a lavaliere microphone improperly—too far away from the mouth or under clothing that will muffle the sound
11. Clapping with your hands near your lavaliere microphone

One common problem requires some elaboration. The sound of paper being bent, turned over, or shuffled is the mark of an amateur. Learn to handle scripts in such a way as to avoid paper rattling. *Never* work from a script that is stapled or held together with a paper clip. *Never* turn script pages over as you move from one page to another; always slide the pages you are discarding to one side. Needless to say, all scripts should be typed on one side of the paper only. When working with practice material from this or other texts, make typed copies on 8½-by-11-inch paper, double-spacing or even triple-spacing them.

Camera
Consciousness

Just as a microphone initiates the process of sending your voice to your listeners, a camera is the first element in the transmission of your physical image. Camera consciousness begins with understanding the needs and limitations of cameras and with recognizing the problems camera operators face. The discussion that follows covers only those technical aspects that are relevant to you as a performer.

First, a few words about light and optics. A television camera picks up reflected light in much the same manner as the human eye. Like the eye, a camera has a lens, an iris or diaphragm, and a surface on which images are focused—a retina for the eye, a photosensitive surface in the camera pickup tube. The lens focuses the picture, the iris opens or closes to control the amount of light entering the system, and the photosensitive surface converts the light patterns into electrical impulses.

Unlike the human eye, the television camera does not do all its work automatically. Camera operators are responsible for focusing, while video engineers maintain the proper iris opening. (Field production cameras *do* have automatic iris controls, however.)

Another difference between the eye and the camera is that the eye does not have a built-in zoom. The zoom lens allows a stationary camera to select anything from a wide shot to an extreme close-up. With the eye, a person standing 10 feet away will always be on a "medium shot," so to speak.

A final difference is that we can rapidly move our heads approximately 180 degrees horizontally, leaving a focus on one object and fixing it on another at the end of our head movement, without any sensation of blurring; the camera cannot.

Keep these elementary facts about cameras in mind as they are applied to several aspects of television performance.

Hitting Marks Hitting marks means moving to an exact spot in a studio or in the field marked by a piece of gaffer's tape or a chalk mark. When movement is called for—for instance, moving 10 feet toward the camera, stopping, and delivering an introduction (a *stand-up intro*)—it is important to be exact in your movements and to come to rest in the predetermined position. Here are some reasons for precision in hitting marks.

1. Focus. The amount of light entering a lens determines the *f*-stop setting of the iris; the *f*-stop setting in turn determines the *depth of field*. Depth of field refers to an area in front of a camera in which everything is in focus; objects closer or farther away will be blurred. The greater the amount of light entering the lens, the smaller the iris opening and the greater the depth of field. Because zoom lenses have a great deal of glass through which the light must pass, because prompting devices cut down further on light entering the lens system, and because studio lighting is kept to the lowest possible level for the comfort of performers, the iris generally is quite open, and this reduces depth of field considerably. To put it plainly, if you don't hit your marks, you may be out of focus.

2. Another reason for hitting marks precisely is that the camera operator is responsible for the composition of the picture. Because it has been determined earlier where you should stand for the best composition, you must follow through in order to enable a camera operator to do a professional job.

3. A third reason for being meticulous about hitting marks is that studios often feature area lighting, which means that not all parts of the studio are illuminated equally. If you miss your mark, you may be outside the area specifically prepared for your presentation.

Standing on Camera　　When standing on camera, you must stand still and avoid rocking from side to side. Weaving or rocking from one foot to the other can be distracting when on a long shot and disastrous when on a close-up. In Figure 3.1, Terry Lowry shows how a little rocking looks on a medium shot; Figure 3.2 shows the same movement on a close-up. In a television studio, a monitor will be placed where you can see it, and thus you will know when the camera has you on a wide, medium, or close-up shot, so you will be aware immediately if you are moving out of the picture. In the field you most likely will not have a monitor, and thus you will have no way of knowing whether you are moving out of the frame. The moral is to practice standing with a minimum of movement at all times, except when movement is called

FIGURES 3.1 AND 3.2
Talk show hostess Terry Lowry shows how rocking from side to side looks on a wide shot and on a close-up. (Courtesy KGO-TV, San Francisco)

for. To reduce a tendency to rock, stand with your feet slightly apart and with one foot turned out to form a 15-to-20-degree angle with the other foot; the turned foot should be about 4 or 5 inches in front of the other. Standing in this manner should make it all but impossible to rock.

Sitting on Camera   You will find it easier to avoid excessive random movement when seated, but remember that most movements are exaggerated on television. If you find that you habitually move your upper torso and head in rapid or wide-ranging motions, you should work to reduce such movement—without at the same time seriously reducing your natural energy level. Sideways movement can be very annoying, especially on close-ups. Movement toward and away from the camera can take you in and out of focus.

Telegraphing Movement   When rising or sitting down and when moving from one part of the studio (or exterior location) to another, you must move somewhat more slowly than you ordinarily would, and you must *telegraph* your movement. To telegraph is to begin a movement with a slow and slight motion, to pause, and then to follow through with the intended movement. Camera operators are trained to follow even fast-moving athletes, but you should not rely on their skill when a little thoughtfulness on your part can guarantee that you will not thwart their efforts.

   For the most part, you should not sit down or stand up on camera unless the movement has been planned in advance or signaled by the floor director.[3] When the camera is on a head shot of a standing performer and the performer suddenly sits, the head drops right out of the picture. When the camera is on a head shot of a seated performer who suddenly stands, the result is even worse: the viewer is treated to the infamous "crotch shot!" In Figures 3.3 and 3.4, Fred LaCosse shows us how this movement looks on television. If you find that you must stand up, even though no such movement was planned, telegraphing the movement is imperative—it will give the director time to zoom out to a wider and safer shot.

---

[3] Three terms, *floor director*, *floor manager*, and *stage manager*, replaced the term *floorman* when terminology was changed to eliminate sex-referent language. Stations are divided in their usage of the three terms and sometimes use them interchangeably.

FIGURES 3.3 AND 3.4
Talk show host Fred LaCosse shows what happens when he suddenly rises without telegraphing movement. (Courtesy KGO-TV, San Francisco)

Cheating to the Camera   To *cheat* is to position yourself so as to create the impression that you are talking to another person (as in an interview), while still presenting a favorable appearance to the camera. Cheating has no relevance to the performer who makes a direct address to the camera, as a news anchor does. But when speaking to a guest or a co-host on television, we want two things that would be mutually exclusive if it were not for cheating: we want to see the faces of both persons, and we want to feel that they are speaking to one another rather than to us. So, instead of presenting only their profiles as they speak, interviewer and guest position themselves at about a 25-degree angle from one another—thus opening themselves up to the camera—while continuing to speak as though they were facing one another directly.

When standing or sitting with another person, as in conducting an interview, position yourself nearer the other person than you would if you were talking with that person off-camera. We are all surrounded by an invisible area that we consider our very own psychological or personal space. When talking with others, most of us sit or stand at a comfortable distance from them. Television, however, is no respecter of psychological space. The intimacy of television is best exploited when interviewer and guest can at times both be seen in a medium shot. To sit or stand too far from another performer is to force the director to settle for close-ups and wide shots. In unrehearsed programs, the director wants to have an acceptable *cover shot,* a shot that can be used regardless of which person is speaking. If the only cover shot available is a long shot, the director's job is quite difficult.

Addressing the Camera   When directly addressing the camera (the viewer, actually), look straight into the lens of the taking camera— denoted by an illuminated red light called a tally light—and focus your gaze about a foot behind the glass lens, for that is where your viewer is.

In a studio production, you can expect to work with from two to four cameras; three are standard. This means that from time to time you will have to change your gaze from one camera to another, on cue. The cuing sequence begins when the floor director points both hands to the taking camera. On a signal from the director, the floor director rapidly moves one or both hands to point to the camera to which you are to turn. When you are performing as a news anchor, the procedure is to notice the cue, glance down at your script, and then raise your head in the direction of the second camera. In Figures 3.5 through 3.10, Janet Zappala shows how to make a clean movement from one camera to another.

When searching for a thought or a word, many of us tend to raise our eyes toward the ceiling as we pause for inspiration. This is distracting and unflattering, and if you have this habit, you should work to overcome it.

Make certain you don't try to freeze on a smile while waiting for the director to go to black or to another camera. In most instances, it is best to continue small and natural movements while you wait. In Figure 3.11, Jack Hanson shows how one can look when a director stays on a shot too long while the performer attempts to hold a smile. This is called the egg-on-face look.

Finally, don't forget to use nonverbal communication when performing on camera. Facial expressions and head, hand, and torso movements *that are not overdone* can add much to your communicative abilities.

Holding Props   A *prop*, short for *property*, is an object that a performer holds, displays, or points to. Typical props are goods used in demonstration commercials, the food and utensils used in cooking shows, and books or album covers displayed by talk show hosts and hostesses.

FIGURES 3.5–3.10
Anchor Janet Zappala shows how to move, on cue, from one camera to another. (Courtesy KGO-TV, San Francisco)

When holding maps, sketches, books, products, or other props, hold them with a steady hand. Chances are the director will want an extreme close-up of the object, and even a slight movement can take the object out of focus or off-camera. Position the prop so that the taking camera has a good view of it.

When pointing at an object or a portion of it, move your hand, with the index finger extended, slowly and evenly toward the spot to be highlighted. Then, hold that hand as steady as possible. Do *not* make quick motions here and there—the camera cannot follow them. Always rely on a television monitor to check both your positioning and your hand movements.

When holding any object that has a reflective surface, such as a dust cover on a book or an album liner, use your monitor to make sure you are holding it at a correct angle. Studio lights reflected from any glossy object can totally wash out the details of the prop you are holding. In Figures 3.12 and 3.13, talk show hostess Terry Lowry illustrates the wrong way and the right way to hold a prop with a reflective surface on camera.

When demonstrating a product or a procedure on camera, do not feel compelled to keep up a nonstop narration. Most of us have

FIGURES 3.12 AND 3.13
Talk show hostess Terry Lowry shows the wrong way and the right way to hold a reflective object on camera. (Courtesy KGO-TV, San Francisco)

difficulty speaking fluently while using our hands to show how something is done or used. Because television is a visual medium, some things are best left to sight alone. Of course, there are times when commentary is helpful or even necessary, so you should practice and perfect the skill of simultaneously speaking and demonstrating. The point is that constant chatter, especially when marred by hesitancy and repetitions, is not good communication.

Holding Scripts Scripts are used in live television primarily by news anchors. They are usually a back-up to a prompting device. In the event that the prompter fails, or the person feeding it falls behind or rushes ahead of your delivery, you will need to refer to your script. And, at some stations, you will have no prompter and must work entirely from a hand-held script. Comments on working with a prompter are to be found in a later section of this chapter, but the proper way to hold a script is appropriate to the present discussion of camera techniques.

When working with a script, hold it with both hands and hold it above the desk. Have it tilted toward you at a comfortable angle for reading. There are three important reasons for holding your script above desk level. First, as you look down to the script and then up to the camera, the degree of up-and-down motion is reduced. Second, as you move from camera to camera, you can move the script so as to keep it in front of you, thereby eliminating diagonal head movements.

Finally, if the script were flat on the surface of a desk, you would have to bend your head down in such a way as to restrict the air flow and thus impair your vocal quality.

Using Peripheral Vision   A periphery is a boundary. If you look straight ahead, you will find that the left and right boundaries of your vision extend in an arc of about 150 degrees. This is the range of your peripheral vision, and you should be able to pick up movements—such as hand signals—given to you within this area. For practical purposes, you need use only about a 45-degree arc of your peripheral vision, because floor directors will give you signals as close as possible to the camera you are addressing. When receiving signals, do not allow your head or even your *eyes* to turn toward the signaler. In Figure 3.14, Terry Lowry shows how a slight movement of the eyes to pick up a cue can look on camera.

There is a natural tendency to acknowledge that one has received and understood a hand signal. Experienced performers working with professional crews do not send back a signal "message received, will comply." At some stations, however, and especially when new, unre-

FIGURE 3.14
Terry Lowry shows what happens when a performer on close-up looks for a cue. (Courtesy KGO-TV, San Francisco)

hearsed, or unusually complex programs are being produced, performers are asked to acknowledge hand signals. In some instances this means an unobtrusive hand or finger movement; in others it may call for a larger gesture. Follow the practice preferred by the director or producer of the show for which you work.

Clothing and Makeup   When performing on television, plan your clothing carefully. If your television system uses chroma-key matting, you should avoid any shade of the color used for chroma-keying—in most instances, blue or green. Chroma-keying is a process that allows a picture from one camera to be "keyed in" to a portion of the picture from another camera. If blue were the color of chroma-key backdrops at your station, and you were to wear a blue shirt or blouse, a second picture would appear in the area of your blue clothing whenever a chroma-key matte was used.

Avoid every article of clothing that has small checks or narrow stripes. The television camera cannot handle fine, high-contrast patterns, and a wavy, shimmering picture, called the *moiré effect*, results. Also avoid black-and-white clothing; it can be accommodated by the television camera system if both lighting and background are compatible, but it makes problems for engineers. Pastel shades are best for nearly all broadcast purposes and are complimentary to people of all skin shades. Performers with extremely dark faces should wear clothing somewhat darker than that worn by people with light skin tones. The principle you should follow is: avoid excessive contrast between your face and clothing, and avoid clothing the same shade and color as your skin.

Jewelry can cause video problems, as can sequins. Studio lights reflected directly into the camera lens cause flaring. This effect may be useful in asserting the glamour of a particular guest, but it is very distracting if created regularly by a program host or hostess.

Makeup for television performers is usually quite simple and quickly applied. Makeup is used to reduce skin shine, eliminate five o'clock shadow, improve skin color, and hide minor blemishes. Makeup is seldom used to drastically change the appearance of a television performer. Close-ups are too revealing of cosmetic attempts to change basic facial features. If your complexion is very sallow, you must be careful to cover your entire face, neck, and ears with makeup because the contrast between near-white and almost any color of makeup would be most noticeable. Max Factor pancake number 4N or 5N would suit your complexion best. If your skin is a medium-tan Caucasian, Max Factor pancake number 6N or 7N should blend in well. Max Factor pancake 10N or 11N is best if you are a Black announcer with skin color ranging from café-au-lait to near-black. Some men, even when freshly shaven, display a gray-blue cast in the beard and mustache area. Pancake makeup helps cover this, but there is a special beard-stick that eliminates the problem for nearly everyone.

Working with Cue Cards   Cue cards are used at most television stations for the following purposes: to give the script of a short announcement to be made by an on-air host or hostess; to give a list of items to be ad-libbed, such as the names and professions of program guests; and to give some bit of information to the performer, such as a telephone number to be called or a reminder to *tease* an upcoming segment of the show.[4] For lengthy messages that must be read by on-air announcers, electronic prompters are used by nearly all television stations, large and small.

At the same time, the majority of college departments of broadcasting do not own prompting devices, and students who must deliver lengthy messages verbatim must rely either on memorization or on cue cards. Memorization involves a greater risk of disaster than do cue cards. The pressure of performing before one's peers added to the normal distractions of the television studio—bright lights in one's face, time cues, signals from a floor director to change cameras—make concentration on a memorized script quite difficult. For most learners, cue cards are the best answer.

Cue cards are generally made in two configurations. If the message is brief enough to fit onto one sheet of poster board, the cue card may measure 28 by 44 inches. The script is written on the card with a broad black felt pen. During rehearsals and performance, a floor director holds the card to the right of the camera lens; as the performer reads the card, it is slowly moved upward so that the line being spoken is always alongside the lens. Although the standard poster board is 28 inches wide, it is best to leave a wide right margin so that the reader-performer will have a minimum of left-to-right head movement.

For longer messages, smaller cards should be used. Cards should be no wider than two feet, and no more than 12 to 15 inches in height. Less information can be placed on each of these smaller cards—a 30-

[4]A *tease* is a brief promotion of another program or of an upcoming segment of a program.

FIGURE 3.15
Guest Rita Jenrette waits to move to the set, while a talk show host introduces her from information on a cue card. (Courtesy KGO-TV, San Francisco)

second commercial requires several cards—but they help you maintain better eye contact with the viewer than do the larger cards. Cards should be held as close to the lens as possible, the best placement being just below the lens; this allows you to look directly at the viewer. If your script calls for a switch from one camera to another, the cards must either be duplicated, with one set at each camera, or they must be divided according to what lines are to be addressed to which camera.

When working with cue cards—especially with multiple cards—it is imperative that you practice with the person or persons who will be holding them during your performance. Even a slight hesitation in changing the cards can cause you to stop in midsentence.

As you read your script from cue cards, practice looking as directly as possible into the lens, using your peripheral vision to its greatest degree. It isn't easy, but you can develop this skill with regular practice.

Working with Prompters   Most television stations use prompting devices to enable performers to maintain eye contact with the lens of the taking camera. Some prompters are entirely electronic; scripts are typed on a word processor (a kind of computer terminal), briefly stored, and transmitted to a display terminal. Other prompters are a combination of mechanical and electronic components. A script made up of pieces of paper taped together is run under the lens of a fixed camera; the image appears on a black-and-white monitor attached to the top of each television camera; a mirror reflects the monitor image down onto a sheet of glass mounted at a 45-degree angle in front of the camera lens. The performer sees the script while looking directly at the camera lens. The speed of the moving script is regulated to match the reading speed of the news anchor.

Prompters are used most extensively on television newscasts. On talk, interview, game, variety, and other types of programs that are predominantly ad-libbed, prompters are used only for short scripts that must be delivered verbatim and, in some operations, to pass on such information as the nature of an upcoming program segment that is to be teased.

When delivering a short piece (a commercial or a station editorial, for example), you will seldom have a script in your hands or on a desk in front of you. Nearly all such performances are taped and can be repeated if the prompter malfunctions. During a live newscast, on the other hand, it is imperative that you have a complete script to turn to in the event that the prompter ceases to work or gets out of phase with your reading.

In preparing for a television newscast, you may have the script typed on an electronic keyboard and then duplicated in the number of copies required for production, or it may be typed directly onto *copy sets*, which produce as many as eight copies, each of a different color. Copies go to each of the co-anchors, the producer, the director, the prompter operator, the tape librarian, and management, and one spare copy goes in the files. The prompter operator feeds the copy onto a moving belt, and the pages are rolled under the lens of a fixed camera.

When you go on the air for a 60-minute newscast, you will have 60 minutes of script, but you can expect it to be revised or replaced during the broadcast. Runners will bring new copy to you and to the prompter operator. Voiced instructions to toss to a reporter in the field or to a co-anchor in the newsroom will be given to you by the director or producer over an IFB, a small earphone.[5] You will also receive instructions passed on by the floor manager during breaks, reports from the field, or taped stories.

[5] At some stations, the IFB is called "interrupted foldback," and at others, "interrupted feedback." Foldback is the term for an earphone system, so "interrupted foldback" is the correct name for the system. You can expect to hear both terms used.

Because you will not have had an opportunity to study those portions of your script that are written and delivered after the start of the newscast, skill in sight reading is extremely important. You may have a chance to skim the new copy for names of people, places, or things that you may have trouble pronouncing, but there is no guarantee that anyone in the studio or control room will be able to help you with the pronunciation. For this reason, you should establish an understanding with people in the newsroom—news writers, assignment editors, or associate producers—that unusual words or names will be phoneticized on the copy that goes to you and the prompter. Figure 3.16 shows one way in which such information can be passed along. In this case, where the name of a scarcely known sweetener appeared, the news writer took the phoneticized spelling from the pronouncer included in the wire-service copy from which the story was taken. *Pronouncer* is the term used by news services for words and names that have been transcribed into wire-service phonetics.

**INSTRUCTIONS
AND CUES**

Most radio and television announcers work as members of teams and must therefore develop harmonious relationships and efficient means of communicating. Disc jockeys and others who work solo do not, of course, have the same kinds of communication needs, but because you cannot be certain that you will always work independently, you should learn to coordinate your efforts with those of others.

Instructions and cues are given to television performers by floor directors and producers. Floor directors use both oral and visual means of communicating, depending on whether the instruction comes at a time when the floor director can issue instructions orally. Television producers communicate by way of an IFB. On-air radio announcers and performers working in a recording studio may receive instructions from an engineer or a producer. These instructions may be given orally over an intercom connecting a control room with a studio, through a headset, or as hand signals.

In general, instructions from floor directors and engineers are confined to details such as cuing, indicating an upcoming program break, and signaling the improper use of equipment or, in television, of lights. Producers usually concern themselves with matters of interpretation or changes of plan, such as dropping a news story.

Regardless of who issues the instructions, it is your responsibility to carry them out promptly and effectively. Several considerations are

SWEETENER

VAL   O.C.

"AZ-PART-AIM"

A new sweetener has
has been approved
by the F.D.A., but
there is still some
controversy over
it's safety.
    It's "Aspartame,"
180 times as sweet
as sugar, but with
only a fraction of
the calories.
The F.D.A. with-
drew it's approval
of the sweetener
seven years ago,
after tests showed
it caused brain
damage in lab
animals.
    According to a
study by an outside
panel of experts,
there are still
some serious
questions as to

VO/ENG

AT   :08 ENG/SOT

Aspartame's safety,
but the F.D.A. has
decided to overrule
their findings.
        (ENG/SOT)

FIGURE 3.16
Prompter copy showing phoneticized spelling added by news writer.

involved in developing effective working relationships. First, as an announcer you do not have to act as a mindless automaton. There will be ample opportunity for you to discuss your ideas and concepts with others. However, when a program is being broadcast, it is no time to exercise independent judgment and ignore instructions. Follow your instructions when they are issued; if appropriate, discuss them later.

Second, when rehearsing or when making a number of takes of a performance under the coaching of a producer or a director, as when recording the narrative for a documentary or when recording commercials, do your best to implement suggestions. If your director welcomes it, you may discuss alternative ways to deliver lines, but always remember that the producer's word is final. One effective way to express your opinion is to say, "What if I tried it this way?" This approach is tactful and nonthreatening and will most likely be productive.

During rehearsals, do not feel compelled to constantly explain why you did something this or that way or why you made a mistake. No one is interested, and alibis and explanations only delay the project.

During rehearsals and performances, always remain alert for cues and instructions. Sometimes you will wait an eternity for a problem, usually a technical one, to be ironed out. This is no time for daydreaming and certainly no time to leave your position. When the problem is corrected you will be needed, and needed at once.

Always treat every member of the production team with respect. No one is unimportant, and your success—and the success of the show— depends on the degree of commitment and the quality of performance of every member.

Taking a Level   Before nearly every performance, you will be asked to take a level. The purpose of taking a level is to give the audio engineer a chance to adjust the volume control associated with your microphone. Because so much time can be wasted in taking voice levels and because getting faulty results is often detrimental to the announcer and the production, it is worthwhile to dwell on this procedure.

Before taping or going on the air, the engineer must know the volume level of all audio inputs. In the simplest production, this means the volume level of the announcer; in elaborate productions, it might mean the levels of several voices, music, and sound effects. The engineer's job is to mix or blend audio inputs in the proper volume proportions and with optimum audio quality. When taking a level, an engineer can tell you if you are off-mic, if you are too loud or too soft, or if you are popping or creating excessive sibilance. *Popping* is an air blast when plosives are sounded; *plosives* are the consonants *p*, *b*, *t*, *d*, *k*, and *g*. *Sibilance* is the hissing sound made when the letter *s*, and sometimes *sh* and *z*, is sounded. You cannot sound your best if you are misusing your mic. An audio engineer can help you make the most effective use of your voice, but you must cooperate. When you are asked to take a level, *it is imperative that you read from the actual script to be used (or, if ad-libbing, that you speak at exactly the same volume you will use during the show); that you position yourself in relation to the mic exactly as you will during the show; and that you continue reading or ad-libbing until the engineer is satisfied with the result.* The following vignette only slightly exaggerates what happens when undisciplined amateurs are asked to take a level. The vignette assumes that the medium is radio and that the engineer is separated from the announcer in a control room, with a sound-proof glass window between them.

> (*The* ENGINEER *is waving hands impatiently, trying to attract attention of the* ANNOUNCER. *In the studio, the* ANNOUNCER *is doing imitations—W. C. Fields, James Cagney, and Rich Little doing an impression of Richard Nixon.*)
>
>   ANNCR: Play it again, Sam. . . .
> ENGINEER: What's the matter with that dodo?
>   ANNCR: Reminds me of a slight peccadillo I once was involved in. . . .
> ENGINEER: (*finally giving up, and reaching for the intercom button*) Hey, you in there. How about giving me a level?
>   ANNCR: OK. Yah-tah-tah, yah-tah-tah. Is that enough?
> ENGINEER: (*who missed all but the question*) Is *what* enough? I haven't heard anything yet.
>   ANNCR: (*now decides to give the engineer a fighting chance and starts counting*) Testing, one—two—three—four. . . .
> ENGINEER: (*with resignation*) Well, at least it proves he watched "Sesame Street."

To make matters worse, this announcer, on receiving the cue, moves a foot nearer the mic and raises the volume by six decibels. "Yah-tah-tah" and counting are nearly useless to an audio engineer in setting levels.

In taking a level, follow these procedures. (1) As you sit or stand before a mic or wait after a lavaliere or other miniaturized microphone has been clipped on, remain silent. Unnecessary chatter is distracting and potentially embarrassing if your mic is open. (2) Wait patiently and alertly for a signal to take a level; the signal will probably be given orally by a floor director (television) or by an engineer over an intercom (radio). In any arrangement wherein you must depend on a *visual* signal, keep watching the engineer. (3) On receiving the signal, move into the exact position and posture you will use during the performance, *and read or speak exactly as you will later on.* (4) When working with a script, read from that script, using all of the vitality, emotion, and other aspects of performance that you intend to use in performance. Do not hold back, thinking that it is wise to save yourself for the real thing. (5) As you read or speak, remain alert for any hand signals given by the floor director or engineer, such as those that might indicate "louder," "softer," or "move closer to (or away from) the mic." (6) As you continue to make adjustments (if any), continue to speak until the signal is given that everything is satisfactory.

Hand Signals

Radio and television sometimes use hand signals for communication between members of a working team. Hand signals were developed in the early days of radio because sound-proof glass partitions separated directors and engineers from performers. Over the years, many aspects of broadcasting have changed. Television came along, and much of radio turned to recorded music, with most music announcers doing their own engineering. Today, not all radio stations even have a control room adjacent to an announce booth or studio. Despite this, some hand signals are still used in both radio and television, and students of announcing should understand and be able to use them.

Some hand signals are used in radio only, some in television only, and others in both.

Radio and Television:

1. *Attention.* This signal, a simple waving of the hand, usually precedes the stand-by signal. In radio it is given by an engineer; in television, by the floor director.

2. *Stand by.* The stand-by signal is made by holding the hand slightly above the head, palm toward the announcer. The stand-by signal is given at any time when the announcer cannot judge the precise moment at which to pick up a cue, such as at the beginning of a radio or

Attention

Stand-by

Cue

Cut

Slow down or stretch

Speed-up

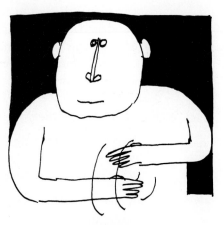

Wrap-up

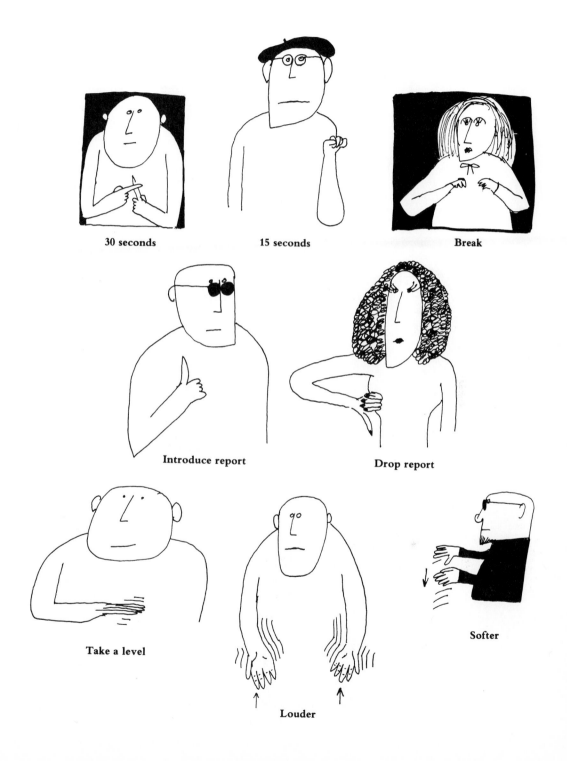

30 seconds

15 seconds

Break

Introduce report

Drop report

Take a level

Louder

Softer

Move closer to mic

Move back from mic

Commercial

Cart

Headlines

Sounder

television program. (A different stand-by signal is used in television when cuing the anchor from one camera to another.)

3. *Cue*. The cue signal is made by rapidly lowering the hand from the stand-by position, with the index finger extended and pointing directly at the person being cued. In nearly every instance, the cue signal follows the stand-by signal; neither signal is normally given alone. In some radio operations, the cue signal is given as often by the announcer as by the engineer. Music and fast-paced news programming require timing to the split second, and cues are given by the person who is in the best position to coordinate the elements of production.

4. *Cut*. The cut signal is made by drawing the index finger across the throat. This is an emergency sign; on receiving it, stop speaking at once. After stopping your performance, wait for oral or visual signals before beginning again.

5. *Slow down, or stretch*. This signal is made by a television floor director or an audio engineer or director. It is made by pulling the hands apart, as though pulling taffy. Because to slow down and to stretch mean two different things, you must rely on the context in which the signal is given to know how to interpret the sign. When reading from a script, the signal means to slow down; when ad-libbing, the signal means to stretch (in other words, to keep talking until a further signal is given). On receiving this signal, you should slow down the pace of your delivery.

6. *Speed up*. The speed-up signal is given by holding the hand before the body, index finger extended, and then rotating the hand. On receiving this signal, you should increase the pace of your delivery. The signal is imprecise, because it does not tell you how much or for how long you should speed up. Later directions, such as *on the nose*, or *slow down*, will give you this information. *This signal must not be used for, nor confused with, the wrap-up sign.*

7. *Wrap up*. This signal is made by holding both hands in front of the torso, and then rotating them about 8 inches apart. The hands are rotated so that one hand, first the left and then the right, is above the other. On receiving this signal, bring the program or the segment to a close as soon as possible in a smooth and natural way.

8. *Time signals.* As a program nears its conclusion or as a segment of a program nears a station break, it is important for an announcer to know the exact number of remaining minutes or seconds. These signals are given in the same manner for both radio and television, though television uses them often and radio uses them only occasionally. The time signals are as follows.

Three minutes   three fingers held up and waved slowly
Two minutes   two fingers held up and waved slowly
One minute   the index finger held up and waved slowly
Thirty seconds   the index finger of one hand crossing the index finger
    of the other (in television, the right and left arms are crossed)
Fifteen seconds   a clenched fist held upright and near the head
Ten to zero seconds   In circumstances wherein extremely close timing is
    required (as in going from a live segment on television to a commercial), the floor director will pass on signals from the control room by
    first holding up all ten fingers on both hands, and then lowering one
    finger for each count until all fingers have been lowered: this will be
    your cue to end your comments.

Television:

9. *Stand by to switch cameras.* This signal, most often used in newscasts, tells the anchor to prepare to be waved from one camera to another. It is made by holding both hands next to the lens of the taking camera. Figure 3.7 shows this signal.

10. *Switch cameras.* On this signal, your glance should move immediately to the camera to which you have been waved. The floor director will have moved from the stand-by signal to the switch-camera signal by moving one or both hands from the first to the second camera. An earlier section of this chapter, "Addressing the Camera," tells how this move is best made when working with a script.

11. *Break.* This signal, used chiefly on interview and talk programs, tells you that you should wrap up the present segment for a commercial break. The signal is made by holding the hands as though they were grasping a brick or a stick of wood, and then making a breaking motion.

12. *Introduce/drop report.* A thumbs-up signal is given to a news anchor to indicate that a planned report from the field is ready to go on the air.

A thumbs-down signal means that the report is not to be introduced. Reports may be dropped because of technical difficulties or because of time pressures.

Radio: The following hand signals are used exclusively in radio, though some may be seen occasionally in an audio recording studio.

13. *Take a level.* This signal is made by holding the hand palm down, and then moving it back and forth as though smoothing a pile of sand. In some operations the signal is given by holding a hand at face level, with the tip of the thumb touching the fingers; the hand is then opened and closed rapidly, as though to say "go on and gab." This usage should be discouraged for two reasons: first, as indicated earlier, the engineer will find gabbing—yah-tah-tah-tah—all but useless in setting a level; second, the gab signal can be confused with the signal for an upcoming tape cart.

   Although the signal to take a level is not often used—an oral cue being preferred by most audio engineers—there are times when it, together with four other hand signals, can be used for efficiently directing a performer to make the best use of a microphone. These signals are *louder, softer, move closer to the mic,* and *move back from the mic.*

14. *Louder.* The signal to increase volume is made by holding the hand before the body, palm up, and then raising the hand.

15. *Softer.* The signal to reduce volume is made by holding the hand before the body, palm down, and then lowering the hand.

16. *Move closer to the mic.* This signal is made by holding the hands apart, palms toward each other, and then moving the hands so as to bring them together. This signal is sometimes used in television to tell a performer to move closer to another person on the set.

17. *Move back from the mic.* The hands are held in front of the body, close to one another, with the backs of the hands facing one another; the hands are then moved away from each other.

18. *Commercial.* The commercial signal is made by touching the index finger of one hand to the palm of the other. It may be given by an engineer or an announcer to indicate that a recorded commercial will follow.

19. *Cart.* Cart is an abbreviation for an audiotape cartridge. The signal is made by holding up one hand in the shape of a U or a C, as though the hand were holding a tape cartridge. In news operations, the cart signal indicates that the news item coming up includes a carted segment, usually a recorded report from a reporter in the field.

20. *Headlines.* The headlines signal is made either by drawing the index finger across the forehead or by tapping the top of the head. The signal is given by a news anchor to tell the engineer that news headlines will follow the news item then being read. The engineer is to play the headlines sounder.

21. *Sounder.* The sounder signal is made by holding the hand flat, palm down, and moving it from right to left while simultaneously making the hand flutter. Sounders, also called *logos* or *IDs*, include jingles for sports reports, consumer action reports, business news, and similar regular features. The signal is given by a news anchor to tell the engineer that the next scheduled feature is coming up, and that the appropriate sounder is to be played on cue.

FIGURE 3.17
Floor director Patsy Wheeler gives a hand signal to Buzz Luttrell during a live telecast. (Courtesy WBZ-TV, Boston. Photo by Sarah Hood.)

PREPARING FOR A PERFORMANCE

Conscientious preparation for a performance is necessary for all but the most seasoned veterans, and proper preparation involves several considerations.

First of all, if you are working with a script, you should study and mark it. Underline words to be stressed. Write, in phonetics, the correct pronunciation of difficult words or names. Note any words that might be mistaken for others, and mark your copy accordingly. For example, the following words are sometimes confused because of similar spellings:

though—through	trial—trail
county—country	mediation—meditation
uniformed—uninformed	complaint—compliant
united—untied	impudent—imprudent

To eliminate the possibility of reading errors on such words, mark your copy. You might write *tho* and *thru* for the first pair of words and use hyphens for the others: *coun-ty, coun-try, un-in-formed, uni-formed, u-nited, un-tied,* and so on.

The final ten minutes before your performance are critical. You must try to separate yourself from any distracting activities and *concentrate* on your upcoming performance. If you are excessively nervous, try to relax; if you are totally apathetic, try to psych yourself up to an appropriate degree of energy. (See "Overcoming Mic and Camera Fright," the first section of this chapter.)

If your performance is to be ad-lib, go over its objectives, and make determinations about how you will structure your ideas within the allotted time. How much time will you give to your opening? How much will you give to your conclusion? How much time does this leave for the body of your presentation?

Note the placement of microphones and, if this is to be a television presentation, the cameras. Note where you will sit or stand, and decide where you will hold or place your script. For television, check out the lighting, and decide exactly where you will stand or sit and how far you may be able to move in each direction without moving into shadows. If necessary, check with the floor director to be sure you know which camera is to be called up to open the scene, and be sure you know of any critical or unusual camera shots to follow.

If you are to hold or demonstrate an object, decide exactly where and how you will hold it and for which camera you are presenting it.

Finally, remind yourself that you are going to control any tendency you have to speak too rapidly; that if you make an error, you will correct it as naturally and unobtrusively as possible and continue; and that if you stumble, you will move on, putting the error behind you (dwelling on it will divide your attention and make further stumbles almost inevitable). Above all, do *not* stop and ask if you may begin again *unless* such a possibility has been agreed to in advance. Always adopt the attitude that your performance, even though it may never actually leave the classroom/studio, is going out live over the airwaves.

Achieving a Conversational Style

A conversational style is one that is natural to you, is appropriate to the intimacy of the broadcast media, and, when you are reading from a script, sounds as though you are talking rather than reading. You can best achieve a conversational style by remembering a few simple principles.

First of all, don't hesitate to smile or laugh when it is appropriate. Don't be afraid to pause as you silently grope for an idea or a word because this is perfectly natural. Fear of doing so can lead either to "ers" and "uhs" (vocalized pauses) or to spouting inanities as you try to fight your way back to where you left off.

Conversational quality is totally destroyed by reading "AY" instead of "UH" for the article *a*. Read this sentence, pronouncing the article *a* as "AY."

> ANNCR: A good way for a person to make a fortune is to open a savings account in a bank.

Now read the sentence, but do *not* stress any of the "uhs."

> ANNCR: Uh good way for uh person to make uh fortune is to open uh savings account in uh bank.

Note how stilted the sentence sounded the first time you read it and how much more natural and conversational it was when you said "uh" for the article *a*.

The article *the* is sometimes pronounced "THEE" and sometimes "THUH." The general rule is to say "THEE" before a word beginning with a vowel sound and "THUH" before a word beginning with a consonant:

> ANNCR: The appetite is the best gauge of the health of the average person.
> (THEE appetite is THUH best gauge of THUH health of THEE average person.)

At times, we break this general rule for purposes of emphasis, as in "It is THEE best buy of THUH year!"

When reading a telephone number that includes an area code, read it as follows:

> SCRIPT: Phone (332) 575-6666
> READ AS: "Phone Area Code three-three-two, five-seven-five, six-six-six-six." (Pause after each unit of the phone number.)

When reading a telephone number that includes zeros, read it as follows:

> SCRIPT: Phone 924-0077
> READ AS: "Phone nine-two-four, zero-zero-seven-seven." (Do not say "OH" or "OUGHT.")

When making a tape recording, do not use the phrase "coming to you live." This cliché has been so overused by announcers that it has apparently lost its true meaning for some students of announcing. The term is to be used (if at all) only on *live broadcasts*.

When performing, as in a newscast, commercial, or interview, do not do take-offs *unless* the assignment calls for it. You may amuse yourself and others by burlesquing your material, but it really affords you no useful practice, unless, of course, you intend to make a career of doing spoofs and take-offs. This does not rule out humorous commercials or humor-oriented interviews, as long as they are realistically related to your growth as an announcer.

Developing a Sense of Time

Announcers must develop a keen sense of time, for split-second timing is a part of every radio or television broadcast. In radio, delivery of the live portion of a donut commercial must be brought off in exactly the allotted time.[6] Disc jockeys often must provide an ad-libbed introduction to a song that will end exactly when the vocal portion begins. Newscasters and engineers must work together so that there are neither unwanted pauses nor overlaps when going from announcer to tape or vice versa.

In television, you will be given time signals by a floor manager or floor director. In a newscast or an interview-talk show, you often will be given a countdown into a taped insert. Typically, you will receive a five-count to introduce videotaped stories. The floor director will first hold up the correct number of fingers and then, on instructions from the director, will lower the fingers, one at a time. When the countdown is completed, the director has gone to tape.

At other times during a program, you may be given a 10-second signal, meaning that you have 10 seconds in which to wrap up. You will also be given hand signals to show that there are 3 minutes, then 2 minutes, then 1 minute left in the program or in a segment of it. It is important to develop a sense of how long a second or an accumulation of seconds is. Smooth transitions and unhurried endings require accurate timing. To develop this sense, you must practice extensively, using a stopwatch. Without looking at the watch, start it and then stop it when you think that a given number of seconds has passed. At first, you will typically think that a minute has passed when the actual elapsed time is closer to 30 or 40 seconds. With practice you should become quite accurate. Your job is not yet finished, however. Now you must practice speaking and reading lead-ins and program closings, matching your words with a predetermined number of seconds.

**IMPROVING
PERFORMANCE
SKILLS**

To close this chapter on performance, a few final suggestions are in order. First, there is no substitute for *practice*. Theoretical knowledge of broadcasting is important, and such knowledge will enhance your development, but without practice you will never become truly professional. You do not need to confine your practice to class assignments. You can practice nearly anywhere, and you can practice without a single item of equipment. When reading newspapers, magazines, and books, isolate yourself from others and read at least some of the printed material aloud.

Second, invest if possible in a few basic items of equipment. Most

[6]For donut commercials, see Chapter 9.

practical is a good-quality cassette tape recorder. With it, you can practice any type of announcing that appeals to you—news, interviewing, sports play-by-play, music announcing, or commercial delivery. Before investing in a tape recorder, check it out through actual use. A recorder that cannot accurately record and play back your voice clearly is of little use to you. A good-quality microphone might be your next purchase.

Third, become honestly self-critical. Listen to playbacks as though the voice you hear is that of another person. Listen for communicative values. Listen for voice quality, precise diction, and correct pronunciation. Experiment. Try different styles of delivery, different levels of energy, different rates of delivery. You should not try these things in imitation of another performer; rather you should experiment to find ways of bringing out the best that is in *you.*

You can practice television delivery with or without equipment. Unless you are an unusual student, performing before a mirror will only distract you. Instead, place some object on a wall (a drawing of a television lens will serve you well) and use it to practice eye contact. An audio recorder can help you even in television practice, though there is no perfect substitute for performing before a camera, with subsequent playbacks for critical evaluations. If possible, volunteer as talent on the projects of others. Perhaps you can even get on-camera experience at a local cable station.

Finally, save your recordings and review them from time to time to measure your progress. If you compare performances made four or five months apart, your improvement will be both impressive and encouraging—if you *practice!*

RADIO AND TELEVISION PERFORMANCE CHECKLISTS

Critical self-evaluation is the mark of the true professional in any of the performing arts. Please note that here "critical" does not mean disparaging; it means careful, objective, and exact evaluation. It involves, too, the development of a mature attitude toward one's performance. A superior performance does not make you a superior person any more than a wretched performance makes you a wretched person. Learn to distinguish between yourself as a person and your performance on any given assignment. Growth and improvement depend on your ability to learn from your mistakes rather than be disheartened by them.

Two checklists follow. The first may be used to measure vocal performance for both radio and television. The second covers the physical aspects of television performance.

Radio and Television Performance Checklist

Pitch	Good ____	Too low ____	Too high ____
Pitch variety	Good ____	Too little ____	Too much ____
Volume	Good ____	Too weak ____	Too loud ____
Tempo	Good ____	Too slow ____	Too fast ____
Tempo variety	Good ____	Too little ____	Inappropriate Variations ____
Vitality	Good ____	Too little ____	Too much ____
Articulation	Good ____	Underarticulated ____ Overarticulated ____	

Voice quality   Good ____ Nasal ____ Husky ____ Thin ____
Other _____

Sibilance	Good ____	Excessive ____
Plosives	Good ____	Excessive ____
Use of microphone	Good ____	Note any problems _____

Pronunciation—note any mispronounced words

_____
_____
_____
_____

Overall evaluation

_____
_____
_____
_____

Work on

_____
_____
_____
_____

*Television
Performance
Checklist*

Eye contact	Good _____ Needs work _____
Use of peripheral vision	Good _____ Needs work _____
Posture	Good _____ Needs work _____
Standing on camera	Steady _____ Rocking _____
Moving on camera	Telegraphed movement? _____
	Moved smoothly? _____
	Sat correctly? _____
	Stood up correctly? _____
Switch cameras	Smooth transition? _____
Property holding	Well-held for cameras? _____
Pointing	Pointing clear and even? _____
Use of cue cards	Maintained camera eye contact? _____
Cues	Responded correctly to cues? _____
Dress	Dressed appropriately? _____
Facial animation	Appropriate? _____ Too much? _____
	Too little? _____

Work on: _____

_____

_____

_____

Areas that showed improvement: _____

_____

_____

_____

_____

4
RADIO EQUIPMENT

This chapter provides basic information about standard broadcast equipment operated by radio announcers. The chapter discusses operational aspects of broadcast equipment and a few basic details of automated radio. (Tips about television equipment are found in Chapters 3, 10, and 12.) As a radio announcer, you must master many aspects of broadcasting in addition to good delivery. Some of these skills are identifying, selecting, and using microphones; cuing and playing records and audiotape cartridges; operating audio consoles; and performing the special functions required at automated radio stations.

As a radio announcer you will be surrounded by costly and delicate equipment; if it is abused or improperly operated, it can defeat your best announcing efforts. Television announcers seldom touch broadcast equipment, but they must know how to conduct themselves in the presence of cameras and microphones. Radio announcers, however, are frequently expected to operate everything in a small station's on-air studio: microphones, turntables, compact disc players, rack-mounted tape recorders, tape cartridge units, and audio consoles. This chapter is an elementary introduction to equipment. You should supplement your reading with practice, for no book can develop your manipulative skills or train your ears to make audio judgments.

MICROPHONES

When sound waves enter a microphone, they set in motion a chain of events culminating in the apparent re-creation of the sound on a radio or television receiver. As the first link in the chain, the microphone is of primary importance. If a microphone is improperly selected, improperly used, or damaged, the sound will be affected adversely throughout the remainder of its trip to the listener and will appear distorted.

Microphones transform sound waves into electrical impulses and are usually classified by internal structure, pickup or polar pattern, and intended use. As an announcer you will probably not select the microphones you use, but you should be able to recognize the types given to you so that you can use each one to the best advantage.

Internal Structure   *Ribbon, or Velocity, Microphones*   The ribbon microphone contains a metallic ribbon, supported at the ends, between the poles of a permanent magnet. The ribbon moves when sound waves strike it, generating voltage that is immediately relayed to the audio console. The straight ribbon, or velocity, microphone is extremely sensitive to all sounds within a great frequency range; is flattering to the human voice; is unaffected by changes in air pressure, humidity, and temperature; and is not prone to picking up reflected sound. You should consider requesting an RCA 77-DX or a Shure SM33 if you want your voice to sound deeper and more resonant, if you have problems with excessive sibilance, or if you tend to pop your plosive consonants. When using a ribbon mic, it is best to stand or sit approximately a foot from it and speak directly into it. This range with a ribbon mic usually makes voice quality deeper, so if you find you have voice reproduction problems at close range, speak at an oblique angle across its front screen.

The RCA 77-DX is widely used in radio. It can be adjusted to a variety of pickup patterns and sound characteristics. Your work will be affected by the way it is set. For voice work the ribbon mic is significantly more flattering when the set screws are turned to "Voice 1" and "Bidirectional."

Dynamic, or Pressure, Microphones   In the dynamic, or pressure, mic, a lightweight molded diaphragm attached to a small wire coil is suspended in a magnetic field. Sound waves striking the diaphragm are relayed to the coil, and the movement of the coil within the magnetic field transforms physical energy into electrical impulses. The dynamic microphone has a number of advantages. It is more rugged than other types; it can be used outdoors with less wind blast; it can be made as small as a person's finger tip; and it can perform better in a wider range of applications than any other type of mic. Only a well-trained audio operator is likely to be bothered by the fact that it does not reproduce the subtle colorations achieved by a high-quality ribbon or condenser mic. In using a dynamic mic, you should stand or sit about a foot away and to one side of the front screen of the instrument. By talking slightly across the screened surface, you should project your voice quality at its best; this is doubly true if you have a tendency to shout or are given to sibilance or popping.

Condenser Microphones   Condenser mics are most often seen in profes-sional recording studios and at stereo FM stations. The condenser is similar to the pressure mic in that it has a diaphragm, but instead of a coiled wire, it has an electrode as a backplate. A capacitance between the diaphragm and the electrode varies with the minute movements of the diaphragm as they reflect the sound waves. If you are asked to work with a high-quality condenser mic, you should treat it as you would a dynamic microphone. If you find that the extreme sensitivity of the condenser is giving you sibilance or popping problems, try working farther away from it and try speaking at an angle. One or both of these adjustments should correct the problem.

Despite continual improvement of internal diaphragm suspension systems, lavaliere condenser mics must be used carefully to avoid pick-ing up unwanted noise. A script being thumbed or rattled three inches away from the lavaliere will be as loud as or louder than a voice coming from a foot or more away. Clothing brushing against the surface of the mic will sound like a forest fire. Nervous toying with the microphone cable will transmit scratching and rumbling sounds directly into the microphone.   If you tend to pop on mic as you sound plosives such as *p, t,* or *k* or if you have excessive sibilance, you may benefit from having a windscreen placed over the face of the microphone. Several manufacturers supply open-cell polyurethane foam windscreens that only slightly affect the frequency response by eliminating some of the highs.

Pickup Patterns   The pickup pattern of a microphone is the shape of the area around it where it picks up sounds with maximum fidelity and volume. Nearly all microphones can pick up sounds from areas outside the ideal pat-tern, but their quality is not as good. For best results, you, the sound source, should be within the pickup pattern, generating enough vol-ume to allow the engineer to keep the volume control knob at a min-imal level. If you are *off mic*—that is, out of the pattern—or if you speak too softly, the audio operator will have to turn up the volume control and the microphones will automatically distort your voice and transmit unwanted sounds from outside the pattern. When you use a stand, hand-held, or control-room mic, you cannot ignore the pickup pattern of the instrument. You are expected to position yourself properly and adjust yourself and the mic to improve the sound.

Manufacturers classify microphones according to four pickup or polar patterns: (1) unidirectional, in which only one side of the microphone is live; (2) bidirectional, or figure eight, in which two sides of the mic are live; (3) omnidirectional (also called nondirectional and hemispherical), in which the mic is live in all directions; and (4) multidirectional (polydirectional or switchable), in which two or more patterns can be achieved by adjusting a control. Unidirectional microphones, except for a few veterans found from time to time, are all cardioid, or heart shaped. Cardioid polar patterns range from normal, to wide, to narrow (or tight), to hypercardioid (or supercardioid). Hypercardioid mics are used chiefly as boom mics in television applications. They have a narrow front angle of sound acceptance and pick up very little sound from the sides.

Descriptions and engineering diagrams (see Figure 4.1) of microphone pickup patterns are inadvertently misleading for two reasons. They do not show the three-dimensionality of the pattern, and they do not indicate that the pattern changes when the relationship between instrument and sound source changes. Because cardioid mics can be placed in every conceivable position between instrument and sound source, the patterns vary in design and are especially difficult to understand from engineering diagrams. The complex cardioid pattern, shown in two dimensions on engineering data sheets, is significantly different when the mic is hand held and when it is stand mounted at a 30-degree angle. The data sheet will show you whether a particular cardioid microphone has a narrow or a wide angle of front sound acceptance, as well as the areas of rear acceptance and rejection, but only actual practice with cardioid mics will teach you how to position them. As you study the typical pickup patterns shown in Figure 4.1, remember that the actual pattern is three-dimensional and that the illustrations for cardioid patterns show the mic lying flat with the screen pointed toward zero degrees, whereas omnidirectional illustrations show the screen pointing directly toward you.

Selecting Microphones

Radio utilizes diverse production methods, thus microphones have become increasingly specialized. A microphone of one design may be ideal for one kind of work but inappropriate for another. One dynamic omnidirectional mic may have been designed to be hand held and another may have been made in miniature for use as a lavaliere. As an announcer, you may expect to work with a number of different mics over the years. Microphones can be classified according to their intended or best use, as explained on page 96.

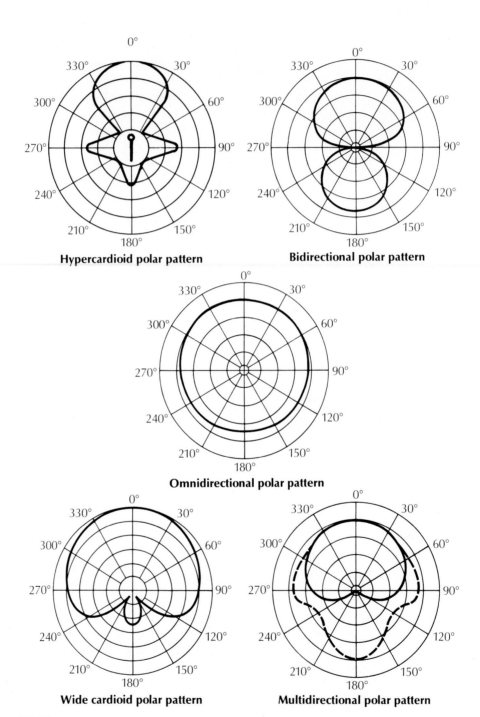

FIGURE 4.1
Microphone polar patterns.

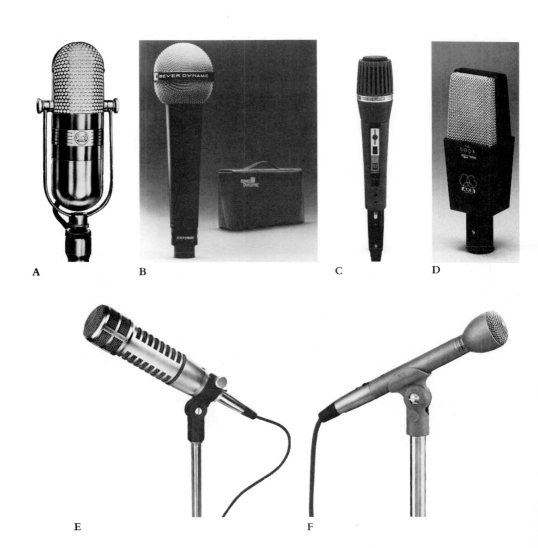

FIGURE 4.2
Types of microphones.   **A.** RCA 77-DX ribbon microphone. (Courtesy RCA)   **B.** Beyer M
500 microphone. Beyer describes this instrument as a ''dynamic ribbon'' microphone. It is
essentially a dynamic mic, but it uses a suspended ribbon rather than a moving coil. (Courtesy Beyer Dynamic, Inc.)   **C.** Shure switchable PE2 microphone. Two built-in filter
switches permit the user to achieve a high-frequency boost and a bass rolloff. (Courtesy
Shure Brothers, Inc.)   **D.** AKG C-414EB multidirectional condenser microphone. (Courtesy
AKG Acoustics, Inc.)   **E.** Electro-Voice RE20 dynamic cardioid microphone. (Courtesy Electro-Voice, Inc.)   **F.** Electro-Voice 635A dynamic omnidirectional microphone. (Courtesy
Electro-Voice, Inc.)

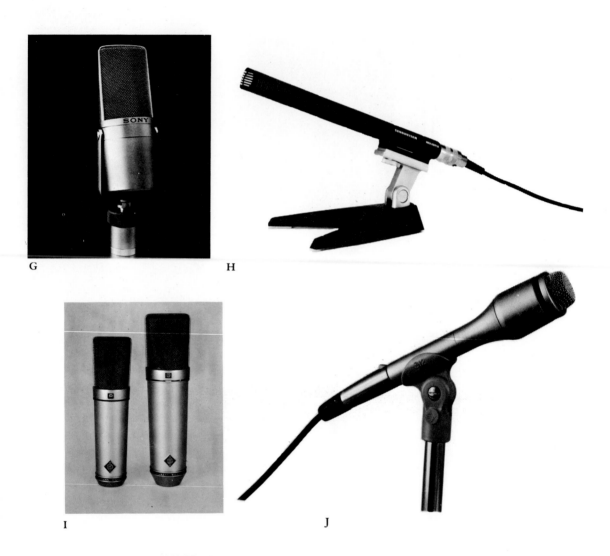

G   H

I   J

FIGURE 4.2
Types of microphones (continued).   **G.** Sony C-47 condenser microphone, which can be switched to uni- and omnidirectional modes. (Courtesy Sony Corporation of America)   **H.** Sennheiser MKH 416TU condenser microphone. (Courtesy Sennheiser Elec. Corp., New York)   **I.** Neuman U 87 and U 89 multidirectional condenser microphones. (Courtesy Gotham Audio Corporation)   **J.** Electro-Voice DO56, a dynamic omnidirectional microphone. (Courtesy Electro-Voice, Inc.)

FIGURE 4.2
Types of microphones (continued).   **K.** Beyer Dynamic MCE-5 Electret condenser microphone. (Courtesy Beyer Dynamic, Inc.)   **L.** Electro-Voice CO90 condenser lavaliere microphone. (Courtesy Electro-Voice, Inc.)   **M.** Swintek wireless microphone. (Courtesy Swintek Enterprises, Inc.)   **N.** Crown PZM®-3LV lavaliere microphone. (Courtesy Crown International Inc. PZM® is a registered trademark of Crown International Inc.)

Announce Microphones   These are found in radio station announce booths and are also used for off-camera film and television narration. Typical announce mics are the Sony C-37P, the Electro-Voice RE15, RE20, and 635A, and the RCA 77-DX.

Stand Microphones   These are used for off-camera narration and in the production of radio commercials. The RCA 77-DX and Shure SM33 are examples.

Hand-held Microphones   These versatile mics can be used indoors or out and can be hand held or desk mounted. The Electro-Voice 635A and RE55 are widely used hand-held microphones.

Studio Boom Microphones   Whereas lavaliere mics have all but replaced television boom mics because of the lower cost of their operation, some boom mics are still used in some television applications. Typical of such microphones are the Electro-Voice CH15S and CL42S.

Lavaliere Microphones   Lavaliere microphones have many advantages in television applications. They are small and unobtrusive, they save the cost of an audio boom operator, and some can be operated as wireless mics. In general use today are the Sony ECM-50 and the Electro-Voice CO90.

Headset Microphones   Miniaturized microphones connected to headsets have become standard for play-by-play sports announcers. Both dynamic and condenser mics are used, but they must be designed to include a honeycomb pop filter in front of the diaphragm.

Wireless Microphones   Wireless microphones are used for work at remote locations and for studio work in which performers need to move without the restraints of a mic cable. The Electro-Voice CO90 is widely used in television production.

Advances in microphones are constantly being made, and instruments not mentioned here will probably be in use by the time you are ready to work. Despite progress in miniaturization, sensitivity, and fidelity, the principles of microphone use will remain the same for many years.

CUING RECORDS

As an announcer for a music radio station, you most likely will spend part of your time cuing up and playing records. Even if a station plays only carted music (music that has been recorded on cartridges), a part of your workday may be spent dubbing discs to carts. Little attention need be given to *playing* carts because you can learn to use them properly in a few minutes. A cart is loaded with a looped, endless audiotape that automatically rewinds as it plays. You insert the cart into the slot in the playback machine (cart machine) and press a button to start the tape. After the tape has played, allow it to run until it stops by itself; it has automatically recued and is ready for the next playing. If you stop the tape before it recues, you will get dead air at the start of its next playing, and it will automatically stop when it reaches the cue position.

Your station may feature compact disc players (CD players), and cuing and playing CDs are simple matters. Compact discs are small—4.7 inches in diameter—and are encoded with digitally recorded music. In digital recording, sound is translated into computer-type on-off pulses. After being recorded, the disc is decoded by a laser beam. Because there is no contact with the disc's surface, there is an absence of surface noise. A typical professional CD player includes displays that show track elapsed time, track remaining time, disc elapsed time,

FIGURE 4.3
Tapecaster stereo cartridge recorder. (Courtesy Auditronics, Inc.)

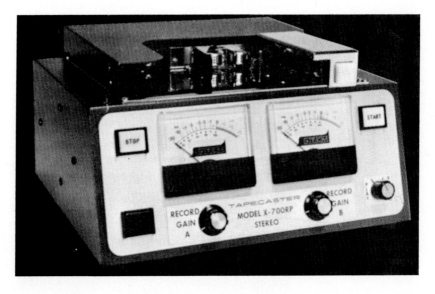

FIGURE 4.4
Studer A725 professional
compact disc player.
(Courtesy Studer Revox
America, Inc.)

and disc remaining time. The disc spins at speeds ranging from 200 to 500 revolutions per minute (rpm) and gets up to speed almost instantly. To play a CD, you load the small disc into its playing compartment, press *busses* (buttons) that program the machine to play a particular cut, press "pause," and, when ready, press the "play" bus.

It is unlikely that your station will play compact discs exclusively, so you should learn how to operate a conventional turntable. Most broadcast turntables have the following components: (1) a rotating table that is connected to the motor, (2) a pickup or tone arm, (3) a pickup cartridge, (4) an off-on switch, (5) a variable equalizer, (6) a speed switch, and (7) an attachment for playing large-holed 45 rpm discs.

1. *Rotating table (turntable).* This is usually made of metal and may be covered by a felt or rubber pad. The pad is not attached to the metal,

FIGURE 4.5
A Technics professional
turntable and tone arm.
(Courtesy KTIM, San
Rafael, California)

and some announcers cue the record, hold the pad, turn on the power, and release the pad (and the record on it) when it is time to play the music. This is called *slip starting*. A direct drive turntable is, in effect, an electric motor. Motors are composed of a stationary part, the stator, and a rotating part, called the rotor. The turntable acts as a rotor on direct drive turntables. Older turntables may have a rim-driven mechanism, but most such old-timers have been phased out.

2. *Pickup or tone arm*. Pickup arms used for broadcast are both counterbalanced and damped to prevent damage to records. The tone arm is adjusted to put less than one gram of pressure on the grooves of the record, and viscous damping, using fluid silicone in a hydraulic application, prevents the arm from making sharp or sudden movements.

3. *Pickup cartridges and styluses*. Turntables are equipped with plug-in cartridges. Styluses are spherical or elliptical in shape. Spherical styluses are generally found on home equipment, and elliptical styluses are preferred in broadcast applications.

4. *Off-on switch*. All turntables are equipped with a power switch. Most disc jockeys now start their records by pressing the "on" switch instead of slip starting them.

5. *Variable equalizer*. Some older turntables are equipped with variable equalizers, or filters, that allow you to control the frequencies being transmitted. Discs poorly recorded or pressed can be made to sound better by eliminating high frequencies. At most stations, records in need of equalization are dubbed to tape carts with appropriate corrections made in the board.

6. *Speed switch*. Turntables are provided with speed-selector switches, offering a choice of 33⅓ or 45 rpm.

7. *45-rpm attachment*. Many turntables have a recessed metal hub in the center. By turning the hub, you can raise it to accommodate large-holed 45-rpm discs. Some turntables require an adapter which fits over the center spindle.

Discs have dead grooves before the sound begins. Because you do not want several seconds of dead air between your announcement and the start of the recording, you must *cue up* your records. Cuing involves the following steps. (1) While one record is being broadcast, place the next selection on a spare turntable. (2) Using a control on the audio console, activate the cue box or cue speaker. (3) Place the stylus on the outside groove of the record. (4) Disengage the drive mechanism so that the table spins freely. (5) Spin the table clockwise until you hear the start of the sound on the cue speaker. (6) Stop the table and turn the record counterclockwise. (7) When you hear the sound—now being played backward—stop, continue spinning the record a short distance into the dead air grooves. (8) Engage the drive mechanism at the proper operating speed. To play the disc on the air, you need only open the volume control and turn on the power switch.

The reason for turning the record back to a point in the dead air is to allow the turntable to reach its operating speed before the sound begins. All turntables need a little time to go from zero rpm to operating speed; before they reach operating speed, sound is distorted. This *wowing* is as unacceptable as several seconds of dead air; a little practice with a particular turntable should enable you to cue records unerringly.

AUDIO CONSOLES

Most radio announcers will, at one time or another, have to operate an audio console, or board. Disc jockeys almost always work their own boards, and although announcers on all-news stations and hosts and hostesses on talk shows seldom work the board, they probably were required to do so earlier in their careers.

The audio console picks up the electrical impulses coming from microphones, cart machines, or turntables; mixes the sound in proper proportions if more than one signal is coming in; controls the amplitude of the electrical impulse; amplifies the sound; and sends it, by means of another amplifier, to the transmitter. A microphone is positioned on or very near the console. Several audiotape cartridge machines are placed within reach of the console operator, and two turntables usually are positioned, one on either side of the operator. The physical arrangement may vary in small details, but it is usually similar to the KTIM on-air studio shown in Figure 4.6. Most disc jockeys, as well as announcers reading station breaks, news bulletins, or live commercials, work in an on-air studio and operate their own console. Combining engineering and announcing is called *working combo*.

Audio consoles may seem a bit intimidating at first glance, but they actually are simple to operate. On-air boards (those used by DJs) require the operation of only a few controls. Production boards are more complex, and those who operate them must have special training beyond that needed for the operation of on-air boards. Production con-

FIGURE 4.6
Michael Fox plays big
band music, using a
Ramko Research console,
an Electro-Voice RE20
dynamic microphone,
and Technics turntables.
(Courtesy KTIM, San
Rafael, California)

soles are equipped with equalization, compression, noise-reduction, and assorted *sweetening* features that make possible the production of commercials, station promos, musical IDs or logos, and other program material of high quality. As an announcer, you probably will not have to operate a production console. As an announcer-engineer, however, especially at a smaller station, you probably will be asked to operate the production board. This book cannot give you all details of audio control and sound mixing; if you are heading toward a career that may require sophistication in audio production, you should enroll in appropriate courses of instruction. A sophisticated production console, as well as other production equipment, is shown in Figure 4.7.

Standard Console Features

Most boards, however different they may seem at first glance, are essentially the same. You will find two types of consoles in general use: those that feature a row of rotating volume controls (*potentiometers,* or *pots*), and those that use vertical faders. Most boards with rotating pots are made as a single unit; most boards with vertical faders are made up of several plug-in modules, and elements can be shifted as desired. Each station uses the input potential of its board in a unique way, so you should not merely learn to operate one board by rote. If you understand the reasons for doing what you do, you will be able to transfer to other consoles with little additional instruction.

FIGURE 4.7
Production Director Albert Lord operates an ABX-34 production console, Technics turntables, Tomcat tape cart machines, Tascam cassette machines, Otari reel-to-reel tape recorders, and Sennheiser 441 microphones. (Courtesy Albert Lord and KFRC, San Francisco)

A stereo board is no problem for the radio combo operator. Stereo discs are already balanced, so the operator does not have to correct them on the board. Program announcements are usually given over only one of the two broadcast channels, but even when both channels are used, the console's controls will maintain an even balance. If the stereo signal reaching the transmitter is distorted, the combo operator merely notes it and asks the telephone company to check the lines.

The following description of a simple monaural console stresses

FIGURE 4.8
Auditronics 700 Series audio mixing console—a production board. (Courtesy Auditronics, Inc.)

function, rather than electronics, to show you how the board relates to your work.

The sounds of radio begin with the electrical impulses from microphones, cart machines, or turntables. Suppose we are designing a console, adding elements as we perceive a need for them, to serve an AM station of moderate size. Because the station does not broadcast in AM stereo, a monaural board will serve our needs. The station has three production areas: an *on-air studio* where the board will be housed; a *newsroom;* and a small *production studio,* which will have its own production console.

Our first problem is to feed the outputs of the announce mic and the newsroom mic into the board. Mics generate weak signals, so the output of each must be boosted, or amplified, before we can send its signal out of the board to a recorder or a transmitter. The amplifiers that receive and boost signals from mics are *preamplifiers (preamps);* the one that collects, boosts, and sends the sounds to the transmitter or tape recorder is the *program amplifier.*

In addition to the two microphones, we also need to feed through the board four tape cartridge players, two turntables, and two rack-mounted open-reel tape recorders, as well as lines from a network, UPI Radio, a mobile van, and a remote line. With the microphones, this adds up to fourteen inputs, so there would seem to be a need for fourteen channels, but we can economize here by installing *input selector switches,* which will allow us to feed more than one signal through each input channel. The two microphones have one input channel each because they need to have their sound boosted by preamps, but the other twelve inputs—which do not need preamps—can be selectively fed through six input channels. With the two mic channels, this makes a total of eight input channels to handle fourteen inputs.

We now see two problems calling for more controls: we need to vary the volume of sound, and we need a switch for opening and closing microphones. We regulate volume by adding potentiometers, or pots. A pot, also known as a *fader, mixer, attenuator,* and *gain control,* can be in the form of a rotating knob or a vertical slider. For the two microphones (on-air announce mic and newsroom mic), we use three-position selector switches, with one position delegated to "off," one to the mic ("on"), and one spare for any unanticipated future use. We give each of the other input channels three-position selector switches. This gives us a position for off, and two channels for sending signals; if we had only one channel, we could not use the board for two functions

FIGURE 4.9
Auditronics 200 Series
on-air broadcast console.
(Courtesy Auditronics,
Inc.)

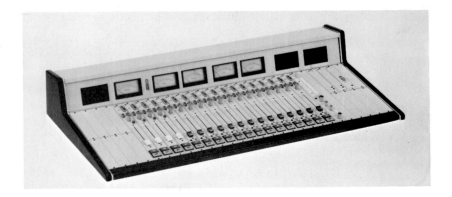

FIGURE 4.9
Auditronics 200 Series
on-air broadcast console.
(Courtesy Auditronics,
Inc.)

at the same time. With two channels we can broadcast a news roundup from our newsroom while simultaneously receiving and recording AP Radio news for later broadcast. Each of the two channels gets its own program amplifier, so we now have four amplifiers for the board—two preamps for the microphones, and two program amplifiers. Our board has become a two-channel, monaural audio console.

In adding volume controls, we have raised another problem: how can we judge the volume? We cannot listen to ourselves on an air monitor because the sound of our broadcast would reenter the mic and create an unearthly howl called *feedback,* so we add a meter that gives us a picture of the sound. Our meter may be an *LED* (light-emitting diode) meter, a series of dots that are illuminated according to the strength of the signal. Many portable AM-FM cassette decks use LED meters, so most people are familiar with them. We may, instead, install a meter with a swinging needle, called a *VU* (volume unit) meter or *VI* (volume indicator) meter. The VU meter has a swinging needle that registers volume on a calibrated scale. A semicircular black line registers volume units from 1 to 100, at which point it becomes a red line. If we are too low on the scale, we are said to be "in the mud," and if we are too high we are "bending the needle," "in the red," or "spilling over." If we peak too high on the scale, we can distort the signal and possibly damage the equipment. We install two meters, one to show us the signal going out over the air, the other for auditioning a signal that is not being broadcast. We place the meters at the top and center of the board, where they are easily visible. Stereo boards require a separate meter for each channel.

We now have everything we need to pick up sounds from our two mics and send them through the board to the transmitter or a tape

FIGURE 4.10
A VU or VI meter.

recorder. We can open and close the mics, mix the signals from the mic with those from tape carts or turntables, boost the signal strength of the mics, see the volume level, and regulate the volume. Now we have the following configuration on our board (see Figure 4.11):

SOUND SOURCE	POT NUMBER
on-air announce mic	1
newsroom mic	2
cart #1 and turntable #1	3
cart #2 and turntable #2	4
cart #3 and tape recorder #1	5
cart #4 and tape recorder #2	6
network and UPI Radio	7
mobile van and remote line	8

To avoid the difficulties that would arise in manually balancing the inputs of more than one sound source, we add a *master pot* that can raise or lower at the same time the volume of all sounds being mixed. After balancing of the microphone and turntable pots, for instance, the VU meter may tell us that the mixed sound is too weak or too strong; all we have to do to correct the problem is adjust the master pot.

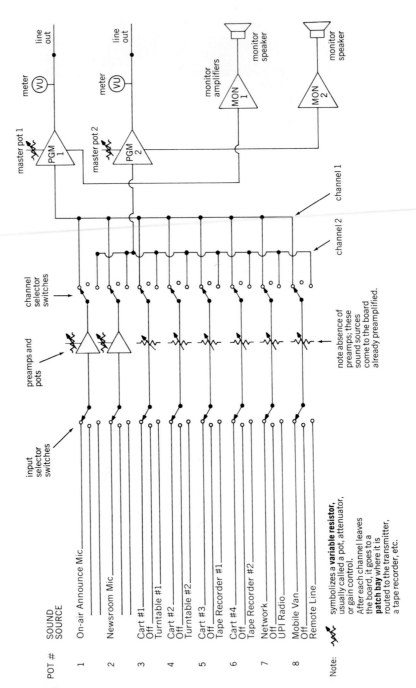

FIGURE 4.11
Schematic drawing of mixing board.

In order to hear material being broadcast or recorded, we add a *monitor speaker* for each of the two channels. If we have patched channel 1 to the transmitter, we can listen to our programming on monitor speaker 1; monitor speaker 2 can be used to audition material not then being broadcast or to listen to program material being recorded for later broadcast. The monitor speakers need amplifiers of higher power than the program amplifiers to boost the signal to the level needed to activate the loudspeakers. Each has its own *monitor pot* so that we can raise and lower the volume of sound in the control room. We also install a *channel monitor switch* so that we can selectively monitor channels 1 and 2. *Muting relays* are installed to cut off the monitor speakers whenever the control room mic is opened.

Before broadcasting discs we must cue them up, and this means we must be able to hear them without broadcasting the sound. We add a *cue speaker* or cue box with its own cue amplifier fed by all nonmicrophone pots. When each of these pots is turned to an extreme counterclockwise position, the cue amplifier and speaker are automatically activated. We could use other arrangements, but this one seems best. With a turntable or tape pot turned completely off and into cue, there is no possibility of accidentally sending our cuing sounds out over the air—unless, of course, the control room mic were open at the same time. To make sure that we do not confuse cuing sounds with program sounds, we place the monitor speakers and the cue speaker in different parts of the control room.

Finally, we add a *headphone jack* for *headphones* so that we can listen to either channel without having sound emanate from the monitor or cue speakers; both speakers automatically cut off when we plug in. This feature allows us to talk over music on the air. We can listen to the balance between our voice and the music without using the monitor speaker, which, of course, would create feedback. We also use phones to cue records when working combo. With the cue speaker dead, there is no chance of cuing sounds accidentally being broadcast over the control room mic.

Now the audio console is complete. We could, of course, add feature after feature, but nothing more is really needed for most modern radio applications. Many radio stations are now installing far simpler consoles than the board we have put together, but you cannot reasonably expect to find one at every station. The board we have created is a practical compromise between the extremes of simplicity and the complexity that is characteristic of production boards.

AUTOMATED RADIO STATIONS

In the past twenty years, many radio stations have become automated. Most of this automation has been in FM or AM stereo, with some monaural AM stations having become automated as well. Automation provides the following advantages for station owners: stations can be operated with fewer employees; owners of both AM and FM stations can use the AM staff to program the FM station; a small station can have a "big city" sound; and disc jockeys can do their day's announcing work in a half-hour, which helps them sustain energetic delivery.

Opponents of automated radio are offended by the sacrifice of instantaneousness, long thought to be radio's most valuable characteristic. Opponents also claim that automated radio sounds canned and that even the most sophisticated equipment and the most skilled operators cannot make an automated station sound live. Overweighing these complaints is one based on economics: automated radio means fewer jobs for announcers.

Regardless of the arguments, automated radio is here to stay, and you should become familiar with the essentials of automation. Because several automation systems are in use today, you will have to learn the details of each particular system on the job. This brief overview is designed to make you aware of automation, to provide you with an idea of how an automated radio station works, and to expose you to some of the terms used in automated radio.

Most automated systems rely on three components. A *controller*, or *brain*, is programmed by an operator; a series of reel-to-reel tape reproducers play the station's music; and a bank of tape cartridge machines stores commercials, public-service announcements, voice-track program openers, station jingles, time announcements, news headlines, weather reports, and network access announcements. Such systems also include an automatic logging device and an internal clock programmed to give accurate time signals that can be used to join and leave a parent network's hourly newscasts.

The controller's chief function is to intersperse music with other program elements. A middle-of-the-road station might use four large music reels—one containing music from the current charts, a second playing golden hits of the past, a third containing up-tempo music to be played at the start of each hour following station identification, and a fourth made up of the music director's favorites. Nearly all such stations have a rigid format that is repeated hourly.

As an announcer for an automated station, you will be expected to spend some of your time programming the controller and the rest of your working day performing a variety of tasks: recording music introductions, weather reports, commercials, and newscasts; loading the cart machines and replacing carts that have served their purpose; and, in many stations, providing preventive maintenance for the equipment. Obviously, both recorded weather reports and newscasts are recorded a short time before being broadcast.

5
PHONETIC TRANSCRIPTION

As an announcer, you face unique and challenging problems in pronunciation. In news, commercial, and classical music copy you frequently must read words of foreign origin, and you are expected to read them fluently and correctly. In newscasting you are expected not only to pronounce foreign words and names with accuracy and authority, but also to know when and how to Americanize many of them. Unlike your British counterpart, you are not allowed to Anglicize categorically, and you would be seen as odd or incompetent if you said DON KWICKS-OAT for Don Quixote or DON JEW-UN for Don Juan, as do British announcers.

English pronunciation is subject to few rules, thus English is one of the most difficult languages to learn. Whereas in Spanish the letters *ch* are always pronounced as in the name *Charles*, in American English *ch* may be pronounced in the following ways:

sh as in *Cheyenne*
tch as in *champion*
k as in *chemist*
two separate sounds, as in the name *MacHeath*

Other examples can be cited. In the sentence fragment "I usually used to use this," the letter *s* is sounded differently in the words *usually*, *used*, and *use*. The letter *a* is pronounced differently in such words as *cap, father, mate, care, call, boat,* and *about*. Similar variations are seen in all other vowel sounds and in most consonants as well. For example, *th* is pronounced differently in *Thomas, though,* and *then*; *r* is pronounced differently in *run, fire,* and *boor*. At times letters are silent as in *mnemonic, Worcester,* and *Wednesday*. At other times and for as little reason, a word is correctly pronounced only when all letters in it receive some value as *misunderstood* and *plenipotentiary*. The letters *ie* are sometimes pronounced "eye" as in *pie*, and sometimes "ee" as in *piece*. Two words with almost identical spellings, *said* and *maid*, have quite different pronunciations. In short, the only constants are variation and change.

Of course, common words do not cause difficulty. But try to determine the correct pronunciation of the following words according to your knowledge of language and any rules of pronunciation you may have learned:

quay	flaccid	dais
mortgage	interstices	gunwale
medieval	forecastle	brooch
egregious	cliché	phthisic

Correct pronunciation of these words may be found at the end of this chapter. After checking the pronunciation of these words, you will certainly agree that no amount of puzzling over them, and no rules of pronunciation, would have helped.

Correct American pronunciation of English is not only inherently illogical but also changes with time and common usage, generally tending toward simpler forms. It is becoming more and more acceptable to pronounce *clothes* KLOZE, for example, to leave the first *r* out of *February*, and to slide over the slight "y" sound in *news* so that it becomes NOOZ.

The whole problem of English pronunciation was reduced to its most obvious absurdity by George Bernard Shaw, who wrote the letters *ghoti* and asked how his manufactured word was to be pronounced. After all attempts had failed, Shaw answered that it was to be pronounced "fish." The *gh* is pronounced "f" as in *enough*, the *o* is pronounced "i" as in *women*, and the *ti* is pronounced "sh" as in *motion*.

If you have difficulty pronouncing words whose spelling offers little help, you may be doubly perplexed by American personal names and place names derived from foreign originals. As a sportscaster, for example, you cannot assume that a player named Braun gives his own name the correct German pronunciation "Brown." He may pronounce it "Brawn" or "Brahn." If you tried to pronounce every foreign-derived name as it would be pronounced in the country of origin, your audience would wince every time you failed to follow established custom.

American place names present the same problem. In Nebraska, *Beatrice* is pronounced BEE-AT'-RIS. In South Dakota, *Pierre* is pronounced PEER. In California, *Delano* is pronounced DUH-LANE'-O. In Kentucky, *Versailles* is pronounced VER-SALES'. In Georgia, *Vienna* is pronounced VYE-EN'-UH. Any community, of course, has the right to pronounce its name as it pleases. In the Southwest, Spanish place names are conventionally pronounced neither as the Spanish original nor as they seem to be spelled. The *San* in *San Jose* is pronounced SAN (as in sand) rather than the Spanish SAN (as in *son*net), and HO-ZAY is used rather than an Americanized JO-ZAY or the Spanish HO-SAY. Because the only standard for pronouncing place names is the common practice of the natives of the region, you must be on guard to avoid error. All American communities have specialized and capricious ways of pronouncing street names and the names of suburbs, nearby towns, and geographical landmarks. Radio and television announcers who are new to an area and who consistently offend listeners with mispronunciations may not be around long enough to learn regional preferences. Bostonians may not care if you mispronounce *Pago Pago,* but they will be outraged if you make *Quincy* rhyme with *mince-ee.*

It is not surprising that the problems inherent in the pronunciation of American English have given rise to various systems of phonetic transcription. Three of these systems are outlined here, the first two in brief, and the third—the International Phonetic Alphabet—in some detail.

WIRE-SERVICE PHONETICS

Several news agencies provide radio and television stations with news stories, sending them over telephone lines to teleprinters. When a word or a name that might cause pronunciation problems is transmitted, that word often is phoneticized—given a *pronouncer*—as in this example:

```
(SYDNEY, AUSTRALIA)  THE ISLAND NATION OF VANUATU

(VAHN-OO-AH'-TOO)--FORMERLY THE NEW HEBRIDES--WAS HIT TO-

DAY BY A STRONG EARTHQUAKE.
```

Wire-service phonetics are suitable for most purposes, though a few sounds defy accurate transcription. With a little practice—and some ingenuity—you can make wire-service phonetics into a handy tool.

Consonants are easiest to master because most of them represent only one sound. Thus T, D, S, Z, and M, for instance, can hardly cause confusion. Other consonant sounds need two letters to represent them, as with TH (THIN), CH (CHAT), and SH (SHOP). One consonant, Y, is used for two sounds—one a consonant and one a diphthong. As a consonant, it appears in the word *yeoman* (YO'-MUN); as a diphthong, it represents an entirely different sound, as in *sleight* (SLYT).

The TH symbol is the most troublesome, for it represents the initial sounds in *think* and *then*. Context can help in some instances, but not in all. It works in *hearth* (HAHRTH), but not in *calisthenics*. Anyone seeing (KAL-UHS-THEN'-IKS) would read THEN as the common English word, and this is not the correct sound.

Some vowel sounds are a bit troublesome, but they can usually be differentiated by their contexts. The letters OO, for example, stand for the vowel sounds in *food* and *poor*, which are not, of course, the same sound. Here is how context can distinguish between them:

buoy (BOO'-EE)   *Purim* (POOR'-IHM)

In these examples, the common words *boo* and *poor* tell us which sound we are to give the OO in these words.

All of the symbols of wire-service phonetics follow, arranged in the same order in which they appear in the International Phonetic Alphabet. Remember, we are dealing with *speech sounds*, so alphabetic arrangement has no relevance. Key words have been chosen for reasons of clarity, so most are quite commonplace. Where two symbols are given for the same sound, it is to give users an option. For example, in the second vowel listed, I works well for the word *impel*, but IH works better for *Bethesda*. If this word were transcribed as BI-THEZ'-DUH, a reader might pronounce the first syllable as in the English word *by*.

Vowels

SYMBOL	KEY WORD	PHONETIC TRANSCRIPTION
EE	*believe*	(BIH-LEEV')
I or IH	*impel, Bethesda*	(IM-PEL') (BIH-THEZ'-DUH)
AY	*bait*	(BAYT)
E or EH	*pester, beret*	(PEST'-ER) (BEH-RAY')
A	*can*	(KAN)
AH	*comma*	(KAH'-MUH)

SYMBOL	KEY WORD	PHONETIC TRANSCRIPTION
AW	*lost*	(LAWST)
O	*host*	(HOST)
OO[1]	*mooring*	(MOOR'-ING)
OO[1]	*pool*	(POOL)
ER	*early*	(ER'-LEE)
UH	*sofa*	(SO'-FUH)

Diphthongs

SYMBOL	KEY WORD	PHONETIC TRANSCRIPTION
Y[2]	*lighting*	(LYT'-ING)
AU	*grouse*	(GRAUS)
OY	*oiling*	(OY'-LING)
YU	*using*	(YUZ'-ING)

Consonants

(*Note:* The consonants P, B, T, D, K, G, F, V, S, Z, H, M, N, L, W, and R are pronounced as in English. The symbol G is always pronounced as in *green,* never as in *Gene.*)

SYMBOL	KEY WORD	PHONETIC TRANSCRIPTION
TH[3]	*think*	(THINGK)
TH[3]	*then*	(THEN)
SH	*clash*	(KLASH)
ZH	*measure*	(MEHZH'-ER)
CH	*church*	(CHERCH)
J	*adjust*	(UH-JUST')
NG	*singing*	(SING'-ING)
Y[4]	*yeoman*	(YO'-MUN)

The key words used are commonly known, and it is not for such words that wire-service phonetics were developed. Here are some typical words that might be given pronouncers by a wire service:

Beirut (BAY-ROOT')   *Sidon* (SYD'-UN)
Bayreuth (BY'-ROYT)   *Coelho* (KWAY'-LO)

[1] As indicated previously, OO stands for two different sounds.
[2] Note that the Y symbol is used for two different sounds.
[3] Note preceding discussion of the use of the same symbol for these two different sounds.
[4] As indicated earlier, Y is used both as a diphthong and as a consonant sound.

Clio (KLY'-O)   *Ojai* (O'-HY)
Schuylkill (SKUHL'-KIL)   *Yosemite* (YO-SEM'-IH-TEE)
Faneuil (FAN'-UHL)   *Hamtramck* (HAM-TRAM'-IK)

At times you will have to read a news story for which no pronouncers are given. In a "rip and read" operation, you will have to attempt difficult copy without adequate preparation time. When time permits, you should do your own transcribing of difficult words:

(NASHVILLE, TENNESSEE) MEDICAL RESEARCHERS REVEALED TODAY A STUDY SHOWING THAT AS FEW AS TWO CUPS OF COFFEE CAN CUT THE BLOOD FLOW TO YOUR BRAIN BY 10 TO 20 PERCENT. DR. WILLIAM WILSON, ASSISTANT PROFESSOR OF PSYCHIATRY AT VANDERBILT UNIVERSITY, AND CO-AUTHOR OF THE STUDY, SAID: "WHILE THE BLOOD-FLOW REDUCTION DOES NOT SEEM SEVERE ENOUGH TO CAUSE PROBLEMS IN NORMAL INDIVIDUALS, IT IS UNCLEAR WHETHER IT MAY INCREASE THE RISK OF TRANSIENT ISCHEMIC (IZ-KEE'-MIK) ATTACKS AND CEREBRAL INFARCTIONS (SEH-REE'-BRUHL IN-FARK'-SHUNZ) IN HIGH-RISK INDIVIDUALS OR THOSE RECOVERING FROM CEREBROVASCULAR (SEH-REE'-BRO-VAS'-KYU-LER) ACCIDENTS." CAFFEINE COULD ALSO MAGNIFY THE EFFECTS OF CERTAIN DRUGS, SUCH AS THE DIET DRUG PHENYLPROPANOLAMINE (FEEN'-UHL-PRO-PAN-OHL'-UH-MEEN), WHICH ALREADY CONTAINS CAFFEINE.

Wire-service phonetics work well in this example, but there are times when the system will not work. There is simply no foolproof way of using the twenty-six letters of the English language to represent more than forty speech sounds. Furthermore, the wire-service system does not use symbols for most foreign speech sounds that do not occur in English. Until a few years ago, teletype machines were limited to the same symbols found on an ordinary typewriter. Today's teleprinters, however, can be programmed to reproduce any symbol desired, so the time may come when additional pronunciation symbols will be added to the twenty-six letters now in use. A good starting point would be to add these symbols:

[ð] for the initial sound in *then*
[ʊ] for the vowel sound in *go͝od*

At the end of Chapter 7, "Foreign Pronunciation," there is news and commercial copy featuring names and words in a variety of foreign languages. For practice in using wire-service phonetics it is suggested that you transcribe these names and words into phonetics and then read the copy aloud. Work with this—and other practice copy—until you find it easy to transcribe into wire-service phonetics, and until you can read such copy without errors or hesitation.

DIACRITICAL MARKS

Dictionaries use a system of phonetic transcription that features small marks placed above the vowels *a, e, i, o,* and *u,* as well as a few additional symbols for sounds such as *th* as in *thin* and *zh* as in *vision*. Although diacritical marks are not totally standardized, variations from dictionary to dictionary are slight. *The American Heritage Dictionary* uses these symbols:

ă pat / ā pay / â care / ä father
ĕ pet / ē be
ĭ pit / ī pie / î pier
ŏ pot / ō toe / ô paw
o͞o took / o͞o boot
th thin / *th* this
ŭ cut / û urge
zh vision
ə about

The American Heritage Dictionary uses 17 symbols to indicate the vowel sounds of the English language. *Webster's Collegiate Dictionary,* on the other hand, uses 30 symbols. If you decide to use diacritical marks to indicate correct pronunciation on your scripts, it is important to adopt *one* system of marks and stick with it. Going from one dictionary to another could be confusing.

Diacritical marks have at least three important limitations. First, they are rather difficult to learn and to remember. The publishers of American dictionaries recognize this fact, and they reproduce a guide to pronunciation at the bottom of every page. A second disadvantage is that diacritical marks were not designed for use by oral readers. The marks are small and vary only slightly in their configurations. When accuracy under pressure is demanded, diacritical marks often fail to meet the test. A final limitation of the dictionary method of transcription is that the key words used to identify symbols vary in pronunciation from area to area. To learn that *fog* is pronounced as *dog* tells a Texan that "fawg" rhymes with "dawg," just as it tells a Rhode Islander that "fahg" rhymes with "dahg." Some modern dictionaries have developed rather sophisticated pronunciation guides. They have eliminated some ambiguity through the use of more standardized key words; have added fairly extensive discussions of pronunciation, as well as symbols to indicate foreign speech sounds not heard in the English language; and have included a few symbols from more sophisticated systems of phonetic transcription. They remain less than satisfactory, however, for serious students of speech.

THE INTERNATIONAL PHONETIC ALPHABET (IPA)

The International Phonetic Alphabet (IPA) was devised to overcome the ambiguities of earlier systems of speech transcription. Like any other system that attempts to transcribe sounds into written symbols, it is not totally accurate, but it comes closer to perfection than any other system in widespread use. The International Phonetic Association has assigned individual written symbols to all the speech sounds of the major languages of the world. Thus, whether the language is French, German, or English, the symbol [e] is always pronounced "ay" as in *bait*. Speech sounds not found in English have distinct symbols—for example, [x] represents the sound *ch* as in the German word *ach* and no other sound, and [y] represents the sound *u* as in the French word *lune*.

IPA is a system of encoding correct pronunciation for efficient and accurate retrieval, but you can use it only when you know the correct pronunciation of the word to be encoded. Obviously, your use of IPA will be reserved for the few names and words that appear in your copy and require you to turn to a dictionary, gazetteer, or similar source of information. *The Associated Press Style Book* (Lorenz Press, Dayton, OH,

1977) suggests the following sources for determining correct pronunciation in each of several different problem categories:

CATEGORY	SOURCE
Persons	The individual featured in the story; failing that, members of the family or associates
Foreign names	Appropriate embassy or consulate
Foreign place names	*Columbia Lippincott Gazetteer of the World*
State or regional place names	State or regional historical societies or highway patrol
Members of legislatures	Clerk of legislature

To this useful list should be added Kenyon and Knott, *A Pronouncing Dictionary of American English* (G. & C. Merriam, Springfield, Mass., 1953) and the *NBC Handbook of Pronunciation* (Thomas Y. Crowell, New York, 1964) for American and foreign place names and for the names of famous composers, authors, artists, scientists, and history makers.

Once you have determined the correct pronunciation of a word, you can render it in IPA symbols directly above the problem word in your script. Having done so, you should be able to read it on the air with little chance of stumbling. Here is a sample script:

```
                THE MAYOR OF THE SMALL NORTH CAROLINA TOWN OF
['kɪmbl̩tən]
KIMBOLTON SAID TODAY THAT HE IS SKEPTICAL ABOUT REPORTS OF

FLYING SAUCERS ABOVE HIS COMMUNITY.
```

In this example, a glance at the *Pronouncing Dictionary of American English* would show that *Kimbolton* is pronounced KIM-BOLT'-UN [kɪm'boltn̩] in the Ohio community of that name, but that a town of the same name in North Carolina is pronounced KIM'-BUL-TUN ['kɪmbl̩tən]. The correct pronunciation of the name of this town may seem of slight importance to some, but to a professional announcer it is a matter of pride to be as accurate as time and resources permit.

Though IPA seems formidable at first, it actually is easier to learn than the system of diacritical markings found in dictionaries. You will find many uses for IPA, and you should make a sincere effort to learn it. Because spoken language is the communication medium used by announcers, mastery of any aspect of human speech will benefit your work. It is true that only a small (but growing) number of professional announcers are familiar with IPA, but it also is true that all would benefit from knowing and using it. Those who do not know IPA usually follow the principles of wire-service phonetic encoding, adding to that system symbols of their own as necessity demands. Such a system is capable of handling most of the pronunciation problems that arise in a day's work, but it falters often enough to warrant being replaced by a more refined and accurate system. IPA has several advantages. (1) It is an unvarying system of transcription in which one symbol represents only one speech sound. (2) Every sound in any language, however subtle it may be, is invested with a separate symbol. (3) Once the correct pronunciation of each sound is learned, it allows almost no possibility of error because of regional dialect. (4) It is the most nearly perfect system of describing human speech sounds yet devised.

As time goes by, IPA commands more and more attention. The excellent *NBC Handbook of Pronunciation*—virtually a must for any announcer—transcribes names and places into IPA. Many foreign-language dictionaries and texts use IPA to indicate correct pronunciation. Drama departments use IPA to help teach dialects, and music departments use it to teach singers foreign pronunciation. The Kenyon and Knott *A Pronouncing Dictionary of American English* transcribes exclusively into IPA.

Like any system for indicating correctness in speech sounds, IPA defines each sound in terms of its use in a particular word. Thus, in indicating the correct sound of the symbol [i], IPA tells us that it is pronounced like the vowel sound of the word *bee*. Though this poses no problem where the key word is pronounced uniformly throughout the United States and Canada, a distinct problem arises where regional variations in the pronunciation of the key words exist. For example, in southern British, as well as in the speech of eastern New England, the sound [ɑ], as in *father*, is not used in words spelled with *o*, and the sounds [ɒ], as in the eastern New England *wash*, and [ɔ], as in *bought*, are not differentiated; thus *bomb*, *wash*, and *bought* are all pronounced with the same vowel sound, which varies from [ɒ] to [ɔ]. The speech sounds and the key words used in describing them are found in General American speech, unless otherwise indicated. General American speech is defined as that spoken by well-educated citizens of the Canadian and United States Midwest and Far West.

Please note that if you live in a region of the United States or Canada where General American is not spoken, you may experience some difficulty in learning the IPA symbols. If, for example, you live in the southeastern United States, and you pronounce the word *bait* as most Americans pronounce *bite*, then the key words used to explain the IPA may confuse you. But a little extra effort can turn the IPA into a useful tool for you.

IPA symbols represent vowel sounds, diphthongs or glides, and consonants. In this section of the book, only the sounds in American speech will be listed. Symbols for foreign speech sounds are discussed in Chapter 7.

Vowels

Vowel sounds are classified as front vowels and back vowels, depending on where they are formed in the mouth. The front vowels are produced through the vibration of the vocal folds in the throat and are articulated by the tongue and teeth near the front of the mouth. The back vowels are produced in the same manner but are articulated by the tongue and mouth opening in the rear of the mouth. The front vowels are:

[i]   This sound is pronounced "ee" as in *beet*. Phonetically, then, *beet* is spelled [bit].

[ɪ]   This sound is pronounced "ih" as in *bit*. Phonetically, *bit* is spelled [bɪt].

[e]   This sound is pronounced "ay" as in *bait*. Phonetically, *bait* is spelled [bet].

[ɛ]   This sound is pronounced "eh" as in *bet*. Phonetically, *bet* is spelled [bɛt].

[æ]   This sound is pronounced "aah" as in *bat*. Phonetically, *bat* is spelled [bæt].

[a]   This sound is pronounced "aah," as the word *bath* is pronounced in the eastern United States. This sound is not usually heard in General American speech, but the symbol must be learned because it is a part of two of the diphthongs to be considered later. *Bath*, spelled phonetically as an Easterner would pronounce it, is [baθ].

These, then, are the front vowels:

VOWEL	KEY WORD
[i]	*beet* [bit]
[ɪ]	*bit* [bɪt]
[e]	*bait* [bet]
[ɛ]	*bet* [bɛt]
[æ]	*bat* [bæt]
[a]	*bath* [baθ]

If you pronounce each of these sounds in turn, beginning at the top of the list and running to the bottom, you will find your mouth opening wider as you move from one sound to the next. As your mouth opens, your tongue is lowered and becomes increasingly relaxed. These symbols—like all phonetic symbols—should be written with characters of equal size. No capitals are used, even for proper nouns.[5]

Before moving on to the back vowels, we should discuss the two front vowels [i] and [ɪ]. If you look in an American or English dictionary, you may be surprised to discover that the final sounds of words such as *Friday, busy,* and *worry* are given the pronunciation [ɪ], as in *ill.* Now there can be no doubt that in General American speech, as well as in the speech of most other sections of the country, these words have a distinct [i] sound. Kenyon and Knott, in their *Pronouncing Dictionary of American English,* take note of this fact but indicate that minor variations in the pronunciation of this sound are too complex to pin down. Like most other American dictionaries, they simply use the [ɪ] symbol for words in which the sound may actually be either [ɪ] or [i]. Thus they arrive at the pronunciation [sɪtɪ] (sɪH-tɪH) for *city.* Though it is doubtful that more than an infinitesimal number of Americans actually pronounce the word in this manner, most Americans *do* pronounce the final sound in the word somewhere between a distinct [ɪ] and a distinct [i].

Kantner and West, in their excellent book *Phonetics,* address themselves to the problem of [i] and [ɪ] in the transcription of human

---

[5] All IPA symbols have been enclosed in brackets throughout this book, and the use of brackets has been restricted to IPA symbols. Thus all letters and words that appear in brackets can be identified immediately as being IPA symbols rather than ordinary Roman letters.

speech. They note that some authorities use the symbol [ɪ] to represent the sound that is halfway between [i] and [ɪ]. They express reservations, however, about the use of a symbol that otherwise is confined to narrow phonetic transcription. They conclude that in rapidly spoken speech the [ɪ] symbol is closer to the sound actually articulated in the final syllables of words such as *body, mighty, likely,* and *city* than is the [i] symbol. We suggest that you follow these principles in determining your personal use of the symbols involved:

1. If your speech tends toward eastern or British pronunciation, the [ɪ] symbol is appropriate for your use.
2. If you speak General American, you might want to develop a narrow transcription approach to the vowel sounds in this section. Therefore, you might use [i] for the final sound in *candy,* the symbol [ɪ] for the medial sound in *merciful,* and the narrow transcription symbol [ɪ] for the word *mighty* in the clause "the mighty Casey has struck out." Here the [i] symbol might well be used for the name *Casey.*

In conclusion, it is worth noting that the essential purpose of IPA is to help with pronunciation problems. The examples used here and throughout this chapter are included for clarity, not in the expectation that you actually have problems pronouncing *mighty, Casey,* or *city.*

We move now to the back vowels.

[ɑ] This sound is pronounced "ah" as in *bomb.* Phonetically, the word *bomb* is spelled [bɑm]. (*Note:* Because the English language makes much use of unsounded letters, like the final *b* in *bomb,* there is frequently an unconscious tendency to include these in phonetic transcriptions. You should remember that you are transcribing sounds, not letters, and should disregard all letters not sounded in the original spelling of the words.)

[ɔ] This sound is pronounced "aw" as in *bought.* Phonetically, *bought* is spelled [bɔt].

[o] This sound is pronounced "o" as in *boat.* Phonetically, *boat* is spelled [bot].

[ʊ]   This sound is pronounced "ooh," as in *book*. Phonetically, *book* is spelled [bʊk].

[u]   This is pronounced "oo" as in *boot*. Phonetically, *boot* is spelled [but].

VOWEL	KEY WORD
[ɑ]	*bomb* [bɑm]
[ɔ]	*bought* [bɔt]
[o]	*boat* [bot]
[ʊ]	*book* [bʊk]
[u]	*boot* [but]

If you pronounce each of these vowel sounds in turn, you will find your mouth closing more and more and the sound being controlled at a progressively forward position in your mouth.

Only two other vowel sounds remain, "er" and "uh"—unfortunately the two that cause the most trouble to students of phonetics. Before getting to their symbols, let us look at two words: *further* and *above*. In *further*, two "er" sounds appear. Pronounce this word aloud and you will discover that, because of a stress on the first syllable, the two "ers" sound slightly different. The same is true of the two "uh" sounds in *above*. Because the first syllable of this word is unstressed and the second is stressed, there is a slight but definite difference between the two sounds. IPA makes allowances for these differences by assigning two symbols each to the "er" and "uh" sounds:

[ɝ]   stressed "er," as in the first syllable of *further*

[ɚ]   unstressed "er," as in the second syllable of *further*

[ʌ]   stressed "uh," as in the second syllable of *above*

[ə]   unstressed "uh," as in the first syllable of *above*

The word *further*, then, is spelled [fɝðɚ] in IPA, and *above* is spelled [əbʌv]. The unaccented "uh" sound—[ə]—is given a special name—the *schwa* vowel. Naturally, in a one-syllable word with an "uh" or an "er" sound, the sound is stressed. For this reason, in all one-syllable words both "er" and "uh" are represented by their stressed symbols:

bird [bɝd]	*sun* [sʌn]
church [tʃɝtʃ]	*come* [kʌm]

One exception to this rule occurs in foreign phrases, where a phrase such as *Voici le chapeau* is so run together as to make the "uh" in the *le* become a schwa: [vwɑsiləʃɑpo].

Diphthongs   A diphthong, or glide, is a combination of two vowel sounds. If you say aloud the "ow" of *how*, you will notice that it cannot be completed without moving the lips. There is no way of holding the sound of the entire diphthong; you can hold only the last of the two vowels of which it is formed. The diphthong "ow" as in *how* is actually the rapid movement from the vowel [a] to the vowel [ʊ]. The English diphthongs are as follows.

[aɪ]   This sound is pronounced as a rapid combination of the two vowels [a] and [ɪ]. The key word is *bite*, spelled [baɪt] in IPA.

[aʊ]   This sound is pronounced as a rapid combination of the two vowels [a] and [ʊ]. The key word is *how*, transcribed as [haʊ] in IPA.

[ɔɪ]   This sound is pronounced as a rapid combination of the two vowels [ɔ] and [ɪ]. The key word is *toy*, transcribed [tɔɪ] in IPA.

[ju]   This sound is pronounced as a rapid combination of the two sounds [j] and [u]. The key word is *using*, transcribed as [juzɪŋ] in IPA.

[ɪu]   This sound is pronounced as a rapid combination of the two vowels [ɪ] and [u]. The key word is *fuse*, transcribed as [fɪuz] in IPA. (Note the subtle difference between the sounds of the last two diphthongs.)

In addition to these diphthongs, the vowel [e], as in *bait*, is actually a diphthong, because its pronunciation in a word such as *say* involves a glide from [e] to [ɪ]. In other instances—the word *fate*, for example— the [e] is cropped off more closely. Because it changes according to context, the [e] sound may be transcribed either as a pure vowel, [e], or as a diphthong, [eɪ]. It will be found as such in various dictionaries and other words using IPA.

The diphthongs, then, are:

DIPHTHONG	KEY WORD
[aɪ]	*bite* [baɪt]
[aʊ]	*how* [haʊ]
[ɔɪ]	*toy* [tɔɪ]
[ju]	*using* [juzɪŋ]

DIPHTHONG	KEY WORD
[ɪu]	*fuse* [fɪuz]
[eɪ]	*say* [seɪ]

Consonants

With few exceptions, the IPA symbols for consonant sounds are their American English equivalents. The consonants are, therefore, easiest to learn.

In general, consonants may be classified as either voiced or unvoiced. If you say aloud the letters *b* and *p*, cutting off each without adding a vowel sound, you will notice that each is produced in exactly the same way, except that *b* involves phonation (a vibration of the vocal folds) and *p* is merely exploded air, with no phonation at all. Because most consonants are related this way, they will be listed in their paired relationships rather than alphabetically.

[p]   This is exploded air with no phonation, as in *poor* [pʊr].

[b]   This is a phonated explosion as in *boor* [bʊr].

[t]   This is exploded air with no phonation, as in *time* [taɪm].

[d]   This is a phonated explosion, as in *dime* [daɪm].

[k]   This is exploded air with no phonation, as in *kite* [kaɪt].

[g]   This is a phonated explosion, as in *guide* [gaɪd].

[f]   This is escaping air with no phonation, as in *few* [fɪu].

[v]   This is escaping air with phonation, as in *view* [vɪu].

[θ]   This is escaping air with no phonation, as in *thigh* [θaɪ]. It is similar to the consonant [f] but has a different placement of the tongue and lips. The Greek letter theta [θ] is its symbol, making it easier to remember.

[ð]   This is escaping air but with phonation, as in *thy* [ðaɪ].

[s]   This is escaping air without phonation, as in *sing* [sɪŋ].

[z]   This is escaping air with phonation, as in *zing* [zɪŋ].

[ʃ]   This is escaping air without phonation, as in *shock* [ʃɑk].

[ʒ]   This is escaping air with phonation, as in *Jacques* (French) [ʒɑk].

[tʃ]   This is an unvoiced, or unphonated, combination of [t] and [ʃ]. It is pronounced as one sound, as in *chest* [tʃɛst].

[dʒ] This is a voiced, or phonated, combination of [d] and [ʒ]. It is pronounced as one sound, as in *jest* [dʒɛst].

These are the paired consonants. The following consonants have no direct counterparts.

[h] This is an unvoiced sound, as in *how* [haʊ].

[hw] This is an unvoiced sound, as in *when* [hwɛn].

[m] This is a voiced sound, as in *mom* [mɑm].

[n] This is a voiced sound, as in *noun* [naʊn].

[ŋ] This is a voiced sound, as in *sing* [sɪŋ].

[l] This is a voiced sound, as in *love* [lʌv].

[w] This is a voiced sound, as in *watch* [wɑtʃ].

[j] This is a voiced sound, as in *yellow* [jɛlo].

[r] This is a voiced sound, as in *run* [rʌn].

Most consonants present relatively little difficulty, but a few are potential sources of confusion and deserve special consideration.

The word *fire* is usually pronounced [faɪɚ] in the United States, but is frequently transcribed as [faɪr] by the authors of dictionaries and phonetics texts. The problem here is that the "r" sound in a word such as *run* is really quite different from the "r" sound in the word *fire*, which is to say that the "r" sound differs depending on its position in a word. Beyond this, there is yet another difference: the *r* in *boor* is different from the *r* in *fire*, even though both are in the same position in the words and both follow vowel sounds. This difference stems from the fact that it is easy to produce an [r] after the vowel [ʊ] but difficult to produce an [r] after the diphthong [aɪ]. If you transcribe *fire* in the conventional manner as a one-syllable word—[faɪr]—you must be careful to avoid having it become [fɑr], as it is often pronounced in the South.

Certain combinations of sounds may be transcribed in two ways, either of which is as accurate as the other. The word *flattery*, for example, may be transcribed either [flætɚi] or [flætəri]. The difference in the way [ɚ] and [ər] are pronounced is imperceptible to most ears.

Another potential source of trouble comes from the plural ending *s*. Years of conditioning have taught us that most plurals end in an "s," though in actuality they end in a "z" sound—*brushes, masters, dozens, kittens,* and so on. Make certain, when transcribing into IPA, that you do not confuse the two symbols [s] and [z].

The common construction *-ing* tends to make one think of a combination of [n] and [g] when transcribing a word like *singing.* Many students transcribe this as [sɪŋgɪŋ]. In IPA a distinct symbol, [ŋ], is used for the "ng" sound. The correct transcription of *singing* is [sɪŋɪŋ]. Another common error is to add a [g] after the [ŋ]. To do so is incorrect.

The symbol [j] is never used to transcribe a word like *jump.* The symbol [dʒ] is used for this sound. The symbol [j] is always pronounced as in *young* [jʌŋ], *yes* [jɛs], and *William* [wɪljəm]. The symbol [y] is used only to represent a sound in the French and German languages.

Note that many of the consonants change their sounds as they change their positions in words or are combined with different vowel sounds. We have already seen how the "r" sound does this. A similar change takes place in the "d" sound. Notice it in the first syllable of the word *dazed.* Because the initial *d* is followed by a vowel sound, [e], the *d* is sounded. But when the *d* appears in the final position of the word, it is merely exploded air and is only slightly different from the sound a *t* would make in the same position. The only way the final *d* could be sounded would be if a slight schwa sound were added.

Three of the consonants, [m], [n], and [l], can be sounded as separate syllables without a vowel sound before or after them. Though a word such as *button* may be pronounced [bʌtən], in colloquial speech the [ə] sound is often missing, and the word is represented [bʌtn̩]. In such a transcription, the syllabic consonant is represented by a short line under the symbol. A few words using the syllabic consonants follow:

button [bʌtn̩]	*punkin* [pʌŋkn̩]
see 'em [sim̩]	*hokum* [hokm̩]
saddle [sædl̩]	*apple* [æpl̩]

Accent and Length Marks

Accent Marks Thus far most of the words transcribed into IPA have been of one syllable. Polysyllabic words must be transcribed with accent marks to indicate the relative stress to be placed on the various syllables. In the word *familiar* we have three syllables, [fə], [mɪl], and [jɚ]. In General American speech the first of these syllables receives little stress, the second receives the primary emphasis, and the third receives about the same degree of emphasis as the first. To indicate relative stress in a word, IPA uses a mark ['] *before* the syllable being modified. If the mark is placed above the syllable, as before the first syllable in the word *facing* ['fesɪŋ], it indicates that the syllable is to receive the primary accent in the word. If the mark is placed below the syllable, as before the first syllable of *farewell* [ˌfɛr'wɛl], it indicates that the syllable is to receive secondary accent. A third degree of stress is possible for which no mark is provided—namely, an unstressed sound. To clarify this, let us take the word *satisfaction*. A continuous line, drawn under the word to indicate the degrees of accent or stress we place on the syllables when uttering them, would look about like this:

sæt ɪs fæk ʃən

From this line we can see that there are three rather distinct degrees of emphasis in the word. This word would be transcribed [ˌsætis'fækʃən]. The primary mark is used for the syllable [fæk], the secondary mark for the syllable [sæt], and no mark at all for the two unstressed syllables [ɪs] and [ʃən]. Because secondary stress varies from slightly less than primary stress to slightly more than the unstressed syllables in a word, the secondary accent mark is used for a wide range of emphasis, although it is used only once per polysyllabic word.

The following list of related words (related either in meaning or in spelling) shows how stress or accent marks are used to assist in pronunciation.

consequence ['kɑnsəˌkwɛns]   *consequential* [ˌkɑnsə'kwɛnʃəl]
overalls ['ovɚˌɔlz]   *overwhelm* [ˌovɚ'hwɛlm]
interim ['ɪntɚɪm]   *interior* [ɪn'tɪriɚ]
mainspring ['menˌsprɪŋ]   *maintain* [men'ten]
contest (n.) ['kɑntɛst]   *contest* (v.) [kən'tɛst]
Oliver ['ɑləvɚ]   *Olivia* [o'lɪviə]
invalid (sick) ['ɪnvəlɪd]   *invalid* (not valid) [ɪn'vælɪd]

Because the schwa vowel [ə] and the unaccented [ɚ] vowel are by definition unstressed, they need no further mark to indicate stress. Because the [ʌ] vowel and the [ɝ] vowel are by definition stressed, they, too, need no additional mark where they appear in a word. The words *further* [fɝðɚ] and *above* [əbʌv] may thus be transcribed without accent marks of any kind.

The Length Mark   The colon [ː] appearing after any phonetic symbol indicates that the sound immediately preceding it is to be prolonged. This is most common in foreign words and names, as in the name of the Italian composer Puccini [puˈtʃiːni].

Using the IPA

For handy reference, all IPA symbols used to transcribe General American speech are listed below.

Vowels

IPA SYMBOL	KEY WORD	IPA SYMBOL	KEY WORD
[i]	*beet* [bit]	[ɑ]	*bomb* [bɑm]
[ɪ]	*bit* [bɪt]	[ɔ]	*bought* [bɔt]
[e]	*bait* [bet]	[o]	*boat* [bot]
[ɛ]	*bet* [bɛt]	[ʊ]	*book* [bʊk]
[æ]	*bat* [bæt]	[u]	*boot* [but]
[ɝ]	*bird* [bɝd]	[ʌ]	*sun* [sʌn]
[ɚ]	*bitter* [bɪtɚ]	[ə]	*sofa* [ˈsofə]

Diphthongs

[aɪ]	*bite* [baɪt]	[ju]	*using* [ˈjuzɪŋ]
[aʊ]	*how* [haʊ]	[ɪu]	*fuse* [fɪuz]
[ɔɪ]	*toy* [tɔɪ]	[eɪ]	*say* [seɪ]

Consonants

[p]	*poor* [pʊr]	[ʃ]	*shock* [ʃɑk]
[b]	*boor* [bʊr]	[ʒ]	*Jacques* [ʒɑk]
[t]	*time* [taɪm]	[tʃ]	*chest* [tʃɛst]
[d]	*dime* [daɪm]	[dʒ]	*jest* [dʒɛst]
[k]	*kite* [kaɪt]	[h]	*how* [haʊ]
[g]	*guide* [gaɪd]	[hw]	*when* [hwɛn]
[f]	*few* [fɪu]	[m]	*mom* [mɑm]
[v]	*view* [vɪu]	[n]	*noun* [naʊn]
[θ]	*thigh* [θaɪ]	[ŋ]	*sing* [sɪŋ]
[ð]	*thy* [ðaɪ]	[l]	*love* [lʌv]
[s]	*sing* [sɪŋ]	[w]	*watch* [watʃ]
[z]	*zing* [zɪŋ]	[j]	*yellow* [ˈjɛlo]
		[r]	*run* [rʌn]

These examples show the IPA symbols in a variety of applications:

IPA SYMBOL	WORD	IPA SPELLING
[i]	*free*	[fri]
	peace	[pis]
	leaf	[lif]
	misdeed	[mɪsˈdid]
	evening	[ˈivnɪŋ]
[ɪ]	*wither*	[ˈwɪðɚ]
	pilgrim	[ˈpɪlgrɪm]
	kilowatt	[ˈkɪləˌwɑt]
	ethnic	[ˈɛθnɪk]
	lift	[lɪft]
[e]	*late*	[let]
	complain	[kəmˈplen]
	La Mesa	[ˌlɑˈmesə]
	coupé	[kuˈpe]
	phase	[fez]
[ɛ]	*phlegm*	[flɛm]
	scherzo	[ˈskɛrtso]
	Nez Perce	[ˈnɛzˈpɝ·s]
	pelican	[ˈpɛlɪkən]
	bellicose	[ˈbɛləˌkos]
[æ]	*satellite*	[ˈsætl̩aɪt]
	baggage	[ˈbægɪdʒ]
	campfire	[ˈkæmpˌfaɪr]
	Alabama	[ˌæləˈbæmə]
	rang	[ræŋ]
[ɑ]	*body*	[ˈbɑdi]
	collar	[ˈkɑlɚ]
	pardon	[ˈpɑrdn̩]
	padre	[ˈpɑdre]
	lollipop	[ˈlɑliˌpɑp]
[ɔ]	*fought*	[fɔt]
	longwinded	[ˈlɔŋˈwɪndɪd]
	rawhide	[ˈrɔhaɪd]
	Kennesaw	[ˈkɛnəˌsɔ]
	awful	[ˈɔfl̩]
[o]	*closing*	[ˈklozɪŋ]

IPA SYMBOL	WORD	IPA SPELLING
	Singapore	[ˈsɪŋgəˌpor]
	tremolo	[ˈtrɛməˌlo]
	odor	[ˈodɚ]
	Pueblo	[ˈpwɛbˌlo]
[ʊ]	*looking*	[ˈlʊkɪŋ]
	pull	[pʊl]
	took	[tʊk]
	tourniquet	[ˈtʊrnɪˌkɛt]
	hoodwink	[ˈhʊdˌwɪŋk]
[u]	*Lucifer*	[ˈlusəfɚ]
	cuckoo	[ˈkuˌku]
	losing	[ˈluzɪŋ]
	nouveau riche	[nuvoˈriʃ]
	cruel	[ˈkruəl]
[ɝ]	*absurd*	[əbˈsɝd]
	early	[ˈɝli]
	curfew	[ˈkɝfju]
	ergo	[ˈɝgo]
	hurdle	[ˈhɝdl]
[ɚ]	*bitter*	[ˈbɪtɚ]
	hanger	[ˈhæŋɚ]
	certificate	[sɚˈtɪfəˌkɪt]
	Berlin	[bɚˈlɪn]
	flabbergast	[ˈflæbɚˌgæst]
[ʌ]	*lovelorn*	[ˈlʌvlɔrn]
	recover	[ˌrɪˈkʌvɚ]
	chubby	[ˈtʃʌbi]
	Prussia	[ˈprʌʃə]
	hulled	[ˈhʌld]
[ə]	*lettuce*	[ˈlɛtəs]
	above	[əˈbʌv]
	metropolis	[ˌməˈtrɑpļɪs]
	arena	[əˈrinə]
	diffidence	[ˈdɪfədəns]
[aɪ]	*dime*	[daɪm]
	lifelong	[ˈlaɪfˈlɔŋ]
	leviathan	[ləˌvaɪəθən]
	bicycle	[ˈbaɪˌsɪkļ]
	imply	[ˌɪmˈplaɪ]

IPA SYMBOL	WORD	IPA SPELLING
[aʊ]	plowing	['plaʊˌɪŋ]
	endow	[ˌɛn'daʊ]
	autobahn	['aʊtoˌbɑn]
	council	['kaʊnsl̩]
	housefly	['haʊsˌflaɪ]
[ɔɪ]	toiling	['tɔɪlɪŋ]
	oyster	['ɔɪstɚ]
	loyalty	['lɔɪl̩ti]
	annoy	[ə'nɔɪ]
	poison	['pɔɪzn̩]
[ju][6]	universal	[junə'vɝ·sl̩]
	euphemism	['jufəmɪzm̩]
	feud	[fjud]
	refuse	[rɪ'fjuz]
	spew	[spju]
[p]	place	[ples]
	applaud	[ə'plɔd]
	slap	[slæp]
[b]	break	[brek]
	about	[ə'baʊt]
	club	[klʌb]
[t]	trend	[trɛnd]
	attire	[ə'taɪr]
	blast	[blæst]
[d]	differ	['dɪfɚ]
	addenda	[ə'dɛndə]
	closed	[klozd]
[k]	careful	['kɛrfəl]
	accord	[ə'kɔrd]
	attack	[ə'tæk]
[g]	grand	[grænd]
	aggressor	[ə'grɛsɚ]
	eggnog	['ɛgˌnɔg]
[f]	finally	['faɪnl̩i]
	affront	[ə'frʌnt]
	aloof	[ə'luf]

[6][ju] and [iu] are all but indistinguishable, and speakers tend to use one or the other, depending on the preceding sound.

IPA SYMBOL	WORD	IPA SPELLING
[v]	*velocity*	[vəˈlasəti]
	aver	[əˈvɝ]
	love	[lʌv]
[θ]	*thrifty*	[θrɪfti]
	athwart	[əˈθwɔrt]
	myth	[mɪθ]
[ð]	*these*	[ðiz]
	although	[ˌɔlˈðo]
	breathe	[brið]
[s]	*simple*	[ˈsɪmpl̩]
	lastly	[ˈlæstli]
	ships	[ʃɪps]
[z]	*xylophone*	[ˈzaɪləˌfon]
	loses	[ˈluzɪz]
	dreams	[drimz]
[ʃ]	*shock*	[ʃɑk]
	ashen	[æʃən]
	trash	[træʃ]
[ʒ]	*gendarme*	[ˈʒɑnˈdɑrm]
	measure	[ˈmɛʒɚ]
	beige	[beʒ]
[tʃ]	*checkers*	[ˈtʃɛkɚz]
	riches	[ˈrɪtʃɪz]
	attach	[əˈtætʃ]
[dʒ]	*juggle*	[ˈdʒʌgl̩]
	adjudicate	[əˈdʒudɪˌket]
	adjudge	[əˈdʒʌdʒ]
[h]	*heaven*	[ˈhɛvən]
	El Cajon	[ˌɛl ˌkəˈhon]
	cahoots	[ˌkəˈhuts]
[hw]	*when*	[hwɛn]
	Joaquin	[hwɑˈkin]
	whimsical	[ˈhwɪmzɪkl̩]
[m]	*militant*	[ˈmɪlətənt]
	amusing	[əˈmjuzɪŋ]
	spume	[spjum]
[n]	*nevermore*	[ˌnɛvɚˈmɔr]
	announcer	[əˈnaʊnsɚ]
	sturgeon	[ˈstɝˈdʒən]

IPA SYMBOL	WORD	IPA SPELLING
[ŋ]	*English*	[ˈɪŋglɪʃ]
	language	[ˈlæŋgwɪdʒ]
	pang	[pæŋ]
[l]	*lavender*	[ˈlævəndɚ]
	illusion	[ɪˈluʒən]
	medial	[ˈmidil̩]
[w]	*wash*	[wɑʃ]
	aware	[əˈwɛr]
	equestrian	[ɪˈkwɛstriən]
[j]	*yellow*	[ˈjɛlo]
	William	[ˈwɪljəm]
	Yukon	[ˈjukɑn]
[r]	*Wrigley*	[ˈrɪgli]
	martial	[ˈmɑrʃəl]
	appear	[əˈpɪr]

For additional practice, transcribe any of the passages in this book into IPA. As you become proficient, begin to look up and transcribe only words or names with which you are unfamiliar. Remember always that IPA is taught by using common words but that it is most useful with words you otherwise might stumble over or mispronounce. You might mark a news script with *Pago Pago* in it, for example, as [ˈpæŋgo ˈpæŋgo], whereas a commercial script with *fungicide* or *tricot* might be marked [ˈfʌndʒəˌsaɪd] and [ˈtriˌko], respectively.

Also remember that IPA is used to transcribe sounds, not written words. Pronounce the word as you transcribe it, breaking the word down into its component sounds. In transcribing the word *broken,* for instance, say to yourself the first sound, "b," then add the second, "br," then the third, "bro," and so on. Because one sound in a word may condition the sound that precedes or follows it, you should use an additive system rather than one that isolates each sound from all others.

Correct pronunciation of words listed on page 111:

WORD	WIRE-SERVICE PHONETICS	DIACRITICS	IPA
quay	KEE	kē	[ki]
mortgage	MOR'-GIDJ	môr'gĭj	[ˈmɔrˌgɪdʒ]

WORD	WIRE-SERVICE PHONETICS	DIACRITICS	IPA
medieval	MEE-DEE-EE'-VUHL	mē'dē-ē'vəl	[midi'ivl̩]
egregious	IH-GREE'-JUS	ĭ-grē'jəs	[ɪ'gridʒəs]
flaccid	FLAK'-SID	flăk'sĭd	['flæksɪd]
interstices	IN-TER'-STIH-SEEZ	ĭn-tûr'stĭ-sēz	[ɪn'tɝ·stɪsiz]
forecastle	FOHK'-SUHL	fōk'səl	[foksl̩]
cliché	KLEE-SHAY'	klē-shā'	[kli'ʃe]
dais	DAY'-ISS	dā'ĭs	['de͵ɪs]
gunwale	GUHN'-UHL	gŭn'əl	['gʌnl̩]
brooch	BROTCH	brōch	[brotʃ]
phthisic	TIZ'-IK	tĭz'ĭk	['tɪzɪk]

6
VOICE AND DICTION

Your voice is the most important tool of communication that you possess. Whether or not you intend to enter the field of broadcast announcing, you will use your voice daily for the rest of your life. For this reason, you should make every effort to refine your speaking voice; to eliminate harsh or shrill sounds; to enunciate your words clearly; and, in short, to develop the most pleasant and effective speaking voice you are capable of producing. Although you may not have an innately pleasant voice, you can improve the quality of the voice you have.

Most professional broadcast announcers have excellent voices. Both men and women announcers tend to have rather low, resonant voices. They speak at an ideal rate of speed for easy comprehension, and they articulate words and phrases with clarity and precision. Some sports announcers, disc jockeys, and commercial *pitchmen* (announcers of commercials, usually men, who speak at a rate in excess of 200 words a minute) are exceptions to the general rule, but news anchors and reporters, talk show hosts, interviewers, and announcers on classical or middle-of-the-road music stations must have pleasant voices and must use them well.

This chapter is intended to help you identify any problems of voice or diction that you may have and to provide exercises for speech improvement. It is not designed as a substitute for speech therapy where significant problems may exist. In discussing the speech sounds of the American English language, the symbols of both the International Phonetic Alphabet (IPA) and the more conventional (though less accurate) wire-service transcription system will be used.

Your speech personality is made up of seven variables: (1) *pitch,* including pitch range; (2) *volume* (degree of loudness); (3) *tempo,* or rate of delivery; (4) *vitality,* or enthusiasm; (5) *pronunciation;* (6) *voice quality,* including timbre and tone; and (7) *articulation* (the movement of speech organs to make speech sounds).

All the qualities and characteristics that make up your "speech personality" can, to a degree, be isolated and worked on for overall speech improvement. Using appropriate exercises, you can work consciously on your pitch, for example, without at the same time working on volume or tempo. Eventually, however, your efforts must come together if your speech is to avoid affectation and to blend successfully into the aural representation of the person you want to project to others. You have by now developed a personality. You may or may not like some aspects of it, but one of the most positive results you can hope for through your study of announcing is a considerable improvement in your speech personality.

PITCH

Pitch is that property of a tone that is determined by the frequency of vibration of the sound waves. Generally speaking, low-pitched voices are more pleasant than high-pitched voices. Exceptions occur when a voice is pushed so far down the pitch scale as to sound unnatural or even grotesque. Barring this extreme, you should speak near the lowest pitch level that is comfortable. If you have a naturally low-pitched voice, be careful not to push it down so low as to sound strained or guttural. Whatever your pitch, you should make sure that you are not *consistently* speaking at your lowest pitch, because good speech demands *variety* in pitch. If you always speak at your lowest level, you have no way of lowering your pitch for selected words. Furthermore, a voice that remains down in the cellar sounds strained and monotonous.

Pitch is determined by the rate of vibration of the vocal folds; the faster they vibrate, the higher the pitch. The vocal folds of a mature woman generally vibrate about twice as fast as those of a mature man. For this reason, a male voice is generally about an octave lower than a female voice. To make the best use of your voice, you should find and develop your optimum pitch.

There are several methods for determining your optimum pitch. One system effective for many speakers is based on the theory that the optimum pitch is at that level where the greatest amount of resonance is produced. To find that point, place your palms on your cheekbones and read a series of short sentences, each at a different pitch level. Resonance is the result of vibrations in the nose and cheekbones, so you should be able to feel your optimum pitch. By recording and playing back the test sentences, you will be able to hear, without the distraction of bone-conducted sound, what you sound like when you are at or very near your optimum pitch.

Most of us sound best when we are speaking in the lower half of our available pitch range. Although careless speakers make little use of their range, with practice nearly everyone can achieve a range of between one and two octaves. Another useful method of determining optimum pitch involves a piano. Sitting at the piano, sing the scale as low and as high as you comfortably can, striking the note that corresponds with each sound. If your singing voice covers two octaves, your optimum speaking voice should be at about the midpoint in the lower of the two octaves. In other words, optimum pitch is very close to a quarter of the way up from your bottom to your top pitch capability. Having determined the note that corresponds to your optimum pitch, start reading a prose passage. When you reach a vowel sound that can be prolonged, hold the tone and strike the piano key that matches your optimum pitch. You can easily tell if you are consistently above, on, or below your optimum pitch level.

Because the vocal cords are actually two muscles, they are subject to contraction. In a taut, contracted state, they vibrate at a more rapid rate than when they are relaxed, and the faster they vibrate, the higher the pitch. It follows that some degree of speech improvement can be achieved by relaxing the vocal folds, but this cannot be done in an isolated way. To relax the throat muscles, you must simultaneously relax the rest of your body. Because an announcer is a performer, and because performing usually causes tension, it is important that you learn to relax. A professional announcer with several years of work experience usually has no problem with nervousness. But the inexperienced announcer, performing before an instructor and fellow students or auditioning for that precious first job, may very well expect to experience nervousness. *Mic fright* (fear of the microphone), stumbling over words, and a raised pitch may be the result. To help you confront and control mic and camera fright, a section of Chapter 3 discusses the causes and cures of these common maladies.

In present radio and television practice, some announcers speak above their optimum pitch level for a variety of reasons. As we have said, disc jockeys on some stations featuring the latest pop music are expected to shout, and it is not possible to do so without raising one's pitch. Second, some sports reporters apparently believe that a frenetic, mile-a-minute delivery enhances the significance of their reports, and both the frenzy and the volume level tend to raise their pitch. Finally, some announcers attempt to project their voices to the camera, rather than to the lavaliere microphone that is only 10 or 12 inches from their mouths, thus throwing the voice 10 or 15 feet. This raises the volume level and that, in turn, raises the pitch. Use your medium; electronic communication does not usually require high volume. Speak softly, and the pitch of your voice should remain pleasantly low.

Practice: Achieving a Low Pitch

Use the following commercial to try to achieve a low pitch. If you have a very low voice, make sure that you do not creep along the bottom. Regardless of pitch, work for variety.

```
Mellow. Smooth and mellow. That's the way to describe

Dairyland Longhorn Cheese. We use the finest Grade A milk

from happy cows. Nothing but pure, natural ingredients. We

take our time, letting the cheese age to the peak of per-

fect taste. We package Dairyland Longhorn in cheesecloth

and wax, just like in the old days. And we speed it to your

grocer, so that you get it at its flavorful best. Dairy-

land Longhorn Cheese. It's smooth and mellow.
```

Try to read this commercial in exactly 30 seconds. If you read it in less time, you are probably not savoring the key selling words in the commercial, and your speed may be interfering with the achievement of optimum pitch.

Inflection refers to the altering of the pitch or tone of the voice. It is repetitious inflection that makes some voices sing-song, and it is the lack of inflection that causes others to speak in a monotone. Good speech avoids the extremes and reaches a happy medium. Untrained speakers often fail to use variations in pitch sufficiently, whereas some overtrained speakers sound pretentious. You should be very self-critical about the degree and style of your pitch variations. Listen intently to tape recordings of your speech. If you feel that improvement is needed, use the following exercises, always speaking aloud, and always taping, replaying, and noting your progress.

Say these sentences, inflecting on the italicized word or words:

"When did *you* get here?"	"When did you *get* here?"
"I *hope* you're right."	"I hope you're *right.*"
"Which one *is* it?"	"*Which* one is it?"
"Which *one* is it?"	"Which one is *it*?"
"We *lost* the *game!*"	"*We* lost the game!"
"Don't say *that.*"	"Don't *say* that."
"*She* found the key."	"She *found* the key."
"The *dog* ate the steak."	"The dog ate the *steak.*"

Now, inflect these words in isolation:

"What?"	"Tremendous!"
"Certainly!"	"Ridiculous!"
"Maybe."	"Surely."
"Awful!"	"Life?"
"Sure!"	"How?"
"Try!"	"Stop."
"Go!"	"Caught?"

(Note that the challenge is greatest with one-syllable words. The word "Life?" for example, asked as a question, can easily accommodate both an upward and a downward inflection without becoming a two- or three-syllable word.)

For additional practice in increasing your pitch range, see the drill material in Chapters 10 and 12.

VOLUME

Volume level is seldom a problem in broadcast speech, except for lay persons who do not know how to use the broadcast media, and for reporters or sportscasters who are covering events that produce a high level of ambient noise. In a studio or control room environment, sensitive microphones pick up and amplify all but the weakest of voices. An audio engineer will see to it that the proper volume of speech is going through the audio console and on to the transmitter. Always remember that your listener is very close to you and speak in a normal voice, as you would in a face-to-face conversation.

Outside the studio environment, volume level can be a problem. The ambient noise from a parade, a political convention, or a sports event may require a louder voice. Under these circumstances, a good result may be obtained from moving in closer to the mic and actually reducing your volume level. On the other hand, if conveying the excitement of the event dictates increased volume, back away from the mic and speak up. Your pitch may go up as you do so, but that might enhance the excitement of your actuality.

Most radio and television speech is at its best when it is delivered at conversational level. Because this level remains relatively constant for each of us, it follows that for each of us there is an optimum distance from mouth to mic to achieve speech whose quality is suited to the event. A weak voice, too distant from the microphone, will require the engineer to increase the gain on the console or tape recorder; this in turn will increase the volume of ambient noise. On the other hand, a speaker with a high volume level who is positioned too close to a microphone is apt to produce popping, excessive sibilance, and an unpleasant aspirate quality. *Popping* is a term used to describe the sound made when a plosive (such as an initial *p, b, t, d, k,* or *g*) is made too close to the microphone. *Sibilance* is the sound made by the fricatives *s, sh,* and sometimes *z,* as well as the *z* sound in *vision.* Sibilance is a characteristic of American English, and to totally avoid it is to develop a lisp. The microphone tends to exaggerate sibilant sounds, so it is important to avoid excessive sibilance. To *aspirate* is to release a puff of breath, as in sounding the word *unhitch.* Like sibilant sounds, aspirate sounds are a part of our spoken language; again, these sounds tend to be exaggerated by microphones. If you find that you pop on microphone, practice the exercises that deal with the plosives; practice with the fricative exercises to overcome excessive sibilance; and use the exercises that are given for the letter *h* to work on problems of overaspiration. A windscreen will eliminate popping, but it also will eliminate the higher frequencies.

Establishing your optimum volume level and microphone placement (distance from the mouth) should be one of your first priorities as a student of announcing. Because microphones vary in sensitivity, pickup pattern, and tonal reproduction, it is important to experiment with each type of microphone that you are likely to use.

TEMPO

Your rate of delivery is often determined for you by the number of words to be read in a given period of time. In general, newscasts and hard-sell commercials are read quite rapidly, whereas documentary narration, classical music copy, and institutional commercials are read more slowly. In ad-lib announcing, you must judge what speed is appropriate to the mood of the event (whether it is an interview, a live report from the field, or a description of a sports event) and adjust your rate of delivery accordingly.

There is no correct rate at which to speak or read. When no time limit is imposed, gear your reading speed to the mood of the copy. But keep in mind that most of us speak too rapidly much of the time. Speed is often the enemy of clear articulation. The sentence "So give to the college of your choice," if read at too rapid a rate, becomes "Sgive tuhthukallage uvyer choice." There is an absolute limit to the reading speed one can achieve without sacrificing good articulation. Few of us are good judges of our own speech; this is doubly true when it comes to judging tempo. Aside from soliciting help from others, the best way to learn to achieve your optimum speaking or reading rate is by constantly using an audiotape recorder. Isolate the one problem of tempo or rate of delivery and work on it until a good speed becomes automatic.

Aside from a good basic rate of delivery, you also should work for variety in speed. Speeding up for throwaway lines and slowing down for emphatic words or phrases will help you give more meaning to your message. Current throwaway phrases include "member, FDIC," "substantial penalty for early withdrawal," and "your mileage may vary."

Practice: Varying Your Tempo

The following commercial provides good opportunities for shifts in reading speed.

SFX: SOUND OF GRIZZLY MOTORCYCLE IN DISTANCE, GRADUALLY

APPROACHING.

ANNCR: I can hear it in the distance. (PAUSE) Can you? (PAUSE)

The "grrrr-ing" of the Grizzly motor bike. (PAUSE) No, not

a "purring," a "grrr-ing." What's the difference? A "purr"

comes from a contented cat--a "grrr" is made by a hefty

Grizzly, looking for adventure. Cats are great, but

they're usually gentle. The Grizzly is wild, but not

unmanageable.

SFX: GRIZZLY VOLUME CONTINUES TO INCREASE.

ANNCR: The Grizzly doesn't "putt-putt," and it doesn't purr. It

has a warm, furry sound, as befits a creature of the wild.

(PAUSE) Here's the Grizzly, speaking for itself. (PAUSE)

SFX: SOUND UP FULL, THEN BEGIN FADE.

ANNCR: There it goes! (PAUSE) "Grrrr-ing" its way to where it's

going. Hear the "grrrr?" You can own the "grrrr"--if you

don't want a pussy-cat, and think you can tame a Grizzly.

Check us out. (PAUSE) We're in the Yellow Pages. The

Grizzly. (PAUSE) It's for people who want something on the

wild side.

SFX: SOUND OF GRIZZLY TO CLOSE.

In the diagnostic reading called "William and His Friends" (see page 156), there are two obvious speed traps. If you try to speak too fast on "This is the story," or ". . . joyous though they were," you will probably trip over your tongue. There are other less obvious traps in the piece. Your challenge is to keep the reading moving, while avoiding stumbles.

VITALITY

Two speakers with nearly identical speech qualities may sound quite different if they vary greatly in vitality or enthusiasm. Though a sense of vitality is often communicated by rapid speaking or reading, this is not always the case. Some speakers are able to communicate a feeling of energy and vitality even when speaking slowly; other speakers may be fast but unenthusiastic.

All other things being equal, you should strive for two objectives in your announcing work. You should use a degree of vitality that is appropriate to your personality, and you should gear the degree of vitality to the mood of the event being described. Above all, do not push yourself up to a level of vitality that is forced, unnatural to you, or inappropriate to the occasion. Most announcers are at their best when they are being themselves. You may need years of study and practice to develop your latent speaking potential, but you will certainly waste your time if you try to substitute someone else's personality for your own.

On the other hand, many beginning students of announcing are more subdued (and therefore less vital) in performing assignments than they are in their normal, out-of-class behavior. Your objective might well be to lift yourself up to your customary level of vitality.

PRONUNCIATION

To *pronounce* means to form speech sounds by moving the articulators of speech—chiefly the jaw, tongue, lips, and glottis. There are many different and acceptable ways of pronouncing American English because the language is spoken differently in various parts of the United States and Canada. Think of the differences in speech of a native-born Georgian, a Texan, a New Englander, a New Yorker, a Hoosier, and a person from Colorado. Despite the language's richness, as represented by regional differences in pronunciation, broadcasters have always favored General American speech—roughly defined as that spoken by well-educated Americans and Canadians of the Midwest and Far West. Even regionally, one hears General American spoken by broadcast announcers in every part of the United States.

There are signs of change (most noticeable at the local station level) and it is now possible to hear—occasionally, at least—voices that are identifiably Black, Hispanic, Southern, Eastern, and "Down-Eastern." This trend will undoubtedly continue and accelerate, but your chances of succeeding as a professional announcer will still be enhanced if you employ General American speech. As a student of announcing, you must consider the question of pronunciation: if you do not speak General American, you must decide whether you want to cultivate it. Because overall pronunciation is an important part of your speech personality, a decision to change it is not to be made lightly.

If regional variations in speech are not substandard (except in the eyes of many broadcast executives), what *does* constitute incorrect pronunciation? One or more of the following problems can cause mispronunciation:

1. *Sloppy or incorrect articulation.* If you say *air* for *error* or *Wih-yum* for *William,* you are mispronouncing because of laziness in the use of your

articulators. Say these words aloud, first *air*, then *error*. Note that *air* can be sounded by a simple closing of the mouth and a drawing back of the tongue. *Error*, however, requires more effort: two distinct movements of the lips and two movements of the tongue. Articulation, which is related to pronunciation, is discussed in some detail later in this chapter. If you are guilty of sloppy articulation, you should work extensively with the exercises in the "Voice Quality and Articulation" section of this chapter.

2. *Physical impairment*. Missing teeth, a fissure in the upper lip, a cleft palate, nasal blockage, or any degree of facial paralysis may make it impossible for a speaker to pronounce words correctly. If you have a correctable physical impairment, such as missing teeth, you should consult an appropriate specialist.

3. *Misreading*. Mispronunciations may result from a simple mistake, such as reading *amenable* for *amendable, outrage* for *outage,* or *through* for *though*. If you are a consistent misreader of words, you may have a learning impairment or a problem with your vision, and either condition calls for consultation with specialists.

4. *Affectation*. Some Americans who employ General American for nearly all their vocabulary pick up a Britishism here and there, and this practice can be jarring to a listener. Saying *eye-thuh* for *either* works well with New England or Southern speech, but it sounds out of place when used by a Far or Midwesterner. Affectation can be worked on and eliminated, but this requires a keen ear and, in many instances, calls for the help of a qualified speech teacher.

5. *Ignorance of correct pronunciation*. Most of us have a reading vocabulary that is far greater than our speaking vocabulary. From time to time, we err when we attempt to use a word known to us only through our eyes. The word *coup*, for example, might be pronounced *koop* by one who knew it only through the printed page. Ignorance of correct pronunciation may be due to having a limited speaking vocabulary, to having grown up in a home where American English was poorly pronounced, or to having learned English as your second language. It can be overcome only by a systematic effort to become somewhat of a linguist. To be truly professional, you must develop an extensive vocabulary and cultivate accuracy and consistency in pronunciation. There are many books that can help you build your vocabulary, but be sure you are not simply adding to your *reading* vocabulary. Appendix B

provides a list of about 300 words selected because they are often mispronounced or because they are uncommon words that might turn up in broadcast copy.

6. *Vowel and diphthong distortion.* Some people have grown up in environments where scores of words were mispronounced due to the distortion of vowels and diphthongs. Those who say *melk* for *milk* or *be-kuz* for *because* are guilty of vowel distortion. To say *kawl* for *coil* is to distort a diphthong. Vowel and diphthong distortions can be corrected, but first they must be identified. Both vowel and diphthong distortion are discussed in subsequent sections of this chapter.

Speech Sounds of the American English Language

Speech sounds may be classified in a number of ways. We classify sounds as vowels, diphthongs, and consonants. A vowel is defined rather loosely as a pure phonated (sounded) tone that does not use the articulators and can be held indefinitely without changing. If you say aloud the vowel [ɑ] (AH), you will notice that you can hold it as long as your breath lasts without substantial change in its sound. Now say aloud [ɔɪ] (OY), a diphthong. You will notice that it glides from [ɔ] (AW) to [ɪ] (IH) and that you cannot hold its entire sound. You *can* hold the last part of this diphthong indefinitely, but only because it turns into [ɪ] (IH), a pure vowel. Now try to say aloud the consonant [p]. You will notice that you cannot do so unless you add to this sound some vowel sound. The [p] is merely exploded air and cannot be prolonged. Other consonants, such as [n], *can* be prolonged; but as soon as you stop using your articulators (in this instance the tip of the tongue has been placed on the gum ridge behind the upper front teeth) the sound turns into the vowel [ʌ] (UH). Consonants, then, may or may not use phonation but necessarily use the articulators.

There is a point at which it becomes impossible to say whether an unacceptably uttered word has been mispronounced or sloppily articulated. Saying "mirr" for *mirror*, for example, could be the result of either not knowing the correct pronunciation or simply not bothering to force the articulators to do their job. Many so-called pronunciation problems can be overcome by frequent use of the articulation exercises given later in the chapter.

Vowels The English language contains twelve vowel sounds (called phonemes), if we do not consider the three or four sounds that lie between members of these twelve and occur rarely—and only region-ally—in American speech. (See Chapter 5.) These sounds are usually classified according to the placement of the tongue in the mouth, the tongue being the only articulator that materially affects their produc-tion. Here are the twelve vowel sounds.

[i]   The vowel [i] (EE), as in *beet* [bit], is formed by holding the mouth slightly open, placing the tip of the tongue on the back surface of the lower front teeth, and arching the tongue toward the front of the mouth so that the sides of the tongue are in contact with the molars.

[ɪ]   The vowel [ɪ] (IH), as in *bit* [bɪt], is formed by placing the tip of the tongue on the back surface of the lower front teeth and lowering and relaxing the tongue slightly more than for [i].

[e]   The [e] (AY) sound, as in *bait* [bet], is formed much the same as the [ɪ] sound, but the mouth is in a more open position and the tongue lies almost flat in the mouth.

[ɛ]   The [ɛ] (EH) sound, as in *bet* [bɛt], finds the mouth still farther open than for the [e] sound but with the tongue in just about the same relative position.

[æ]   The [æ] (AAH) sound, as in *bat* [bæt], finds the mouth quite open and the tongue lying flat on the bottom of the mouth. A certain tenseness in the jaws is noticeable.

[ɝ]   The [ɝ] and [ɚ] (ER) sounds, as in *bird* [bɝd] and *bitter* [bɪtɚ], are formed by holding the mouth slightly open and holding the tongue back in the mouth, with the tip poised somewhere about the midpoint between the hard palate and the floor of the mouth.

[ʌ]   The [ʌ] and [ə] (UH) sounds, as in *sun* [sʌn] and *sofa* ['sofə], are formed by holding the mouth slightly open with the tongue flat on the bottom of the mouth. The tongue is quite relaxed. As indicated in Chapter 5, [ʌ] (UH) and [ə] (UH) are pronounced in the same way, the difference is that the first symbol is used when the sound is stressed, and the second when it is unstressed.

[u]   The [u] (OO) sound, as in *boot* [but], is formed by holding the front of the tongue in approximately the same position as for the [i] sound but with the rear of the tongue in a raised position. The lips are rounded and extended.

[ʊ]   The [ʊ] (ooh) sound, as in *book* [bʊk], is formed in much the same way as the [u], except that the lips are more relaxed and slightly more open.

[o]   The [o] (oh) sound, as in *boat* [bot], is made by rounding the lips and raising the tongue slightly in the rear of the mouth.

[ɔ]   The [ɔ] (aw) sound, as in *bought* [bɔt], is made by holding the lips open (but not rounded) and raising the tongue slightly in the rear. The tip of the tongue lies low on the gum ridge under the front lower teeth.

[ɑ]   The [ɑ] (ah) sound, as in *bomb* [bɑm], is made with the mouth quite open and the tongue lying flat and relaxed in the mouth.

Vowel Distortion   It is not uncommon for speakers of American English to distort one or more vowel sounds. This statement does *not* refer to those who speak with regional accents such as are found in New England, the Eastern seaboard, or the deep South. It is not incorrect for an Easterner or a Southerner to say *an-suh(r)* for *answer*, ['ænsə(r)] for ['ænsɚ], but it is substandard for speakers of American English any-where to say *fer-give* for *forgive* or *jist* for *just*. It is with this type of vowel distortion that the present section is concerned. Throughout this unit, General American (or broadcast speech, as it is sometimes called) will be used.

Five main distortions occur with some regularity among Americans in any part of the United States and Canada, and several occur less frequently. It is not surprising that these distortions take place between vowel sounds that are next to one another in the list that arranges vowel sounds according to placement in the mouth. As mentioned before, there are front and back vowels. In saying these sounds aloud in order, the mouth gradually opens for the front vowels and gradually closes for the back vowels: [i] (ee), [ɪ] (ih), [e] (ay), [ɛ] (eh), [æ] (aah), [ɑ] (ah), [ɔ] (aw), [o] (oh), [ʊ] (ooh), [u] (oo). The chief vowel distortions are:

[ɛ]   (eh) for [e] (ay)

[æ]   (aah) for [ɛ] (eh)

[ɛ]   (eh) for [æ] (aah)

[ɑ]   (ah) for [ɔ] (aw)

[ɪ]   (ih) for [i] (ee)

The readings that follow should help you (1) discover whether you have any problems of vowel distortion and (2) provide you with practice material to help you overcome such problems.

[ɛ] *for* [e]   (EH) *for* (AY)

ANNCR: The pale graduate of Yale hailed the mail delivery daily. She failed to go sailing, for fear of gales and whales, but she availed herself of the tall tales told her by the mail deliverer. "I shot a quail out of season and was sent to jail," he wailed, "but a female friend put up bail, so they failed to nail me." The pale Yale graduate did not fail to hail the mail deliverer's tale.

Note that those who may distort the [e] (AY) sound, turning it into an [ɛ] (EH), usually do so only when the vowel sound is followed by an [əl] (UL) sound. This is because it is quite easy to sound the (AY) in a word such as *pay* but more difficult to sound the (AY) in the word *pail*. Say, in turn, the words *pail* and *pell,* and you will see why some speakers slip into the easier of the two and thus distort the vowel sound of this and similar words.

[æ] *for* [ɛ]   (AAH) *for* (EH)

Unlike the vowel problem we have just described, this distortion tends to be of regional and ethnic origin, and it is not brought about because one manner of pronunciation is easier than another. Cities or large areas of cities where there is a sizable German American population are most prone to make this vowel distortion. *Fance* for *fence* and *talephone* for *telephone* are examples of this vowel problem.

ANNCR: My friend, who is well but elderly, helped me mend my fence. I telephoned him to let him know when to get here, but he didn't answer the bell, so I guess he'd left. He's a mellow friend who never bellows, but he sometimes questions everything a fellow does. He took some lessons on television about fence mending, or else he wouldn't be able to help me mend my fence.

[ɛ] *for* [æ]   (EH) *for* (AAH)

Many Americans do not distinguish between the vowel sounds in the words *Mary* and *merry,* giving both the [ɛ] (EH) sound. It was because of widespread distortion of these two vowel sounds that *catsup* became *ketchup* in common usage. Whereas the [æ] (AAH) sound is not often a source of trouble in the sounding of words such as *bat, champion,* and *sedan,* it often slips off into [ɛ] (EH) in words wherein it is more difficult to sound the [æ] (AAH), as in *shall.*

> ANNCR: Mary left the Caribbean to visit Paris. She carried her clothes in a caramel-colored carriage. Mary tarried at the narrow entrance of the barracks. There was a caricature of Mary that chilled her marrow. Mary said, "I shall never tarry in Paris again."

Note the difficulty of hitting the [æ] (AAH) sounds when so many words using this sound appear in rapid succession. Note, too, how the passage begins to sound foreign to American ears. The [æ] (AAH) sound will remain in American English speech, but there is no doubt that it is gradually disappearing in words wherein its manufacture is difficult.

[ɑ] *for* [ɔ]   (AH) *for* (AW)

Some speakers do not distinguish between these sounds, giving the same vowel sound to the words *bought* and *bomb.* Two brief exercises will be offered for your diagnosis and assistance. The first uses words for which the [ɔ] (AW) sound is correct; the second mixes words using both sounds.

> ANNCR: We all talked about the day in the fall when Loretta sawed off the longest stalk. Our jaws dropped in awe of her raw courage. She caught the stalk in a bolt of gauze and waited for the dawn to prevent the loss of all her awful morbid, haunted house of horror.

> ANNCR: I saw them haul the bomb from the bottom of the water-fall. All around, I saw the awesome possibility of large-scale horror. Lost souls watched in a state of shock. The bomb slowly fought its way clear of the pond. Water

dripped from the bottom of the bomb. I lost my fear, for I saw that the bomb was not awfully large.

[ɪ] *for* [i]   (IH) *for* (EE)

Sounding [i] (EE) before an *l* calls for slightly more effort than sounding [ɪ] (IH) in the same construction. For this reason, some speakers habitually say *rilly* for *really* and *fil* for *feel*.

ANNCR: Sheila Fielding really had a strong feeling that something really bad would come of her deal to have the keel of her boat sealed. She wanted to shield the keel, so that peeling paint wouldn't be a real big deal. Sheila really hit the ceiling when she saw the bill. As Sheila reeled, she took the wheel and dragged the keel with the peeling paint across the pier and into the field, where her feelings were really healed.

Aside from these major problems of vowel distortion, one occasionally hears several others. Speakers who commit these distortions (with some exceptions) tend to be quite consistent. Each of these distortions will be listed, followed by examples of correct and incorrect pronunciation.

[ɔ] *for* [ʊ]   (AW) *for* (OOH), as in *book*

WORD	CORRECT PRONUNCIATION	DISTORTION
poor	[pʊr] (POOHR)	[pɔr] (PAWR)
your	[jʊr] (YOOHR)	[jɔr] (YAWHR)
sure	[ʃʊr] (SHOOHR)	[ʃɔr] (SHAWHR)
tourist	['tʊrɪst] (TOOHR'-IST)	['tɔrɪst] (TAWR'-IST)
jury	['dʒʊri] (JOOHR'-EE)	['djɔri] (JAWHR'-EE)

[ɝ] *for* [ʊ]   (ER) *for* (OOH), as in *book*

WORD	CORRECT PRONUNCIATION	DISTORTION
jury	['dʒʊri] (JOOHR'-EE)	['dʒɝi] (JER'-EE)
sure	[ʃʊr] (SHOOHR)	[ʃɝ] (SHER)
insurance	[ɪn'ʃʊrəns] (IN-SHOOHR'-UNS)	[ɪn'ʃɝəns] (IN-SHER'-UNS)
mature	[mə'tjʊr] (MUH-TYOOHR')	[mə'tʃɝ] (MUH-TCHER')
assure	[ə'ʃʊr] (UH-SHOOHR')	[ə'ʃɝ] (UH-SHER')

[ɪ] *for* [ɛ]   (IH) *for* (EH)

WORD	CORRECT PRONUNCIATION	DISTORTION
tender	['tɛndɚ] (TEN'-DER)	['tɪndɚ] (TIHN'-DER)
get	[gɛt] (GEHT)	[gɪt] (GIT)
send	[sɛnd] (SEND)	[sɪnd] (SIHND)
engine	['ɛndʒən] (EN'-JUHN)	['ɪndʒən] (IHN'-JUHN)
friend	[frɛnd] (FREHND)	[frɪnd] (FRIHND)

[ɚ] *for* [ə], [ɔ], *or* [ɪ]   (ER) *for* (UH), (AW), *or* (IH)

WORD	CORRECT PRONUNCIATION	DISTORTION
familiar	[fə'mɪljɚ] (FUH-MIL'-YER)	[fɝ'mɪljɚ] (FER-MIL'-YER)
forget	[fɔr'gɛt] (FAWR-GET')	[fɚ'gɛt] (FER-GET')
congregate	['kaŋgrɪ,get] (KANG'-GRIH-GAYT)	['kaŋgɚ,get] (KANG'-GER-GAYT)
garage	[gə'rɑʒ] (GUH-RAHZH')	[gɚ'rɑʒ] (GER-AHZH')
portray	[pɔr'tre] (PAWR-TRAY')	[pɚ'tre] (PER-TRAY)
lubricate	['lubrɪ,ket] (LOO'-BRIH-KAYT)	['lubɚ,ket] (LOO'-BER-KAYT)

[ɛ] *for* [ɪ]   (EH) *for* (IH)

WORD	CORRECT PRONUNCIATION	DISTORTION
milk	[mɪlk] (MIHLK)	[mɛlk] (MEHLK)
since	[sɪns] (SINSS)	[sɛns] (SEHNSS)
fill	[fɪl] (FIHL)	[fɛl] (FEHL)
think	[θɪŋk] (THINGK)	[θɛŋk] (THENGK)

[ɪ] *for* [ɛ]   (IH) *for* (EH)

WORD	CORRECT PRONUNCIATION	DISTORTION
cent	[sɛnt] (SENT)	[sɪnt] (SIHNT)
men	[mɛn] (MEHN)	[mɪn] (MIHN)
helicopter	['hɛlɪkɑptɚ] (HEL'-IH-KAHP-TER)	['hɪlɪkɑptɚ] (HIL'-IH-KAHP-TER)
many	['mɛni] (MEHN'-EE)	['mɪni] (MIHN'-EE)

A rare vowel distortion—rare in that those who use it seldom distort similar-sounding words—is the substitution of [æ] (AAH) for [e] (AY) in the word *graham,* making it [græm] (GRAM), rather than ['greəm] (GRAY'-UM).

Other vowels that are occasionally distorted include the following.

[ə] for [ɪ] — (UH) for (IH)

it (as in *get it?*) becomes *uht*

[ʌ] for [ɔ] — (UH) for (AW)

because becomes *be-kuz*

Diphthongs The diphthong, or glide, as it is sometimes called, is a combination of two vowel sounds spoken in rapid order, with a glide from one sound to the other. The diphthongs are represented in the alphabet of the International Phonetic Association by a combination of the two vowels that form them. Unfortunately for the learner, however, IPA has chosen to use [a] instead of the more common [ɑ], and [ɪ] instead of the more nearly correct [i] in some of these symbols. The diphthongs and their symbols follow.

[aɪ]   as in *bite* [baɪt]

[aʊ]   as in *bout* [baʊt]

[ɔɪ]   as in *boy* [bɔɪ]

[ju]   as in *beauty* ['bjuti]

The vowel [e], as you may detect by saying it aloud, is actually a glide, because the sound quite definitely goes from [e] (AY) to [ɪ] (IH). It is therefore sometimes considered a diphthong and given the symbol [eɪ] in IPA.

Diphthongs are a source of trouble for some speakers. Diphthong distortion tends to be regional and, while not necessarily substandard, is not compatible with General American speech. Here are a few common diphthong distortions.

WORD	CORRECT PRONUNCIATION	DISTORTION
bike	[baɪk] (BYKE)	[bak] (BAHK)
cow	[kaʊ] (KAU)	['kæˌaʊ] (KA'-OW)
toy	[tɔɪ] (TOY)	[tɔ] (TAW)
news	[njuz] (NYUZ)	[nuz] (NOOZ)
pail	['peḷ] (PAY'-UL)	[pɛḷ] (PELL)

Practice: Pronouncing Diphthongs

If you have trouble with diphthongs, practice making each of the vowel sounds that form them and then speak them with increasing rapidity. The following exercises will help only if you are producing the sounds of the diphthongs correctly.

[aɪ]
1. I like my bike.
2. Lie in the silo on your side.
3. Fine nights for sighing breezes.
4. Why try to lie in the blinding light?
5. Si tried to fly his kite.
6. My fine wife likes to fly in my glider.
7. Try my pie—I like it fine.
8. Shy guys find they like to cry.
9. My sly friend likes to be wined and dined.
10. Like all fine and right-minded guys, Mr. Wright liked best to try to find the slightest excuse to lie about his life.

[aʊ]
1. Flounce into my mouse's house.
2. Cows allow just about too much proudness about them.
3. Round and round went the loudly shouting lout.
4. A mouse is somewhat louder than a louse in a house.
5. A bounding hound went out on the bounding main.
6. Grouse are lousy bets when abounding results are found.
7. A cow and a mouse lived in a house.
8. The louder they proudly cried, the more the crowd delighted in seeing them trounced.
9. They plowed the drought-stricken cow pasture.
10. Allow the grouse to shout louder and louder, and you just about drown out the proud cows.

[ɔɪ]
1. A toy needs oiling.
2. The soybeans are joyously coiling.
3. Floyd oiled the squeaky toy.
4. Goya painted Troy in oils.
5. His annoying voice was boiling mad.
6. The oyster exploited the joyous foil.
7. Roy and Lloyd soiled the toys.
8. Joy, like a spoiled boy, exploited her friends.
9. Hoity-toity men make Lloyd boil.

10. What kind of noise annoys an oyster? A noisy noise annoys an oyster.

[ju] 1. A few beautiful girls are using perfume.
  2. I used to refuse to use abusive news.
  3. The kitten mewed, but I refused to go.
  4. The music was used to imbue us with enthusiasm.
  5. The beautiful view used to confuse.
  6. June was beautiful.
  7. The newest pupil was wearing his suit.
  8. The cute kitten mewed.
  9. He eschewed responsibility for the news.
  10. The few new musical numbers were confusing to the beautiful girl.

VOICE QUALITY AND ARTICULATION

The remainder of this chapter is concerned with voice quality and articulation, the two most important and demanding aspects of human speech. Speech is the process of making meaningful sounds. These sounds are created in the English language by vibration of the vocal folds or cords, nasal resonance, and exploded air. Speech sounds are controlled and patterned by the degree of closure of the throat, the placement of the tongue, and the use of the teeth, lips, and nasal passages. Problems arising from improper use of vocal folds and resonance cavities are problems of *quality;* improper placement or use of the articulators gives rise to problems of *articulation.*

Practice: Diagnosing Problems

The following readings are designed to help you discover minor problems in voice quality and articulation. In each, all speech sounds of American English appear in initial, medial, and final positions, except for a few instances in which a sound is never used in a certain position. Each sound is given at least once; the more common sources of speech difficulty are given at least twice. The passages are nonsensical, but you should read them as though they make a great deal of sense. Try to use your regular patterns of inflection and stress and use your normal rate of delivery; only by doing so can you detect errors in voice quality and articulation. It is highly recommended that you record your performance of these exercises and that, after making a diagnosis of your problems, you retain the tape so that you can measure your progress.

WILLIAM AND HIS FRIENDS

This is the story of a little boy named William. He lived
in a small town called Marshville. Friends he had galore,
if one may judge by the vast numbers of children who
visited his abode. Every day after school through the
pathway leading to his house, the little boys and girls
trudged along, singing as though in church. Out into the
yard they came, a vision of juvenile happiness. But, joyous though they were, they served only to work little William up into a lather. For, although he assuaged his pain
with comic books and the drinking of milk, William ab-
horred the daily routine. Even Zero, his dog, was aghast
at the daily appearance of the running, singing, shuf-
fling, open-mouthed fellows and girls. Beautiful though
the sight may have been, William felt that they used the
avenue leading to his abode as an awesome item of lush
malfeasance. Their little oily voices only added fuel to
the fire, for William hated music. "Oooo," he would say,
"they mew like cats, baa like sheep, and moo like a cow.
My nerves are raw." Then back into his ménage the little
gigolo would scamper, fast action earnestly being his
desire.

Here is an alternate reading.

THE BATTLE OF ATTERBURY

The big battle was on! Cannons thundered and machine guns
chattered. The troops, weary after months of constant

struggle, found themselves rejuvenated by a vision of triumph. Atterbury, the junction of three main roads, was on the horizon. Using whatever annoying tricks he could, Jacques Deatheridge, the former millionaire playboy, was much in charge as he eyed the oil capital of the feudal republic. Few men would say that the Beige Berets had not cashed in on Jacques's flash of genius. Then the rather uncommon English fellow, a zany half—wit to many who now would writhe in agony, looked puzzled for a moment; the mob on top of Manhasset Hill was frantically throwing him a signal. He snatched the message from the courier. "My gracious," he muttered. "Atterbury is our own capital!" Elated, nonetheless, he invited his overawed band to play in his honor. After a solo on the drums, Jacques spoke to the multitude: "Rejoice, my fellow citizens! All is not bad! At least our troops have won <u>one</u> victory!"

Problems of Voice Quality

The most common problems associated with voice quality are nasality, huskiness, and thinness or lack of resonance. Each can be worked on, and most can be overcome to some extent. The first step is to diagnose your problems. You will probably need help with this, for few of us are objective about the sounds of our own voices. Once you have identified specific problems of voice quality, you should follow the suggestions and exercises that apply to your case.

Nasality Nasality is caused by improper use of the nasal passage and the speech organs associated with it. Pinch your nostrils and speak a sentence or two; you will find that by preventing air from passing through your nose you have produced a nasal vocal quality. Nasality can also be the result of allowing too much air to pass through the nasal passage. Without holding your nose, try to speak with a nasal tone. You will find that the sound can be generated only by forcing air up through the nasal passage. Proper use of the nasal passage involves selectively closing off sound—by the lips or the front or rear of the tongue—to force it through the nasal cavity. If you will say, in turn, *sim, sin,* and *sing,* holding on to the last sound of each word, you will find that for *sim* your lips close off the "m" sound, for *sin* the front of your tongue against the upper gum ridge (alveolus) creates the "n" sound, and for *sing* the rear of your tongue against the soft palate (or velum) produces the "ng" [ŋ] sound. These are the three nasal sounds, and they are properly produced only by the correct placement of your articulators and an unblocked nasal passage.

If you have nasality, your first problem is to determine whether it is caused by not properly sending the "m," "n," and "ng" sounds up through your nose or whether it is the result of sending non-nasal sounds through the nasal passage. The following sentence should help you do this. Read it very slowly, pausing to prolong every vowel sound that can be held without change. Record and play back the results. All the sustained "m," "n," and "ng" sounds should have nasal resonance associated with them (as a matter of fact, unless these sounds are allowed to pass through the nose, they can barely be sustained), whereas all non-nasal vowels should have no taint of nasality.

Many men and women can do this in many differing manners.

Besides evaluating the results of your taping, you should check for nasal resonance by placing the tips of your fingers lightly on either side of your nose. When holding a nasal vowel, you should feel a distinct vibration; when prolonging a non-nasal vowel, you should not. If you speak the word *women,* for example, the first prolonged vowel sound, "wiiii" [wɪ], should not have nasal resonance and you should not, therefore, feel any vibration. The "wiiiii" then gives way to "wimmmmm" [wɪm], and this should produce nasal vibration. The next vowel sound is "ihhhhhh" [ɪ], and this should be free from vibration. The final sound, "nnnnnnn" [n], should bring back the vibration. If you find that your nose does not produce vibrations on the nasal vowels, your problem is representative of the most common type of nasality. If, on the other hand, you find that you are nasalizing vowels that should not be nasalized, you have a less common and more difficult problem to work on.

If you are not nasalizing the nasal vowels *m, n,* and *ng,* your problem may be physiological or you may simply be experiencing nasal congestion. In either case, there is no point in working on speech exercises as long as the blockage exists. Do whatever is appropriate to end the blockage, whether this means a trip to a speech therapist, a naso-pharyngologist, or an allergist.

If you have no physiological or congestion problem and still lack resonance on the nasal vowels, the following exercises should help. Like all the exercises in this book, they should be spoken aloud. Speak each of the pairs of nasal and non-nasal words in turn, keeping the tips of your fingers lightly on the sides of your nose. Work for vibration in the first word of each of the pairs and for a lack of it in the second.

M VOWEL	*N* VOWEL	*NG* VOWEL
aim—aid	earn—earth	link—lick
arm—art	barn—bard	bank—back
atom—attar	bane—bathe	blank—black
balm—bock	fawn—fall	wink—wick
calm—cot	band—bat	singer—sinner
beam—beet	bend—bed	bunko—bucko
farmer—father	bin—bit	tongue—tuck
bump—butt	win—will	ming—mick
summer—Sutter	own—oath	manx—Max
ram—rat	friend—Fred	trunk—truck

If your problem is nasalization of non-nasal vowels, these same exercises should help. Work to avoid any nasal resonance in each of the non-nasal words, but do not try to eliminate it from the words that legitimately call for nasality.

Huskiness   A husky or excessively hoarse voice is usually the result of a medical problem. Laryngitis, smoker's throat, infected tonsils, and infected sinuses can all cause a husky voice. Quite obviously, you should seek medical attention for these conditions, for they are a handicap in radio and television work. To some extent, huskiness can arise as the result of excessive nervous tension. If yours is an unpleasantly husky voice and if there is no medical explanation for it, you might improve your performance by using the relaxing exercises mentioned in Chapter 3. Speaking exercises will help you overcome excessive huskiness or hoarseness only if your problem is the result of a gross misuse of your speech organs.

Thinness or Lack of Resonance   A good voice for the electronic media is one with resonance. A sensitive, top-quality microphone, such as a condenser mic, can enhance your natural resonance. But even the best equipment can work only with what you give it, and a voice that is thin or lacking in resonance can be significantly improved only by its owner. The sound vibrations that emanate from your vocal folds are weak and colorless. They need resonators to strengthen and improve the quality of sound. The chief resonators are the bones of the chest and face, the windpipe (trachea), the larynx (connecting the trachea and the pharynx and containing the vocal folds), the pharynx (between the mouth and the nasal passages), the mouth, the nose, and the sinuses.

In general, thinness of voice comes from one of three causes or a combination of them: shallow, weak breathing; speaking at too high a pitch (in general, the higher the pitch, the less the resonance); or inadequate use of the resonators that can be moved (the pharynx, the larynx, and the tongue as it affects nasal resonance or resonance in the mouth).

As with any other speech problem, the first step is diagnosing it. Do you have a thin voice? What causes it? What do you need to do about it? The following passage is provided for diagnostic purposes. Read it slowly, working for your most resonant quality. Record it, using a sensitive professional microphone and a top-quality tape recorder. If possible, seek the help of a person qualified in assessing both the quality of your voice and the apparent causes of thinness. Begin this reading approximately five feet from the microphone, using a volume level appropriate to that distance. With each section, move forward about six inches, until you are reading the final sentences about eight inches from the mic. Adjust your volume as you move in. On playback, determine whether your resonance is significantly affected by distance and volume level. Unless other negative qualities show up (excessive sibilance, popping, nasality), you should in this way find and use your optimum microphone position to bring out resonance.

```
     1. Johnny has an IQ of 170, but he can't read.

The words are jumbled, upside down. Mirrored.

     2. He has dyslexia. A learning disability that

affects one out of every ten children.
```

3. Johnny goes to school and faces frustration, humiliation, and ridicule.

4. It's a tragedy because the techniques are there to help the dyslexic child. He can learn to read and write. And survive in school.

5. He can even go to college. If--and only if-- dyslexia is diagnosed early. And dealt with.

6. Today, there are over a dozen centers in Massachusetts that can diagnose dyslexia--even among pre- schoolers.

7. To find out more, call 1-872-6880.

8. 1-872-6880.

9. One out of every ten kids has dyslexia.

10. And every one of them needs help.[1]

If yours is a thin, colorless voice, you should be able to increase resonance by following these suggestions:

1. Practice deep breathing. Learn to breathe from the diaphragm. Speak or read while you consciously try to increase the force of air coming from your lungs.
2. Make sure you are moving your articulators. Use the exercises that follow and work for an exaggerated use of tongue and lips.
3. Make sure that there is no blockage of your nasal passages.
4. Try to lower your pitch. (See the suggestions for pitch given earlier in this chapter.)
5. Read passages that emphasize vowel sounds (nineteenth-century British poetry is excellent for this), prolonging vowel sounds when they occur and trying to keep your throat as open as possible.
6. Discover the best mic for your voice, and establish your optimum distance from it.

[1] Courtesy Ingalls Associates, Inc., Boston, Massachusetts.

Improving
Articulation

Articulation problems arise from too fast a rate of delivery and from the improper placement or faulty use of the articulators: the jaw, the tongue, and the lips. Because many American and Canadian speakers suffer from poor articulation, the remainder of this chapter is devoted to exercises intended to improve articulation. Analysis of your performance with the two diagnostic readings "William and His Friends" and "The Battle of Atterbury" should tell you if you have inarticulate speech or if you have difficulty with one or another of the speech sounds. If you find that you have problems, you should use the exercises daily for as long as necessary. The exercises will do you no good, however, unless you read them aloud and unless you make a conscious effort to form successfully every syllable of every sentence. It is wise to exaggerate articulation at first, gradually moving toward normally articulated speech.

The exercises that follow are based on the correct sounding of consonants. Please note, however, that vowel and diphthong sounds (which have already been discussed) are present in every exercise and must be sounded correctly in order to achieve good American English speech.

Consonants   There are twenty-five consonant sounds (phonemes) in the English language. They may be classified in a number of ways, the most basic of which is according to whether they are voiced or not. Thus, the letter *b*, spoken with a vibration of the vocal folds, is called a voiced consonant, whereas *p*, formed in exactly the same way but not phonated, is called an unvoiced consonant. In a more detailed and more useful system of classification, describing how the sound is formed, the consonants are classified as follows:

1. *Plosives*. These sounds begin with the air from the throat blocked off, and the sound is formed with a release of the air. The plosive consonants are [p], [b], [t], [d], [k], and [g].

2. *Fricatives*. These sounds are created by the friction of air through a restricted air passage. The fricative consonants are [f], [v], [θ] (as in *thin*), [ð] (as in *the*), [z], [s], [ʃ] (as in *shoe*), [ʒ] (as in *vision*), [j] (as in *yellow*), [h], and [hw] (as in *when*).

3. *Nasals*. These sounds are resonated in the nasal cavity. The nasal consonants are [n], [m], and [ŋ] (as in *sing*).

4. *Semivowels.* These sounds are similar to the true vowels in their resonance patterns. The consonants [w], [r], and [l] are the semivowels.

5. *Affricates.* These sounds combine a plosive with a fricative. The consonants [tʃ] (as in *choose*) and [dʒ] (as in *jump*) are the affricates.

One final method of classifying speech sounds must be mentioned—the system that describes the consonants according to their place of articulation. In this classification the consonants are described as follows.

1. *Labial or bilabial.* The lips are primarily responsible for these consonants. Labial consonants are [p], [b], [m], [w], and, in a less obvious way, [hw].

2. *Labiodental.* In forming these sounds, the lower lip is in proximity to the upper teeth. Labiodental consonants are [f] and [v].

3. *Interdental or linguadental.* In these sounds the tongue is between the upper and lower teeth. Interdental consonants are [θ] (as in *thin*) and [ð] (as in *then*).

4. *Lingua-alveolar.* In these consonants the tip of the tongue (lingua) is placed against the upper gum ridge (alveolus). The lingua-alveolar consonants are [n], [t], [d], [s], [z],[2] and [l].

5. *Linguapalatal.* In these sounds, the tip of the tongue touches (or nearly touches) the hard palate just behind the gum ridge. Linguapalatal consonants are [j] (as in *yellow*), [r] (as in *rain*), [ʃ] (as in *shoe*), [ʒ] (as in *vision*), [tʃ] (as in *chew*), and [dʒ] (as in *jump*).[3]

6. *Linguavelar.* In these sounds, the rear of the tongue is raised against the soft palate (velum), and the tip of the tongue is lowered to the bottom of the mouth. Linguavelar consonants are [k], [g], and [ŋ] (as in *sing*).

7. *Glottal.* The glottal consonant, [h], is formed by the passage of air between the vocal folds but without vibration of those folds.

---

[2]Many people form [s] and [z] with the tip of the tongue against the lower gum ridge. If no speech difficulty results from this, there is no reason to change it.

[3]Some speech authorities classify [ʃ], [ʒ], [tʃ], and [dʒ] as lingua-alveolar sounds, but the preponderance of modern scholarly opinion places them in the linguapalatal category.

These various methods of classification will prove helpful in discussing the consonants, because they quite accurately describe the most significant characteristics of the consonants.

Practice: Pronouncing Consonants

In the following practice, as in Chapter 5, voiced and unvoiced consonants formed in the same way are considered together.

[b] The consonant [b] is a voiced, labial plosive. It is formed by first stopping the flow of air by closing the lips and then releasing the built-up air as though in an explosion.

1. Big Bill bent the bulky box.
2. The Boston bull was bigger than the boy.
3. Libby lobbed the sobbing lobster.
4. The ribbing was robbed from the jobber.
5. Bob could rob the mob.
6. The boxer baited the big boy, while the mobster hobbled about the sobbing, crabby boy named Bob.

[p] The consonant [p] is an unvoiced labial plosive. It is formed exactly the same as [b], except that it is unvoiced. It is, therefore, merely exploded air.[4]

1. Pretty Paula peeked past the platform.
2. Peter Piper picked a peck of pickled peppers.
3. Happy people appear to approach unhappiness happily.
4. Approximately opposed in position are Dopey and Happy.
5. Stop the cap from hitting the top.
6. Apparently the perfect approach to happiness is practiced by the popular purveyor of apoplexy, Pappy Perkins.

[t] The consonant [t] is an unvoiced, lingua-alveolar plosive. As this description suggests, [t] is formed by the release of unvoiced air that has been temporarily blocked off by the pressure of the tongue tip against the upper gum ridge. Note that [t], like [p], is best softened for radio and television speech.

1. Tiny Tim tripped toward the towering Titan.
2. The tall Texan tried to teach the taxi driver twenty tall tales of Texas.

[4]In working with plosive exercises, try to keep the popping under control. The blast of air that accompanies these sounds is magnified by the microphone.

3. Attractive though Patty was, the battling fighters hesitated to attempt to please her.
4. The bottled beetles were getting fatter.
   (For extra work with the medial *tt,* try saying the following with increasing speed: beetle, bittle, bayttle, bettle, battle, bottle, boottle, berttle, buttle.)
5. The fat cat sat in the fast-moving draft.
6. Herbert hit the fat brat with the short bat.

The medial *t* is a problem for many American speakers. In the West and Midwest, it often is turned into a *d,* as in saying *baddle* for *battle.* In some parts of the East Coast, the medial *d* is turned into a glottal stop, as in *bah-ul* ['baʔl] for *bottle.* To help you determine whether you have a medial *t* problem, record and listen to this exercise:

The metal kettle was a little more than half full. I settled for a little bit of the better stuff, and waited while an Irish Setter begged for a pitiful allotment of the fatter part of the kettle's contents. The Setter left, disgusted and a little bitter over the matter of the lost battle for more of the beetle stew.

[d] The consonant [d] is a voiced lingua-alveolar plosive. Except that it is voiced, it is the same as [t]. (Say *tot* and then *dod,* and you will find that your articulators repeat the same positions and movements for each. Deaf people who read lips cannot detect any difference between voiced and unvoiced pairs and must therefore rely on context for understanding.)

1. Don dragged the dull, drab dumptruck up to the door.
2. The dry, dusty den was dirtier than Denny's delightful diggings.
3. The ladder added to the indeterminate agenda.
4. The sadly padded widow in the middle looked addled.
5. Around the lad the red-colored rope was twined.
6. Glad to lead the band, Fred allowed his sad friend to parade around.

[k] [k] is an unvoiced linguavelar plosive. It is formed by releasing unphonated air that has been blocked momentarily from passage by the pressure of the rear top of the tongue against the hard palate.

1. Keep Kim close to the clothes closet.
2. A call came for Karen, but Karen wasn't caring.
3. Accolades were accorded to the picnicking dockworkers.

4. Action-back suits were accepted on occasion by the actors playing stock *commedia* characters.
5. Like it or not, the sick man was picked.
6. Rick kept count of the black sacks.

[g] The consonant [g] is a voiced linguavelar plosive and is formed like the unvoiced [k].

1. The good girl with the grand guy glanced at the ground.
2. One glimpse of the good, green earth, and the goose decided to go.
3. Agog with ague, the agonizing laggard stood agape.
4. Slogging along, the haggard, sagging band lagged behind.
5. 'Twas brillig, and the rig did sag.
6. The rag bag was big and full, but the sagging trigger was clogged with glue.

[f] The consonant [f] is an unvoiced labiodental fricative. It is formed by releasing air through a restricted passage between the front teeth and the lower lip.

1. The fish fry was a fairly fashionable affair.
2. Flying for fun, Freddy found the first fairly fast flying machine.
3. Affairs of affection are affable.
4. The affected *aficionado* was afraid of Africa.
5. The laugh graph showed a half-laugh.
6. The rough toff was off with his calf.

[v] The consonant [v] is a voiced labiodental fricative and is formed exactly the same as [f], except that it is phonated.

1. A vision of vim, vigor, and vitality.
2. Viola was victorious with Vladimir's violin.
3. Avarice, averred the maverick on the avenue, is to be avoided.
4. An aversion to lavender obviously prevents the inveterate invalid from involving himself avidly in mauve.
5. A vivid avarice was obviously invested in the avoidance of the man on the avenue.
6. Live, live, cried the five live jivesters.

[θ] The consonant [θ] (as in *thin*) is an unvoiced interdental fricative. [θ] is frequently a source of trouble, because the microphone tends to amplify any slight whistle that may be present. In making this sound, place the tongue up to, but not into, the space between the upper and lower teeth, held about one-eighth inch apart. Air passing over the top of the tongue and between its tip and the upper front teeth makes this sound.

1. Think through thirty-three things.
2. Thoughts are thrifty when thinking through problems.
3. Cotton Mather lathed his bath house.
4. The pathway to the wrathful heath.
5. The thought of the myth was cutting as a scythe.
6. Thirty-three thinking mythological monsters, wearing pith helmets, wrathfully thought that Theobald was through.

[ð]   The consonant [ð] (as in *them*) is a voiced interdental fricative and is formed the same as [θ], except that it is phonated.

1. This, the man then said, is older than thou.
2. The man therein was thereby less than the man who was theretofore therein.
3. Other people lather their faces further.
4. I'd rather gather heather than feathers.
5. Wreathe my brow with heather.
6. I seethe and breathe the truths of yore.

[s]   The consonant [s] is an unvoiced lingua-alveolar fricative. It is one of the more common sources of trouble for the announcer. A slight misplacement of the articulators may cause a whistle, a thick, fuzzy sound, or a lisp. There are two methods of producing [s], neither of which seems clearly superior to the other. In the first, the sides of the tongue are in contact with the upper teeth as far forward as the incisors. The tip of the tongue is held rather high in the mouth, and a fine stream of air is directed at the tips of the upper front teeth. The teeth, meanwhile, are held slightly apart. The second method of making [s] finds the tongue fairly low in the mouth at the rear and at the tip, with the tongue just behind the tip raised in the mouth to make a near contact with the gum ridge. A fine stream of air is permitted to flow through this passage, down toward the front teeth, which are held slightly apart. Because most microphones tend to exaggerate any slight whistle or excessive sibilance, work for a softened [s].

Because the sibilant *s* is a source of trouble to announcers, a diagnostic exercise is included here. Read the following passage into a tape recorder, play it back, and determine whether you have the problem of excessive sibilance. Before working to soften this sound, however, you should experiment with microphone placement and even the use of a windscreen or pop filter, for you may find that the problem is with the equipment or the way you are using it, rather than in your speech.

ANNCR: How long has it been since you saw a first-rate side-show? Some of us certainly should be sad over the disappearance of the classic circus side-show, once a staple of civic celebrations. Six or seven acts, set forth in circumstances that seemed awesome, or at least mysterious. Certainly, side shows were sometimes scandalous, and sometimes in questionable taste, but they served to keep our curiosity in a steady state of astonishment.

1. Should Samson slink past the sly, singing Delilah?
2. Swimming seems to survive as a sport despite some circumstances.
3. Lessons on wrestling are absurd, asserted Tessie.
4. Assurances concerning some practices of misguided misogynists are extremely hysterical.
5. The glass case sits in the purse of the lass.
6. Past the last sign for Sixth Place the bus lost its best chance to rest.

[z] The consonant [z] (as in *zoom*) is a voiced lingua-alveolar fricative and is formed exactly as [s], except for phonation.

1. The zippy little xylophone had a zany sound.
2. The zoological gardens were zoned by Zola for the zebras.
3. The fuzzy, buzzing bees were nuzzling the trees.
4. He used the music to arouse enthusiasm in the buzzards.
5. Was the buzz that comes from the trees caused by the limbs or the bees?
6. His clothes were rags, his arms were bare; yet his features caused his admirers to gaze as though his misery were a blessing.

[ʃ] The consonant [ʃ] (as in *shoe*) is an unvoiced linguapalatal fricative. It is made by allowing unvoiced air to escape with friction from between the tip of the tongue and the gum ridge behind the upper front teeth. Although this sound is not a common source of difficulty, guard against its becoming a thick, unpleasing sound. To form [ʃ], make certain that air does not escape around the sides of the tongue and keep the central portion of the tongue fairly low in the mouth.

1. Shortly after shearing a sheep, I shot a wolf.
2. The shapely Sharon shared her chateau with Charmaine.
3. Mashed potatoes and hashed cashews are flashy rations.
4. The lashing gale thrashed; lightning flashed and the Hessian troops gnashed their teeth.
5. A flash flood mashed the cash into trash.
6. Fish wish that fishermen would wash their shoes.

[ʒ] The consonant [ʒ] (as in *vision*) is a voiced linguapalatal fricative and is formed the same as [ʃ] but with phonation. It is seldom found in an initial position in English.

1. Jeanne d'Arc saw visions in the azure sky.
2. *Measure for Measure* is not the usually pleasurable Shakespearean play.
3. A hidden treasure was pleasurably unearthed from the beige hill with great precision.
4. The seizure was leisurely measured.
5. The edges of his incision had the *noblesse oblige* to form an elision.

[h] The consonant [h] is an unvoiced glottal fricative. It is seldom a source of difficulty to the speaker, but many announcers tend to drop the *h* in certain combinations. Note that the *h* is definitely present in most words beginning with *wh*. Note that the consonant [h] depends entirely on the sound that follows it and cannot, therefore, be articulated at the end of a word.

1. The huge hat was held on Henrietta's head by heaps of string.
2. Halfway home, the happy Herman had to have a hamburger.
3. Manhattan abhors one-half the upheaval of Manhasset.
4. "Ha-ha-ha," said the behemoth, as he unhitched the horse.

[tʃ] The consonant [tʃ] (as in *charm*) is an unvoiced linguapalatal affricate. It is, by this definition, formed with the tongue against the gum ridge behind the upper teeth and consists of both the pent-up release of air of the plosive and the friction of the fricative.

1. Chew your chilly chop before you choke.
2. Choose your chums as cheerfully as children.
3. An itching action follows alfalfa pitching.
4. The richly endowed Mitchells latched on to much money.

[dʒ]   The consonant [dʒ] (as in *justice*) is a voiced linguapalatal affricate and is formed exactly as [tʃ], except for phonation.

1. The junk man just couldn't joust with justice.
2. Joan jumped back in justifiable panic as Jud jettisoned the jet-black jetty.
3. Adjutant General Edgewater adjusted his midget glasses.
4. The edgy fledgling was judged unjustifiably.
5. The edge of the ledge was where Madge did lodge.
6. Trudge through the sedge and bridge the hedge.

[m]   The consonant [m] is a voiced labial nasal. It is articulated with the lips completely closed; the phonated sound does not pass into the mouth, as with most other speech sounds, but into the nasal cavity through the nasopharyngeal port. When [m] occurs in a final position, the mouth remains closed. When it occurs in an initial position the mouth must open, not to sound [m] but to move immediately to the sound that follows. The same sound, printed [m̩], indicates that the sound is to be formed by itself, independent of any vowel sound. It occurs in speech constructions such as *keep 'em clean,* which would be transcribed phonetically as [kip m̩ klin].

1. Mother meant more than my miserable money.
2. Merton moved my midget mailbox more to my right.
3. Eminent employers emulate immense amateurs.
4. Among amiable emigrants, Ermgard admitted to mother, him, and me inestimable immaturity.
5. Slim Jim and Sam climbed the trim limb.
6. Rhythm hymns they perform for them.

[n]   The consonant [n] is a voiced lingua-alveolar nasal. Unlike [m], it can be sounded with the mouth open or closed, since the tongue, rather than the lips, blocks off the air and forces it through the nasal cavity. [n], too, can be used as a complete unit of speech, and it appears as [n̩] in the International Phonetic Alphabet. The commonly heard pronunciation of a word like *meeting,* in which the [ŋ] sound is dropped, would thus be transcribed as [mitn̩]. [n] is responsible for much of the excessive nasality characteristic of many irritating voices. If you detect, or someone detects for you, a tendency to overnasalize sounds, spend several sessions with a tape recorder learning how it feels to soften and improve these sounds.

1. Ned's nice neighbor knew nothing about Neil.
2. Now the new niece needed Nancy's needle.
3. Indigestion invariably incapacitated Manny after dinner.
4. Many wonderful and intricate incidentals indirectly antagonized Fanny.
5. Nine men were seen in the fine mountain cabin.
6. Susan won the clean garden award and soon ran to plan again.

[ŋ] The consonant [ŋ] (as in *sing*) is a voiced linguavelar nasal. It is formed much as the consonant [g] is formed, but it lacks the plosive quality of that sound. One of the most common problems involves the advisability of turning this sound into [n] in words that end with *ing*. The announcer must, of course, determine whether it is appropriate on the particular occasion to drop this sound. The newscaster will undoubtedly decide not to. Disc jockeys and sports announcers, depending on their speech personality, may decide that it is permissible. One additional but not widespread pronunciation problem involving this sound is the practice in some parts of the eastern United States of adding [g] in words such as *singing* [sɪŋgɪŋ] and saying.

1. The English singer was winning the long contest.
2. He mingled with winged, gaily singing songbirds.
3. The long, strong rope rang the gong.
4. Running and skipping, the ringleader led the gang.
5. Among his long songs, Engel mingled some lilting things.
6. Along the winding stream, the swimming and fishing were finding many fans.

[l] The consonant [l] is a voiced lingua-alveolar semivowel. In forming [l], the tip of the tongue is placed against the upper gum ridge, and phonated air escapes around the sides of the tongue. [l] presents little difficulty when in an initial or final position in a word, but it is so frequently a source of trouble in a medial position that a special discussion of this sound is in order. If you say aloud the word *William*, you will notice that the tip of the tongue is placed low in the mouth for [wɪ], raised to the upper gum ridge for [l], and returned to the floor of the mouth for [jəm]. Quite obviously, it is easier to speak this name without moving the tongue at all. When this is done, the name then sounds like [wɪjəm], and the [l] sound is completely lost. Unlike some of the English speech sounds that may in informal delivery be softened or

dropped without loss in effectiveness, the lost medial [l] is definitely substandard and should never occur in the announcer's speech. Note that [l], like [m] and [n], is capable of forming a speech entity by itself, in a word such as *saddle* [sædl̩].

Here is a diagnostic exercise for the medial [l].

ANNCR: Millions of Italians filled the hilly sector of Milan. The willing celebrants whirled all along the palisades, down by the roiling river. The lilting lullabys, trilled by Italian altos, thrilled the millions as they willingly milled along the boulevard. "It's really thrilling," said William Miller, a celebrant from Valley Forge. "I willingly call this the most illustrious fellowship in all of Italy."

1. A million silly swallows filled their bills with squiggling worms.
2. Willy Wallace willingly wiggled William's million-dollar bill.
3. Lilly and Billy met two willing fellows from the hills.
4. A little melon was willingly volunteered by Ellen and William.
5. Bill filled the lily pot with a million gallons of water.
6. The mill filled the foolish little children's order for willow leaves.
7. William wanted a million dollars, but he seldom was willing to stop his silly shilly-shallying and get to work.
8. Phillip really liked Italian children, although he seldom was willing to speak Italian.
9. Enrolling in college really was thrilling for William, even though a million pillow fights were in store for the silly fellow.
10. Billy Bellnap shilled for millions of collegians, even though his colleagues collected alibis galore in the Alleghenies at Miller's celebration.

[w] The consonant [w] is a voiced labial semivowel. It is formed by moving the lips from a rounded, nearly closed position to an open position. The tongue is not in any particular position for [w] but is positioned according to correct placement for the following vowel sound. A common speech fault is occasioned by insufficient movement of the lips in making [w].

1. Worried Willy wouldn't waste one wonderful word.
2. The wild wind wound round the woody wilderness.
3. The wishing well was once wanted by Wally Williams.
4. Wouldn't it be wonderful if one walrus would wallow in the water?
5. Walter wanted to wash away the worrisome watermark.

6. Always sewing, Eloise wished the wonderful woman would want one more wash dress.

[hw] The consonant [hw] is an unvoiced labial fricative. It is a combination of the two consonants [h] and [w] and is achieved by forming the lips for the [w] sound but releasing the air that makes the [h] sound first. [w] follows immediately, and [h] is thus barely heard. Although the [h] sound in words such as *when* is lost by most speakers, the radio or television announcer should include the sound at least until such time as it drops out of our language altogether, which it seems to be doing.

1. Mr. Wheeler waited at the wharf.
2. Wherever the whippoorwill whistled, Whitby waited.
3. Why whisper when we don't know whether or not Mr. White's whelp is a whiz?
4. Why not wholesale,[5] whispered the white-bearded Whig?
5. Whitney whittled the white-headed whistle.
6. On Whitsun, Whittier was whipping Whitman on a whim.

[j] The consonant [j] (as in *yellow*) is a voiced linguapalatal fricative. As in saying [l], [w], and [r], a slight glide is necessary during the delivery of this sound. Although it causes little difficulty when in the initial position in a word, the medial [j] frequently follows a double l (*ll*) construction and therefore is sometimes involved in the speech problem that arises from dropping the medial [l]. Americans often mispronounce the name *William* as [wɪjəm] and the word *million* as [mɪjən].

1. Young Yancy used yellow utensils.
2. The millionaire abused the useful William.
3. Yesterday the youthful Tillyard yelled "Yes."
4. The Yukon used to yen for yokels.
5. Yorick yielded to the yodeler from Yonkers.
6. The yegg yelled at William.

[r] The consonant [r] is a voiced linguapalatal semivowel. In certain areas of the United States and in England, [r] is frequently softened or completely dropped. In General American speech, however, all [r]s are sounded, though they need not and should not be prolonged or formed too far back in the throat. A voice described as harsh quite

[5]Where the word begins with a distinct [h] and does not move immediately to [w], [w] is dropped.

frequently overstresses the [r] sounds. A word of warning is in order. In attempting to soften your [r]s, be careful to avoid affectation; a pseudo-British accent is unbecoming to Americans and Canadians. Few speakers can successfully change only one speech sound. The slight softening of [r] should be only one part of a general softening of all harsh sounds in your speech.

1. Rather than run rapidly, Rupert relied on rhythm.
2. Robert rose to revive Reginald's rule of order.
3. Apparently a miracle occurred to Herman.
4. Large and cumbersome, the barge was a dirty hull.
5. Afraid of fire and sure of war, the rear admiral was far away.
6. The bore on the lower floor left his chair and went out the door.

7
FOREIGN PRONUNCIATION

Despite the fact that nearly all Americans have their ethnic roots embedded in a foreign culture, most Americans are familiar with only one language—American English. This presents a problem to most American announcers, who must daily read words and names of foreign origin. News stories originating in any of a hundred different nations, featuring the names of places and people and organizations, must be read with accuracy and authority by professional news announcers. Announcers on classical music stations must deal with Spanish, Italian, French, German, and Russian names and music titles in a typical one-week shift. Commercials for a variety of goods and services—international restaurants, foreign tours, exotic perfumes, foreign films, and Oriental rugs, to name a few—often require the ability to pronounce foreign names and words. It is no exaggeration to state that your career as a professional announcer will be seriously handicapped unless you develop skill and ease in pronouncing words from at least the major modern languages of the world.

Several years of study of every major language would prepare you ideally for your work, but because time and capacities do not usually permit such thoroughness, the next-best solution is to learn the rules of pronunciation of the languages you are most likely to need. This chapter provides a detailed discussion of Spanish, Italian, French, and German pronunciation and a brief mention of other European and Asian languages. The drill section includes commercial and news copy drawing on several languages.

Although correct foreign pronunciation is stressed in this chapter, proper pronunciation for radio and television is not always the same as the correct pronunciation. In Chapter 5 you saw that the names of American people and places derived from foreign words are usually

Americanized. Similarly, conventional pronunciations of foreign cities, nations, personal names, and musical compositions, though not correct, are usually preferred on radio and television. Here are some examples:

SPELLING	CORRECT PRONUNCIATION	CONVENTIONAL PRONUNCIATION
Paris	PAH-REE' [pɑ'ri]	PAIR'-IS ['pɛrɪs or 'pærɪs]
Copenhagen	KOEBN-HAU'-N [købn'haʊn]	KOPE'-UN-HAIG'-UN ['kopən 'hegṇ]
Berlin	BEAR-LEEN' [bɛr'lin]	BER-LIHN' [bɚ'lɪn]

You are expected to use correct foreign pronunciation for certain words and to modify it for others. This amounts to knowing when it is correct to be incorrect. This problem poses at least three possibilities when you are pronouncing foreign or foreign-derived words. (1) You may pronounce them as the natives do in the country of origin. (2) You may modify them to conform to conventionally accepted American usage. (3) You may completely Anglicize them. There are regrettably few rules to guide you. The absolutist position that the correct pronunciation is never wrong offers no help. Even the most extreme advocate of correct pronunciation would admit that an announcer who begins a news bulletin with PAH-REE', FRĀHS [pa'ri frɑːs] is affected.

GUIDELINES FOR ANNOUNCERS

In the absence of ironclad rules, the following suggestions, which are in accord with the best practice among topflight announcers in the United States and Canada, are offered. They seek order in a situation that is by definition disorderly, so they cannot guarantee answers to all pronunciation questions that may arise.

1. *Give the names of cities and countries the familiar, conventionalized pronunciation current in the United States.* The citizens of Germany call their country *Deutschland;* the word *Germany* is not even a German word. If it were, its German pronunciation would differ considerably from that used by Americans. There is no point in either applying the German rules of pronunciation to the name *Germany* or calling Germany *Deutschland* in this country.

In most instances, we spell foreign city names as they are spelled in their own country but pronounce them in conventionalized ways true neither to their original pronunciations nor to any rational system of Anglicization. This presents no problem when the name is in more or less constant use, as Paris, Berlin, and Copenhagen are. The problem arises when a city relatively unknown to Americans, such as Eleusis [ɛ'lusɪs], São Paulo [ˌsāu'paulʊ], or Rheims [ræːs], is suddenly thrust into the news. Here, if pronunciation rules do not help, you should check a standard pronunciation guide. Several are to be found in almost every broadcast station, and at least one should be in the personal library of every announcer. The Kenyon and Knott *A Pronouncing Dictionary of American English* (G. & C. Merriam, Springfield, Mass., 1953) and the NBC *Handbook of Pronunciation* (Thomas Y. Crowell, New York, 1964) give conventional pronunciations of foreign place names for broadcast use. To repeat, there is often no virtue in using the correct foreign pronunciation for a foreign place name. The correct Japanese pronunciation of Iwo Jima is EE-WAW'-DJEE-MAH [i'wɔdʒimɑ], but it is customary in this country to say the technically incorrect EE'WO DJEE'-MUH ['iˌwo'dʒimə].

2. *Pronounce the names of American cities derived from foreign namesakes as the natives of that American city pronounce it.* Vienna, Versailles, Marseilles, and Alhambra are all names of American cities, and not one of them is correctly pronounced like its foreign counterpart. Pronunciation guides will give you the correct local pronunciations of these and other cities and towns.

3. *In pronouncing the names of foreigners, adopt one of the following rules.* (a) If the person's preference is known, use the preferred pronunciation. (b) If the person is well known and a conventional pronunciation has developed, use that pronunciation. (c) If the person is not well known and you do not know the person's preference, follow the rules of pronunciation for his or her language.

4. *In pronouncing the names of Americans derived from foreign names, adopt one of the following rules.* (a) If the person's preference is known, use that pronunciation. (b) If the person's preference is not known, pronounce the name the way other Americans of the same name do. For example, if the name is DuBois and the person is American, you will be safe pronouncing it DUE-BOYZ, rather than as if it were the French DUH-BWAH.

5. *In pronouncing the titles of foreign musical compositions, let the following rules guide you.* (a) If the title is in common use and the customary

pronunciation is quite close to the original, use that pronunciation. (b) If the title is little known and has no conventional pronunciation, pronounce it according to the rules in its country of origin. Although it may sometimes be desirable to soften some foreign words slightly for American ears, you cannot in this instance go wrong by being correct.

In this chapter the correct rules of foreign pronunciation will be discussed and illustrated. In each instance the correct pronunciation will be transcribed into IPA symbols as well as the less precise symbols of the radio and television wire services. Before taking up each language in detail, one word of caution is in order. Because most modern European countries comprise many formerly independent states, regional variations in pronunciation abound. The pronunciations given in this chapter follow those established by qualified natives as standard pronunciations. Deviations are not necessarily substandard.

SPANISH PRONUNCIATION

Spanish, unlike English, is a strictly phoneticized language. Once you have mastered the rules of Spanish pronunciation, you will know how to pronounce any Spanish word you see in print. Although a few letters have more than one speech sound, the surrounding letters in the word are an infallible guide to their pronunciation.

Stress

Spanish words have one strongly stressed syllable. All other syllables receive no stress at all. There is no such thing as secondary stress; every syllable in a word is either stressed or not, with no middle ground.

Many Spanish words carry an accent mark over one of the vowels— for example, **médico**—and this indicates that the syllable the accented vowel appears in receives a strong stress. Unlike the accent marks in French, the Spanish accent mark does not affect the pronunciation of the vowel. Two general rules govern words that carry no mark:

1. Words ending in a consonant other than **n** or **s** are stressed on the *last* syllable, as in **usted** [u'stɛd], **canal** [ka'nal], **señor** [se'ɲɔr].
2. Words ending in **n, s,** or a vowel are stressed on the *penultimate* (next-to-last) syllable, as in **joven** ['xoven], **señores** [sen'jɔres], **hombre** ['ɔmbre].

Spanish Vowels

Spanish has five vowels—**a, e, i, o,** and **u.** Whether the vowel is stressed or unstressed, it seldom moves from its customary sound. The chief exceptions are **i** and **u** when they form part of a diphthong. No vowel ever becomes the schwa [ə], as, for example, the letter *a* does in English *about*.

a   The vowel **a** is always pronounced "ah" [ɑ], as in *father*. Examples: **balsa** ['bɑlsɑ] (BAHL'-SAH); **casa** ['kɑsɑ] (KAH'-SAH).

e   The vowel **e** is pronounced "ay" [e], as in English *bait*, but it sometimes becomes more like "eh" [ɛ], as in *met*, depending on its context. When it has the "ay" sound, it is never prolonged and allowed to glide into an "ee" sound. Examples: **meses** ['meses] (MAY'-SAYS); **deberes** [de'beres] (DAY-BAY'-RAYS); **gobierno** [go'βjɛrno] (GO-BYEHR'-NOH).

i   The vowel **i,** except when part of a diphthong, is always pronounced "ee" [i], as in English *machine*. Examples: **definitivo** [defini'tiβo] (DAY-FEE-NEE-TEE'-VO); **pipa** ['pipɑ] (PEE'-PAH).

o   The vowel **o** is usually pronounced "oh" [o], as in English *hoe*, but depending on its context it may become more like "aw" [ɔ]. Examples: **contrata** [kon'trɑtɑ] (KOHN-TRAH'-TAH); **pocos** ['pokos] (POH'-KOHS); **hombre** ['ɔmbre] (AWM'-BRAY).

u   The vowel **u,** when not part of a diphthong, is pronounced "oo" [u], as in English *rule*. Examples: **luna** ['lunɑ] (LOO'-NAH); **público** ['publiko] (POO'-BLEE-KO).

Spanish Diphthongs

ia, ie, io, and iu   If you pronounce the sounds "ee" and "ah" together very rapidly, they form a sound very much like "yah." A similar change occurs in rapidly saying aloud the two component vowels in **ie** ("yay"), **io** ("yo"), and **iu** ("you"). These sounds, called diphthongs because they are a combination of two vowels, are represented as follows in IPA: [jɑ], [je], [jo], [ju]. In pronouncing them, sound both component sounds but make sure that the **i** becomes [j]. Examples: **piano** ['pjɑno] (PYAH'-NO); **mientras** ['mjentrɑs] (MYAYN'-TRAS); **naciones** [nɑ'sjones] (NAH-SYONE'-AYS); **viuda** ['vjudɑ] (VYOO'-DAH).

ei   Spanish **ei** is pronounced "ay" [e], as in English *rein*. Example: **seis** [ses] (SAYSS).

ai   The Spanish **ai** is pronounced "eye" [aɪ]. Example: **bailar** [baɪ'lɑr] (BY-LAHR'). (*Note:* At the ends of words, **ei** and **ai** are spelled **ey** and **ay**.)

oi   Spanish **oi** is prounced "oy" [ɔɪ], as in *loiter*. Example: **heroico** [ɛr'ɔɪko] (EH-ROY'-KO).

ua, ue, ui, and uo   Spanish **u** preceding another vowel is pronounced like English *w* [w]. Examples: **cuatro** ['kwɑtro] (KWAH'-TRO); **puente** ['pwɛnte] (PWEN'-TAY); **cuidar** [kwi'dɑr] (KWEE-DAR'); **cuota** ['kwotɑ] (KWO'-TAH). (But note the exceptions under **gu** and **qu**.)

au   Spanish **au** is pronounced "ow" [aʊ]. Example: **autobus** [aʊto'bus] (OW-TOE-BOOS').

eu   Spanish **eu** is pronounced by running "eh" [ɛ] and "oo" [u] together rapidly. Example: **deuda** [dɛ'udɑ] (DEH-OO'-DAH).

Spanish Consonants

b   At the beginning of a word or after **m**, this is pronounced like English *b* [b]. Examples: **bueno** ['bweno] (BWAY'-NO); **nombre** ['nombre] (NOHM'-BRAY). In other positions it is more like English *v*, although it is produced with both lips instead of the upper teeth and lower lip. The IPA symbol for this sound is [β]. Example: **alabar** [ɑlɑ'βɑr] (AH-LAH-BAHR'). (*Note:* There is no way of indicating this sound with conventional type, and the B is used in the wire-service example to avoid confusion.)

c   Spanish **c** has two values. (1) Before **e** or **i** it is soft. Castilian speech—fairly standard in most of Spain—pronounces this as *th* in *thin*. In southern Spain and in Spanish America it is pronounced as *s* in *say*. You should base your choice on the origin of the person or title, unless a large Spanish-speaking audience in your area would consider Castilian pronunciation affected. Example: **ciudad** [sju'dɑd] (SYOU-DAHD'), or [θju'dɑd] (THYOU-DAHD'). (2) In all other positions, **c** is pronounced "k" as in *car*. Examples: **cura** ['kurɑ] (KOO'-RAH); **acto** ['ɑkto] (AHK'-TOH). The sound of "k" preceding **e** or **i** is spelled **qu** (see below).

cc   The first **c** is by definition hard, and because **cc** appears only before **e** or **i**, the second **c** is soft. Example: **acceso** [ɑk'seso] (AHK-SAY'-soh), or in Castilian Spanish [ɑk'θeso] (AHK-THAY'-SO).

ch   Spanish **ch** is pronounced as the *ch* [tʃ] in *church*. Example: **muchacha** [mu'tʃɑtʃɑ] (MOO-CHA'-CHA).

d   At the beginning of a word, or after **n** or **l**, Spanish **d** is much like English *d* [d]. Examples: **dios** [djos] (DYOS); **caldo** ['kɑldo] (KAHL'-DO). In other positions it is more like a weak-voiced *th* [ð], as in English *weather*. It is made by extending the tongue a short distance beyond the front teeth and thus weakening the sound. Example: **padre** ['paðre] (PAH'-THRAY). (*Note:* This sound is still more [d] than [ð], so the [d] will be used in this chapter.)

f   Spanish **f** is pronounced like English *f* [f]. Example: **flores** ['flores] (FLO'-RAYS).

g   The **g** has two values. (1) Before **e** or **i**, **g** is pronounced much like German *ch* [x], as in *ach,* or Scottish *ch,* as in *loch.* It is a guttural sound, with tightening and some rasp in the rear of the mouth but no vibration of the vocal folds. Examples: **general** [xene'ral] (KHAY-NAY-RAHL'); **gente** ['xente] (KHAYN'-TAY). (2) In all other positions, **g** is hard, as in *gag.* Examples: **gala** ['gala] (GAH'-LAH); **largo** ['largo] (LAHR'-GO). (*Note:* Because the sound [x] does not occur in English, the wire services have difficulty transcribing it. Sometimes they use CH and sometimes KH. When CH is used there is no way of knowing whether [x] or [tʃ] is intended. We shall transcribe it as KH in this chapter, but you should be alert to the frequent inconsistencies in transcribing this sound when you come to the wire-service drill material later in this book.)

gu   When the sound of hard **g** occurs before **e** or **i**, it is written **gu.** In this convention **u** is merely a marker and has no sound of its own. Example: **guia** ['gia] (GHEE'-AH).

gü   The two dots over **ü,** when it is between **g** and **e** or **i** (**güe, güi**), indicate that **ü** is part of a diphthong, to be sounded like *w.* Example: **agüero** [a'gwero] (AH-GWAY'-RO).

h   Except in the combination **ch** previously discussed, **h** is a superfluous letter—the only one in the Spanish language. Examples: **habas** ['aβas] (AH'-BAHS); **adhesivo** [ade'siβo] (AHD-AY-SEE'-BO).

j   Exactly like the first pronunciation of Spanish **g** given above. Example: **junta** ['xunta] (KHOON'-TAH).

l   Very similar to English *l,* although the Spanish keep the rear of the tongue flat. Example: **labios** ['laβjos] (LAH'-BYOS).

ll   In Castilian Spanish, **ll** is pronounced much like *lli* [lj] in the English word *million.* However, in most parts of Spanish America, **ll** is pronounced like *y* [j] in *yes.* Example: **calle** ['kalje] (KAH'-LYAY) or ['kaje] (KAH'-YAY).

m   Like English *m.* Example: **cambio** ['kamβjo] (KAHM'-BYO).

n   There are three pronunciations for the letter **n**. (1) Before **ca, co, cu, qui,** and **que** (that is to say, before any "k" sound) and before **g** or **j**, it is pronounced *ng* [ŋ] as in *sing*: **tango** ['taŋgo] (TAHNG'-GO). (2) Before **f, v, p,** or **b**, it is pronounced like English *m*: **confiado** [kom'fjaðo] (KOM-FYAH'-DO). (3) In all other instances it is pronounced like English *n*: **manojo** [man'oxo] (MAH-NO'-KHO).

nn   Very rare. Both **n**s are sounded. Example: **perenne** [pe'ren:e] (PAY-RAYN'-NAY).

ñ   Spanish **ñ** is pronounced *ny* [ɲ], as in English *canyon*. Example: **señor** [se'ɲor] (SAY-NYOR').

p   Like English *p*. Example: **padre** ['paðre] (PAH'-THRAY).

qu   Like hard **c**, with **u** never sounded. This occurs only before **e** or **i**. Examples: **qué** [ke] (KAY); **aquí** [a'ki] (AH-KEE').

r   Spanish **r** has two values, neither of which is like the English. (1) At the beginning of a word or after **l, n,** or **s**, the tongue is trilled against the roof of the mouth. Examples: **rico** ['riko] (RREE'-KO); **honrado** [on'rado] (OWN-RRAH'-DO). (2) In other positions it is a single flip of the tongue against the roof of the mouth. Example: **caro** ['karo] (KAH'-RO).

rr   The **rr** is used to indicate a full trill where the rule would call for a single flip of the tongue were single **r** used.

s   There are two pronunciations of this letter. (1) Before **b, d, g, l, m, n, r,** and **v**, it is pronounced like English *z*. Example: **mismo** ['mizmo] (MEEZ'-MO). (2) In other instances it is pronounced like English *s* in *sea*. Example: **cosa** ['kosa] (KOH'-SAH).

sc   In both Castilian and non-Castilian, **s** plus hard **c**, or [s] plus [k], are always pronounced separately. Example: **disco** ['disko] (DEES'-KO). In non-Castilian, **s** plus soft **c**, being identical sounds, are merged. Example: **discernir** [diser'nir] (DEE-SAIR-NEAR'). In Castilian, **s** plus soft **c**, which is actually [θ], are pronounced separately. Example: **discernir** [disθer'nir] (DEES-THAIR-NEAR').

t   Much like English *t*. Example: **trato** ['trato] (TRAH'-TOE).

v   The same as Spanish **b**, with the same positional varieties.

x   Normally like English *x* [ks] in the word *vex*. Example: **próximo** ['proksimo] (PROCK'-SEE-MO). Before a consonant, the Castilian pronunciation is like Spanish **s: expreso** [ɛs'preso] (ESS-PRAY'-SOH). The words for *Mexico* and *Mexican* are pronounced with the **j** [x] sound: **México** ['mexiko] (MAY'-KHEE-KO).

y Much like English *y* in *year*. Example: **yerba** ['jɛrbɑ] (YEHR'-BAH). In certain instances, instead of representing a consonant, the letter **y** substitutes for the vowel **i:** (1) the second element of a diphthong at the end of a word, **rey** [re] (RAY); (2) the initial in a few proper names, **Ybarra** [i'bɑrɑ] (EE-BAH'-RAH); (3) the word for *and*, **pan y vino** [pɑni'vino] (PAHN-EE-VEE'-NO).

z The letter **z** follows the same rules as soft **c.** Examples: (Castilian) **jerez** [xe'reθ] (KHAY-RAYTH'); (Spanish-American) **jerez** [xe'res] (KHAY-RAYSS').

Practice: Pronouncing Spanish Words
Practice pronouncing the following Spanish words:

Toledo	Ramírez	Cabezón
Guernica	San Sebastián	*Danzas españolas*
Falange	Albéniz	*Pepita Jiménez*
Cuernavaca	Manuel de Falla	Oviedo
Segovia	Granados	picante
García	Sarasate y Navascuez	servicio

ITALIAN PRONUNCIATION

Italian, like Spanish, has a phonetically strict writing system. Although it is not quite as thorough as Spanish spelling, which tells you everything about the pronunciation of a word, it is a very businesslike system. Italian conventional spelling does not consistently mark stress, and in the unmarked words certain vowel qualities are likewise undifferentiated. Aside from this, Italian presents few difficulties to the student.

Stress

Italian words have one strongly stressed syllable, whereas the other syllables are completely unstressed. Unlike English, Italian has no half-stresses. The relatively small number of words stressed on the last syllable are always marked with an accent over that vowel—for example, **sarà** [sɑ'rɑ] (SAH-RAH'). Most Italian words are stressed on the penultimate syllable: **infinito** [infi'nito] (EEN-FEE-NEE'-TOE). Many words are stressed on the antepenultimate syllable: **medico** ['mediko]

(MAY'-DEE-KOE). A few Italian printing houses mark such words with a grave accent over the vowel in the syllable to be stressed, but this is not the general rule. To help in the examples in this chapter, an accent mark will be used to show stress on some syllable other than the penultimate. The grave accent will also be used to indicate an open **e** [ɛ] or an open **o** [ɔ], but this should cause no confusion, because syllables containing open **e** and open **o** are always stressed in Italian.

Italian Vowels   Italian has seven basic vowel sounds but uses only the five letters **a, e, i, o,** and **u** to represent them. Stressed or unstressed, each keeps its distinctive quality, though stressed vowels tend to be lengthened before single consonants—the first vowel of **casa** is longer than that of **cassa,** for example.

a   The vowel **a** is always pronounced "ah" [ɑ], as in *father*. Examples: **là** [lɑ] (LAH); **pasta** ['pɑstɑ] (PAH'-STAH).

e   Italian **e** varies from "ay" [e] to "eh" [ɛ]. Although there are ways of determining the correct pronunciation in each instance, the rules are complex and of no concern here. Most northern and southern Italians, including the best educated, have just one **e,** which may vary somewhat according to the consonants that precede or follow it. This pronunciation is understood and accepted everywhere. Where accent marks are given, the acutely accented **é** tells you that the pronunciation is [e], whereas the grave accent, **è,** tells you that the pronunciation is [ɛ]. Examples: **débole** ['debole] (DAY'-BO-LAY); **prèsto** ['prɛsto] (PREH'-STOE).

i   Much like English *i* in *machine*. Example: **pipa** ['pipɑ] (PEE'-PAH).

o   Speakers who distinguish between two **e** sounds also distinguish two qualities of **o:** a closed **o** [o], as in *go,* and an open **o** [ɔ], as in *bought*. Dictionaries sometimes indicate the closed **o** with an acute accent—**pólvere** ['polvere] (POHL'-VAY-RAY)—and the open **o** with a grave accent—**còsta** ['kɔstɑ] (KAW'-STAH). As with the open and closed **e,** the difference between the two varieties of **o** is minor, and most speakers who use only one **e** sound likewise use only one **o** sound.

u   Much like English *u* in *rule*. Examples: **luna** ['lunɑ] (LOO'-NAH); **futuro** [fu'turo] (FOO-TOO'-ROH).

Italian
Diphthongs

The Italian vowels **a, e, i, o,** and **u** form many different combinations to produce the diphthongs. Although they may seem somewhat complex at first glance, they are quite easily mastered.

ia — The **ia** diphthong, except when it follows **c** or **g,** finds **i** becoming "y" [j] and **a** retaining its regular pronunciation. Example: **piano** ['pjɑno] (PYAH'-NOH). When **ia** follows **c,** the **i** merely serves as a silent marker to indicate that **c** is soft, [tʃ] like the *ch* in *chair.* Example: **Ciano** ['tʃɑn‚o] (TCHAH'-NOH). When **ia** follows **g,** the **i** merely serves as a silent marker to indicate that **g** is soft, [dʒ] like the *g* in *gem.* Example: **Gianinni** [dʒɑ'nini] (DGAH-NEE'-NEE).

ie — The **ie** diphthong, except for the few instances in which it follows **c** or **g,** finds **i** becoming "y" [j] and **e** retaining its regular pronunciation. Examples: **pièno** ['pjeno] (PYAY'-NOH); **cielo** ['tʃɛlo] (TCHEH'-LOH). Like the **ia** diphthong, **ie** following **c** or **g** serves to indicate that the soft pronunciation is to be used, and the **i** has no other function.

io — The **io** diphthong, except where it follows **c** or **g,** finds **i** becoming "y" [j] and **o** retaining its regular pronunciation. After **c** or **g,** the **i** serves only as a silent marker to indicate that the soft pronunciation is to be used. Examples: **Mario** ['mɑrjo] (MAHR'-YO); **bacio** ['bɑtʃo] (BAH'-TCHOH); **Giorgio** ['dʒɔrdʒo] (DGAWR'-DGOH).

iu — The **iu** diphthong, except where it follows **c** or **g,** finds **i** becoming "y" [j] and **u** retaining its regular pronunciation. Following **c** or **g,** the **i** serves as a silent marker to indicate that the preceding sound is soft. Examples: **iuta** ['jutɑ] (YOU'-TAH); **acciuga** [ɑ'tʃugɑ] (AH-CHEW'-GAH); **giù** [dʒu] (DGOO).

ai, oi, and ui — These diphthongs are merely the glide from **a, o,** and **u** to the "ee" sound. Examples: **mai** [maɪ] (MY); **pòi** [pɔɪ] (POY); **guida** ['gwidɑ] (GWEE'-DAH).

ua, ue, and uo — These diphthongs all find **u** becoming *w* (as in *will*) and **a, e,** and **o** each retaining its permanent sound. Examples: **guàio** ['gwɑjo] (GWAH'-YOH); **sàngue** ['sɑŋgwe] (SAHNG'-GWAY); **cuòre** ['kwɔre] (KWAW'-RAY).

au — The **au** diphthong is pronounced like *ow* [aʊ] in English *how.* Example: **Làura** ['laʊrɑ] (LAU'-RAH).

Italian Consonants

An all-important feature of Italian pronunciation is the occurrence of both single (or short) and double (or long) consonants. In Italian, a written double consonant (**cc, rr, zz**) always means a spoken double consonant. The nearest thing in English to the Italian double consonant is the effect produced in two-word expressions such as *ought to, guess so,* or *sick cat.* These have their counterparts in the Italian words **òtto, messo,** and **seccare.** Note that this is not really a doubling of the sound as much as a prolonging of it. Before a double consonant (as in **canne**), a stressed vowel is perceptibly shorter than before a single consonant (as in **cane**). In the following discussion of the Italian consonants, several words will be listed without phonetic spellings for practice.

b　Like English *b.* Examples: **barba, bianco, buòno, bambino, babbo, sàbbia, labbra.**

c　The **c** has two values. (1) Before **e** or **i,** it is soft, like *ch* [tʃ] in *church.* Examples: **cena, cènto, fàcile, Lècce, spicci, accènto.** When the sound of soft **c** [tʃ] occurs before **a, o,** or **u,** it is written **ci** (**ciò**), and **i** is merely a silent marker with no sound of its own. Example: **bacio** ['batʃo] (ʙᴀʜ'-ᴛᴄʜᴏʜ). (2) In all other positions, **c** is hard, like *c* in *call* [k]. Examples: **caldo, cura, clèro, bocca, sacco, piccolo.**

ch　The **ch** occurs only before **e** or **i,** where it represents hard **c** [k]. Examples: **che** [ke] (ᴋᴀʏ); **vècchio** ['vɛkːjo] (ᴠᴇʜᴋ'-ᴋʏᴏʜ).

d　Much like English *d.* Examples: **dardo, duòmo, càndido, freddo, rèd-dito, iddio.**

f　Like English *f.* Examples: **faccia, fiato, fiume, gufo, bèffa, ràffio, soffiare.**

g　The **g** has two values. (1) Before **e** or **i,** it is soft, like *g* in *gem* [dʒ]. Examples: **gènte, giro, pàgina, legge, viaggi, suggèllo.** When the sound of soft **g** [dʒ] occurs before **a, o,** or **u,** it is written **gi** (**già**), and the **i** serves only as a silent marker with no value of its own. Example: **Giovanni** [dʒo'vanːi] (ᴅɢᴏʜ-ᴠᴀʜɴ'-ɴᴇᴇ). (2) In all other positions, except as described below, **g** is hard, like *g* in *good* [g]. Examples: **gamba, góndola, guèrra, lèggo, agganciare.**

gh　Occurs only before **e** or **i,** where it represents hard *g* [g]. Example: **ghiàccio** ['gjatʃːo] (ɢʏᴀʜᴛᴄʜ'-ᴏʜ).

gli Italian **gli** is like English *lli* in *million*. When another vowel follows, as it usually does—in the next word in the case of the definite article **gli** (*the*)—the **i** is a silent marker and represents no sound of its own. Inside a word, the consonant sound is always double. Remember that the **g** in **gli** has no value whatsoever, and that, when the word is followed by another vowel, the **i** has no value. The entire sound, then, becomes [l] plus [j]. Examples: **figlio** ['fiʎːjo] (FEE'-LYOH); **paglia** ['paʎːja] (PAH'-LYAH); **pagliacci** [paˈʎjatʃːi] (PAH-LYAHCH'-CHEE); **gli altri** ['ʎaltri] (YAHL'-TREE).

gn Like English *ny* [ɲ] in *canyon* (Spanish ñ). Inside a word the sound is always double. Examples: **signore** [siˈɲːore] (SEEN-NYO'-RAY); **giugno** ['dʒuɲo] (JOON'-NYOH).

h Except in the combinations **ch** and **gh, h** is the only superfluous letter in Italian. In native words it occurs only at the beginning of four related forms of the verb **avere** (*have*). The word **hanno,** then, is pronounced exactly like the word **anno** ['anːo] (AHN'-NO).

j The letter **j** is not regularly used in Italian, except as a substitute for the letter **i** in proper names (**Jàcopo** for **Iàcopo**) or in a final position as a substitute for **ii** in plurals (**studj** for **studii**).

l Can be pronounced like English *l,* though the Italians pronounce it with the tongue flat and unraised in the back of the mouth. Examples: **lavoro, lièto, Itàlia, giallo, bèlla, nulla.**

m Like English *m.* Examples: **mièle, mùsica, fame, mamma, gèmma, fiammiferi.**

n Like English *n,* including [ŋ] (*ng* as in *thing*) where it precedes hard **c** or hard **g.** Examples: **nòno** ['nɔno] (NAW'-NOH); **bianco** ['bjaŋko] (BYAHNG'-KOH); **inglese** [iŋˈgleze] (ING-GLAYZ'-AY).

p Much like English *p.* Examples: **papa, prète, capo, dòppio, zuppa, appòggio.**

q The same as hard **c** and always followed by **u,** which is always sounded [w] as part of a diphthong. Examples: **quadro, quindi, dunque, quèrcia.** When doubled, it appears as **cq: acqua, nacque, acquistare.**

r Where single **r** appears, it is manufactured with a single flip of the tongue tip against the roof of the mouth. Where double **r** appears, it is a trill of the tongue tip, as with Spanish **rr.** Examples: **Roma, rumore, dramma, carro, burro, orrore.**

s   In most positions, Italian **s** is pronounced like English *s* in *sea.* Examples: **sole** ['sole] (SO'-LAY); **sfida** ['sfida] (SFEE'-DAH); **rosso** ['ros:o] (ROHS'-SOH). Before any of the voiced consonants, **b, d, g, l, m, n, r,** or **v,** the **s** is pronounced like *z* in *zoo.* Examples: **sbaglio** ['zbal:jo] (ZBAH'-LYOH); **disdegno** [di'zdeɲo] (DEE-ZDAY'-NYOH); **slancio** ['zlantʃo] (ZLAHN'-CHOH). Single **s** between vowels is pronounced either [s] or [z], with [s] generally preferred in Tuscany and [z] elsewhere. Examples: **casa, francese, còsa.**

sc   Before **e** or **i, sc** is pronounced [ʃ] like English *sh* in *shoe.* Inside a word, it is pronounced double. Examples: **scelto** ['ʃelto] (SHAYL'-TOH); **pesce** ['peʃ:e] (PAYSH'-SHAY). When this sound occurs before **a, o,** or **u,** it appears as **sci.** In this convention, the **i** is merely a silent marker and is not pronounced. Examples: **sciame** [ʃame] (SHAH'-MAY); **asciutto** [a'ʃ:ut:o] (AHSH-SHOOT'-TOH). The spelling **scie** is the same as **sce.** In all other positions, **sc** is pronounced like *sk* in *ski.* Examples: **scale** ['skale] (SKAH'-LAY); **tasca** ['taska] (TAH'-SKAH).

sch   The **sch** occurs only before **e** and **i,** where it represents *s* as in *say* plus hard *c* as in *come.* Example: **schiavo** ['skjavo] (SKYAH'-VOH).

t   Much like English *t.* Examples: **tèsta, tòrto, triste, gatto, sêtte, prosciutto.**

v   Like English *v.* Examples: **vivo, Verona, vuòto, bevve, òvvio, avviso.**

z   Italian **z** is ambiguous, representing both [ts] like *ts* in English *cats* and [dz] like *ds* in *beds.* In the initial position, there is no firm rule for its pronunciation. Examples: **zèlo** ['dzɛlo] (DZEH'-LOH); **zio** ['tsio] (TSEE'-OH). Internally, [ts] is general after **r** and **l: fòrza** ['fɔrtsa] (FAWR'-TSAH). A single **z** between vowels is [ts]: **azione** [a'tsjone] (AH-TSYOH'-NAY).

Practice: Pronouncing Italian Words

Practice pronouncing the following Italian words:

Arcangelo Corèlli	*Il barbiere di Siviglia*
Giovanni Pierluigi Palestrina	*La cenerentola*
Ottorino Respighi	*L'Italiana in Algeri*
Gioacchino Rossini	*Tosca*
Doménico Scarlatti	*Chi vuole innamorarsi*

Giuseppe Tartini   *Il matrimonio segreto*
Beniamino Gigli   *Le nozze di Figaro*
Dusolina Giannini   *La finta giardiniera*
Franco Ghione   *Cosi fan tutte*
Giàcomo Puccini   *La gioconda*

FRENCH PRONUNCIATION

French, like English, uses complicated spelling conventions including numerous superfluous letters, sequences of letters representing single sounds, several ways of writing one sound, and the use of one letter to represent several sounds. But on the whole, French spelling is more systematic than English, and with practice one can learn to read French with an acceptable pronunciation.

Stress

French words, as well as entire phrases and sentences, have about equal accent on each syllable up to the last one, which is a little more heavily stressed. In the name of the French composer **Debussy** [dəbysi] (*),[1] the syllable **-sy** gets a slight extra stress if you pause or stop after it but not if you do not. In the sentence **Debussy est bien connu** (*Debussy is well known*), only the final sound of the phrase gets that extra bit of stress: [dəbysi ɛ bjɛ̃ kɔ'ny] (*).

French Oral Vowels

French has three classes of vowel sounds: twelve oral vowels, four nasal vowels, and three semivowels. Because a single speech sound in French may have as many as six different spellings, the vowels, nasal vowels, and semivowels will be grouped by sound rather than alphabetically.

Many of the sample words include a sound somewhere between [o] (OH) and [ɔ] (AW). In IPA the symbol for this sound is [ǫ], but it is not much used in French dictionaries, so there is little point in using it here. Authoritative reference works use the symbol [ɔ] to describe **o** and **au** in **école** and **Paul**, even though the actual sound is probably closer to [o]. To avoid confusion, sample words will be transcribed as they are in standard reference works. As you become familiar with the French language, you may want to modify conventional transcriptions to suit your own standards of accuracy.

[1] French **u** and German **ü** are both represented by the IPA symbol [y]. This sound does not occur in English, and no combination of English letters can approximate it phonetically. An asterisk enclosed in parentheses (*) is used throughout to indicate words and sounds that cannot be approximated with wire-service phonetics.

French has a number of speech sounds that do not occur in English, and each has been given an IPA symbol. Most of them are described here, but two need early and special explanation. The French tend to prolong a final l or r sound in an unvoiced, recessive manner. These sounds are especially noticeable when the words they are in terminate a phrase or are sounded separately. IPA invests each of them with a small circle—[l̥], [r̥]—to distinguish them from other l and r sounds. These symbols differ from the English syllabic consonant symbols [l̩] and [r̩], and they sound quite unlike anything in the English language. There is no satisfactory way of approximating these sounds in wire-service phonetics, but you will find them represented in this book in this manner.

WORD	IPA	WIRE SERVICE
siècle	[sjɛkl̥]	(SYEH-KL(UH))
mettre	[mɛtr̥]	(MET-R(UH))

IPA SYMBOL	DESCRIPTION OF SOUND	FRENCH SPELLING	EXAMPLES
[a]	Between *a* in *father* and *a* in *bat*	a	**patte** [pat] (PAHT)
		à	**déjà** [deʒa] (DAY-ZHAH)
[ɑ]	Like *a* in *father*	a	**phase** [fɑz] (FAHZ)
		â	**pâte** [pɑt] (PAHT)
[e]	Like *e* in *they* but without the final glide	e	**parlez** [pɑrle] (PAR-LAY)
		é	**été** [ete] (AY-TAY)
		ai	**gai** [ge] (GAY)
[ɛ]	Like *e* in *met*	e	**mettre** [mɛtr̥] (MET-R(UH))
		ê	**bête** [bɛt] (BET)
		è	**frère** [frɛr] (FREHR)
		ei	**neige** [nɛʒ] (NEHZH)
		ai	**frais** [frɛ] (FREH)
		aî	**maître** [mɛtr̥] (MET-R(UH))
[i]	Like *i* in *machine*	i	**ici** [isi] (EE-SEE)
		î	**île** [il] (EEL)
		y	**mystère** [mistɛr] (MEES-TAIR)
[o]	Like *o* in *hoe* but the final glide toward an "oo" sound is omitted	o	**chose** [ʃoz] (SHOZ)
		ô	**hôtel** [otɛl] (O-TEL)
		au	**haute** [ot] (OAT)
		eau	**beauté** [bote] (BO-TAY)
[ɔ]	Like *ou* in *bought* but shorter	o	**école** [ekɔl] (AY-KAWL)
		au	**Paul** [pɔl] (PAUL)

IPA SYMBOL	DESCRIPTION OF SOUND	FRENCH SPELLING	EXAMPLES
[u]	Much like *u* in *rule*	ou	**vous** [vu] (VOO)
		où	**où** [u] (OO)
		oû	**coûter** [kute] (KOO-TAY)
[y]	Pronounced with the tongue as for [i] but with the lips rounded as for [u]	u	**lune** [lyn] (*)
		û	**flûte** [flyt] (*)
[ø]	Pronounced with the tongue as for [e] ("ay") but with the lips rounded as for [o] ("oh")	eu	**feu** [fø] (*)
		œu	**vœux** [vø] (*)
[œ]	Pronounced with the tongue as for [ɛ] ("eh") but with the lips rounded as for [ɔ] ("aw")	eu	**seul** [sœl] (*)
		œu	**sœur** [sœr] (*)
[ə]	This is the schwa vowel, a simple "uh" sound, like the sound of *a* in *about*. It occurs mainly in pre-final syllables.	e	**semaine** [səmɛn] (SUH-MEN)
			neveu [nəvø] (*)

The [ə], or "uh" sound, occurs also in nine common little words consisting solely of a consonant plus this vowel—namely **ce, de, je, le, me, ne, que, se,** and **te**—most of which are always prefinal in a phrase, as in **je sais** [ʒəse] (ZHUH-SAY) and **le roi** [lərwa] (LUH-RWAH). If you listen carefully to a French speaker, you may decide that the vowel sound in each of these short words is closer to [œ] than to [ə]. Despite what your ears tell you, all standard French dictionaries transcribe these words with the schwa. This practice will be followed here to avoid confusion, but you should be careful not to give these words a fully Americanized [ə] (UH) sound.

At the end of many words, an extra **e** is written after one or another of these words. This so-called mute **e** has no effect on the pronunciation. Examples are **épée** [epe] (AY-PAY) and **craie** [krɛ] (KREH) or (KRAY).

Obviously, certain spellings fail to distinguish between pairs of vowel sounds: **a** represents both [a] and [ɑ]; **e** and **ai** represent both [e] and [ɛ]; **o** and **au** represent both [o] and [ɔ]; **eu** and **œu** represent both [ø] and [œ]. Following consonants often give clues—for example, before **r** in the same syllable [ɛ], [ɔ], [œ] always appear and never [e], [o], [ø]—but there are no sure rules. Fortunately, it does not matter too much because the distinctions between two members of a given pair are rarely important in conversation, and many educated speakers of French do not scrupulously observe all of them.

French Nasal Vowels

In producing the nasalized vowels, which have no counterpart in English, the breath passes through the mouth and nose simultaneously, giving a quality sharply and importantly distinct from that of the oral vowels. There is no way to signify these sounds with wire-service phonetics, so the pronunciation of words using nasalized vowels will be transcribed only in IPA symbols.

The nasalized vowels are the sounds that result when [ɑ], [ɛ], [ɔ], or [œ] precedes **m** or **n**. In such constructions, **m** or **n** is not pronounced as an entity. It serves only to indicate that the preceding vowel and sound is nasalized.

IPA SYMBOL	DESCRIPTION OF SOUND	BEFORE *M*		BEFORE *N*	
[ɑ̃]	Nasalized [ɑ]	am	chambre [ʃɑ̃br̥]	an	avant [avɑ̃]
			champagne [ʃɑ̃paɲ]		français [frɑ̃sɛ]
		em	tempel [tɑ̃pl̥]	en	entente [ɑ̃tɑ̃t]
			semblable [sɑ̃blabl̥]		pensée [pɑ̃se]
[ɛ̃]	Nasalized [ɛ]	im	simple [sɛ̃pl̥]	in	cinq [sɛ̃k]
		ym	symphonie [sɛ̃fɔni]	yn	syntaxe [sɛ̃tæks]
		aim	faim [fɛ̃]	ain	bain [bɛ̃]
		eim	Rheims [rɛ̃ːs]	ein	peintre [pɛ̃tr̥]

IPA SYMBOL	DESCRIPTION OF SOUND	BEFORE *M*	BEFORE *N*
[ɔ̃]	Nasalized [ɔ]	**om sombre** [sɔ̃br̥] **rompu** [rɔ̃py]	**on pont** [pɔ̃] **bonbon** [bɔ̃bɔ̃]
[œ̃]	Nasalized [œ]	**um humble** [œ̃bl̥]	**um lundi** [lœ̃di]

Kenyon and Knott's *Pronouncing Dictionary of American English* substitutes the symbol [æ̃] for [ɛ̃] and the symbol [õ] for [ɔ̃]. But most French dictionaries follow the practice given here. You should be aware, however, that nasalized [ɛ] is actually closer in sound to nasalized [æ] and that nasalized [ɔ] is actually closer to nasalized [o].

French Semivowels

Certain combinations of French vowels or of vowels and consonants combine to form new sounds as follows.

IPA SYMBOL	DESCRIPTION OF SOUND	FRENCH SPELLING	EXAMPLES
[j]	Before the vowel, like English *y* in *yet*	i	**hier** [jɛr] (YEHR) **Pierrot** [pjɛro] (PYEH-ROH)
		ï	**païen** [paɪjɛ̃] (*) **aïeux** [aɪjø]
		y	**payer** [pɛje] (PEH-YAY) **yeux** [jø] (*)
	After the vowel, like *y* in *boy*	il	**travail** [trɑvaɪj] (TRAH-VAHYUH) **soleil** [sɔlaɪj] (SAW-LEHYUH)
		ill	**œil** [œj] (*) **Marseille** [marsɛj] (MAR-SEHYUH)
		ll	**faillite** [fajit] (FAH-YEET) **bouillon** [bujɔ̃] (*) **fille** [fij] (FEE-YUH) **sillon** [sijɔ̃] (*)

Written **ill** is ambiguous, because it represents either the diphthong [ij], as in the last two examples, or the sequence **il,** as in **mille** [mil] (MEEL) or **village** [vilaʒ] (VEE-LAZH).

In the diphthong [jɛ̃], the nasal vowel is written **en: ancien** [ɑ̃sjɛ̃]; **rien** [rjɛ̃].

IPA SYMBOL	DESCRIPTION OF SOUND	FRENCH SPELLING	EXAMPLES
[w]	Like English *w* in *win*	**ou**	**oui** [wi] (WEE) **ouest** [wɛst] (WEST) **avouer** [ɑvwe] (AH-VWAY)

The diphthong [lwa] is written **oi**, as in **loi** [wa] (LWAH). When it is followed by another diphthong beginning with [j], the letter **y** is used between the diphthongs: **foyer** [fwaje] (FWAH-YAY); **joyeux** [ʒwajø]. The diphthong [wɛ̃] is written **oin**, as in **point** [pwɛ̃], **joindre** [ʒwɛ̃dṛ].

[ɥ]	Pronounced with the tongue as for [j] but with the lips rounded as for [w]; occurs mainly before the letter **i**	**u**	**suisse** [sɥis] (*) **nuit** [nɥi] (*) **cuir** [kɥir] (*)

French Consonants

With a few exceptions, the French consonants do not represent as many different sounds as the vowels do; for this reason, they have been arranged alphabetically.

The French letters **b, d, f, m, n, p, t, v,** and **z** represent one sound each and are pronounced much the same as in English. With some exceptions treated separately, doubled consonant letters (**nn, rr, tt**) have the same values as the corresponding singles.

c   Before **e, i,** or **y** or with the cedilla (**ç**) before any vowel, **c** is soft like English *c* in *city* [s]. Examples: **cent** [sɑ̃] (*); **grâce** [grɑs] (GRAHSS); **cité** [site] (SEE-TAY); **précis** [presi] (PRAY-SEE); **ça** [sɑ] (SAH); **reçu** [rəsy] (*). Before **a, o, u,** or a consonant, or in a final position, or when it is without the cedilla, it is hard like English *c* in *cat* [k]. Examples: **calme** [kalm] (KAHLM); **encore** [ɑ̃kɔr] (*); **cri** [kri] (KREE); **siècle** [sjɛkl̩] (SYEH-KL(UH)); **sec** [sɛk] (SECK). Double **cc** represents [ks] or simply [k], depending on the following letter; thus **accident** [aksidɑ̃] (*) but **accord** [akɔr] (A-KAWR).

ch   Usually like English *sh* in *shoe* [ʃ]. Examples: **chapeau** [ʃapo] (SHAH-POH); **Chopin** [ʃɔpɛ̃] (*); **riche** [riʃ] (REESH); **marché** [marʃe] (MAR-SHAY). In a few newer words of Greek derivation, **ch** stands for hard *c*: **psychologie** [psikɔlɔʒi] (PSEE-KAW-LAW-ZHEE) or (PSEE-KOH-LOH-ZHEE).

g   Before **e, i,** or **y** it is soft, like English *z* in *azure* [ʒ]. Examples: **geste** [ʒɛst] (ZHEST); **mirage** [miraʒ] (MEE-RAZH); **agir** [aʒir] (AH-ZHEER). The combination **ge**, with mute **e**, represents soft English *g* before **a** or **o**. Example: **bourgeois** [burʒwa] (BOOR-ZWAH). Before other vowels or consonants (other than **n**), **g** is hard like English *g* in *gag* [g]. Examples: **garçon** [garsɔ̃] (*); **goût** [gu] (GOO); **règle** [rɛgl] (REG-L(UH)). The combination **gu**, with mute **u**, represents hard *g* before **e, i,** or **y**. Example: **vogue** [vɔg] (VAWG) or (VOHG).

gn   Much like English *ny* in *canyon* [ɲ]. Note that this represents a different sound from the similar [ŋ]. Examples: **Mignon** [miɲɔ̃] (*); **Charlemagne** [ʃarləmaɲ] (SHAR-L(UH)-MAH-NY(UH)).

h   Except in **ch** and **ph**, this letter represents no sound at all. Examples: **histoire** [istwar] (EES-TWAHR); **honnête** [ɔnɛt] (AW-NET) or (OH-NET). Between two vowels, however, **h** indicates that the vowels form separate syllables rather than a diphthong. Example: **envahir** [ãvair] (three syllables, the nasalized "ah," followed by "vah," and completed with "eer").

j   Like English *z* in *azure* [ʒ]; the same as French soft **g**. Examples: **jardin** [ʒardɛ̃] (*); **Lejeune** [ləʒœn] (*).

l   Can be pronounced like English *l,* although the French pronounce it with the tongue flat and not raised at the back. Examples: **lache** [laʃ] (LAHSH); **ville** [vil] (VEEL—one syllable). At the end of a word, where **l** is pronounced separately, the French make **l** voiceless. The IPA symbol for this is [l̥]. Example: **débâcle** [de'baːkl̥] (DAY-BAHK-L(UH)).

ph   The same as **f**. Example: **philosophie** [filɔzɔfi] (FEE-LAW-ZAW-FEE) or (FEE-LOH-ZOH-FEE).

q   Like English *k.* It is normally followed by **u**, which is always mute. Examples: **quatre** [katr̥] (KAHT-R(UH)); **cinq** [sɛ̃k] (*). The **q** is doubled by writing **cq**, as in **acquitter** [akite] (AH-KEE-TAY).

r   Not like English *r.* It is pronounced by most speakers as a guttural sound, with tightening and vibration in the region of the uvula. Examples: **rose** [roz] (ROSE); **terre** [tɛr] (TEHR). French **r**, when final after a voiceless consonant, is frequently spoken with a voiceless sound that is scarcely audible. IPA indicates this sound with the symbol [r̥]. The closest approximation of it in wire-service phonetics is R(UH), with (UH) representing a very deemphasized "uh" sound. Example: **Joffre** [ʒɔfr̥] (ZHAW-FR(UH)) or (ZHOF-FR(UH)).

s   Between vowels like English *z* in *crazy* [z]. Examples: **désir** [dezir] (DAY-ZEER); **raison** [rɛzɔ̃] (*); **Thérèse** [terɛz] (TAY-REZ). Single **s** in other positions and double **s** always are like English *s* in *sea* [s]. Examples: **Seine** [sɛn] (SEN); **message** [mɛsaʒ] (MEH-SAZH).

sc   Before **e, i,** and **y** it is soft, like English *sc* in *science*. Example: **descendre** [desɑ̃dr̩] (*). Elsewhere, as [s] plus [k]. Example: **escorte** [ɛskɔrt] (ES-KAWRT) or (ES-KORT).

x   Usually like English *x* in *extra*. Example: **expliquer** [ɛksplike] (EX-PLEE-KAY). An initial **ex-** before a vowel becomes [gz]. Example: **exercise** [ɛgzɛrsis] (EGGZ-AIR-SEES).

French Final Consonants

Generally, consonants written at the ends of French words are not sounded; examples are **trop** [tro] (TROH); **part** [pɑr] (PAR); **voix** [vwa] (VWAH); **allez** [ale] (AH-LAY). An almost complete exception is **l**, as in **national** [nasjɔnal] (NAH-SYAW-NAHL) or (NAH-SYOH-NAHL). Often **c, f,** and **r** are sounded at the ends of words, as in **chic** [ʃik] (SHEEK); **chef** [ʃɛf] (SHEF); **cher** [ʃɛr] (SHAIR). When final **r** is preceded by **e** (**er**), the **r** is usually silent and the vowel is like *e* in *they* [e]. Example: **papier** [papje] (PAY-PYAY).

On the other hand, all the consonant sounds are pronounced at the ends of the words when they are followed by mute **e**. Examples: **place** [plas] (PLAHS); **garage** [garaʒ] (GAH-RAZH); **rive gauche** [riv goʃ] (REEVE-GOASH). This includes **m** and **n**, which before final mute **e** have their regular values and do not indicate that the preceding vowel is nasal. Examples: **aime** [ɛm] (EM); **pleine** [plɛn] (PLEN). Contrast these with **faim** [fɛ̃] (*f* plus nasalized *eh*) and **plein** [plɛ̃] (*pl* plus nasalized *eh*).

In all these cases, the addition of **s** (often the plural sign) after a consonant plus or minus mute **e** has no effect on pronunciation. Thus **places** is the same as **place, parts** is the same as **part,** and **temps** is the same as **temp.** Likewise, the addition of **nt** (a plural sign in verbs) to a word ending in mute **e** does not change anything—**chantent** and **chante** both are pronounced [ʃɑ̃t] (*sh*, as in *shoe*, plus the nasalized *ah*, plus a final *t*).

The French call it a liaison, or a linking, when the ordinarily silent consonant at the end of a word is sounded before a word beginning with a vowel sound. In liaison, *d* is pronounced [t], *g* is pronounced [k], *s* and *x* are pronounced [z], and nasalized *n* is sometimes denasalized. Examples: **grand amour** [grɑ̃tamur] (*); **sang impur** [sɑ̃kɛ̃pyːr] (*); **les autres** [lɛzotr̩] (LEH-ZOH-TR(UH)) or (LAY-ZOH-TR(UH)); **deux hommes** [døzɔm] (*); **mon ami** [mɔnami] (MOH-NAH-MEE).

Practice: Pronouncing French Words

Practice pronouncing the following French words:

Georges Bizet	Prosper Mérimée
Gabriel Fauré	Marcel Proust
Camille Saint-Saëns	*L'enfant prodigue*
Vincent d'Indy	*Danseuses del Delphes*
Maurice Chevalier	*Jardins sous la pluie*
Benoit Coquelin	*La demoiselle élue*
Rachel	*Le chant des oiseaux*
Guy de Maupassant	*Si mes vers avaient des ailes*

GERMAN PRONUNCIATION

The English spelling system contains a great many excess letters. French resembles English in this respect, but German, like Spanish and Italian, is economical in its spelling system, with every letter (or combination of letters, such as **sch**) usually representing one sound in the pronunciation of a word.

German is actually easier to pronounce than it first appears to be. Most long German words are simply combinations of stem words with prefixes and suffixes. When you know how to identify these elements, you know where to break each word into syllables, and then pronunciation is quite simple. The formidable word **Arbeitsgemeinschaft,** for example, is easily divided into **Arbeits, gemein,** and **schaft** by anyone familiar with the way German words are put together. Also, all German nouns are capitalized, which should help you identify parts of speech, making for better interpretation of German titles and phrases.

Stress

Most German words are accented on the first syllable, as in **stehen** ['ʃteːən] (SHTAY'-N), though not when they begin with a prefix, as in **verstehen** [fɛr'ʃteːən] (FER-SHTAY'-N). Words foreign to German are often accented on some syllable other than the first, to conform with their native pronunciation: **Philosophie** [fiːloːzoː'fi] (FEE-LOH-ZOH-FEE'). In compound words, the first component is usually accented: **Götterdämmerung** ['gœtərˌdɛmərʊŋ].[2]

---

[2] This word is impossible to represent with wire-service phonetics because of the unique way Germans sound the syllable **er** at ends of words or word components. This sound is transcribed [ər] in IPA, but rendering it UHR or UR would be misleading. In German speech, the "r" sound is almost completely lost, and the unaccented "uh" [ə] is nearly all that remains. The sound is quite different from French [ɾ], so the same wire-service phonetics cannot be used. Throughout this section, German **er** will be transcribed (UH(R)). **Götterdämmerung** would then be (GUH(R)-TUH(R)-DEM-MER-RUNG).

The German syllable **en,** when final in a word or word component, is deemphasized so that it is nearly lost. The syllabic consonant [ṇ] would be a fair way of representing this sound in IPA, but all standard German reference works transcribe it as [ən]. Standard practice will be followed for IPA transcriptions, but in wire-service phonetic equivalents, N without a preceding vowel sound is given. Example: **geben** [geːbən] (GAYB'-N).

At the end of a word and when otherwise unaccented (as, for example, when it appears in an unaccented prefix), the German letter **e** is pronounced as the schwa vowel—that is, as an unaccented "uh," the IPA symbol for which is [ə]. Examples: **sehe** ['zeːə] (ZAY'-UH); **gesehen** [gə'zeːən] (GUH-ZAY'-N).

German Short Vowels

German has four classes of vowel sounds: seven short vowels, seven long vowels, three diphthongs, and one special vowel that occurs only unaccented. Like the French vowels, they will be arranged according to sound rather than by their German spelling.

IPA SYMBOL	DESCRIPTION OF SOUND	GERMAN SPELLING	EXAMPLES
[a]	Like English *a* in *father*, but much shorter	a	**Gast** [gɑst] (GHAST) **fallen** ['fɑlən] (FAHL'-N)
[ɛ]	Like English *e* in *bet*	e	**Bett** [bɛt] (BET) **essen** [ɛsən] (ESS'-N)
	The spelling **ä** is used for this sound when the basic form is **a**	ä	**Gäste** [gɛstə] (GUEST'-UH) **fällt** [fɛlt] (FELT)
[ɪ]	Like English *i* in *hit*	i	**blind** [blɪnt] (BLIHNT) **Winter** ['vɪntər] (VIHN'-TUH(R))
[ɔ]	Like English *au* in *caught* but much shorter	o	**Kopf** [kɔpf] (KAWPF) **offen** ['ɔfən] (AWF'-N)
[œ]	Pronounced with the tongue as for "eh" [ɛ] but with the lips rounded as for "aw" [ɔ]	ö	**Köpfe** ['kœpfə] (*) **öffnen** ['œfnən] (*)

IPA SYMBOL	DESCRIPTION OF SOUND	GERMAN SPELLING	EXAMPLES
[ʊ]	Like English *u* in *put*	**u**	**Busch** [bʊʃ] (BUSH)
			Mutter [mʊtər] (MUH'-TUH(R))
[y]	Pronounced with the tongue as for "ih" [ɪ] but with the lips rounded as for "oo" [u]	**ü**	**Büsche** ['byʃə] (*)
			Mütter ['mytər] (*)

Note that the German spelling generally shows when an accented vowel is short by writing two consonant letters or a double consonant letter after it.

German Long Vowels

IPA SYMBOL	DESCRIPTION OF SOUND	GERMAN SPELLING	EXAMPLES
[ɑ]	Like English *a* in *father*	**a**	**ja** [jɑː] (YAH)
			Grab [grɑːp] (GRAHP)
		ah	**Kahn** [kɑːn] (KAHN)
		aa	**Staat** [ʃtɑːt] (SHTAHT)
[e]	Much like English *e* in *they* but without the final glide	**e**	**geben** [geːbən] (GAYB'-N)
		eh	**gehen** [geːən] (GAY'-N)
		ee	**See** [zeː] (ZAY)
	When spelled **ä** or **äh,** the pronunciation usually is still "ay" [e]	**ä**	**Gräber** ['greːbər] (GRAY'-BUH(R))
		äh	**Kähne** ['keːnə] (KAY'-NUH)
[i]	Much like English *i* in *machine*	**i**	**Schi** [ʃiː] (SHE)
			Lid [liːt] (LEET)
		ih	**Ihn** [iːn] (EEN)
		ie	**Lieder** ['liːdər] (LEE'-DUH(R))
[o]	Like English *ow* in *blow* but without the final glide	**o**	**so** [zoː] (ZO)
			oben ['oːbən] (OB'-N)
		oh	**Lohn** [loːn] (LOAN)
		oo	**Boot** [boːt] (BOAT)
[ø]	Pronounced with the tongue as for "ay" [e] but with the lips rounded as for "oh" [o]	**ö**	**Römer** ['røːmər] (*)
		öh	**Löhne** ['løːnə] (*)

IPA SYMBOL	DESCRIPTION OF SOUND	GERMAN SPELLING	EXAMPLES
[u]	Much like English *u* in *rule*	u	**du** [duː] (DOO)
			Mut [muːt] (MOOT)
[y]	Pronounced with the tongue as for "ee" [i] but lips rounded as for "oo" [u]	ü	**Brüder** [bryːdər] (*)
		üh	**rühmen** ['ryːmən] (*)

Note that German spelling has four ways of showing that an accented vowel is long. (1) The vowel is at the end of a word: **ja, je, schi.** (2) The vowel is followed by only one consonant: **Grab, haben, wen.** (3) The vowel is followed by an unpronounced *h:* **Kahn, gehen, ihn.** (4) The vowel is written double: **Staat, See, Boot.** (The long **i** is never doubled; **ie** is used as the lengthening sign, as in **Lieder.**) There are relatively few words in which long vowels are not indicated in this way. Two exceptions are **Papst** [pɑːpst] (PAHPST) and **Mond** [moːnt] (MOANT).

The double dot over **ä, ö,** and **ü** is called an umlaut. The old-fashioned spellings for these umlaut vowels, **ae, oe,** and **ue,** still survive in a few names: **Goebbels, Goethe, Huebner.** You will also encounter these spellings when a type font (as, for example, on the wire-service machines) has no special umlaut letters. Typewriters can simulate the umlaut with quotation marks, but wire-service machines cannot return, as a typewriter carriage can, to add the marks after the letter has been transmitted.

German Diphthongs

IPA SYMBOL	DESCRIPTION OF SOUND	GERMAN SPELLING	EXAMPLES
[aɪ]	Like English *ai* in *aisle*	ei	**Leid** [laɪt] (LIGHT)
			Heine ['haɪnə] (HIGH'-NUH)
		ai	**Kaiser** ['kaɪzər] (KY'-ZUH(R))
		ey	**Meyer** ['maɪər] (MY'-UH(R))
		ay	**Bayern** ['baɪərn] (BUY'-URN)
[aʊ]	Like English *ou* in *house*	au	**Haus** [haʊs] (HOUSE)
			Glauben ['glaʊbən] (GLOUB'-N)
[ɔɪ]	Like English *oi* in *oil*	eu	**Leute** ['lɔɪtə] (LOY'-TUH)
		äu	**Häuser** ['hɔɪzər] (HOU'-ZUH(R))

BRANDT, BUT HAS BEEN STRENGTHENED BY MORE RECENT CHANCEL-
LORS. RELATIONS CONTINUE TO IMPROVE. EAST GERMAN PREMIER,
ERICH HONECKER, IS EXPECTED TO MAKE AN UNPRECEDENTED VISIT
TO BONN NEXT YEAR.

(FORSYTH, GEORGIA) ANDRES GRUENTZIG, WHO REVOLUTIONIZED
THE TREATMENT OF HEART DISEASE, DIED YESTERDAY IN A PLANE
CRASH. GRUENTZIG, WHO WAS FORTY-SIX, WAS KILLED WHILE FLY-
ING TO ATLANTA FROM ST. SIMONS ISLAND. GRUENTZIG, WHO DE-
VELOPED THE "BALLOON" TECHNIQUE TO CLEAR FATTY DEPOSITS
FROM THE HEART, WAS BORN IN DRESDEN, NOW EAST GERMANY. HE
WAS AWARDED AUTOMATIC U.S. CITIZENSHIP IN 1980. HIS BAL-
LOON TECHNIQUE, ALSO KNOW AS PERCUTANEOUS TRANSLUMINAL
CORONARY ANGIOPLASTY, WAS DEVELOPED WHILE HE WORKED AT THE
UNIVERSITAT POLICLINIC HOSPITAL IN ZURICH, SWITZERLAND.

(LIMA, PERU) REPORTS REACHING LIMA YESTERDAY CLAIMED THAT
FIFTY-NINE PEOPLE IN TWO VILLAGES WERE SHOT OR STABBED TO
DEATH BY PERUVIAN SOLDIERS LAST MONTH. NEMESIO GUTIERREZ,
WHO CLAIMED TO BE AN EYEWITNESS, SAID THAT THE MASSACRE
WAS CARRIED OUT IN THE VILLAGES OF BELLAVISTA AND UMARO.
IF CONFIRMED, IT WOULD BE THE SECOND MASSACRE OF PEASANTS
BY PERUVIAN SOLDIERS SINCE ALAN GARCIA WAS INAUGURATED
PRESIDENT IN JULY. THE PERUVIAN ARMY HAS BEEN FIGHTING THE
MAOIST SENDERO LUMINOSO GUERRILLAS. IN AN UNRELATED DEVEL-
OPMENT, THE GOVERNMENT CLAIMED THAT FIFTY-ONE SENDERO
LUMINOSO REBELS SURRENDERED SATURDAY IN AYACUCHO.

(ROME) ITALY HAS A NEW GOVERNMENT TODAY. PRIME MINISTER-
DESIGNATE BETTINO CRAXI HAS REPORTED TO PRESIDENT
FRANCESCO COSSIGA THAT HIS CABINET IS NOW COMPLETE.
GIOVANNI SPADOLINI, FORMER DEFENSE MINISTER, WAS THE LAST
HOLDOUT IN FORMING THE NEW GOVERNMENT. IT IS SAID THAT A
WRITTEN AGREEMENT BETWEEN CRAXI AND REPUBLICAN PARTY
LEADER SPADOLINI WAS WORKED OUT BY CRAXI'S TOP ADVISOR,
ANTONIO BALDINI. THE AGREEMENT GUARANTEES INCREASED CON-
SULTATION BY THE MINORITY PARTY OF GIOVANNI SPADOLINI.

(NEW YORK) CELLIST MSTISLAV ROSTROPOVICH (MISS-TEE'-SLAHV
RAHS-TRAH-PO'-VICH) WAS PRESENTED WITH A MAJOR AWARD IN NEW
YORK LAST NIGHT. ROSTROPOVICH, WHO SHELTERED SOVIET DISSI-
DENT AUTHOR ALEXANDER SOLZHENITSYN (SOL-ZHEN-EET'-SUN),
WAS THE RECIPIENT OF THE ALBERT SCHWEITZER MUSIC AWARD.
THE CREO SOCIETY CITED ROSTROPOVICH AND HIS WIFE, SOPRANO
GALINA VISHNEVSKAYA (GAH-LEEN'-UH VISH-NEV-SKY'-UH), FOR
THE POLITICALLY DANGEROUS BUT HUMANITARIAN GESTURE IN
SHELTERING SOLZHENITSYN. THE AWARD WAS PRESENTED BY RHENA
SCHWEITZER-MILLER, THE ONLY CHILD OF ALBERT SCHWEITZER.

Commercials

CLIENT: Cafe L'Europa

LENGTH: 60 seconds

ANNCR: When you think of good food, you probably think of Paris,
          Copenhagen, or Rome. But, now, right here in the center of
          America, you can find the best of European and Asian

cuisine at a price that will surprise you. The CAFE
L'EUROPA, on Highway 40 at White's Road, is under the
supervision of Chef Aristide Framboise. Chef Framboise
earned his Cordon Bleu at the famous Ecole des Quatre
Gourmandes in Cannes, France. The Chef's staff of European
and Asian cooks have been personally trained for the
exacting work of pleasing you, regardless of your culinary
preferences. Whether you like poulet sauté marseillais or
gedämpfte Brust, spaghetti all' amatricianna or calamares
en su tinta, you'll thrill to your candlelight dinner at
CAFE L'EUROPA. Dial 777-3434, and ask our Maître D' for a
reservation soon. That's 777-3434, the CAFE L'EUROPA, at
White's Road on Highway 40.

Pronunciation guide.

Aristide Framboise (AR-EES-TEED FRAM-BWAH)

Ecole des Quatre Gourmandes (AY-KOHL DAY KAT GOOR-MAHND)

poulet sauté marseillais (POO-LAY SO-TAY MAHR-SAY-AY)

gedämpfte Brust (GEH-DEMFT'-UH BRUST)

spaghetti all'amatricianna (SPAH-GET'-EE AL AHM-AH-
   TREECH-YAH'-NAH)

calamares en su tinta (KAHL-AH-MAHR'-EES EN SU TEEN'-TAH)

Maître D' (MET'-RUH DEE)

CLIENT: Cafe L'Europa

LENGTH: 60 seconds

ANNCR: How long since you've enjoyed a special evening of your
         own creation? Not a birthday. Not an anniversary. Not a

holiday. But an evening you've set aside to tell that
special someone, "I appreciate you!" The CAFE L'EUROPA is
the perfect restaurant for this and all other very special
celebrations. The CAFE L'EUROPA features delicacies
from around the world. Sukiyaki from Japan. Nasi
Goereng from Indonesia. European cuisine includes Pfannekoeken from Holland, Cochifrito from Spain, and
Ratatouille from France. Or, perhaps you'd prefer an English Rarebit or German Sauerbrauten. Whatever your taste,
you're sure to enjoy candlelight dining at CAFE L'EUROPA.
Make a date now, and call our Maître D' for a dinner
reservation. Dial 777-3434, and prepare yourself for an
unforgettable evening of dining at the CAFE L'EUROPA. Your
significant other will appreciate your thoughtfulness.

Pronunciation guide.

Sukiyaki (SKEE-AHK'-EE)

Pfannekoeken (PFAHN'-KUK-UN)

Ratatouille (RAT-UH-TOO'-EE)

Nasi Goereng (NAZ'-EE GEHR'-ING)

Cochifrito (COACH-EE-FREE'-TOE)

Sauerbraten (SOUR'-BRAHT-UN)

CLIENT: Kuyumjian's Rug Bazaar

LENGTH: 60 seconds

ANNCR: Kuyumjian's has just received a large shipment of new and
         used oriental rugs which must be sold at once. These rugs
         are being sold to settle tax liens against a major import

firm. So, their misfortune is your gain. Here is your
chance to own a genuine oriental rug at a fraction of its
regular cost. Gulistan, Kerman, Sarouk, Shiraz, and
Baktiary rugs at unheard-of prices. Time does not permit a
complete listing, but here are a few specials: a
five-by-seven Faridombeh rug in antique gold, only $288. A
three-by-five Feraghan in ivory and pistachio, just $375.
An extra-large, nine-by-fourteen virgin wool Ispahan
ivory, $1,000. Small Yezd, Oushak, and Belouj scatter rugs
at less than $100. All sizes are approximate, and
quantities of each style are limited. Visit Kuyumjian's
this week, and become the proud owner of an original,
hand-woven, virgin wool oriental rug. Kuyumjian's Rug
Bazaar, on the downtown mall opposite the State Theater.

Pronunciation guide.

Kuyumjian's (KY-OOM'-JUNZ)

Gulistan (GOO'-LIS-TAHN)

Kerman (KEHR'-MAHN)

Sarouk (SAH-ROUK')

Shiraz (SHEE'-RAHZ)

Baktiary (BAHK-TEE-AR'-EE)

Faridombeh (FAHR-EE-DOME'-BAY)

Feraghan (FEHR-AH-GAHN')

Ispahan (EES'-PAH-HAHN)

Yezd (YEZD)

Oushak (OO'-SHAHK)

Belouj (BELL-OODG')

CLIENT: Hough's House of Fabrics

LENGTH: 60 seconds

ANNCR: Hough's House of Fabrics announces its annual spring
          fashion yardage sale. Beginning this Thursday and running
          for one full week, you can save dollars while you pre-
          pare for a colorful spring and summer. Synthetic fabrics
          that never need ironing, in a variety of textures and
          patterns--appliqué puff, crêpe de chine, etched peau di
          luna, your choice, only $2.49 a yard. Or look for
          summertime sheers--batiste, voile, or crushed crepe, at
          just $1.09 a yard. Hough's has a complete collection of
          dazzling Hawaiian prints, too. Wahini poplin, Kahului
          broadcloth, or Niihau jacquard weave--with prices ranging
          from 99¢ to $2.89 a yard. And, yes, Hough's has patterns,
          notions, and everything else you need to create your
          wardrobe for the coming season. So, why don't you save
          money and get started on your own versatile and original
          spring ard summer wardrobe right now? Remember, Hough's
          House of Fabrics, in the Northfield Shopping Center, just
          out of town on Marsh Road. That's Hough's--on Marsh Road.
          Sale ends a week from Thursday.

          Pronunciation guide.

          Hough's (HUFFS)

          appliqué puff (AP-LIH-KAY' PUFF)

          crepe de chine (KREP DUH-SHEEN')

          peau di luna (PO DEE LUN-UH)

batiste (BA-TEEST')

voile (VOIL)

crepe (KRAYP)

Wahini (WAH-HEE'-NEE)

Kahului (KAH-HOO-LOO'-EE)

Niihau jacquard (NEE-EE-HOW' JUH-KARD')

8
AMERICAN ENGLISH USAGE

To be an announcer is to be a user of words. It follows that every serious student of announcing will undertake a systematic study of American English. This means engaging in several different but related studies. It means making a lifelong habit of consulting dictionaries. It means becoming sensitized to nuances of language and striving to find the precise, rather than the approximate, word. It means changing your vocabulary as changes in our language occur. It means cultivating and practicing the art of plain talk. And it means perfecting both American English pronunciation and foreign pronunciation. Chapter 6 discusses vowel and diphthong distortion. Appendix B provides a list of frequently mispronounced words. Chapter 7 reviews the principles of pronunciation of some of the major languages of the world. Chapter 8 examines American English usage from the standpoint of the broadcast announcer and discusses our changing language.

Top professional announcers use words with precision and manage to sound conversational while honoring the rules of grammar. Unfortunately, some broadcast announcers are not perfect, and listeners and viewers suffer daily from a variety of errors in usage. During a randomly chosen two-week period, the following mistakes were made by announcers at local and network levels:

"The French farmers have thrown up barrages across the major highways leading out of Paris." The announcer meant *barricades*, not *barrages*.

"The deputy sheriffs are still out on strike, and it doesn't look like they'll be back to work before long." "Soon" would be acceptable in place of "before long."

"General _____, who last year authored an unsuccessful coup . . . "

Author is a noun, not a transitive verb, but even if it were, it is doubtful that the announcer meant that the general "wrote" an unsuccessful coup.

"The fishing boat was loaded to the gills." Fish may possibly be loaded to the gills, but boats are loaded to the gunwales.

"The little girl was found in the company of an unidentified man." Does the announcer mean that the man's identity was unknown or that his identity was not disclosed?

"The secretary of state reportedly will visit South America late this summer." There are many kinds of visits—long visits, brief visits, surreptitious visits—but no one can make a reported visit. The announcer meant "it is reported that the secretary of state . . ."

"Three kids died when their house slid down a hill during the storm." "Kids" is slang, and is acceptable under some circumstances, but not when reporting a tragedy.

"After being surrounded by the policemen, the suspect came out with his hands up." The term *policemen* has been replaced by *police officers* by the U.S. Department of Labor.

"Firefighters rescued an elderly Oriental man . . ." The term *Oriental* is offensive to most persons of Asian ancestry and should be avoided.

"The government of Kenya is making a serious effort to eliminate poaching in its national parks." The announcer said KEEN'-YUH. The citizens of this nation call it KEN'-YUH, and consider KEEN'-YUH an unwelcome reminder of colonial days.

News reporters, interviewers, commentators, disc jockeys, talk show hosts and hostesses, sportscasters, and weather, environmental, and consumer reporters must frame their own thoughts into words and must choose those words well and pronounce them correctly. To do this, they must be proficient with their language. The sections that follow cover a portion of the territory that is the province of professional announcers.

AGE REFERENTS

It is as offensive to a young adult to be called a boy or a girl, as it is to a middle-aged person to be called elderly. Announcers must be sensitive to the feelings of those described by age category *and* of listeners and viewers who may object to the age classifications.

Age is, of course, not always an appropriate referent. To report that a musician triumphed at a concert, it is not necessary to give that musician's age—unless the musician was extremely young or very old. On the other hand, in a reported death of a well-known person, age is a legitimate item of information. When the age of a person is known, and when age is of some significance (as with athletes, prodigies, or people who have reached an unusual age, such as 100), give the correct age and avoid using an age category.

At times, it is appropriate to state that a given person is within a recognized age group. When this occurs, let the following criteria guide you:

Child   any person between birth and puberty (approximately 12 or 13)

Boy or *girl*   a person of the appropriate sex who has not yet reached puberty

Young and *youth*   when used collectively, persons between puberty and legal age (approximately 13–18)

Youth   when singular, a young person between puberty and legal age

Young adult   a person of either sex, between the ages of 18 and 25

Juvenile   between the ages of 13 and 18

Adolescent   approximately 12–16

Teen-ager   13–19, inclusive

Man or *woman*   any person over the age of 18

Adult   any person over the age of 18

Middle-aged   approximately age 40 to age 65

Elderly   past late middle-age (above 70)

Old   a person of advanced years (above 75)

Senior   a person beyond retirement age (usually above 70)

Elderly people are often referred to as *senior citizens,* but many do not like the term. *Seniors* is somewhat more acceptable, though there always will be some individuals who resent being classified by an age category.

The term *kid,* for a young person, is sometimes acceptable and at other times in poor taste. We are safe when speaking of our kid sister, or in saying, "Your kids will love this!" When we become narrower in our focus and speak of a specific person, we run the risk of provoking resentment: a child up to the age of 12 or 13 probably will accept the term *kid;* adolescents gradually begin to object as they approach the age of 14 or 15. The term is *never* appropriate when describing a tragedy. In general, slang words, or words that seem flippant, are never appropriate when reporting a tragedy.

JARGON AND VOGUE WORDS

Every profession and social group has a private or semiprivate vocabulary. From time to time, words or phrases from such groups enter the mainstream of public communication. It is useful and enriching when expressions such as *inner city, Gestalt therapy,* or *skinny-dip* are added to the general vocabulary. But as an announcer, you should guard against picking up and overusing expressions that are trite, precious, deliberately distorting, or pretentious. Here are a few recent vogue words with some very frank (and slightly cynical) translations.

From the military:

Deescalate   To give up on a lost war

Balance of power   A dangerous stand-off

Nuclear deterrent   The means by which war can be deterred when antagonistic nations possess enough nuclear weapons to destroy the world

Preemptive strike   First attack

Debrief   To ask questions of someone

From government:

At home and abroad   Everywhere

Nonproliferation   Monopolization of nuclear weapons

Disadvantaged   Poor people

Department of Human Resources Development   The unemployment office

Decriminalize   To make legal

From academe:

Operant conditioning   Learning by trial and error

Quantum leap   A breakthrough

Deaestheticize   To take the beauty out of art

Dishabituate   To break a bad habit

Dehire   To fire someone

Microencapsulate   To put in a small capsule

Found art   Someone else's junk

Megastructure   A large building

Pass-fail grading system   A reduction of the five-point grading scale to two points in the name of improved evaluation of student work

A few other words that should be used precisely and sparingly, if at all, are *rhetoric* when meaning "empty and angry talk," *charisma, relevant, obviate, facility* when meaning a building, *viable,* and *meaningful*. Vogue phrases that have already become clichés should be avoided; some of these are *a can of worms, a breakdown in communication,* and *generation gap*.

Tacking *-wise* onto nouns in awkward ways is possibly one of the most offensive speech habits that has arisen in the past several years. Familiar examples of this are: "Culturewise, the people are _____," "Foodwise, your best buy is _____," and "National securitywise, we should _____." Outrages against American English are perpetrated by people who have found such habits an effortless means of avoiding proper sentence construction. The suffix *-wise* does, of course, have a proper use in words such as *lengthwise, sidewise,* and *counterclockwise,* but the authority of these words does not sanction an indiscriminate tacking of suffixes onto words with results that sound trite, silly, or camp.

Three particularly contagious vogue words that seem to strike their victims as a team are *like, man,* and *y'know*. The following example is not an exaggeration:

"Like, man, y'know, it's lousy man. Like, here I am, man, y'know, looking for a house, and, like this guy comes up to me, y'know, and like he says, 'Hey, man, like what're you doing here?' y'know."

Boring and ineffective speech is not the exclusive property of any particular ethnic or social group. Contagious fashions spread alarmingly through our society. Obviously such words replace *uh* and other annoying affectations in the speech of many who find a need for verbalized pauses to compensate for lack of fluency. Awareness of your speech patterns, together with an adequate vocabulary, should help you eliminate most vogue words from your speech.

REDUNDANCIES

To be *redundant* is to be repetitive. At times, as in a commercial, redundancy may be useful in driving home a point or a product advantage. At most other times, redundancy may be seen as needlessly repetitive. *Close proximity* is redundant because *close* and *proximity* (or *proximate*) mean the same thing. A *necessary requisite* is redundant because *requisite* contains the meaning of *necessary.* Spoken English is plagued with needless redundancy, and constant watchfulness is required to avoid contamination. Here are some redundancies heard far too often on radio and television:

Knots per hour A knot is a nautical mile per hour, so *per hour* is redundant.

Abundant wealth *Wealth* means having a great amount.

More preferable Use this only if you are comparing two preferences.

Totally annihilated *Annihilate* means to destroy totally.

Still remains If something *remains,* it must be there *still.*

True facts There can be no untrue facts.

Divide up *Up* is superfluous.

Hallowe'en Evening *Hallowe'en* includes *evening* in an abbreviated form.

Sierra Nevada Mountains *Sierra* means rugged mountains.

Sahara Desert *Sahara* means *desert.*

Serious crisis It is not a crisis unless it has already become serious.

Cooperate together To *cooperate* means that two or more work together.

Completely surround, completely abandon, completely eliminate To *surround,* to *abandon,* and to *eliminate* are to do these respective things completely.

Joint partnership *Partnership* includes the concept of *joint.*

End up, finish up, rest up, pay up, settle up All are burdened by the unnecessary *ups.*

General consensus Consensus means *general agreement.*

Universal panacea *Panacea* means a cure-all and is automatically universal.

Habitual custom *Custom* and *habit* mean the same thing.

Both alike, both at once, both equal *Both* means *two,* and *alike, at once,* and *equal* all imply some kind of duality.

Important essentials   To be essential is to be important

Equally as expensive   If something costs what another does, then inevitably their costs are equal. (The correct form is *equally expensive* or *as expensive*.)

An old antique   There can be no such thing as a new antique.

Novel innovation   To be innovative is to be novel.

Visible to the eye   There is no other way a thing can be visible.

Exchanged with each other   An exchange is necessary between one and some other.

I thought to myself   Telepathy aside, there is no one else one can think to.

That person set a new record   All records are new when they are set.

Most unique, most perfect   A thing is unique or perfect or not. There are no degrees of either.

Develop a keen ear for redundancies. Recognizing errors in usage is the first step toward avoiding them in your own speech.

CLICHÉS

A *cliché* is an overused expression or idea. Most popular clichés once were innovative and effective. They became clichés by being overused and, in most instances, misapplied by people who were no longer aware of their original meanings. Many who use the cliché *as rich as Croesus* have no idea who Croesus was or the degree of his wealth. Similarly, the expression *as slow as molasses* is used by many who have never seen or used molasses. Good use of our language demands that we think before we fall back on the first cliché to enter our minds. A few commonly heard clichés are:

As sharp as a tack

Quick as a flash, quick as a wink

Dead as a doornail

Dry as a bone

Mad as a hatter, mad as a March hare

Fresh as a daisy

Bright as a button

Sure as rain

As certain as death and taxes

Quiet as a grave, quiet as a tomb

As coarse as gravel

As common as dirt

As cool as a cucumber

As hungry as a bear

As new as tomorrow

The similes listed here and dozens more like them have simply worn out their effectiveness by endless repetition. Good broadcast speech is not measured by our ability to make new and more effective images, but from time to time creative metaphorical expression can make for memorable communication. See what a little thought and time can do to help you use your language creatively. How would you complete the following similes to make novel and effective images?

As anxious as . . .

As awkward as . . .

As barren as . . .

As deceptive as . . .

As desirable as . . .

As friendly as . . .

As quiet as . . .

As strange as . . .

In addition to dead metaphoric language, many words and phrases have become hackneyed by overuse. Sportscasters and reporters seem especially vulnerable to clichés. Here are a few examples of tired language:

In tonight's action

Over in the NBA, over in the American League   Why *over?* Why not simply *in the NBA?*

All the action is under the lights

He was in complete charge   Is there such a thing as being in *incomplete*
   charge?

Off to a running start

Odds-on favorite

Off to a shaky start

Sparked the win

Suffered a sixth setback

Raised the record to

Went the distance

Is the leading candidate

   Not all familiar sports expressions are to be thought of as clichés.
Some clear, direct, and uncomplicated expressions that can hardly be
improved on are *loaded the bases, gave up a walk* (although *yielded a walk*
borders on the unacceptable), *got the hat trick, finished within one stroke
of, knocked out of the tournament, lost the decision.* Be wary of time-worn
sports clichés, but do not be afraid to use common expressions if you
are not able to improve on them.

   Many clichés can be heard on daily newscasts. If you aspire to a
career as a news reporter or newscaster, you should make a careful and
constant study of words that have become meaningless. A few choice
examples follow:

Has branded as ridiculous   Why *branded as?* Why not *called?*

A shroud of secrecy

Deem it advisable

Was held in abeyance

Informed sources at the White House

Has earmarked several million dollars

Augurs well

In no uncertain terms

Tantamount to election

The depths of despair

A flurry of activity

One cliché of the newsroom deserves special attention: *pending notification of the next of kin* is a stilted and clumsy way of saying "until the relatives have been notified."

Many speakers and writers use clichés without knowing their precise meaning. In doing so, it is easy to fall into error. The expressions *jerry-built* and *jury-rigged* sometimes become "jerry-rigged" and "jury-built" when used by people unaware that the first expression means "shoddily built" and the second is a nautical expression meaning "rigged for emergency use."

It is also important to be aware of incorrect literary expressions to avoid mistaken allusions such as these:

"Far from the maddening crowd" is the incorrect version of "far from the madding crowd's ignoble strife," which is from Thomas Gray's "Elegy Written in a Country Churchyard."

The clause "suffer, little children," or "suffer the little children" has been used recently to mean "let the little children suffer." The original expression is in the King James version of Mark 10:14 as "Suffer the little children to come unto me." In its context, *suffer* means "allow": "Allow the little children to come unto me."

"Alas, poor Yorick. I knew him well." This is both corrupt and incomplete. The line from *Hamlet*, Act V, scene i, lines 184–85, reads: "Alas, poor Yorick! I knew him, Horatio: a fellow of infinite jest."

The misquotation "Music hath charms to soothe the savage beast" is a not-very-elegant version of a line from a play, *The Mourning Bride* by William Congreve, and the original version is, "Music hath charms to soothe the savage breast."

The all-too-familiar question "Wherefore art thou Romeo?" is consistently misused by people who think that *wherefore* means "where." The question asks "Why are you Romeo?" not "Where are you, Romeo?"

"Pride goeth before a fall" is actually, in King James Proverbs 16:18, "Pride goeth before destruction, and a haughty spirit before a fall."

"A little knowledge is a dangerous thing" is close, but not close enough, to what Alexander Pope actually wrote: "A little learning is a dangerous thing."

"It takes a heap o' livin t' make a house a home." Edgar Guest's poem opens "It takes a heap o' livin' in a house t' make it a home." The corrupt version is probably an attempt to improve the original.

"I have nothing to offer but blood, sweat, and tears." Winston Churchill really said, "I have nothing to offer but blood, toil, tears, and sweat."

"I see one-third of a nation ill-housed, ill-clad, ill-fed." President Franklin D. Roosevelt used "ill-nourished," not "ill-fed."

These are but a few of the most commonly misquoted clichés. As a broadcast announcer, you should routinely check original sources, and even then use the quotation only if it truly belongs in your work. A handy source for checking the accuracy of oft-used phrases is John Bartlett's *Familiar Quotations*. When in doubt, skip the cliché—even correctly cited clichés are still clichés.

LATIN AND GREEK PLURALS

People who care about broadcast *media* should be meticulous in using *medium* for the singular and *media* for the plural. Radio is a *medium*. Radio and television are *media*. We can speak of news *media* but not of television news *media*. If people who work in broadcast *media* do not reinstate correct usage, no one else will, and the incorrectly used plural *media* will take over the singular form.

Many other words of Latin and Greek origin are subject today to much misuse. Here are some of the more important of these words. Note that the Greek words end in *-on* and the Latin words end in *-um*.

SINGULAR	PLURAL
addendum	addenda
criterion	criteria
datum	data
medium	media
memorandum	memoranda
phenomenon	phenomena
stratum	strata

Data is perhaps the most abused of these words, for it is commonly used as a singular, as in "What is your data?" This sentence should be

"What are your data?" The sentence "What is your datum?" would be correct if the singular were intended.

The words referring to graduates of schools are a more complicated matter, for both gender and number must be considered:

Alumna   Female singular: "She is an alumna of State College."

Alumnae   Female plural, pronounced [əˈlʌmˌni] (UH-LUM'-NEE): "These women are alumnae of State College."

Alumnus   Male singular: "He is an alumnus of State College."

Alumni   Male plural, pronounced [əˈlʌmˌnaɪ] (UH-LUM'-NY): "These men are alumni of State College."

Alumni   Male and female plural, pronounced as the male plural: "These men and women are alumni of State College."

STREET EXPRESSIONS

Slang, the language of the streets, is often brilliantly effective. Expressions such as *crash pad* for a place where a person may sleep without fee or invitation and *glitch* to mean a mishap or, in television, a type of visual interference on the screen are descriptive and, in the proper context, useful additions to our language. As an announcer, you must develop sensitivity to when and how slang adds to or detracts from your message. What might be appropriate in a humorous commercial might be in very bad taste in a newscast.

It is important to remember that one person's slang may not fit another's personality. Many Black American expressions may sound pretentious or condescending when spoken by a non-Black. Similarly, words of foreign origin, such as *mensch* or *schlepping*, may sound out of place when spoken by one who has only a vague notion of their meanings and uses them in inappropriate contexts. Some users of in-group expressions resent nongroup persons who take over their language.

Especially to be avoided are words from the world of crime and drugs. Terms such as *ripped off* to mean stole, *busted* to mean arrested, *stuck* to mean stabbed, *shank* to mean knife or dagger, *bombed* to mean under the influence of a drug, and *spike* to mean the needle used to administer a drug are words devised to remove onus from the object or activity being described. "He was busted for smack" sounds far more innocent and trivial than the more conservative translation "He was arrested for possession of heroin." To *rip someone off* is to steal from a person, and theft is not an activity to be condoned by removing from the language the words that connote illegality. "He was stuck with a shank" means that he was stabbed with a knife or similarly lethal weapon; the slang only attempts to make the event seem less serious than it is and, perhaps, even a little humorous. Though you should avoid using such expressions, you should be aware that a few stations encourage—or even require—announcers to use street expressions. At such a station, an announcer might be directed to use terms appropriate to a certain type of tabloid journalism, such as saying that someone was *butchered* rather than killed or murdered.

SOLECISMS

A *solecism* is a blunder in speech. It is related to a barbarism (a word or phrase not in accepted use), and both should be avoided by broadcast announcers. Surely you do not need to be told that *ain't* is unacceptable or that *anywheres* is not used by educated speakers. A number of words and phrases that we pick up early in childhood are substandard but survive to plague us if we do not become aware of them.

Substandard colloquialisms include the following.

Redhead for *red haired*

Foot for *feet:* "She was five foot tall." Five is more than one, and it demands the plural *feet,* as in "She was five feet tall."

Enthused over for *was enthusiastic about*

Guess as a substitute for *think* or *suppose* as in "I guess I'd better read a commercial."

Expect for *suppose* or *suspect:* "I expect he's on the scene by now."

Try and for *try to:* "She's going to try and break the record."

Unloosen for *loosen:* "He unloosened the knot."

Hung for *hanged* Hung is the past tense of *hang* in every meaning other than as applied to a human being. Correct usages are "I hung my coat on the hook" and "He was hanged in 1884."

Outside of for *aside from:* "Outside of that, I enjoyed the movie" is wrong.

Real for *really* For "I was real pleased" say "I was really pleased."

Lay and *lie* are problem words for many speakers of English. When we refer to people, correct usage is as follows.

Present tense   "I will lie down."

Past tense   "I lay down."

Past participle   "I had lain down."

When you refer to objects, use

Present tense   "I will lay it down."

Past tense   "I laid it down."

Past tense   "I had laid it down."

Hens lay eggs, but they also lie down from time to time.

   This review of common solecisms is necessarily limited, but it may be adequate for your needs. If you habitually make errors described here, you should undertake a study of English usage.

**WORDS OFTEN
MISUSED**

Do not say *anxious* when you mean *eager* or *desirous*. *Anxious* means "worried" and "strained" and is associated with anxiety. *Compose* and *comprise* are trouble words. They relate to the same phenomena, but they should be distinguished with precision, for they are not interchangeable: "The Republic comprises fifty states" but "Fifty states compose the Republic." The logic behind this difference is that *comprise* always refers to the relation of the larger to the smaller. Thus our solar system comprises the sun and nine planets, whereas nine planets and the sun compose the solar system. But note that the solar system is composed of the sun and nine planets, because here we are saying what the solar system is made up of, rather than what the solar system takes in.

   Concoct means to "cook together" and is a word used only in connection with food preparation. It is impossible to "concoct a plot."

   Connive, conspire, and *contrive* are sometimes confused. To *connive* is to "feign ignorance of a wrong," literally to "close one's eyes to something." To *conspire* is to "plan together secretly"; one person cannot conspire, because a conspiracy is an agreement between two or more persons. To *contrive* is to "scheme or plot with evil intent"; one person is capable of contriving.

   Continual and *continuous* are used by many speakers as interchangeable synonyms, but their meanings are not the same. *Continual* means "repeated regularly and frequently"; *continuous* means "prolonged without interruption or cessation." A foghorn may sound continually;

it does not sound continuously unless it is broken. A siren may sound continuously, but it does not sound continually unless the meaning is that the siren is sounded every five minutes (or every half-hour or every hour).

Contemptible is sometimes confused with *contemptuous*. *Contemptible* is an adjective meaning "despicable." *Contemptuous* is an adjective meaning "scornful" or "disdainful." Say "The killer is contemptible" but "He is contemptuous of the rights of others."

Convince and *persuade* are used interchangeably by many announcers. In some constructions, either word will do. A problem arises when *convince* is linked with *to*, as in this sentence: "He believes that he can convince the Smithsonian directors to give him the collection." The correct word is *persuade*. *Convince* is to be followed by *of* or a clause beginning with *that*, as in "I could not convince him of my sincerity" or "I could not convince him that I was honest." The sentence "I could not convince him to trust me" is incorrect. *Persuade* should have been used in this sentence, recently heard on a network newscast: "He did not know whether or not the president could convince them to change their minds."

Distinct and *distinctive* are not interchangeable. *Distinct* means "not identical" or "different"; *distinctive* means "distinguishing" or "characteristic." A distinct odor is one that cannot be overlooked; a distinctive odor is one that can be identified.

Here are six words that some speakers used interchangeably but that should be differentiated by people who want to be precise in their use of American English: *feasible, possible, practical, practicable, workable, viable*. Here are the specific meanings of these terms:

Feasible Clearly possible or applicable: "The plan was feasible" or "Her excuse was feasible."

Possible Capable of happening: "The plan may possibly work."

Practical The prudence, efficiency, or economy of an act, solution, or agent: "This is a practical plan" or "He is a practical person."

Practicable Capable of being done: "The plan is hardly practicable at this time." Note that *practicable* never refers to persons.

Workable Capable of being worked, dealt with, handled: "The plan is workable." Note that *workable* implies a future act.

Viable Capable of living; capable of growing or developing: "It is a viable tomato plant." Recently *viable* has replaced *feasible* in many applications. You should avoid using this overworked word. If you remember that it is derived from the Old French *vie* and the Latin *vita,* both of which mean *life,* it is unlikely that you will speak of "viable plans."

Emanate means to "come forth," "proceed," or "issue." You may say "The light emanated from a hole in the drape." Note that only light, air, aromas, ideas, and other such phenomena can emanate. Objects such as rivers, automobiles, and peaches cannot emanate from the mountains, a factory, or an orchard.

Farther and *farthest* are used for literal distance, as in "The tree is farther away than the mailbox." But *further* and *furthest* are used for figurative distance, as in "further in debt."

Flaunt and *flout* are often used interchangeably but incorrectly. To *flaunt* is to "exhibit ostentatiously" or to "show off." To *flout* is to "show contempt for," or to "scorn." You may say "He flaunted his coat of arms" or "He flouted the officials."

Fulsome originally meant "abundant," but the term has been used for many years to mean "offensively excessive" or "insincere." *The American Heritage Dictionary* advises against using fulsome in a positive sense, as in "fulsome praise," stating that this usage is obsolete.

Hopefully and *reportedly* are among several adverbs misused so pervasively and for so long that some modern dictionaries now sanction their misuse. Adverbs modify verbs, adjectives, and other adverbs; in other words, adverbs tell us how something happened. In the sentence "He runs rapidly," *rapidly* is the adverb, and it modifies the verb *runs.* The adverb tells us how he ran. *Hopefully* means "with hope" or "in a hopeful manner." To say "Hopefully, we will win" is not the same as saying "We hope we will win." "Hopefully, we will win" implies that hope is the means by which we will win. To say "He was reportedly killed at the scene" is not to say "It is reported that he was killed at the scene." "He was reportedly killed" means that he was killed in a reported manner. *Hopefully* is used properly in these sentences: "She entered college hopefully," "He approached the customer hopefully." There is no proper use of *reportedly.* This quasi adverb is of recent origin and does not stand up to linguistic logic because there is no way to do something in a reported manner.

Adverbs such as those previously discussed represent a special problem to announcers: should you go along with conventional misuse? One argument in favor of this says that everyone understands what is meant when these words are used. An argument against it says that widespread misuse of adverbs undermines the entire structure of grammar, making it increasingly difficult for us to think through grammatical problems. Because any sentence can be spoken conversationally without misusing adverbs, it is to be hoped that you will use adverbs correctly.

The adverb *allegedly* is widely misused. It is impossible for a person to steal, kill, or lie in an alleged way. "Twenty people were allegedly killed or injured by the crazed gunman" makes no grammatical sense whatever. *Allegedly* and *alleged* (the adjective) are perhaps the most overworked and misused words in modern broadcast journalism. One may assume that their proliferation stems from announcers' prudence and fairness. To state on a newscast that "Jones allegedly stole eighty typewriters" may make you guilty of poor grammar, but it shows your virtue in having indicated that Jones may be innocent of grand theft. Many news writers, news directors and station managers believe that the use of *alleged* frees the station from legal charges of defamation, but such is not always the case. The only sound reason for using any of the derivatives of *allegation* is that to do so helps preserve the notion that all people are innocent until proven guilty. There are, however, correct and incorrect ways of using the terms of allegation. Here are a few misuses recently noticed:

"The bullet, allegedly fired at the president . . ."

"Jones also will stand trial for alleged auto theft." The notion of a trial carries with it the allegation, by a district attorney, of guilt. *Alleged* is unnecessary in this sentence.

"The experts have examined the alleged bullets used in the assassination." There are many kinds of bullets, but no one has ever examined an alleged one.

When considering the use of any term of allegation, ask yourself these questions. Is it necessary to qualify the statement? Clearly, *allegedly* and *alleged* are superfluous in the three examples here. Is it possible or useful to say who is doing the alleging? "Jones is alleged by his estranged wife to have set fire to the store" is longer and more cumbersome than "Jones, the alleged arsonist," but it contains more useful information and is fairer to Jones than the shorter version. Am I using the terms of allegations correctly? Here are some correct and incorrect uses of these terms:

"The principal alleged that the striking teachers destroyed their attendance records."   Correct

"The striking teachers allegedly destroyed their attendance records." Incorrect

"Benson is alleged to be an undercover agent for a foreign power." Correct

"Benson is allegedly an undercover agent."   Incorrect

"Lindsay allegedly is set to buy the hockey team at the end of the season." This is wrong in two ways—it is not possible to buy anything in an alleged manner, and the terms of allegation should be reserved for instances in which there is possible wrongdoing.

Allegedly, like *hopefully* and *reportedly*, is a poor reporter's cop-out. These words fail to tell us who is doing the alleging, the hoping, or the reporting. To say that "The negotiators are reportedly near an agreement" is only slightly worse than saying "The negotiators are reported to be near an agreement." The second statement is proper grammar, but it would be far better as a news item if it included the source of the information. As a news writer, you may not know who is doing the alleging, the hoping, or the reporting, but as a field reporter it is part of your job to gather such information and include it in your report.

Implicit means "implied" or "understood"; *explicit* means "expressed with precision" or "specific." "He made an implicit promise" means that the promise was understood but was not actually stated. "His promise was explicit" means that the promise was very clearly stated.

To *imply* is to "suggest by logical necessity" or to "intimate"; to *infer* is to "draw a conclusion based on facts or indications." One may say "His grades imply a fine mind" or "From examining her grades, I infer that she has a fine mind." Avoid the common practice of using one to mean the other.

Libel means "any written, printed, or pictorial statement that damages by defaming character or by exposing a person to ridicule." *Slander* means "the utterance of defamatory statements injurious to the reputation of a person." *Defamation* is a more general term meaning both libel and slander. Libel is associated with defamation of a permanent sort; slander is associated with transient spoken statements.

A *loan* is "anything lent for temporary use"; to *lend* is to "give out or allow the temporary use of something." *Loan* is a noun and *lend* is a verb. Say "She applied for a loan" but "He lent me his rake" and "Do not lend money to friends." Avoid using *loan* as a verb, as in "Do not loan money to friends."

Meritorious means "deserving merit." Note that this word can refer only to persons, as in "He was meritorious in his conduct." You cannot have meritorious books, programs, or light bulbs.

A suffix meaning "theory of" is *-ology*. *Methodology* is not the same as method; it is the theory of methods. *Technology* is not the same as the manufacturing of products; it is the theory of a technical world. Broadcast announcers can avoid compounding confusion by obtaining precise definitions of all words ending in *-ology* that they habitually use.

Oral means "spoken" rather than written. *Verbal* means "of, pertaining to, or associated with words." *Aural* means "of, pertaining to, or perceived by the ear." *Verbal* is less precise than *oral*, because it can mean *spoken* or *written*; for this reason, the phrase "oral agreement" rather than "verbal agreement" should be used if the meaning is that the agreement was not written. Although *oral* and *aural* are pronounced nearly the same, the two words are used in different senses: "She taught oral interpretation" but "He had diminished aural perception."

People (not *persons*) should be used in referring to a large group: "People should vote in every election." *Persons* and *person* should be used for small groups and for individuals: "Five persons were involved" and "The person on the telephone." A *personage* is an important or noteworthy person. A *personality* is a pattern of behavior. It is incorrect to call a disc jockey a "personality," even though the term has wide acceptance.

Most dictionaries indicate that *prison* and *jail* can be used interchangeably, but strictly speaking a jail is maintained by a town, city, or county, whereas prisons are maintained by states and the federal government. Jails are usually used to confine prisoners for periods of less than a year; prisons or penitentiaries are for confinement of people with longer sentences.

A *proselyte* is a convert; to make converts, one proselytizes. In other words, *proselyte* is a noun and *proselytize* is a verb. Do not say "She was proselyted."

Repulsion is the act of driving back or repelling; *revulsion* is a feeling of disgust or loathing. Do not say, "His breath repelled me," unless you mean that his breath physically forced you backward.

Reticent means "silent"; *reluctant* means "unwilling." Do not say "She was reticent to leave."

Rhetoric is the art of oratory or the study of the language elements used in literature and public speaking. *Rhetoric* is not a synonym for *bombast, cant,* or *harangue. Rhetoric* is a neutral term and should not be used in a negative sense to mean empty and threatening speech.

A *robber* unlawfully takes something belonging to another by violence or intimidation; a *burglar* breaks into a house to steal valuable goods. Although both actions are felonies, they are different crimes, so *robber* and *burglar* should not be used interchangeably.

Sensuous refers to the senses affected in the enjoyment of art, music, nature, and similar phenomena. *Sensual* specifically applies to the gratification of the physical senses, particularly those associated with sexual pleasure.

Since is not a synonym for *because. Since* means "later in time," whereas *because* refers to a consequence. Do not say "She didn't get the purse since the store was closed."

A *tremor* is a quick shaking or vibrating movement; a *temblor* is an earthquake. Do not mix these two words, either of which may be used to describe an earthquake, by saying "tremblor."

Verbiage is wordiness. Because the word contains the concept of excess, the phrase *excess verbiage* is redundant.

Xerox is the trademark of a corporation that makes copying machines. The company specifies that *Xerox* is the name of the company and, when the name is followed by a model number, it refers to a specific machine. A copy made by this or any other machine is not "a Xerox."

As an announcer, you will at times have to read copy that is ungrammatical, demands poor usage, or requires deliberate mispronunciation. Here are a few examples of copy that falls short of excellence in these respects. "So, buy _____. There's no toothpaste like it!" If there is no toothpaste like it, the advertised product itself does not exist; a correct expression here would be "There is no *other* toothpaste like it." In "So, gift her with flowers on Mother's Day!", the word *gift*, which is a noun, has been used ungrammatically as a transitive verb. You can give her flowers on Mother's Day, but unless all standards of grammar are abandoned, you cannot gift her. When you are asked to commit these and similar barbarisms as an announcer, what should you do?

You may resent the agency that asks you to foist such poor examples of American speech on the public, but there is little you can do. Do not think that advertising writers are ignorant of the standards of grammar, usage, or pronunciation; agency writers and account executives are well educated. The mistakes they pass on to you are deliberate. Their reasons are curious but important. Poor grammar, they believe, is more colloquial and less stilted than correct grammar. Poor usage causes controversy, and to attract attention is to succeed in the primary objective of any commercial message. Mispronunciations, when required, are asked for because the American public, for any of several reasons, has adopted the mispronunciation. You may have to make deliberate mistakes requested of you, but they are seldom consequential enough to force you to quit your job. You should use language correctly in all broadcast circumstances you control; when you are under orders to read ungrammatical copy exactly as it is written, you should follow the line of least resistance—at least as far as your conscience will permit.

OUR CHANGING LANGUAGE

American English is a dynamic, ever-changing language. During periods of relative stability, change is slow, though more or less constant. During times of upheaval, whether political, economic, or social, rapid changes in our language take place. World War II, for example, created many new words. *Blitz, fellow traveler, fifth column, radar,* and *quisling* all became a part of our language during that war. More recently, *cryogenics, Dacron, dashiki, apartheid,* and *bit* (computer science) have been added to our language.

During the 1960s and 1970s, three separate movements brought about many changes in both spoken and written American English. There was the rise of Black[1] awareness, followed by similar movements among other American ethnic groups. Among many other changes, ethnic consciousness demanded that new terms replace *Negro, American Indian,* and other labels of ethnicity. The decline of colonialism saw the emergence of new nations—Tanzania, Namibia, and Sri Lanka, to name but three—and the nouns and adjectives used to identify them and their citizens brought about important changes in our language. Moreover, the women's movement of the 1970s made obsolete—or at least indelicate—terms such as *mankind, manpower,* and *chairman.* Broadcast announcers must be in the forefront of knowledge of our

---

[1]The terms *Black* and *White* are capitalized throughout because they refer to two historically differentiated races rather than to color. Blacks and Whites come in a considerable range of colors; these terms replace *Negro* and *Caucasian,* which, together with *Asian, Oriental, Indian,* and *Native American,* are capitalized.

ever-developing language; we expect professional communicators to reflect the best contemporary usage, and to set an example.

AMERICAN ENGLISH AND ETHNICITY

Changes in designation have been sought by several ethnic groups during the past twenty or thirty years. For some, the change—as from *Negro* to *Black*—has occurred easily and in a relatively brief period of time. For others, change has been hindered because of a lack of consensus on preferred usage. For example, some Americans of Filipino ancestry want to be called *Pilipinos,* but it is not yet clear whether this term will gain general acceptance. As a broadcast announcer, you must carefully watch this and similar movements in our evolving language, so that your speech reflects contemporary usage.

Some members of non-European ethnic groups in the United States resent being given a hyphenated status, as in "Chinese-American." Preferring to be regarded simply as "Americans," they point out that Americans of European descent are never identified in news stories as "German-American," or "Italian-American," nor does the U.S. government apply ethnic terms to European-Americans, lumping them together for most purposes as "Whites." There is no consensus on this among any major ethnic group, however, and nearly any metropolitan telephone directory will list organizations under such headings as "Japanese-American . . . ," "Mexican-American . . . ," and "Afro-American. . . ."

In broadcasting, the racial or national background of Americans is irrelevant in most circumstances, though not all. For instance, if a person of Mexican heritage is interviewed on the subject of soccer or rapid transit, that person's heritage is not an essential or even an appropriate item of comment. On the other hand, if that same person were to be interviewed on the subject of bilingual education or the working conditions of Mexican-American farmworkers, mentioning the heritage of the speaker would be a legitimate means of establishing that person's interest in, and special knowledge of, those topics. There are times, then, when an announcer may legitimately refer to the ethnic background of a person or group. The first principle of ethnic usage is to ignore ethnicity when it has nothing to do with the subject at hand. There is a corollary: do refer to ethnic background when it helps promote understanding.

You must also be accurate in using ethnic terms. Nowhere is the task of correct identification more difficult than in designating the large group of people often referred to as "Spanish surnamed." The difficulty is in the diversity of their ancestry, which may be Spanish, Filipino, Cuban, Mexican, Puerto Rican, Central American, or South American. "Spanish surnamed" embraces all these different cultures and races, but it is both too cumbersome and too general. More specific terms must be applied. For Americans who come from or owe their ancestry to Mexico or the Caribbean or Central or South America, the term *Latin American* is appropriate; the derivatives *Latina* and *Latino* may be used to designate female and male, respectively. *Mexican-American* is acceptable to all or nearly all members of that ethnic group. Some use *Chicano* and *Chicana, La Raza,* or *Mexican* to describe themselves, but not all members of the Mexican-American communities find these terms acceptable.

A person from Cuba may be referred to either as a *Cuban* or a *Cuban-American,* depending on whether that person is a resident alien or a naturalized citizen. Puerto Ricans, because they are citizens of the United States, should *not* have *American* tacked onto their designation. *Spanish-American* and *Filipino-American* are correct designations for people originally from Spain or the Philippines.

In referring to Spanish-surnamed Americans, do not assume that a person from the Southwest is of Mexican ancestry, that a person from Florida is Cuban, or that a person who lives in New York is Puerto Rican. Where ethnic or national background cannot be ascertained, it is better to avoid a term than to guess.

The original inhabitants of the United States were named *Indians* by early European explorers. Five hundred years later, we still have not agreed on the designation of this group of citizens. The U.S. government classifies them as *Native Americans* in many demographic and statistical reports, yet it continues to operate the Bureau of Indian Affairs. Some resent the term *Indian,* yet refer to themselves as members of the American Indian Movement. *American Indian* is acceptable in some parts of the United States but considered derogatory in others. You would be wise to check on sensitivities in your area. Everywhere, it is acceptable to use Anglicized tribal designations—Sioux, Navajo, Nez Perce, Apache, Zuñi, for example. *Native American* may be used but is still misunderstood by many people. The term *native* means "one who belongs to a nation, a state, or a community by birth." Thus *Native American,* linguistically speaking, refers to anyone born in America.

Black Americans prefer the terms *Black* and *Afro-American. Negro* and *colored person* are presently offensive to most Black Americans. The term *Black Muslim,* used for years by news media, is not used by the religious order it is meant to describe. Refer to this group as the *Nation of Islam* or the *Muslim Brotherhood.*

The term *Chinaman* is occasionally heard today. This term is extremely insulting and should be avoided. Americans of Chinese heritage may be referred to as *Chinese, Chinese-Americans, Sino-Americans, Asians,* or *Asian-Americans.* Use *Asian* when referring to people who came from or whose ancestors came from Asia. *Oriental* is no longer acceptable. You may speak of an Oriental rug but not of an Oriental person.

It is not only Americans of so-called third-world ancestry who are concerned about their designation. Others are offended from time to time by insensitive announcers. Scots bridle when they are referred to as "Scotch." People from Scotland are *Scots, Scottish,* or *Scotsmen* and *Scotswomen.* Scotch is an alcoholic beverage manufactured by the Scots. Scots may sometimes drink Scotch. *Scotch* should not, of course, be used as a synonym for *stingy* because it is both as offensive and as false as most stereotypes.

People from Canada are *Canadians* and should never be referred to as "Canucks." Those living near the border between Canada and the United States know this, but others living far from Canada may not realize that "Canuck" is considered derogatory by French Canadians. A professional Canadian hockey team is named the Vancouver Canucks, but it is one thing to call oneself a "Canuck" and another to be called that by a stranger.

People of Polish ancestry are never "Polacks"; a person of Polish ancestry is a *Pole* or a *Polish-American.* Announcers should never say "Polack," even in jest.

You may refer to citizens of Iran as *Iranians* or *Persians* but never as *Arabs.* Iranians share Islamic faith with their Arabian neighbors, but Iranians are not Arabs.

Do not use *Welsh* to mean a failure to pay a debt. Do not say *Irish* or *Dutch* to mean hot-tempered. Do not use the word *Turk* in any construction that means that the person so labeled is brutal or tyrannical, as in "young Turk." Avoid the term *Dutch* in any of several derogatory connotations: *Dutch bargain,* to mean a transaction settled when both parties were drinking; *Dutch courage,* meaning courage from drinking liquor; *Dutch treat,* where each person pays for his or her share; and *Dutchman,* a term used to describe something that conceals faulty construction. Other offensive terms are *Indian giving,* meaning to give something and then take or demand it back, and *Scotch verdict*, meaning an inconclusive judgment.

No list of dos and don'ts can substitute for sensitivity and consideration. If you find yourself using terms such as *Mexican standoff, French leave,* or *Chinese fire drill,* you could find yourself in serious trouble as an announcer.

GENDER IN AMERICAN ENGLISH

The women's movement brought about significant changes in the terminology we use for a great many acts, objects, and occupations. The historic male orientation of our language was the source of three general areas of discontent. The first was the use of *man* and *mankind* to refer to the entire human race. The second was the group of nouns and verbs that have "maleness" built into them—*chairman, spokesman,* and "*manning* the picket lines" are examples. The third was the generic use of *he* and *his* when both sexes are meant, as in "Everyone must pay his taxes."

Over the centuries, the male orientation of our language gradually increased. Originally, *man* was used to refer to the entire human race. In the proto-Indo-European language, the prehistoric base for many modern languages, including English, the word for man was *wiros* and the word for woman was *gwena. Manu* meant human being. As the centuries passed and as language changed, *man* came to be used for both males and the human race. Many of us speak of "the man in the street," the "working man," and "manpower." Many of us are accustomed to saying that "all men are created equal," and that we believe in the "common man."

Because words help determine and define reality, terminology had to be changed to go along with new career opportunities that developed in the 1970s. With the sanction of state and federal laws, official terminology for nearly 3,500 occupations was changed to eliminate discriminatory referents. Publishing houses prepared guidelines for authors with instructions and suggestions for removing male bias from their writings. Linguists seriously proposed that the rules of grammar be changed, so that "Everyone must pay their taxes" would become correct usage.

A large number of words that are thought by some to be sexist actually are not. The Latin word *manus* means "hand," and in this sense it formed the basis of a great many English words, including *manacle, manage, manager, manner, manual, manicure, manifest, manipulate, manufacture,* and *manuscript.*

With change upon us, announcers have a challenging responsibility. Colloquial speech, which is standard for most announcers, does not lend itself to some of the changes that have been proposed. To substitute *humankind* for *mankind* or *human being* for *man* is necessary until something less affected comes along, but it *is* awkward.

It is necessary to phase out nouns such as *chairman* and *spokesman,* even though the proposed substitutes, *chairperson* and *spokesperson* are long and awkward. *Chair* is used increasingly to mean the moderator of a group, as in "the chair of the PTA," and one might propose *speaker* as a substitute for *spokesman* or *spokesperson,* but these and other changes must become generally accepted before this linguistic problem can be considered solved. Broadcast announcers must work with accepted usage, try to coin better expressions than those they do not like, and be alert for the many changes yet to come.

One way of avoiding the use of male terminology when the intent is to include all of us is to use the plural. An awkward statement such as "Everyone should send in his or her entry so that he or she will be eligible for a prize" can easily be turned into "All people should send in their entries so that they will be eligible for prizes." Another way is to use second person: "You should send in your entry so that you will be eligible for a prize."

Appendix C is a compilation of job titles approved by the U.S. Department of Labor.

NATIONS AND CITIZENS OF THE WORLD

Broadcast announcers, and especially news anchors and reporters, can expect to refer at one time or another to nearly every nation in the world. If you were asked to read news stories from Belau, Burkina Faso, or Vanuatu, where would you turn to learn the correct pronunciation of these new nations? And, whereas you undoubtedly know that a citizen of Turkey is a Turk, how do you refer to a citizen of the Ivory Coast? Cameroon? San Marino? Belau is pronounced [be'lau] (BAY-LAU'), and a citizen of San Marino is *San Marinese* [san mari'nese] (SAN-MAHR-EEN-AY'-SAY). Announcers cannot be expected to know pronunciation and terminology for all the nations of the world, but they are expected to know where to find the information. Appendix D provides the name and correct pronunciation for every nation of the world. It also gives the correct noun and adjective to be used when referring to citizens of these nations (for example, He is a Lao [noun]; She is Laotian [adjective]). Where both noun and adjective are the same, as in Omani, only one term is given.

Note that we Americanize the names of many nations. The country we call Albania is properly Republika Popullore e Shqiperise (schk'-yee-puh-ree'-zuh) [ˌʃkjipəˈrizə]. The Ivory Coast is actually République de Côte d'Ivoire (ray-poo-bleek' dih coat-dee-vwar') [ˌrepybˈlik dy ˈkot di ˈvwar]. Because most nations have had their names Americanized, you should try for correct American pronunciation rather than attempting to pronounce the name as a native of the country would pronounce it. This is true even for countries for which we have not changed the spelling. Remember, though, that pronunciation changes over the years. Moreover, there is a growing trend toward giving correct or nearly correct Spanish pronunciation to the names of nations such as Chile, Colombia, and Costa Rica. If you are a Spanish-speaking American announcer, correct pronunciation of such names is acceptable and may even be preferred by your audience and supervisors.

Refer to Appendix D whenever you are unsure of the pronunciation of a nation's name or of the correct noun or adjective for its citizens.

This chapter on American English ends much as it began, with a brief compilation of grammatical errors recently heard on radio and television. The sentences and fragments that follow have one thing in common—all are grammatically incorrect.

"A jockey must learn to handle a horse before they can get regular work."

"But the odds against them overtaking the Democrats are astronomical."

"But what really sold my wife and I was the guarantee."

"And they'll put on a new muffler within thirty minutes or less."

Mistakes of other kinds include the following.

"The _____ remain clustered in their suburban mansion." The reporter meant *cloistered*.

"The Cuban refugees claim that an invasion of Cuba is eminent." The correct word is *imminent*.

"There were a lot of fire fighters at the scene with smutty faces, but
they were smiling." Sooty? Smudged?

"He said he does not believe that such riots are in the offering." In the
offing.

"They amuse themselves by hurtling insults at each other." We *hurtle*
through the field, but *hurl* insults.

This is a brief list of mistakes in usage, to be sure, but it exemplifies
the kinds of mistakes made by professional speakers who should provide us with models of correct speech. If you make mistakes like these
or if you confuse *who* and *whom, shall* and *will, like* and *as,* and *which*
and *that,* this chapter should serve as a notice to you that you should
undertake a serious study of American English.

9
COMMERCIALS AND PUBLIC-SERVICE ANNOUNCEMENTS

Advertising is the lifeblood of American commercial broadcasting. Radio and television would be far different from what they are if there were no commercial advertising. One has only to look at the broadcast services of nations in which tax-supported broadcast systems predominate to see that advertising has brought the American public many more radio and television stations, more daily hours of broadcasts, and a much greater range of program material. While commercials are much maligned, they have provided jobs for writers, producers, directors, sales personnel, and announcers. Because of our commercial orientation, your future as a broadcast announcer will be more secure if you develop the ability to sell products.

Public-service announcements (PSAs) resemble commercials in many respects. Both are brief announcements, lasting from ten to sixty seconds; both are informational in nature; and both are considered nonentertainment program elements.

Radio commercials and PSAs differ considerably from those on television, so the challenges presented by the two media will be discussed separately. Note, however, that suggestions for analyzing and marking copy apply to both.

RADIO COMMERCIALS

Most radio stations aim at a specific target audience. This means that radio relies heavily on local retailers, that it writes and produces many commercials at the local station level, and that commercials are geared to the age, taste, interests, and even the ethnic background and sex of

FIGURE 9.1
Free-lance performer Peter Scott reading a radio commercial. (Courtesy Peter Scott)

the local audience. Aside from hourly newscasts, which may come from a parent network, nearly all radio broadcasts are heard only in a fairly restricted geographical area. Advertisers are careful to scrutinize the demographics of each station's audience before committing advertising money. A product used only by people middle-aged and older will not be advertised on a station that caters to young adults. The commercial approach to a station featuring country music may be quite different from the approach used for the very same product when it is advertised on a Black/urban contemporary station. What all this means to you is that in writing and delivering radio commercials you must know your audience and adapt your presentation to it.

Sponsored programs are the exception on radio, but they occupy a portion of the day on some foreign-language stations, all-religion stations, and sometimes are heard on classical music stations where a local music store or record outlet will sponsor "Opera Classics" or "Symphonic Masterpieces." One type of brief program is also subject to sponsorship, and this is the "Business Briefs," "Farm Report," or "Report from the Produce Mart." Advertisers for such reports want to have their commercials broadcast at a precise time each day to reach a particular audience. For example, a brokerage house may sponsor a business feature weekdays at 7:35 A.M., hoping to reach commuters during morning drive time; a farm products company may sponsor a five-minute program of agricultural news at 5:30 or 6:00 A.M.; and a chain of food stores may sponsor a daily report on the best produce buys of the day at 10:00 A.M. Each of these times is chosen on the basis of assumptions about the listening habits of the target audience. Other advertisers buy time for either rotating spots or wild spots. *Rotating spots* work as follows. The advertiser or agency buys five spots to be broadcast one a day for the five-day work week. The station guarantees that they will be rotated—for example, the spot will be played between 6:00 A.M. and 7:00 A.M. on Monday, between 7:00 A.M. and 8:00 A.M. on Tuesday, and so on. At the end of the week, the fifth and last spot will return to the 6:00–7:00 interval, so that it does not move to a time when the audience falls off. Many radio stations consider the 6:00 A.M. to 10:00 A.M. time block the most valuable, with the largest audience, and they assign this time a category such as AA or AAA time. This designation dictates a higher cost per spot, because cost is directly related to audience size.

Wild spots are more common than rotating spots because they are easier for stations to schedule. A *wild spot* simply guarantees the advertiser that the spot will be played sometime within the time period purchased, whether AA, A, B, or C time.

A radio spot gets to a station and into a program schedule in any of several different ways.

1. An advertising agency time buyer buys time on the station, and a written script is sent to the station to be read or ad-libbed by the announcer on duty.
2. An agency follows this purchasing procedure but the spot is produced on tape by a station announcer. When this is done, the recording announcer receives a special fee.
3. An agency sends a script and a recording, and the announcer reads the written copy at the time agreed to. Generally speaking, such commercials are either *cart with live tag* or *donut* commercials. In the first, the commercial begins with the playing of the taped cart, which may be only a jingle or music with recorded speech, and the station announcer comes in at the end to provide a tag that gives local or updated information. It might simply provide a current price or a local phone number. In other instances, the recorded portion may begin with a brief jingle and then fade under while the announcer reads the entire sales pitch. Donut commercials are similar. A jingle opens the spot, the music is faded for a pitch by the

station announcer, and the music is faded up just as the announcer completes the message. Music begins and ends such a commercial, with the announcer filling in the middle—hence the term *donut.*

4. An agency sends a recorded commercial for which the announcing and other production work has been done at a recording studio.

5. A local merchant comes to the station and is recorded by station personnel for later editing (if necessary), carting, and scheduling.

6. A station sales representative has sold time to a client and has written the commercial copy. The announcer on duty reads the script live as scheduled.

7. A station sales representative has sold time to a client, has written the copy, and works with a station announcer to produce the commercial on tape.

8. A station production specialist, working from a rough script or a fact sheet, produces a commercial for a local account using a musical *bed,* sound effects, voices, and any other appropriate production resource.

Typically, a recorded commercial will come to a station on ¼-inch reel-to-reel tape, and station production personnel will dub this to tape carts. Carts are not sent from the advertising agency because there are several different cart formats, and each is playable only on the machine for which it was designed.

In smaller markets, advertising agencies may supply only 10 percent of the commercials broadcast, the other 90 percent being written and produced by the station on behalf of local merchants. It is typical for an announcer for a popular music station to work a four-hour board shift, and to spend another two hours by contract in the production of commercials. At some stations, you would do the voice work only; at others, you would also select music and sound effects and engineer the spots. Some very small stations expect on-air announcers to spend part of their day selling time on the station. Few smaller radio stations employ full-time continuity writers, so scripts are written by any of a number of people—management personnel, time sellers, announcers, or production specialists. At larger stations, full-time account executives sell time and write and produce commercials, often using station personnel as talent.

Most radio announcers deliver commercials as part of a job that includes other duties, such as music announcing (DJ work), newscasting, or performing as talk show host or hostess. Some staff announc-

FIGURE 9.2
Sandi Lojko, account executive at KSRO, Santa Rosa, prepares to read a local commercial. (Courtesy KSRO, Santa Rosa, California)

ers—particularly DJs—receive a sum of money beyond their salaries if they can perform well as commercial announcers; they may receive an additional $50 to $100 a week for working a stipulated number of hours in the production of carted commercials. Especially valuable to a production manager responsible for recording such spots are announcers who *can act,* including those who can do dialects. Many staff announcers earn additional money by doing free-lance recordings at professional recording studios. These announcers are represented by a talent agency and are hired by advertising agencies.

More than 90 percent of the commercials broadcast by most radio stations will be on tape carts. You will be expected to read some commercials live, however, and your work usually will leave you very little time to study the commercial copy. Sight-reading without stumbling or misreading is expected of you as a professional announcer, but sight-reading in an authoritative and convincing manner is difficult. Take advantage of any and all spare moments to look over the copy you are given to read, even if this means arriving for work earlier than you are scheduled.

Much radio commercial copy, especially that written without the help of a professional agency staff, is uninspired. Most merchants

FIGURE 9.3
Producer Cindy Mills timing one of a dozen "takes" during the recording of a radio commercial. (Courtesy Allen and Dorward Advertising, San Francisco)

want a straightforward catalogue of items and prices, hardly designed to bring out the best in you. Commercial announcing at many (perhaps most) radio stations demands skill in reading unfamiliar copy, concentration during performance, and using otherwise leisure time in *woodshedding* your copy—an old-time radio term meaning reading, rehearsing, and marking your copy. If you are fortunate enough to work for a classical music station, a low-key FM station, or any station at which commercials are limited in frequency, your chances of being effective are greatly improved. Take advantage of such ideal working conditions to woodshed. The results will benefit you, your station, your client, and your listeners.

Analyzing and Marking Commercial Copy

Chapter 2 presented the analysis of several types of broadcast copy, including commercial copy. Because commercials are much shorter than other types of broadcast material, such as newscasts or documentaries, they present a unique challenge to the announcer. Both the *structure* and the *mood* of a commercial must be effectively communicated in sixty seconds or less. For this reason, additional comments on the analysis and marking of commercials are in order. The following scripts used for analysis (other than the one for Webster's) are worthwhile because they represent the greatest challenge to interpreters. Hackneyed scripts tend to repeat the same structural formulas and deserve only a competent performance, delivered with as much energy and persuasiveness as you can muster.

First, let's look at the *structure* of commercials. Most outstanding commercials are both subtle and complex. The commercial that follows makes use of the so-called *rule of three*. This rule, long recognized and practiced, tells us that the sharpness and punch of one's comments are diluted by going beyond three words or phrases in a given sequence. This has important implications for you as the interpreter of commercial scripts. Note that, in the Potato Board commercial that follows, the first grouping of three comes early: "Fast food . . . slow food . . . all kinds?" Also note that the first three sentences (beginning with "Here's another . . ." and ending with ". . . the potato?") form a complete expository unit, and each of the three sentences should be read to give us a sense of a beginning, a middle, and an ending—though not so obvious an ending as to make what follows seem tacked on.

The next set of three is less obvious. Here are the three parts of this segment of the commercial:

1. "Why Americans love potatoes as appetizers . . ."
2. ". . . in soups and salads . . ."
3. ". . . as entrees and side dishes . . ."

Then comes what seems to be the fourth element—". . . even as desserts"—but the ellipses indicate that this is to be set apart from the sequence of three by both a pause and a stressing of the last three words. Even these words become a group of three in themselves if you pause *slightly* between each word—". . . even . . . as . . . desserts." In analyzing and marking this copy, it is important that you *not* see "appetizers," "soups," "salads," "entrees," "side dishes," and "desserts" as *six* points, each to receive equal stress.

The final set of three is ". . . scalloped, hashed, or mashed," "sliced or diced," and "french fried, boiled, or baked." Two of the three phrases in this sequence are made up of three units each.

The copy has been marked for interpretation. Virgules (/) are used to indicate pauses: one for a slight pause, two for a longer pause, and three for a very noticeable pause. Underlined words are to receive emphasis. Two words were underlined by the copywriter; the others were added by the announcer during the study and analysis of the script.

```
  AGENCY:  Ketchum Advertising, San Francisco
  CLIENT:  The Potato Board
 PRODUCT:  Potatoes
   TITLE:  "Versatile"
  LENGTH:  60 seconds

   ANNCR:  Here's another message from The Potato Board.//Don't we

           Americans love food? Fast food . . ./slow food . . ./all

           kinds?//But, above all, don't we love that good food--the

           potato? Today, the potato stands alone as the number one

           vegetable of versatility./And our friends at The Potato

           Board remind us that Americans crave potatoes in any and

           every form,/for every meal./Why, Americans love potatoes

           as appetizers,/in soups and salads,/as entrees and side

           dishes, and///yes . . .//even as desserts. The Potato

           Board says any way you serve the All-American potato,

           you'll be getting an economical vegetable that has lots of

           nutrition, but not--I repeat not lots of calories.//So,

           whether you serve potatoes scalloped, hashed, or mashed

           . . ./sliced or diced . . ./french fried, boiled, or

           baked,/for all their delicious versatility, The Potato

           Board says potatoes are America's favorite vegetable.

           Well, aren't they in your house?
```

Now read the following commercial, and note how the rule of three is employed three times.

```
  AGENCY:  Allen and Dorward
  CLIENT:  New Century Beverage Co.
  LENGTH:  60 seconds
```

ANNCR: Wherever you go in San Francisco (SFX: FOG HORNS), the

          executive bistros (MUSIC: CONTEMPORARY) in the bustling

          financial district, the elegant homes of Pacific Heights

          and Sea Cliff, or the lavish rooms of the major hotels,

          you'll hear the inviting sound of Schweppervescence. (SFX:

          HISS AND POUR) That curiously refreshing sound when the

          mixer meets the ice, is an irresistible call to pleasure.

          And whether you're pouring Schweppes Tonic Water, Club

          Soda, or Ginger Ale, the sound is the same. (SFX: HISS

          AND POUR) But each has a taste all its own. You'll find

          the unchanging quality of Schweppervescence immedi-

          ately apparent in the company of kindred spirits or

          straightaway. That curiously refreshing sensation found

          only in Schweppes that makes your drink so extraordinary.

          San Franciscans are not alone in their refreshing

          appreciation of Schweppes, for Schweppes Mixers are

          accepted around the world by those with a taste for

          quality. The great taste of Schweppes Mixers cannot be

          silenced. (SFX: HISS OF POUR) Tonic Water, Club Soda,

          Ginger Ale. Listen to the sound of Schweppervescence. Call

          for Schweppes. Curiously refreshing since 1783. (SFX: FADE

          OUT HISS)

The three groups of three are

1. the executive bistros in the bustling financial district
2. the elegant homes of Pacific Heights and Sea Cliff
3. or the lavish rooms of the major hotels

The second and third groups are the same:

1. Tonic Water
2. Club Soda
3. Ginger Ale

Now, let's analyze another outstanding commercial, one that requires a British accent. Note how the first 60 percent of the commercial
is to be read in a precise, dignified, and restrained manner. Then,
beginning with "Now, what about the other half . . . ," you must begin
a build in emotion, intensity, volume, and rate of delivery. The commercial has a Monty Python quality, and you should enjoy it as an
exercise in mock disdain. Be sure to avoid a Cockney dialect—it calls
for your best Oxonian accent. As you reach the end of the third-to-last
sentence, begin decelerating on ". . . as forthrightly crisp as Bitter
Lemon." The last two sentences should see you returning to the same
dignified mood as that with which you began.

As you examine this copy, note again how it uses the rule of three.

"We British love the way it looks."
"We love the way it sounds."
"We especially love the way it tastes."

Then, again, the children are

"whining children"
"grubby little urchins"
"youthful upstarts"

Near the middle, we get this sequence of three.

"refreshingly brisk"
"cultivatedly crisp"
"thoroughly Schweppervescent"

AGENCY: Ammirati & Puris, Inc.

CLIENT: Schweppes

LENGTH: 60 seconds

ANNCR: (BRITISH) I have before me a bottle of Schweppes Bitter

           Lemon. The soft drink loved by half of England. We British

           love the way it looks: A fine, sophisticated mist, with

           morsels of crushed whole lemon. We love the way it sounds:

           (BOTTLE OPENS) A particularly masterful rendering of

           Schweppes cheeky little bubbles and we especially love the

           way it tastes: (POURS) Refreshingly brisk, cultivatedly

           crisp and thoroughly Schweppervescent. It's no wonder that

           Bitter Lemon is adored by half of England. Now, what about

           the other half, you might ask? The half that doesn't adore

           Bitter Lemon? Well, let me assure you, they're all whin-

           ing children, grubby little urchins whose opinion is

           completely and totally insignificant. They are youthful

           upstarts and, as such, absolutely incapable of ap-

           preciating anything as forthrightly crisp as Bitter Lemon.

           The frightfully grown-up soft drink from Schweppes. The

           Great British Bubbly.

In analyzing copy, always look for *structure* as revealed by the *parts* of
the copy.

Now, let's consider *mood* in commercial copy. Read the following
two commercials and the brief analysis that follows them; then practice
them aloud, striving for clearly differentiated moods.

AGENCY: Yamashiro Associates

CLIENT: Webster's Department Stores

LENGTH: 60 seconds

ANNCR: Webster's has <u>you</u> in mind!

MUSIC: UP-TEMPO INSTRUMENTAL, UP AND UNDER

ANNCR: Webster's announces the sale of the year! Up to one-half off on thousands of items! Arrow and Van Heusen men's shirts, 50 percent off. All shoes in stock, one-third off. One dollar above our cost for men's three-piece, all wool suits. Save dollars on neckties, belts, socks, and sport shirts. In the women's department, one-third to one-half off on designer pants, blouses, and blazers. Entire dress inventory reduced by 50 percent. Even homewares are going at all-time low prices. Rag rugs from India--were $69, now only $39. Bath and beach towels, all prices cut in half. Fifty-piece stainless tableware, down by one-third. All radios, portables, TVs, and home recorders, just dollars above our cost. Now's the time to take advantage of low, low prices, while enjoying the traditional high value of Webster's! Three Webster's to serve you. Sorry, at these prices, no free delivery and no lay-aways. Come see us today. Webster's has <u>you</u> in mind! Webster's, where you'll save dollars, with no sacrifice of quality!

AGENCY: Ketchum Advertising

CLIENT: Lindsay Olives

LENGTH: 60 seconds

MUSIC: FRIENDLY MUSIC IN BACKGROUND

ANNCR: (FRIENDLY OLIVE) Hi! Hi! How are ya? Good. I'm Ted. I'm a friendly olive. In fact, most of my true-blue friends are olives, too. Yeah, yeah, sure they are. Now, my friends are all mature--strictly high-quality guys. That's why they're Lindsay Olives. We were all very close friends on

our branch. We did everything together: soaked up the sun,

talked to the girl olives, read the classics. Yeah.

Honest. We read the classics. I told you we were high-

quality olives. Well, one day the Lindsay picker came

for the final inspection. He took all my friends, but

rejected me. He said I had a bruise. Yeah, a bruise. I

don't know how I got it--but I got it. We all argued, but

the inspector wouldn't take a flawed olive for Lindsay.

Well, I was quite upset. Upset! 'Cause I knew some day I'd

end up like this in some obscure can of olives, and all my

pals would be Lindsays.

ANNCR: (FEMALE VOICE) An olive is just an olive, unless it's a

Lindsay.

ANNCR: (FRIENDLY OLIVE) Hey, you look friendly. Let's have lunch

some time.

MUSIC: (OUT)

What a difference of mood in these two examples. The first, for Webster's, is designed to hold attention through vitality and the illusion of importance. Every effort is made to encourage direct and rapid action from the listener. The second commercial, for Lindsay Olives, is light, humorous, and wistful. Both pieces of copy contain the same number of words (182), which means that both must be read rather rapidly. Be careful to avoid turning the Lindsay Olive spot into a hard-sell commercial. In practicing these two spots, work for two entirely different moods.

After the analysis of structure and mood comes the marking of copy. As a hard-pressed disc jockey, you may have little time for marking copy; but as a free-lance announcer working with other professionals in a recording studio, you will mark your copy both before and during the recording session. The copy that follows was marked by a professional announcer upon arriving at the recording studio. Read it aloud according to the indications made for pauses and stresses. One virgule (/) means a brief pause; two virgules (//) mean a longer pause. One line under a word means some stress; two lines indicate fairly heavy stress. Note, though, that this is a soft-sell commercial; even your heaviest stress should be consistent with the mood and style of the piece.

AGENCY: Ingalls Associates, Inc.

CLIENT: Middlesex Bank

SUBJECT: Home Improvement

LENGTH: 60 seconds

SFX: CHILLING WIND SOUNDS

VO: This harsh and untimely interruption of summer/is brought to you by/Middlesex Bank. As a reminder that this summer is no time to forget about/next winter.

SFX: UP

VO: The heating. Those storm windows. That leaking ventilating system. If your house could use a little winterizing, summer is the time to do it. Because right now, the prices are right. And right now, Middlesex Bank is standing by, ready with a home improvement loan.//We interrupt this interruption of winter,/with summer.

SFX: SPLASHES OF SWIMMING POOL

VO: As a reminder, that with gas prices the way they are, you might even consider turning your house into a summer place . . .//by putting in a swimming pool. No matter what part of your home you'd like to improve, we've got a Home Improvement Loan to help you do it. We're MIDDLESEX. The Little/Big Bank.

Despite the analyzing and copy marking you have done just before the recording session, be prepared to make changes during the ten, twenty, or more takes that will occur before the person producing the commercial is satisfied. A typical recording setup will require four or five persons: one or two announcers, an agency producer, the writer of the commercial, and an audio engineer. Music will have been recorded in advance and will be added by the engineer.

As each take is recorded, instructions are given for changes to be made. Changes might be made to eliminate awkward phrases, to delete or alter sentences with too many sibilant sounds ("That's because Bonnie's citrus scouts search the finest orange groves"), to change the emphasis of words or phrases, and, most often, to delete words or short phrases to conform to time limits. The producer will offer suggestions for interpreting the copy and will tell you if you are going too fast or too slow. The producer will also tell you if you are mispronouncing a word or if you slurred or had some other articulation problem on the last take. The writer (if the writer is not also the producer) will tell you words to change or cut. As the announcer, you are expected to follow all instructions without comment or argument. Even constructive suggestions from you are unwelcome by most agency writers and producers. Feel your way carefully as you attempt to sense when it is safe to offer suggestions for changes in commercial copy.

FIGURE 9.4
Writer Jim Deasy checks his script to find a way to cut three seconds from it. Engineer Troy Alders checks the volume level on his console. (Courtesy Jim Deasy and TLA Productions, San Francisco)

Working with Commercials During an On-Air Shift

Assuming that most of your commercial announcing will occur during a regular board shift—and this would be true unless you worked with the production department to record carted commercials—here are some of the procedures you are most likely to encounter. The commercial copy for your entire shift will have been logged by the *traffic department*, and you will have a copy of that log.[1] The log indicates the order of the commercials, whether a given commercial is recorded or is to be read live, the cart number for carted commercials, and the time each commercial is to be broadcast. If your station has a tight format, the times will be precise; if your station is casual and relaxed, the times will be approximate.

If you are working at a large station, chances are there will be (in addition to the log) a *copy book*, sometimes called a *continuity book*. Seven such books are prepared weekly by traffic, one for each day of the week. Each book will contain, in order, the commercial copy for spots to be read live, as well as indications of the spots that are carted. Your job in working from a copy book is not difficult; you merely keep track of the sequential placement of the commercials, entering a mark on the program log as each commercial is broadcast. A turn of the page brings you to the next commercial.

At smaller stations, where limited budgets dictate fewer staff members, the work is somewhat more complicated. There is one copy book. Commercials are inserted alphabetically by sponsor name. The program log contains an entry such as "live #4, Malagani Tires" or "cart #23, Red Boy Pizza." The first indicates that you should look up the Malagani copy, commercial number 4, in the alphabetically arranged copy book and read it at the time indicated. The second indicates that, assuming you are working combo, you should locate cart number 23 and play it at the correct time.

In working with commercials that are part live and part recorded, it is necessary to develop split-second timing. A cart with live tag script and analysis follows.

CLIENT: Stonestown Mall

LENGTH: 60 seconds

TYPE: Cart with live tag

---

[1] The traffic department is that unit of a station that prepares program logs, based on information provided by a program director or a sales manager.

```
    CARTRIDGE #:   L-66

         BEGIN:    8/12

      CART L-66

        JINGLE:    (5)

         VOICE:    "Chicago's newest shopping mall"

 CART CLOSE AND

       TAG CUE

         VOICE:    "Open Tuesdays 'til nine."

           SFX:    (1)

     TAG IN AT:    (45)

      LIVE TAG:    Visit the home furnishing display at Bellach's. Fine

                   leather sofas and lounge chairs are on sale at 25% off!

                   Bedroom sets by Heritage now marked down a full 30%!

                   Lamps, end tables, occasional chairs, and desks--all on

                   sale at prices you have to see to believe! Bellach's, at

                   the Stonestown Mall!
```

How do you work from this script? First of all, you must understand the terminology. *Cart* refers to an audiotape cartridge; the numbers identify the particular carts to be played. *Cart with live tag* means that the commercial is a combination of recorded and live copy and that the copy you are to read comes in at the end—hence *tag*. "LENGTH: (60)" tells you that the commercial is to be delivered in sixty seconds. "TAG IN AT: (45)" tells you that you are to come in at the forty-five-second mark and that you have fifteen seconds to read the tag. SFX is the symbol for sound effects. In practicing this commercial, use a stopwatch (preferably a digital watch or clock), and work until you are able to read the tag in exactly fifteen seconds.

Most radio announce booths are equipped with a mounted stopwatch or an electronic digital clock that can be programmed to show either elapsed time or remaining time. In reading commercials of any kind, time is important. Use a stopwatch or clock each time you practice commercial delivery. Split-second timing is most important for carted tags and donuts; time is what radio stations sell, and they want to give clients precisely what they pay for.

Donut commercials require the most accurate timing of all, because only enough seconds have been provided for you to read your copy before the musical background is faded back up. A typical donut begins with music, often with lyrics, and at a precise second the volume is lowered for you to read your copy. At the time indicated on the script, the volume of the music is raised to full volume, and the song or jingle is repeated until the end of the commercial. If you read too rapidly, you will finish while the background music is playing at reduced volume. If you read too slowly or if you stumble and have to repeat a portion of your script, the music will return to full volume while you are still reading. As a professional, you should work for perfection in timing donuts, for you will be judged by your peers and associates on your timing abilities.

Some radio stations have developed a practice that makes split-second timing on donuts of lesser importance. They record the first part of a donut commercial on one cart and the last part on another. The first cart typically includes the opening jingle and the reduced-volume musical bed; the second cart begins with the start of the concluding jingle. The way you would work with this is obvious, and it is equally apparent that this system eliminates almost all possibility of timing error. But you cannot be sure that your station will take the time to dub donuts onto two carts, so you should practice and perfect the skill of reading donuts to the exact times indicated.

At times you may be asked to ad-lib a commercial from a *fact sheet*. Fact sheets provide essential information but do not constitute a script. Here is a typical fact sheet.

```
       CLIENT:  Allison's Pet Center

       LENGTH:  60 seconds

     OCCASION:  Christmas Sale

  MERCHANDISE:  Guppies and goldfish, 29¢ each

                Aquariums, 10-gal., with filter, $19.95 (reg. $29.95)

                White mice, $1.00 a paiг

                Squirrel monkeys, $55.00 each
```

NOTE: CLIENT WANTS HUMOROUS COMMERCIAL

DATES: Dec. 15 'til Christmas Eve

ADDRESS: Corner Fulton and North Streets

The challenges here are two: to ad-lib a humorous commercial and to have it time out to sixty seconds.

RADIO PUBLIC-SERVICE ANNOUNCEMENTS

All commercially licensed broadcast stations provide free time for the reading or the playing of recorded public-service announcements (PSAs). The Federal Communications Commission (FCC) defines a PSA as follows.

> A public-service announcement is an announcement for which no charge is made and which promotes programs, activities, or services of federal, state or local governments (e.g., recruiting, sales of bonds, etc.) or the programs, activities or services of non-profit organizations (e.g., UGF, Red Cross Blood Donations, etc.), and other announcements regarded as serving community interests, excluding time signals, routine weather announcements and promotional announcements.[2]

Most broadcast stations limit their services to organizations that enjoy tax-exempt status, as defined by the Internal Revenue Service.

Despite deregulation, radio stations will continue to carry PSAs. Station management knows that the good will of community members is important to the success of the station. There also is a long tradition of community service on the part of broadcasters. Also, more and more PSAs are being paid for by local merchants who realize that their interests are served by supporting important local causes. Here is a PSA paid for by a brake and tire service.

> ANNCR: *Brandon's Brake and Tire* reminds you that, with the opening of the school year, it's extra important to keep alert on the road. A child often forgets all the safety rules that are taught by parents and teachers. Drive carefully, cau-

---

[2]"NAB Radio–Television Program Log Recommendations," National Association of Broadcasters, revised 1976, Washington, D.C., p. 13.

tiously, and be prepared to stop in a hurry if you see a ball bounce into the street—a child may be right behind it. As adults, we need to do some thinking for children. This message is brought to you by *Brandon's Brake and Tire*, Clement and 14th Streets, in Madison.

PSAs and commercials have much in common, but there also are differences: PSAs tend to be of shorter duration, some constituting only a brief mention on a "Community Billboard" feature; PSAs seldom are augmented by elaborate production, such as music, sound effects, and so forth; and PSAs are more likely to be broadcast during *off hours*, those times of the day that are least attractive to advertisers. More important differences are the different objectives and the motivational devices used. Many commercials present rational arguments to sell a product or a service, such as a supermarket listing the weekend specials. Other commercials are designed to arouse the emotions of fear, greed, or insecurity. Public-service announcements must shun such tactics. Fear, greed, and insecurity are basic human emotions, and it is rather easy to exploit them. A campaign for famine relief or one to save the whales may indeed appeal to basic human emotions, but the producers of PSAs for these causes traditionally avoid emotional overkill. Because of these considerations, you should give PSAs an unadorned, straightforward delivery in nearly all instances.

At a large-market station, the PSAs that you are to read will be neatly typed, duplicated, and placed in your copy book. At many small-market stations, PSAs will come to you in a variety of ways. Where there is a staff member assigned to public affairs, you may find PSAs typed on 3" × 5" index cards. At regular intervals, you will read two or three of the brief messages as a community calendar offering. The following PSA is typical of such notices.

```
MISSION HOSPITAL                                    out: Apr. 5

The Sunrise Unit of Mission Hospital will present the film

"Chalk Talk" and a discussion on alcoholism, on April 5th,

6:30 P.M., at the hospital.

                                            info: 924-9333
```

At an understaffed radio station, you may find yourself working from handwritten copy (see Figure 9.5).

Obviously, skill in ad-libbing when working from what is essentially a fact sheet is required to deliver Dixie School's message successfully.

Practice: Delivering Radio Commercials and PSAs

Appendix A offers a number of commercial and PSA scripts as well as several fact sheets. These exercises provide practice material in most of the types of commercial and PSA scripts heard on radio today. You are encouraged to find additional practice material and to write and deliver some of your own. Fact sheets should be used for ad-lib practice. Here are some suggestions for practicing the delivery of radio commercials and PSAs.

1. Practice reading aloud and recording ten-second, twenty-second, thirty-second, and sixty-second commercials and PSAs, always working with a stopwatch. Listen carefully to playbacks. Ask yourself these questions. Does this voice please me? Does the piece hold my attention? Does the meaning come through? Is the rate of delivery too fast or too slow? Is there variety in pitch, rate, and emphasis? And, most important, am I sold on the product or the cause?
2. Produce on audiotape commercials that require production—sound effects, music, dramatization.
3. Ask a radio station or advertising agency for taped donut commercials, and practice with them until your timing becomes razor sharp.
4. Write and record commercials based on the fact sheets found in Appendix A.
5. Use the fact sheets for practicing ad-lib delivery.

TELEVISION COMMERCIALS

Television commercials differ from radio commercials in several ways. They almost always are briefer than radio commercials, running from fifteen to thirty seconds; they use music and sound effects more often than those on radio; and they almost never are performed live. Because television is a visual medium, most advertisers want to show their products or services, and this, in turn, means that the majority of television commercials feature voice-over narration. As a television commercial announcer, your face may never appear on the screen. Even in commercials that show the announcer, the time of appearance usually is confined to a few moments of introduction at the beginning.

Dixie School
1818 Morgan Drive
Outland, MI

Dear Friends,

      I would appreciate having
the following announcement aired
during your Public Service Announcements.

      Parental Stress Workshop
      Wednesday, February 24
      7:30 p.m.
      Dixie School
      Room 23
* Child care   * Refreshments
      Thank You!
      Janice Hicks
         544-3321 School
         544-5467 Home

FIGURE 9.5
Example of handwritten copy that may serve as the basis for a PSA at a small-market radio
station.

As a television commercial announcer, you would not have to cope with the problem of reading copy cold, as do many radio disc jockeys. With time to prepare and even to discuss interpretation with a copy-writer or agency producer—and with tape recording giving you a margin of safety—you will find commercial announcing for television a manageable challenge.

Television commercials reach the air by a process similar to that of radio commercials. They are sent, almost always on videotape, by an advertising agency; they are produced by a local or nearby production company and are sent to stations by the advertiser; or they are produced by the retail services unit of a television station and are both played on that station and sent to other stations for playing.[3] If you are an announcer specializing in television commercial delivery, you most likely would receive your assignments through a talent agency. You would perform in one of these settings: a sound recording studio (for voice-over commercials), a television station studio, a video or film studio, or in the field, working with an EFP (electronic field production) crew.

Many television commercials that appear to be produced locally actually are produced in major production centers and offered to local merchants as cooperative commercials. A *cooperative commercial* is one in which the national advertiser pays for making the commercial, but the local merchant shares the cost of its broadcast with the national advertiser. The bulk of the commercial is on tape by the time it reaches the local station; at the station—or at a production house—a closing tag on behalf of the local merchant is added. Thus, a cooperative commercial might be produced by a firm such as Serta Mattresses, with provision made for the identification of the local dealer at the end, such as in the following example.

```
AGENCY:   Allen and Dorward

CLIENT:   Breuners

PRODUCT:  Serta Mattresses

LENGTH:   60 seconds
```

---

[3] Few commercials are sent to stations on film, even though they continue to be shot on film in some production centers, particularly Hollywood.

———————VIDEO———————	———————AUDIO———————
MUSIC UNDER:	SHE: I want my Serta!
WOMAN TOSSING AND TURNING IN A TRAIN BERTH.	ANNCR (VO): Here's why people want their Serta——why they're spoiled for any other mattress——only Serta goes
ANNOUNCER STANDING NEXT TO SERTA MATTRESSES.	beyond just being firm, beyond what others do. We top our support with
SUPER: SERTA PERFECT SLEEPER	the extra comfortable Serta surface——
SHOTS OF COILS AND TOP SURFACE.	a unique difference you can feel in a Serta Perfect Sleeper.
ART CARD: SERTA LOGO "I WANT MY SERTA"	BREUNERS ANNCR (VO): Save 50% off original prices on the clearance of
PERFECT SLEEPER HOTEL 50% OFF	all Serta Perfect Sleeper Hotel sleep sets, with no payments 'til November!
(DISSOLVE) NO PAYMENTS UNTIL NOVEMBER	
(DISSOLVE) BREUNERS FINE HOME FUR-NISHINGS SINCE 1856	

As either a radio or a television announcer, you may pick up extra money by moonlighting as a television commercial announcer. Television commercial announcing at the national level pays well, but it is a difficult field to enter. Most performers on national commercial spots live in New York or in the Hollywood area, and relatively few performers dominate the field.

Locally produced television commercials offer employment to many performers, mostly in the voice-over mode. Portable electronic field production equipment, together with character generators, graphics generators, digital video effects (DVE) equipment, and chroma-keying, permits even small local stations to create elaborate and effective commercials.[4] These devices permit their operators to make videotapes on

[4]For more detailed treatment of visual effects, see Herbert Zettl, *Television Production Handbook,* 4th ed. (Belmont, Calif.: Wadsworth, 1983).

location—at a carpet store, an auto parts dealer, a tire and brake service, or a grocery store—and to edit in the camera. During postproduction, they allow for the addition of written information (character generator); images drawn onto the screen (graphics generator); creation and manipulation of multiimages, such as changing a picture into a mosaic or swinging a picture through space (digital video effects); and keying two or more pictures into the same screen. A typical locally produced television commercial will show an announcer at or near the beginning of the spot and then show images of products or services, while the announcer continues voice-over narration.

Voice-over narration for television commercials differs from radio commercial delivery only in that the words must be timed to match the pictures being seen by the viewers. This coordination is achieved in one of three production routines. (1) The announcer reads the script, and the pictures are timed to match the words in postproduction. (2) The visual portion of the commercial is shown on a monitor, and the announcer matches words to pictures. (3) The audiotaped performance is edited to match the pictures, again during postproduction editing. In most instances the announcer is long gone before the commercial is completed, and the announcer may never see the finished product.

A few television commercials are produced in the field, with the announcer playing a visual role, as in the showing of automobiles and trucks for sale at a showroom. To perform as the announcer of this type of commercial, you have to memorize your lines—or work from cue cards—and make a direct address to the camera. Although rare, on-camera commercial delivery is worth practicing. Elsewhere in this book, particularly in the chapters on performance, interviewing, and television news, many suggestions are offered for improving your on-camera performance. Nearly all these suggestions apply equally to television on-camera commercial announcing.

Practice: Delivering Television Commercials

Television commercials usually involve elaborate visual effects, thus students of announcing have difficulty finding realistic opportunities for practice. Appendix A provides many radio scripts and a few television scripts. You can adapt some of the radio scripts for television performance, but you will generally be limited to a straight, on-camera presentation. The following suggestions should make it possible for you to achieve satisfactory results with a minimum of production support.

1. Practice on-camera delivery with some of the simple presentational commercials in the drill material. Use demonstration commercials and commercials incorporating studio cards or one or two slides instead of commercials involving elaborate production. Work for exact timing as well as camera presence. Practice with cue cards and a prompting device.

2. Practice ad-libbing live on-camera television commercials from fact sheets. Some slides or studio cards may be used, but do not overdo the production.

3. Prepare slides or studio cards for voice-over slide presentation of twenty-second, thirty-second, or sixty-second radio commercials or PSAs. Practice synchronizing your off-camera delivery with the visual images as they appear on the screen.

4. Tape commercials off the air. Write a script of the spoken portions of the commercial. Then, with the sound turned off, run the commercials and practice voice-over delivery.

5. Produce a demonstration commercial with one person on camera while you are off camera, delivering the voice-over narration.

The following suggestions for practice are offered:

1. *When performing on camera, dress as you would if you had been hired to deliver the commercials.*
2. Try in each one to *understand and convey the impression the sponsor wants to create.*
3. *Make your movements* in handling props or pointing to signs or products *slow, deliberate, and economical.*
4. If television equipment is available, try to *simulate actual broadcast conditions.*
5. Some of the practice commercials call for animation, film inserts, or properties that will not be available. There is no ideal way of working with such commercials, but they are included here because it would be unrealistic to exclude them. They form a large part of broadcast commercials today.
6. *Make sure you adhere scrupulously to the time limits of the commercials.*

7. When appropriate, *look directly into the camera lens.*
8. In on-camera performance, *practice switching smoothly from one camera to another on cue.*
9. *Do not do a parody or a burlesque of a commercial* unless the assignment calls for it!
10. *Communicate!*

As you practice radio and television commercial delivery, try to reflect your own personality. Some commercials call for a slow, relaxed delivery, others for a hard-sell approach; often sponsors will ask for a particular style of delivery. But appropriately changing pace, volume, and level of energy does not mean you have to transform yourself totally each time the style or mood of a commercial changes. If you do not maintain and project your own personality, you will run the risk of sounding like an impersonator rather than an announcer.

10
INTERVIEW AND
TALK PROGRAMS

Interviews occupy a great many hours of every broadcast day. Some are brief, such as a ten-second actuality or sound bite on a news broadcast, whereas others may take up the bulk of an hour-long talk program.[1] Interviewing eyewitnesses and spokespersons at the scene of a fire, an airplane crash, or similar event for a news broadcast is but a minor aspect of the news-gathering responsibilities of reporters; on the other hand, conducting interviews is the chief activity of talk and interview show hosts and hostesses. Interviewing for news broadcasts is discussed in Chapters 11 and 12. This chapter is devoted to interview practices and techniques appropriate to radio call-in shows, television interview programs, and community affairs programs.

The word *interview* comes from the French and means, roughly, "to see one another." Lengthy interviews sometimes are essentially question-and-answer sessions, often with controversial guests; at other times, interviews are low-key conversations. The difference is in technique, and technique is determined by purpose.

Talk programs are important features of American radio and television. Although the two media approach talk programming in somewhat different ways—television making almost exclusive use of studio guests, radio dividing its time between guests and telephone calls—both are alike in that the key to success is the interviewing ability of the program host or hostess.

Talk shows are naturals for radio and television. Their intimacy suits the media well. They present contemporary issues, are entertaining

---

[1] *Actuality* is the radio term for a brief report featuring someone other than broadcast personnel. *Sound bite* is the television term for the same feature.

FIGURE 10.1
Senior producer Jan
Landis warms up the au-
dience just prior to air
time. (Courtesy "AM
San Francisco," KGO-TV,
San Francisco)

and informative, have variety, and often directly involve the listeners and viewers. They are inexpensive to produce and require a minimum of preparation time. Jobs as talk show hosts and hostesses are not numerous, but they are rewarding and challenging and worth practicing for. You may or may not succeed in having a talk show of your own, but the skills you acquire through practice will be useful to you in a range of announcing specializations. Some talk show skills can be practiced; others cannot. You can practice interviewing, discussing music, sports reporting, commercial delivery, and news reporting—all of which will help you become competent as a talk show facilitator— but the measure of your effectiveness is determined by how well you can put it all together on a live broadcast. Talk show announcers are among the few announcers whose auditions often coincide with their first air experience in this capacity. You may not be able to practice in an integrated way all the skills you need for talk show announcing, but you can study the practices and procedures you would encounter if you were to work as a radio or television talk show host or hostess.

PRINCIPLES OF EFFECTIVE INTERVIEWING

Before listing and discussing a number of suggestions for the conduct of interviews, let us consider two fundamental aspects of interviewing. The first concerns what semanticist S. I. Hayakawa calls the "ladder of abstraction." Simply put, we usually have available several terms for the same phenomenon, some of which are precise and some of which are general. For example, we speak of *food, fruit,* and *apple.* An apple is a specific crop, and it is also a fruit and a food, so all three terms are accurate. Some interviewees consistently speak at a level that is high on the ladder of abstraction, which is to say that they use vague and general terms rather than precise ones. It is your job, as an interviewer, to "pull" a guest down the ladder of abstraction, when appropriate. For example:

> ANNCR: And just what does the administration intend to do about the problems of the inner cities?
>
> GUEST: We're extremely aware of the seriousness of the situation. We feel that the development of human resources in our cities must come before we can expect to overcome the problems of the physical environment.

What the guest is saying is quite simple: We need to find jobs for the people before we can hope to clean up and rebuild. The interviewer's problem is to find a way to get the guest to say this in clear, specific language.

> ANNCR: Please tell us what you mean by "the development of human resources."

A later question would direct the guest toward explaining what she or he meant by the phrase "the problems of the physical environment."

The second major consideration for any interviewer is that of bias. When interviewing a person on a controversial or extremely important subject, one has a natural tendency to accept without question comments *that one agrees with.* This is not a problem when the unsubstantiated statement is a matter of common knowledge, as in this example:

> ANNCR: How do today's college students compare with students of twenty years ago?

FIGURE 10.2
Talk show host Fred
LaCosse interviews guest
Rita Jenrette on the set
of "AM San Francisco."
(Courtesy KGO-TV, San
Francisco)

> GUEST: Well, standardized test scores of college-bound seniors
> have fallen pretty regularly over the past two decades.

This is a matter of record and is generally well known.

> ANNCR: And how do you explain the drop?
> GUEST: Television viewing is the primary culprit.

Assume that you believe this. As a responsible interviewer, you have
an obligation to ask further questions and to bring out any factual
evidence that may have led your guest to the conclusion reached.
Probing may reveal that the statement is based on hard fact, or it may
reveal that the conclusion is simply an unsubstantiated hunch. Whatever the outcome, you owe it to your listeners to question undocu-
mented assertions.

Ernie Kreiling, a syndicated television columnist, has compiled a
helpful list of dos and don'ts, ideas, and pitfalls that are especially
appropriate to radio or television talk show interviews. Because they
provide an excellent framework for our discussion of interviewing, his

suggestions are listed here with appropriate amplification. You should understand at the outset that you need not memorize these points or follow them as religiously as you would a check list for a space launch. Ponder the suggestions and work them into your practice where appropriate. It is also helpful to refer to them after each interview.

Concerning Your Guest

1. *Carefully research your guest's background, accomplishments, attitudes, beliefs, and positions.* Under most circumstances, you will know from one to several days in advance who your guest will be, so you will have enough time to do some research. If your guest has written a book, and if the interview is to focus on it, you should obviously read the book, make notes, and even read representative reviews. Among many sources of information about well-known persons and important topics are *Who's Who* (in politics, in education, in medicine, and so on), the *Europa Yearbook*, the *Book of the States*, and the *Municipal Yearbook*. You can find articles by checking the listings in the *Reader's Guide to Periodical Literature* and the *New York Times Index*. Many radio and television stations have computer access to data banks that will provide information on nearly anyone of importance. When time and circumstances permit, research into your guest's background is as important as all other suggestions combined. Style, personality, smooth performance, and perfect timing cannot compensate for a lack of such knowledge.

2. *Make your guest feel at home.* Introduce your guest to studio and control-room personnel when it is convenient. Show the people you are to interview the areas in which the interview will take place and give them an idea of what is going to happen. Such hospitality should help relax your guests and induce them to be cooperative. With seasoned interviewees, people used to being interviewed, you can plunge right into the interview. With inexperienced people, it helps to spend a few minutes explaining how you will conduct the interview and what you expect of them.

3. *Do not submit questions in advance, unless you would lose an important interview by refusing to do so.* Hostile guests and some politicians may ask you to submit your questions in advance. This is a poor practice, for spontaneity demands that guests not rehearse their answers. On the other hand, it is good practice to let your interviewee know the general areas to be covered. To help relax an inexperienced guest, you might even reveal your first question slightly in advance. One question

always should be mentioned in advance: if you are going to ask your guest for his or her most interesting, funniest, or most unusual experience, advance notice will provide time for reflection. Most interviewees draw a blank when asked such a question abruptly, but a little advance notice may turn it into the highlight of your interview.

4. *Never refer to conversations held before air time.* An audience will feel excluded by a question such as "Well, Pat, I'm sure the folks would find interesting that new hobby you were telling me about just before we went on the air. Will you tell them about it?" They want to feel in on the interview, not as if most of it has already taken place.

5. *Establish your guest's credentials at the start of the interview.* Station personnel have usually selected guests because they believe them to be knowledgeable and responsible, and it follows that the audience should know how and why they are qualified to speak on a particular subject. The significance of a partisan statement about heart transplants differs depending on whether the statement is made by a heart surgeon, religious leader, heart recipient, or politician. One opinion is not necessarily better or more newsworthy than another, but your audience must be aware of the specific credentials of the speaker in order to assess statements in a meaningful way.

6. *Occasionally but indirectly reestablish your guest's name and credentials.* On television this is frequently done with supers at the bottom of the screen. On radio, of course, it must be done orally, and because listeners cannot see your guest, frequent reintroductions are especially important. Because the television audience can see your guest, reintroductions are unnecessary if the guest is well known.

7. *Seek out your guest's deep convictions.* Do not settle for mentally rehearsed platitudes and clichés. Probing usually means that you must reveal something of yourself. Your guest is not likely to open up unless you do.

8. *Be tenacious.* Do not be put off with evasive answers. Keep probing until you see that you cannot get any further. Then drop the line of questioning and turn to something else.

9. *Listen attentively to your guest's replies and react with appropriate interest.* Do not feign interest. If your interest is not genuine, you are either conducting a bad interview or not listening to your guest's responses.

10. *Do not interrupt with meaningless comments.* "I see," "Uh huh," "Oh, yes," and "That's very interesting" add nothing to your interview and actually detract from what your guest is saying. There is an even more pressing reason for not peppering your interview with "Uh huhs." Sometimes interviews are intended for editing (usually for newscasts or documentaries), and in most instances the words of the interviewer are edited out, to be replaced with narration. All announcers should cure themselves of the habit of using *vocal* reinforcement as they interview guests. Practice giving nonverbal reinforcement—a smile, a nod of the head—and work to eliminate voiced reinforcements. At the same time, because a good interview frequently is a conversation, do not be afraid to make comments such as "I can't believe you didn't know about your nomination . . ." (or whatever is appropriate to the conversation).

11. *Do not patronize your guest and do not be obsequious.* Avoid phrases such as "I'm sure our viewers would like to know" and "Do you mind if I ask?" Some people are reluctant or hostile, to be sure, but most come to be interviewed and need no coddling.

12. *Keep cool.* Interviewing is your specialization and you should feel at ease. At times your guest may be a stranger to the interviewing situation and may be awed by the equipment, a bit afraid of you, and

worried about saying something wrong. If you fail to remain calm, and if you are distracted by the signals of floor managers or others, you will only rattle your guest further.

13. *Discuss the subject with your guest.* Do not cross-examine or otherwise bully guests. Because they are probably nervous, it is up to you, no matter how much you may dislike or disagree with them, to put your guests at ease. If you show hostility, unfairness, or lack of common hospitality, both your guests and your audience will resent it.

14. *Remember that the guest is the star.* Very rarely is the interviewer of more interest to the audience than the guest. One famous wit and raconteur consistently upstaged his guests and the audience loved it. In general, however, it is not only contrary to the purpose of the interview—which is drawing the guest out—but it is also simply rude.

15. *Remember that the guest is the expert.* At times, of course, you will be an authority on the subject under discussion and will be able to debate it with your guest. In most circumstances, though, your guest will be the expert, and you will do well to keep your uninformed opinions to yourself. (But with this point, keep in mind the next one.)

16. *Keep control of the interview.* Experienced guests, particularly politicians, can take it away and use it for their own purposes. Keep the questions coming so that guests do not have time to diverge from the subject.

17. *On television, do not have your guest address the camera.* The best television interview gives the illusion that the two participants are so absorbed in their conversation that the camera is eavesdropping.

18. *At the conclusion of the interview, thank your guest warmly but briefly.* Do not be effusive. Then move directly to your concluding comments.

Concerning Your Subject

19. *Be sure the subject to be discussed is of interest or importance.* Although a dull guest can make even the most exciting subject boring, your interview will benefit if the topic itself is truly interesting or important. When practicing interviewing, do not settle for the most readily obtainable guest. Interviews with parents, siblings, classmates, and others well known to you are seldom of interest to anyone, the participants included. A special energy is generated when you interview people who are strangers to you, and an even greater intensity develops when you interview people of real accomplishment. There is an important

exception to this general rule: some outstanding interviews have been conducted between college-age announcing students and their parents when the student is genuinely ignorant of the parents' youth, of grandparents, or of some other interesting facet of the past. Here, lack of knowledge allows for the energy that comes from a surprising answer, while the family bond makes for a high degree of interest.

20. *Where appropriate, limit the number of topics discussed so that they can be discussed in depth.* Depending on the intended length of the interview, it is best to explore only as many topics as can be dealt with in depth during the allotted time. The least interesting interviews are those that randomly skim the surface of one topic after another.

21. *Establish the importance of the topic.* Topics that are obviously important need no special build-up, but the importance of others may benefit from brief amplification. People are interested in almost anything that directly affects them, so your interview will increase in significance if you can establish its relevance to your listeners/viewers. One simple way of doing this is to ask the guest early in the session why the issue is important.

Concerning Your Questions and Commentary

22. *Write out, or at least make notes on, your introduction and your conclusion.* Writing or outlining the beginning and ending of your interview will free you during air time to focus on the body of your interview. A word of warning, however: you must be able to read your opening and closing in a totally conversational manner or the shift from reading to ad-lib speaking will be quite noticeable. Your conclusion should, in most instances, include a summary of important or interesting information revealed during the interview; this cannot, of course, be written in advance, but your prepared conclusion might indicate at what point you will ad-lib your summary.

23. *If you do plan your interview and establish its length, build it toward a high point or climax.* Hold back an especially important question for the end of the interview. If your skill allows you to lead up to that question, so much the better.

24. *Plan at least a few questions to get the interview started and to fill awkward gaps.* Few sights are more pathetic than an interviewer at a loss for a question. (But consider the next point, too.)

25. *In general, base questions on the guest's previous statements.* Do not hesitate to dispense with preplanned questions if more interesting

ones arise naturally from the discussion. The following dialogue is an exaggerated example of failure to switch to a new topic.

>ANNCR: Now, Mayor, your opponent has charged you with a willful and illegal conflict of interest in the city's purchase of the new park. What is your answer?
>
>MAYOR: Well, it hasn't been revealed yet, but I have evidence that my opponent is a parole violator from out of state who served five years as a common purse-snatcher.
>
>ANNCR: *The News-Democrat* claims to have copies of the deeds of sale and is ready to ask for your resignation. Will you tell us your side of the story on the park purchase?

Clinging to a preselected question when a far more interesting one clamors for recognition may result from insensitivity, rigidity, or inattention to your guest's answers. In assessing your taped practice interviews, watch carefully for moments when you tend to sacrifice common sense to a previously determined plan. Have a plan but do not be a slave to it.

26. *In particular, follow up on important contradictions.* Many public figures, especially politicians, make contradictory statements that can be developed into good dialogue. Be wary, however; if you perceive that your guest is going to be evasive, adopt another line of questioning. (And remember point 8.)

27. *Make logical, smooth transitions to new subjects.* Here is a bad example.

>ANNCR: You said a few moments ago that your most memorable experience was the time you nearly drowned. Are you into any other sports besides swimming?

28. *Always be ready with your next question,* but do not allow this to distract you from the comments your guest is making. Be prepared to alter your plan on the basis of an unexpected answer (see point 25), but don't be caught with no question at all in mind. The problem of thinking ahead to the next question without tuning out the present can be solved only with practice and experience.

29. *On television, check your notes openly, rather than furtively.*

"TEASE PHONERS" tells Fred (F), who is the host of this segment, to encourage viewers to call in with questions for the guest. The "BUMPER" is a graphic that billboards a feature of the next day's show, and it "bumps" the program to a commercial break. Two columns show the time of the show: "SEG" shows the time of each segment, and "CUM" shows the cumulative time of the program. "Renee" is the segment producer.

Segment Five reads as follows.

	SEGMENT FIVE (T I&I) MEG		
AREA 5	How Does Your Garden Grow?		
	Bert Bertolero––plants	6:00	43:40
BUMPER	STILL––Famous Amos		
COMMERCIAL FIVE		2:10	45:50

"T" refers to Terry Lowry, and "I&I" means introduce and interview. "Meg" is the segment producer.

The program format ends as follows.

AREA 13	CLOSE/BB (T & F)	CHYR # 38	1:45
	STILL––Tom––Child Support	39	
	STILL––Tom––Zia	34	
	STILL––Tom––Billy Eckstine	35	
	STILL––Tom––Geo. Plimpton		
	VT––Fairmont/Maxwell		
	STILL––Boulangerie		

"CLOSE/BB (T & F)" means that Terry and Fred close the program by billboarding the next day's show. "CHYR," followed by a number, indicates that a character generator superimposes the billboard information. (CHYR is an abbreviation of *Chyron*, the brand name of this equipment.) "Tom" means tomorrow. "VT—Fairmont/Maxwell" indicates that a videotape of a local hotel and a restaurant are shown, with a voice-over indication that guests are accommodated by these establishments. "STILL—Boulangerie" indicates that a local bakery supplied food for the program.

Practice: Interviewing

It should be apparent that interviews serve several different ends. The exercises that follow cover interviewing for talk show programs and person-in-the-street features. The practice section following the chapter on radio news suggests interviews for news packages and documentaries.

Before beginning any interview, decide on its purpose, for this will tell you the general approach to be taken (guarded or open, light or somber), the general length of the interview, and whether you should stay with one topic or go into two or more areas of discussion. Generally speaking, multiple-subject interviews are appropriate when your guest is a many-faceted celebrity who can talk on several subjects; single-subject interviews are proper when your guest is a specialist in some area, such as pediatrics, investments, or gardening. Single-subject interviews are mandatory when doing person-on-the-street interviews, as well as when conducting interviews for later use in a documentary.

Like most other exercises in this book, those that follow are designed for the simplest possible production: the use of a portable audio recorder. Any of these exercises can be adapted to studio or field television production.

1. For a multiple-subject interview, select a person whom you believe to be unusually interesting. In general, it is better to avoid interviewing close friends and family members. There is a quality of freshness and genuine interest on your part when interviewing people not well known to you, which cannot be simulated when you know the answers to the questions you are asking. Make sure you do some research about your guest so that you have at least a general idea of what there is to be discovered and discussed. Notes on areas to be explored are almost a necessity for this type of interview. Plan to interview without stopping your tape recorder for at least ten, and preferably twenty, minutes.

2. For a single-subject interview, choose a specialist whose field is of great interest to you, and interview at length without significantly changing the subject. A list of possible questions should help keep you on course.

3. Choose a topic, and conduct person-in-the-street interviews. (Stations continue to refer to these as MOS—man-on-the-street interviews.) A few suggested topics: "What is the most useless gadget on the market?" "What job would you most like to have?" "What is the worst advice you've ever received?" "Have you ever been fired from a job?" Of course you can also obtain samples of public opinion by asking more serious questions, such as probing people's feelings about an item in the news. Editing the responses and organizing them into packages, with appropriate opening and closing remarks, will complete this exercise.

4. Occasionally, it is useful to conduct an interview with all or most questions written in advance. Such an occasion would arise, for example, when you want to pin down an interviewee to answering a string of precisely worded questions:

"Why did you vote against the treaty?"

"Last May, in your Tulsa speech, did you not say that you favored the treaty?"

"On May 20th, the Tulsa *Record* printed this quote: 'I fully support the administration, and therefore I support the proposed treaty.' Do you still maintain that you never expressed support for the treaty?"

"A quote from the Dallas *Advance,* dated May 30th: 'Senator James stated that, while he had some minor reservations about the treaty, he would support it when it came to a vote.' Did the *Advance* also misquote you?"

Select an interviewee and a topic that lend themselves to a scripted approach and practice this unusual, but sometimes very effective, interview technique.

11
RADIO NEWS

News on radio ranges from brief hourly summaries to in-depth coverage around the clock. At many popular music stations, reports are taken directly from a teleprinter and are read without editing. *Rip-and-read* operations require considerable skill in sight reading, but they do not require the services of a qualified journalist. This chapter is devoted to a discussion of news operations at radio stations where news is taken seriously and where specialized news personnel are employed full time.

Nearly every market now has, or can receive signals from, one or more radio stations that feature news. Some of these stations are all news, some provide news during morning and evening drive times, and some give hourly reports researched and written by a news staff. All these news operations rely to some extent on news from wire services, on audio feeds from UPI, AP, private services, and a parent network, as well as on stories that are paraphrased from local newspapers. At the same time, the most important effort of any station that takes news seriously is that made by field reporters, writers, and anchors.

So-called all-news stations, such as those owned and operated by CBS, offer far more than news. Typical features are stock market and other business reports, sports reports, gardening tips, theater and movie reviews, traffic information, and a community billboard. Some stations also feature hour-long special-interest programs, such as cooking programs featuring local chefs, or a call-for-action consumer complaint program. Some features are performed by station news personnel, and others present outside specialists. As an announcer on a news-oriented station, you might find yourself working in the field, collecting news reports and telephoning them in; you may spend your time in a newsroom and an on-air studio, first writing the news and then delivering it; or you might read news stories written by others and spend several hours of your workday preparing short, recorded features for play during other newscasters' shifts.

As a field reporter, you might spend four hours a day in the field gathering, recording, and phoning in reports and the remainder of your working day at the station, obtaining telephone interviews and editing, writing, and carting them for use by on-air news anchors. As you read the ensuing text about the performance and production aspects of radio news at the local station level, keep in mind that only prosperous and well-staffed stations have the resources to provide the support indicated in the models that follow.

THE RADIO NEWS ANCHOR

At most news radio stations, newscasters prepare most of the copy they read. There are many advantages to this practice. First of all, if you write (or rewrite from wire-service copy) the script you are to read, it is most unlikely that it will contain the kinds of typographical errors that crop up regularly in wire copy. Second, in writing your copy, you gain familiarity with the story, and this will be reflected in better interpretation and clearer communication. Finally, writing your copy helps you develop into a reporter rather than a mere reader of words.

In preparing your script, you will probably work with a news editor. The editor determines what news stories will be broadcast and establishes their sequence. You will have access to a log that shows the sequence of the elements that will make up the newscast during your shift. Most all-news stations follow a cyclical format, repeated on an hourly basis. Typical is one that begins each hour with five or ten minutes of network news, provides world news headlines at the half-hour, and has features such as sports, weather, stock market quotations, and consumer reports at regularly established intervals. Commercials are scheduled at stipulated times and, on most stations, public-service announcements are run in any commercial slots that have not been sold—the purpose being to retain the integrity of the cyclical format. The log plus the material given you by the news editor will determine your task as you prepare for your air shift. In effect, your job is to fill the holes left between commercials, features, and other scheduled elements.

Most radio newscasters and reporters are successful because, in addition to other skills, they have good news judgment. As you face the task of writing and assembling materials for a radio newscast, you can expect to be backed up by the following services.

1. *Audio reports, both live and taped, from station, field, and special assignment reporters.*

2. *AP and UPI news wires.* The Associated Press and United Press International provide similar news services, so a listing of services offered by the AP describes the kind of material available to you regardless of which service is subscribed to by your station. The Associated Press maintains an *A wire,* intended chiefly for newspapers but subscribed to by many radio and television stations. News is sent to stations by the AP through AP DataStream, from computer to computer at 1,200 words per minute. The Associated Press also offers AP NewsPower 1200, designed for radio stations. Again, stories are sent at 1,200 words per minute. News directors select categories of stories that interest them from a *menu,* a list of features such as state news, national news, international news, farm news, business stories, sports scores, sports stories, and weather reports. Features not chosen are not received. News stories in selected categories can be printed directly on paper or stored in a station's computer and printed after a decision has been made to use them. Through the use of the menu, rather different news stories will be received by an all-news station, a rock station, and a classical music station.

Another feature of AP NewsPower (and UPI CustomNews Service) allows a station's news writer to summon up a story paragraph by paragraph. At the push of a button, the paragraph moves to the side of the video display terminal, permitting the operator to paraphrase it by typing the story on the unoccupied portion of the screen. The push of another button directs the computer to print the rewritten story.

A separate service, the AP Radio Wire, sends timely features throughout the year, including special reports on income tax tips, Valentine's day, Mother's and Father's days, the new television season, new automobiles, Thanksgiving day, and a year-end review.

The Associated Press also maintains a slow-speed broadcast wire that carries complete newscasts, developing news stories, bulletins, and 60- and 90-second features on such topics as consumerism, health and medicine, physical fitness, entertainment, and home computers.

3. *AP Network news feeds.* This audio service sends 150 or more taped news reports each day. These reports can be inserted into locally produced newscasts and thereby provide worldwide coverage to sta-

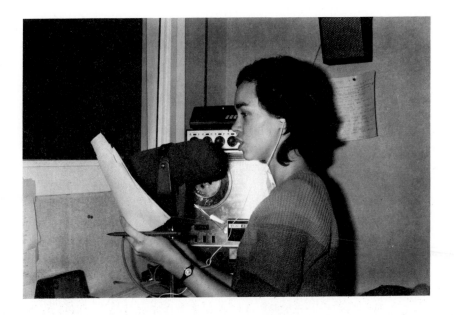

tions that cannot afford teams of correspondents. Other audio services
are provided by *chains*—groups of stations owned by one company—
and by major networks.

4. *A city wire service.* In some markets, the major news services supervise the city wire; in others, it is independently owned and operated.

5. *Interviews or news reports received by telephone.*

6. Depending on the orientation of your station, you may receive both
wire copy and voiced news reports in the Spanish language, or you may
subscribe to *Black Network News.*

   Stories from the wire services leave you four options: to read the
story as you find it; to leave the story without alteration but add a lead-
in of your own; to edit the story to shorten it, sharpen it, or give it a
local angle; or to completely rewrite the story. Whatever you decide,
the story must be properly entered in the running sequence of the
newscast. At some stations, this means making a copy for the engineer
and adding the original copy to a loose-leaf book from which you will
work while on the air. At most stations, engineers work only with the
log and ongoing directions of the anchor.

When preparing for a news shift that will keep you on the air for two hours or more, it is common practice to write, rewrite, and assemble about an hour's worth of live copy; recorded material, features, and commercials constitute a good portion of that first hour on the air. While you are performing, a news writer will be writing and assembling material for the second and, at some stations, the third hour of your shift. If the station for which you work cannot afford news writers, you must prepare in advance for the total amount of time you will be on the air. If timeliness and the constant updating of stories are important in a radio news program, then the preparation in advance of as much as three hours of news is obviously regrettable.

The check list prepared for you by the editor will include the stories to be featured, the order in which they should be given, and the sounds with which you will work. *Sounds* refers to *actualities, wraps, voicers, sceners,* and *raw sound. Sounds* are distinct from *sounders,* short music IDs or logos that identify a particular feature such as traffic or sports reports. An *actuality* is a brief statement made by someone other than station personnel—a newsmaker or an eyewitness—and it is recorded in the field or at the station over the telephone. A *wrap* begins with the voice of a reporter leading into an *actuality,* followed by the reporter's closing comments. The conclusion may be a brief summary, a commentary, or only the tag line. "Bill Hillman, KZZZ News." A *voicer* is a report from a field reporter, usually sent to the station by shortwave radio or by telephone. A *scener* is a report on a breaking event, and it usually is broadcast live. It also may be taped for incorporation into a later broadcast. *Raw sound* refers to news noise—protesters chanting or funeral music with no reporter commentary. Actualities and wraps need lead-ins and lead-outs, sometimes called *intros* and *outros.* During your preparation time for a shift as news anchor, you will have listened to the sounds with which you will work and written introductions and ending statements as appropriate.

In preparing lead-ins and lead-outs, you must follow established practice at your station. Slip-ups during preparation time almost inevitably lead to embarrassing mistakes during the shift. Practices vary from station to station, but you may expect something like the following.

First, either you will edit the actualities, voicers, sceners, and wraps with which you will work or they will have been edited by a field reporter, a news writer, or another newscaster. If your shift is during prime time (usually commuting times), you will probably edit your own tapes. If your shift is during off hours, as in the middle of the night or on the weekend, you will probably rely on tapes prepared by others because your shift will be longer and fewer station personnel will be on hand to help you prepare or furnish you with updated material.

Second, as you edit your tapes, you will usually have available the services of an engineer. Most tapes used in newscasts, aside from taped feature reports, are edited electronically rather than manually. As you listen to each tape, you will make decisions about the fifteen, thirty, or more seconds you would like to use on the newscast. Working with the engineer, you have the tape excerpts you intend to use dubbed to carts. One actuality or taped telephone interview often provides several sounds for a newscast. In your script, you will indicate the words that close each segment of the report so that both the engineer and the announcer who use the tapes will know the outcues. The following is an example of current practice in logging actualities:

ACTUALITY

RADIO NEWS ACTUALITY LOG   EDITOR: CLARK

STORY AND REPORTER: Forest fire, Clark

CART #	SUBJECT	TIME	END CUE
n—35	Mt. Sakea forest ranger James Cleary——fire has burned over 3,000 acres.	:16	"as of now."
n—99	No clear evidence as to cause. Arson not ruled out. Man seen leaving area at high speed in green sports car.	:11	"in a green sports car."
n—83	Should have it sur- rounded by tonight, and contained by midday to- morrow——depending on the weather.	:15	"a lot of tired fire- fighters will be able to go home."

This log shows that the editor (who was also the reporter) was able to edit out three brief actualities from one recorded telephone conversation with a forest ranger. The general nature of each actuality is given under "subject" to enable the person writing the lead-in and lead-out to identify its content, and the end cues are given so that the newscaster can pick up immediately when the carts end. When the precise end cue is spoken earlier in the actuality, the person preparing the log writes "double out" to indicate that fact. For example, if the words *as of now* had been used by the ranger twice in the first actuality, "double out" would have warned the newscaster against picking up the cue prematurely.

Most radio stations that feature news ask reporters to work the *beat check*. This refers to telephone calls to agencies and persons who are most likely to provide news items regularly. A typical beat list includes the names, phone numbers, and speakers for all nearby police, sheriff, disaster, fire, and weather departments; the FBI, the Secret Service, the Alcohol, Tobacco, and Firearms Bureau, civil defense headquarters, and the National Guard; local and nearby jails and prisons; all local hospitals; all nearby airport control towers; and specialized agencies important to listeners in your community (farm bureau, earthquake stations). In working the beat check (also called the *phone beat* or the *phone check*), plan to call each listed agency at the same time each day. Try to establish a personal relationship with the person who is the speaker for the agency. Discover how each speaker prefers to work with you—whether you are allowed to tape the conversation or are permitted only to paraphrase statements. If it fits the news report, give credit to the people who supply your station with news items; most people are pleased to hear their names on the air, but you must respect requests for anonymity.

A related assignment for newsroom personnel is taping recorded messages prepared daily by a variety of government agencies. By telephoning Washington, D.C., you can record three-minute feeds from agencies such as the Department of Agriculture, NASA, and both houses of Congress. Similar services are offered by the U.S. Chamber of Commerce. These sources, of course, have their own purposes to serve, and controversial information should be checked against other sources.

Writing

As a radio journalist, you will be expected to write well and rapidly. To help you develop the necessary writing skills, Chet Casselman, long a news director and formerly national president of the Radio and Television News Directors Association, offers these guidelines. They are for the most part equally applicable to writing news for television.

1. *Write for the ear rather than the eye.* Your audience does not see the script; it only hears it. Sentences should be relatively short, the vocabulary should be geared to a heterogeneous audience, and potentially confusing statistics should be simplified. Specifically,

   a. say it the simple way. Eliminate unnecessary ages, middle initials, addresses, occupations, unfamiliar or obscure names, precise or involved numbers, incidental information, and anything else that slows down or clutters up the story.

b. convert precise or involved numbers to a simplified form. Unless the number is an essential part of the story, it should be dropped. Change a number such as 1,572 to "fifteen hundred," 2.6 million to "slightly more than two-and-a-half million," and 35.7 percent to "nearly 36 percent."

c. express names of famous people and their relatives carefully to avoid confusion. For instance, "Mary Nolan is dead in Chicago at the age of sixty-seven; she was the wife of the famous architect Sydney Nolan" is much clearer than "Mary Nolan, sixty-seven, wife of famous architect Sydney Nolan, died today in Chicago."

d. avoid indiscriminate use of personal pronouns. Repeat the name of the person in the story rather than using "he," "she," or "they" if there is the slightest chance that the reference may be misunderstood.

e. report that a person pleads "innocent" rather than "not guilty." The latter may be too easily misunderstood as its opposite.

f. avoid "Latter," "former," and "respectively," which are excellent print words but should not be used on the air because the listener has no way of referring to the original comment.

g. avoid hackneyed expressions common to newscasts but seldom heard in everyday conversation. Say "run" instead of "flee," "looking for" instead of "seeking," and "killed" or "murdered" instead of "slain."

h. change direct quotations from first person to third person whenever the change will help the listener understand. It is clearer to say, "The mayor says she's going to get to the bottom of the matter" than to say, "The mayor says, and these are her words, 'I'm going to get to the bottom of the matter,' end of quote."

i. always use contractions, unless the two words are needed for emphasis.

A simple and excellent method of checking the clarity of your broadcast news writing has been developed by Irving Fang, who calls his method the easy listening formula (ELF). It is applied as follows: "*In any sentence, count each syllable above one per word.* For example, 'The quick brown fox jumped over the lazy dog' has an ELF score of 2—1 for the second syllable in 'over,' 1 for the second syllable in 'lazy.' " To find your total ELF score, compute the ELF scores of all sentences in your news script and average them. Fang's investigation of a wide variety of broadcast news scripts showed that the ELF scores of the most highly rated news writers average less than twelve. If your sentences are consistently above that figure, chances are that you are not writing well for aural comprehension. Fang points out, however, that no mechanical system of measuring language is infallible. Common sense must be applied at all times in using his formula because "it is easy to devise a confusing sentence with a low ELF score, just as it is easy to devise a simple sentence with a high ELF score. . . . What the Easy Listening Formula shows is tendency and trend."[1]

2. *Avoid confusing words and statements.* The following lead to a news story is seriously misleading: "We have good news tonight for some veterans and their families. A House committee has approved a 6 percent cost-of-living increase." People unfamiliar with the legislative process might assume that the money was as good as in the bank. Confusion can also arise from using a word pronounced the same as a quite different word—for example, "expatriate" might easily be interpreted by a listener as "ex-patriot," with embarrassing consequences.

3. *Avoid excessive redundancy.* Repeating salient facts is advisable, but too frequent repetition is dull. As a bad example, a newscaster might say, "Senator Muncey has called the recent hike in the prime lending rate outrageous," and then we might go to an actuality in which we hear the senator say, "The latest hike in the prime lending rate is, in my opinion, outrageous." Work always for lead-ins that promote interest yet do not duplicate the story to follow.

4. *Use the present tense.* Because the electronic media can report events as they happen, the present tense is appropriate. It automatically gives the news an air of immediacy.

5. *Avoid initials.* Use them only when they are so well known that no ambiguity is possible. A few standard abbreviations are sufficiently well known as to be usable on broadcasts—FBI, US, YMCA, CIA—but most abbreviations should be replaced with a recognizable title, followed later in the story with a qualifying phrase such as "the teachers' association" or "the service group."

6. *Do not give addresses on the air.* You may give them if they are famous or essential to the story. "Ten Downing Street," the home of the British

---

[1] Irving E. Fang, "The Easy Listening Formula," *Journal of Broadcasting*, vol. 11 (Winter 1967), pp. 65, 67.

prime minister, is a safe address to broadcast. The address of a murder suspect or an assault victim is not.

7. *Be careful to use official job descriptions.* Use "fire fighters," "police officers," "mail carriers," and "stevedores" rather than "firemen," "policemen," "mailmen," and "longshoremen." (See Chapter 8.)

8. *Be wary of badly cast sentences.* An example from a wire-service bulletin shows the peril of careless writing: "DETECTIVES FOUND 2½ POUNDS OF ORIENTAL AND MEXICAN HEROIN IN A LARGE WOMAN'S HANDBAG WHEN THE CAR WAS STOPPED IN SOUTH CENTRAL LOS ANGELES." Listeners probably missed the next two news items while trying to decide whether the heroin was found in the handbag of a large woman or in a woman's large handbag.

9. *When referring to yourself, say "I," not "we."*

10. *Do not refer to a suspect's past criminal record.* Also do not refer to any history of mental illness or treatment unless the information is essential to the story and has been checked for accuracy. Not only may the reporting of such information be defamatory, but it may also prejudice the public against a person accused of, but not tried and convicted for, a crime.

Timing

In preparing copy for your newscast, you must have an accurate idea of the number of lines or pages you will read in the allotted time. Time yourself as you read aloud at your most comfortable and effective speed. Determine how many words a minute you average, and use the following chart to judge the approximate number of words you will need for five-minute and fifteen-minute newscasts.

| | NUMBER OF WORDS | |
READING RATE	4:30 NEWSCAST	14:30 NEWSCAST
160 wpm	720	2320
165 wpm	743	2393
170 wpm	765	2465
175 wpm	788	2538
180 wpm	810	2610
185 wpm	833	2683
190 wpm	855	2755
195 wpm	878	2828
200 wpm	900	2900

Wire-service copy is fairly consistent in averaging a certain number of words per line. To use the time chart, count the number of words in ten lines of wire-service copy and divide by ten; this will give you a rough average for the copy with which you will work. If the copy averages 11 words per line and if you read at a rate of 180 words per minute, then you will read approximately 16½ lines each minute. Of course, the time chart is useful only for developing a sense of the relation between space (the physical copy) and time (the newscast). Seasoned reporters have so developed this sense that they can prepare newscasts without conscious thought of lines per minute or of their reading speed. As you work with the time chart, remember that actualities, commercials, and sounds—as well as your desire to vary your pace of reading to match the moods of the stories—will complicate your timing.

Anchor Performance

Once you have written and rewritten the copy you will use during your air shift and once the sounds have been assembled, logged, and delivered to the engineer, you are ready to go on the air. As you sit in the on-air studio, you will have before you the following items:

1. The running log, which follows the established format of your station and indicates the times at which you will give headlines, features, time checks, commercials, and other newscast elements or the times at which they will be played by the engineer.
2. The continuity book, which contains any commercial copy you will read live, as well as notations of recorded commercials to be played by the engineer.
3. Your news script, which will probably be loose-leaf rather than in a ring binder.
4. An elapsed-time clock you can start and stop, to help you time the commercials you will read.
5. Switches or buttons that allow you to open and close your announce mic, to open and close the intercom or talkback mic, and to open a mic in the newsroom for feeding out a news bulletin.
6. One or more lights used to communicate information to you while you are on the air. (For example, a red light might be used to indicate that the newsroom has a bulletin it would like to read. A yellow light might be used to tell you that the station's traffic reporter has a traffic alert.)

The on-air studio will probably be equipped with a comfortable chair without arm rests to restrict your movement and with castered legs that enable you to scoot in and out or from side to side with little effort. The chair may be designed to promote good posture, but no chair alone can make anyone sit up straight. The quality of your voice is directly affected by your posture; remember to sit comfortably, but try to keep your spine as straight as possible. A slumping person cannot breathe correctly, and weakened abdominal muscles and diaphragm cannot push air from your lungs through your phonators and articulators with optimum strength or quality.

Position yourself so that you can observe the engineer and so that you can easily reach the script, the continuity book, and the controls of both the elapsed-time clock and your mic. You will be checking off on the log commercials, PSAs, and other program elements as they occur, so make sure that you are also in a position to reach the running log with your pencil. Unless you have an unusual voice or speech personality, you should position yourself about six to ten inches from the mic. If you experience problems with excessive sibilance or popping or if your voice sounds thin or strident, work with the engineer to find a better way of using your mic.

When you are on the air with the news, you are the anchor. This means that you coordinate the elements of the newscast and act as director. When it is time for a sounder or musical identification, you first give the hand signal for *cart* and then throw the cue for the musical introduction to the weather, the traffic report, or some other feature. The engineer, who has the log to work from, takes this and similar cues from you. At times you may be joined in the booth by a feature reporter, a field reporter who has returned from the scene of a news event, or a second newscaster who will alternate with you in the reading of news stories; at such times, the second announcer will take cues from you.

Most news announcers read copy at about 175 to 200 words a minute. This is considered fast enough to communicate the appropriate degree of importance to what you are reading, yet slow enough to be easily understood. When you read news for a station that features news infrequently and briefly, you may be requested to read at a much faster rate. The overall sound of the station will determine this. To prepare for all eventualities, you should practice reading news in at least four different ways: (1) Practice reading the news slowly and casually, as is preferred by many low-key stations. (2) Read the news at the rate you feel brings out the best in your voice, interpretive abilities, and personality. (3) Practice at a rate of approximately 200 words a minute; this rate will probably be expected of you. (4) Practice reading at your absolute maximum rate, with the understanding, of course, that you are reading too fast if you stumble, have trouble maintaining controlled breathing, have forced your voice into stridency, or have lost significant comprehensibility.

As you read, be prepared for mistakes you may make from misreading or stumbling over words, introducing the wrong cart, or cuing prematurely. Some argue that mistakes should be covered up rather than acknowledged, but the best contemporary practice is to acknowledge mistakes as frankly but unobtrusively as possible. Here are two examples of weak cover-ups:

ANNCR: and they'll have your car ready in a half-hour—or an hour and a half, whichever comes sooner.

The script said "in an hour and a half." The cover-up is inappropriate because it gives false information.

ANNCR: The press secretary delayed and relayed the president's statement on the meeting.

Here the cover-up is so obvious that it would have been far better to have said "The press secretary delayed—sorry, *relayed*—the president's. . . ."

When giving cues to the engineer or to a co-anchor, stop talking after throwing the cue; if you ramble on, you will talk over someone else's opening words. No well-run station will tolerate such sloppiness. In throwing cues, do not think it is amateurish to make your gestures big, clean, and precise. The best professionals never lapse into practices detrimental to the program or their own performance.

You will be handling a great deal of paper during your air shift, so develop skill in shifting papers without allowing the sound of rattling paper to enter your mic. Your chief paper movements will be to lift script pages from the pile in front of you, to move them to one side, and to turn script pages in the continuity book. No materials should be stapled together; there should be no need to turn over pages while on the air.

There will be many times during a normal shift when you will have an opportunity to talk directly with your engineer: during the playing of taped materials or while the network news is being broadcast. Use these opportunities wisely but not too often; it is important to know what your audience is hearing at such times. Check details that might prevent errors; tell the engineer that you are going to shorten or dump a story because you are running late, or ask, in case of doubt, what the next sound is to be. Try at all times to know what is going out over the air. More than one announcer has followed a tragic actuality with an inappropriate wisecrack. Then, too, there is the possibility that the wrong cart has been played. If neither you nor your engineer is listening, you cannot possibly correct the mistake.

Be prepared to make important use of the minutes you have during your shift when are not actually on the air. During breaks thirty to sixty seconds long, bring your logging up to date; check out the next few sounds you will introduce or cue; go over the next commercial you will read and make mental notes about its style, content, and the speed with which you will read it; see whether you are running ahead of, behind, or right on schedule. During longer breaks, you may have to write intros for new actualities or voicers that have been received and edited while you were on the air.

Two-hour and three-hour shifts are not uncommon with stations that feature news. It takes a healthy speech mechanism to continue to perform well day after day. You will very quickly become aware of any misuse of your vocal apparatus because you will suffer from hoarseness, sore throats, or similar afflictions. Obviously, symptoms should be checked out by a doctor. Long before you apply for a position as a newscaster, you should practice performing as you will be expected to perform on the job, not only learning to work with all the elements of a contemporary newscast but also reading the news for extended periods of time. Such practice cannot ordinarily be accomplished in a classroom, and you are encouraged to look for opportunities to perform wherever they present themselves. College radio stations offer realistic challenges to students preparing for careers as radio news personnel.

THE RADIO FIELD REPORTER

Field reporters are responsible for (1) live coverage of events as they occur; (2) taped actualities, voicers, and wraps; and (3) occasional research and production of *minidocs*, a series of brief documentaries, usually broadcast over several days. Field reporters are sometimes called general-assignment reporters, correspondents, or special-assignment reporters. Their work is similar to that of television reporters, with obvious variations dictated by differences in electronic technology.

Live Reporting

It is the live reporter's responsibility to create a *word picture* of a scene, including sights, sounds, smells, tension in the air, and factual details—for example, the extent of a blaze, the names of the victims, or the value of stolen goods.

When reporting live, you most likely will have a portable shortwave radio, either in a small suitcase or in a station-supplied automobile. You use the shortwave radio to indicate when you are ready to give your report, and you hear your cue to begin as the program line is fed back to you on the radio. Even when you are describing events as they occur (a live scener, as opposed to reporting at the conclusion of an event) you may work from notes that you scribbled as you collected information. As you give your report, keep these suggestions in mind:

1. Do not report rumors, unless they are essential to the story, and then report them as only *rumors*.
2. Do not make unsubstantiated guesses as to numbers of injured, or value of a gutted building.
3. Control your emotions, even though a *bit* of genuine excitement in your voice will enhance the significance of your report.
4. Do not identify yourself at the start of the report because this will have been done by the anchor. Do identify yourself at the close of the story, following the policy set down by your station.
5. In the event of physical danger—a police siege or a confrontation between rival groups—do not become so absorbed in your story that you endanger yourself or your station's equipment.
6. Be prepared to discuss the event with the anchor. This means doing sufficient investigation prior to going on the air so that you are able to answer questions.

Voicers, Actualities, Sceners, and Wraps

Most of your work as a field reporter will culminate not in live reports but in the making of packages—wraps, voicers, and edited sceners. When recording in the field, you will use a cassette tape recorder; when making packages at the station, the engineer will record on one-quarter-inch tape. After editing, if editing is necessary, the tape will be

FIGURE 11.3
The Marantz PMD201
portable cassette re-
corder. (Courtesy
Marantz)

dubbed to one or more tape cartridges. These will become *sounds* introduced by news anchors during their shifts.

Field voicers are transmitted to the station by shortwave radio or by telephone. After making notes or, on occasion, a complete script, you notify the station engineer that you are ready to file a report. The engineer either cues up a reel-to-reel tape or inserts a cart into a cart recorder and places the index finger on the start button. You give a brief countdown—"three, two, one"—and start your report; the engineer starts the tape just after hearing "one," and if all goes well the tape and your voice begin at the same time. Voicers made at the station are produced in the same way, although you most likely will work in a small announce booth and have eye contact with the engineer.

Some field reporters must use a telephone to send in field voicers. If you are reporting live, the station engineer simply directs your voice to the transmitter. The process becomes more complicated when you are sending a report that you have previously recorded. Your recorded material may be of two kinds: complete reports that you have recorded at the scene of a news event or recorded statements made by nonstation personnel. The recorded report is a *voicer,* and the second, when you give it a lead-in and a lead-out, is a *wrap.* To phone in the voicer, follow these steps:

1. Cue up the cassette.
2. Plug your microphone into the recorder with the mic switch on.

3. Depress the "record" key. This activates the recorder as a transmitting device, but the tape will not roll because you have not also depressed the "play" key.

4. Insert a cable plug into the jack of the recorder labeled "out" or "aux." The other end of the cable has two alligator clips, and these are connected to the two wire terminals of a telephone. The wire terminals are exposed by removing the mouthpiece cover and the small telephone transmitter.

5. Dial the station engineer and, using your microphone to speak and the telephone earpiece to listen, tell the engineer that you have a voicer to deliver. When the engineer is ready, count down "three, two, one" and begin playing your taped report by hitting the play key. This automatically releases the record key, so the tape rolls and plays without danger of being erased.

A wrap follows much the same procedure, except for the following difference. When all elements are connected, your tape is cued, your mic switch is on, and the record key is depressed, you give the countdown and you begin your report live. When you finish your introduction to the actuality, you depress the play key and the tape rolls. When the actuality is completed you hit the record key; this cancels the play key, so the tape stops rolling while you give your closing tag live.

To use these procedures for phoning in voicers and wraps, you must find a telephone with a removable mouthpiece. Most pay phones have permanently affixed mouthpieces, so office or home telephones must be found. As a last resort, you can send recorded messages to the station by holding the recorder up to the mouthpiece of any telephone. The quality is extremely poor, but an important story, if undeliverable by any other means, may justify this practice.

When possible, use your recorder even for phoning in reports that could be done without it. Sending a live telephone report through your recorder eliminates the small telephone microphone and thus improves audio quality. Some stations, because of either union regulations or station policy, require procedures at variance from those just described. Be prepared to adapt to the requirements of working situations that vary from the norm.

In making voicers at the station, you will first write a script. The log, then, will simply indicate "script attached," the duration of the voicer in seconds, and the end cue, which is always your name followed by the call letters of your station. In making wraps at the station, you begin by making and recording telephone calls. If there is a news story on an impending strike, for example, your phone calls may be to the union leader, the speaker for the company or agency being threatened, and a labor negotiator. From the telephone interviews you should be able to make several usable wraps, carted, timed, and ready to be logged.

Preparing Feature Reports: Minidocs

Many radio stations that emphasize news vary their programming by broadcasting feature reports or short documentaries. Reports often consist of a series of three- or four-minute programs. A series may include as few as three or as many as ten individual segments, each focusing on a different aspect of a common topic. Topics concern people, problems, events, or anything else that is of general interest but lacks the "hard news" character that warrants coverage on a regular newscast. News events frequently inspire feature reports, but such reports differ from news stories in that they provide much more detail, offer greater perspective, and often express a point of view.

Preparing a series of feature reports begins with the selection of a topic. Once you are assigned a topic, your responsibilities will include researching the subject, identifying and interviewing people who will contribute most of the information the public eventually will receive, editing and organizing the taped materials, writing the connective and interpretive narration, voicing the narration, and producing the final mixed versions of the program segments. The steps in creating a series are illustrated in the following example, and the series topic is rape.

1. *Researching the topic.* Your research plan is essential to success. Developing a personal system of research can save hours, reduce the possibility of mistakes, and result in a superior product.

You may want to begin your research in a library, but if your station subscribes to an on-line information service, you may be able to do all your preliminary research at its keyboard. One such system, Nexis, a subsidiary of Mead Data Central, encodes over 160 newspapers, nearly all popular magazines, government documents, encyclopaedias, and many other information sources. The system operates on the basis of key words. In researching rape, you would type that word on the keyboard; the display would then show how many stories are available. Because the number is staggering, you begin to narrow it down—by city or state, by age, by motive, by ethnic group, or by some other criterion. Eventually, you will make your selection of stories and activate a printer to produce hard copy.

If you must do your research at a library, start with the *Reader's Guide to Periodical Literature,* which will provide you a long list of recent stories on the subject of rape. *Facts on File* or a similar reference service will give you statistics. In a few hours you will have learned some of the basic facts and opinions about rape. You will have learned that rape is understood as being usually motivated by hostility rather than sex; that victims of rape are often treated worse than their attackers by the authorities and that many women therefore do not report sexual assaults; that important changes have recently been made in the laws relating to rape; that there are several national organizations devoted to problems caused by rape; and that there are a number of important procedures that should be followed by a victim of a rape assault. Another good starting point for your research is the telephone. Calls to women's shelters, police officials, rape crisis centers, and antirape organizations can provide you with much useful information.

2. *Outlining the series.* Having read several articles and compiled some basic statistics about rape, you are ready to make some tentative decisions about your series. You will decide that the topic is important and complex and that perhaps six or seven segments will be needed to cover it adequately. You may decide that your final segment will provide explicit information to help women cope with rapists. You may decide that the following people should be interviewed: a rape victim, a police officer specializing in the investigation of rape cases, a representative of Women Against Rape, an authority on the causes of rape, a prosecutor, a defense lawyer, a judge, and a convicted rapist. Others will be added to this list, but you now know the people you will need to match the following outline of segments:

Segment 1 Background for the series, basic facts about rape, statistics. Purpose of segment: to show that the problem is large and growing and that any woman can be a rape victim.

Segment 2 What a rape victim goes through. This segment is made up of edited comments made by a victim.

Segment 3 A police view of rape. This segment features the edited comments of a police officer.

Segment 4 The causes of rape. This features comments made by a psychiatrist or some other authority on the subject.

Segment 5 A rapist's view.

Segment 6 What society should do to discourage rape. This segment

is made up of suggestions offered by all persons interviewed for the series.

Segment 7   What women should know about rape. The speaker for
                   Women Against Rape and the police officer suggest dos
                   and don'ts for women who are assaulted.

3. *Interviewing.* All your interviews will be in the field, so this requires
a high-quality, lightweight, battery-operated tape recorder. It also requires a top-quality microphone; the microphones that come with even
the best cassette recorders are inadequate for your purposes. Your
station should supply you with a dynamic mic, but you may have to
prove your point with a demonstration of qualitative differences between microphones. Some unions will not allow you to purchase your
own microphones, but where there is no such prohibition, it is wise to
invest in equipment that will result in better performance. Always
retain, ready for use, the microphone that accompanies the cassette
recorder, however. Unlike most high-quality mics, it has an on-off
switch that can start and stop the tape. As you have seen, this is useful
when phoning in a voicer or a wrap from the field.

Before making dates for interviews, speak with the people you have
tentatively selected for the program. Tell them that you want ideas and

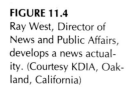

FIGURE 11.4
Ray West, Director of
News and Public Affairs,
develops a news actual-
ity. (Courtesy KDIA, Oak-
land, California)

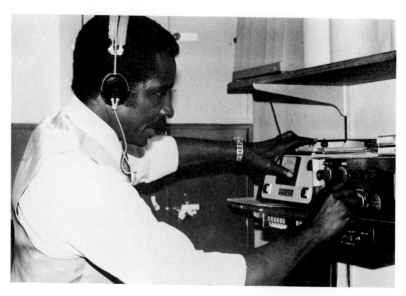

information, but do not invite them to be interviewed until you are satisfied that they are articulate, knowledgeable, and cooperative. You may find that you must look further for your talent.

Before each recording session, prepare a list of questions you want answered. Be as thorough as possible in your preparation, for the audio quality of your program will suffer if you must record the same person on two or more occasions or in different locations. Ambient noise and acoustics should be consistent within each of the program segments. Use your prepared questions, but do not be a slave to them. In addition to the tips on interviewing given in Chapter 10, here are some suggestions for recording material for feature reports.

1. *Test your equipment before beginning the interview, no matter how experienced you are.* Even professionals sometimes complete interviews only to discover that their batteries were down, the machine was not recording, the volume level was too high or too low, or the absence of a windscreen on the mic when recording outdoors resulted in excessive wind blast. Try to test your equipment under the exact conditions and in the precise location of the interview.

2. *Take the time to explain taping and editing procedures to your guest.* It is important for your guest to know that all your comments and questions will be removed from the tape and replaced by narration recorded in the studio. This means that your guest should make direct, complete statements not preceded by references to the questions. To illustrate, here are two responses to the same question:

> ANNCR: Do you feel that there are adequate laws to protect women's rights in rape cases?
>
> ANSWER 1: Well, yes and no. It's all a matter of how they're enforced. And then, too, it varies around the country, and it depends on your social or economic position.
>
> ANSWER 2: There are adequate laws to protect women in rape cases, but they aren't enforced equally. Women who are rich or influential get better treatment than those who aren't.

It is obvious that the second answer will be easier to edit, will provide more precise information than the first answer, and will allow a smoother flow from narration to statement. You cannot expect the person you interview to overcome a lifetime of conversational habit, but you can expect reasonable cooperation. When interviewing a person who simply cannot make direct statements in response to your questions, allow your recorder to run and ask the person to repeat the statement, but this time begin with a paraphrase of the previous answer in the form of a statement.

3. *When you are ready to begin the interview, ask your guest to remain silent and then start recording.* Record about thirty seconds of dead air. This precaution provides you with ambient sound of the room for insertion at any point at which you want an undetectable pause. All rooms other than those designed for scientific tests have ambient noise, and no two rooms are alike. So begin your session with thirty seconds of insurance. You cannot splice in the ambient sound from another interview, and you certainly cannot splice in blank tape, for both would be noticeable to any attentive listener. It is likely that the ambient sounds you record will be needed only infrequently, but when such sound is needed you will be grateful for having developed the habit of recording dead sound before every interview. It is also good practice to allow the tape recorder to run for a few seconds after your guest has stopped speaking. Later, when you are editing and script writing, you may want to do a board fade at the end of one or another of your guest's comments. If you have abruptly stopped the recorder immediately upon the conclusion of your guest's remarks, there is no way to do a fade.

As you interview, avoid giving your guest *oral* reinforcement, such as "uh-huh," "I see," or "Wow!" Such expressions will be impossible to edit out when assembling the program. Nonverbal support— nods of the head, or smiles—is sufficient to encourage your guest to continue.

4. *During the interview, try to keep the recorder running.* Do not hesitate to stop it, however, if the session is going badly. The reason for an uninterrupted take is that most people are more alert and energized when they feel that what they are saying will be heard later on the air. Constant stopping and starting saps energy and reduces concentration. Because you will edit the tape, keep the following hazards in mind: (a) A ninety-minute interview later to be edited as part of a three-minute program segment will cost you hours of production time. Therefore, work for interviews long enough to supply you with the material you will need but not so long as to saddle you with hours of editing. (b) As you interview, keep the format of your station's feature

reports in mind. If, for example, your station prefers to use both your questions and your guest's answers on the final tape, your interviewing technique should reflect the fact. You will not then have to ask guests to answer your question in the form of statements. (c) Some people run words together so habitually and consistently that it is impossible to edit their comments effectively and efficiently. This is often not discovered until time for editing, and by then it is too late. It is possible to train yourself to detect this problem at the time of taping. When you hear that you are working with a slurrer and slider, do your best to slow that guest down. When this fails, ask the guest to repeat single phrases and sentences that seem to constitute the most important contributions you will later use in your report. (d) When recording at any location that has a high level of ambient sound (machinery, traffic, crowds) keep your mic close to your guest's mouth. Authentic background sounds can enhance the realism of your report, but they must not be so loud as to interfere with your guest's remarks. If you will later edit out your questions, you need not move the mic back and forth between you and your guest. If, on the other hand, you are to retain even some of your questions or comments, then you must develop skill in moving the mic. To avoid noise when using a hand-held mic, wrap the mic cord around your wrist. Handling noises are especially troublesome because they can be heard only on playback or by monitoring during the interview, a practice seldom engaged in by people working solo.

5. *After completing each interview, transfer it from cassette to a reel of quarter-inch audiotape.* Cassettes are fine for recording, but they are impossible to edit precisely. When you have finished dubbing the interview, you should make a rough electronically edited version of it by dubbing to a second reel-to-reel machine only those portions of the interview that will conceivably be used in the final report. The rough edit will give you a manageable amount of material with which to begin writing your report. You can, of course, do your rough editing directly from the cassette to the quarter-inch tape, but cassettes are extremely difficult to cue up. They give you only the roughest indication of where you are on the tape, and most cassette recorders are on only when the tape is running, meaning that a brief silence follows when you punch the play button. Because modern quarter-inch tape recorders lose almost no quality when speech is dubbed, you can easily go to three or four generations without detectable loss of quality.

6. *If time permits, make a typescript of the roughly edited interview.* Despite all that one may say about our being a postliterate society, the written word is far easier to identify, retrieve, manipulate, and edit than are words on an audiotape. You will next write a narrative script, so it will be easier to develop a smooth flow and precise lead-ins when working in print. Making a typescript may actually save time.

7. *Having completed the script, do the fine editing of the rough dub.* This should be done by manually cutting and splicing the tape. Electronic editing is done when you have little time to cut and splice, but it has serious drawbacks. Manual editing allows you to remove unwanted pauses, "ers" and "uhs," or even single words. It also allows you to take part of an answer from one part of the interview and join it to an answer from another. Naturally, such editing must preserve the sense of your guest's comments and must not be used for any purpose other than clarifying and strengthening your report.

When you cut your tape, you may find that some statements that looked good in the script do not come out well in sound. Be prepared, therefore, to go back to the roughly edited version to look for substitutes or to rewrite your script to make the points in a narrative manner.

As you cut and splice, leave dead air between all segments of the edited tape; this will make it extremely easy for your engineer to find and cue up each of the statements on the tape. Naturally, you should arrange the edited statements in the sequence in which they will occur in the completed production.

8. *Finally, record your narration.* Often, this means that you will sit in an announce booth or a small production room and do a "real time" recording, with an engineer alternately feeding your voice and the edited statements to a reel-to-reel tape recorder. It is possible for you to record all your narration without the edited inserts and to have an engineer later mix the entire report, but doing so wastes time and effort. It is also detrimental to your interpretation; despite all the wonders of tape editing, there is still something to be said for real-time radio—even when it is on tape.

Practice: Covering Radio News
The following suggestions are offered to assist you in practicing the varied assignments given to radio journalists.

FIGURE 11.5
News director Jeffrey Schaub reads the news from a news studio. (Courtesy KTIM-FM, San Rafael, California)

1. Cover news stories, including news conferences, with a portable cassette tape recorder; then create actualities and wraps with the recorded material. To do this, you must first dub the cassette tape to reel-to-reel tape because, as we have seen, cassettes are extremely difficult to cue up. Then follow the procedures described earlier in writing lead-ins and lead-outs and in logging each with cart identification and out-cues.

2. If telephone taping equipment is available, practice recording statements over the phone to be used as edited wraps.

3. Practice interviewing. It is an important part of all journalists' work.

4. In working with wire-service copy, practice reading five-minute summaries cold. Also practice rewriting wire-service news stories.

5. Practice reading commercials. Some station policies prevent news reporters from reading commercials; most do not.

6. Form a complete news team—including an anchor and co-anchors, field and general-assignment reporters, weather and sports reporters—and assemble and produce a complete news program. Work for split-second timing between news items, program segments, and commercials. Record voicers, wraps, and a range of musical IDs to headline sports news, a traffic alert, and similar features.

12
TELEVISION NEWS

News on television varies from brief voice-over-slide bulletins to the twenty-four-hour coverage of Cable News Network (CNN). Most television stations and networks produce between two and three news programs daily, some thirty minutes in length and some lasting an hour. Typical are news broadcasts at noon, at the dinner hour, and at ten or eleven at night. Except for the smallest local stations, most news departments are large in relation to the station's total employment. Departments range from twenty to more than one hundred employees. Television news programs are put together by reporters, anchors, news writers, videotape crews, mobile van operators, operators of special-effects generators and computer graphics systems, tape editors, and a production crew stationed in the studio, the control room, and the videotape room.

THE REPORTER

Journalists who work away from the station are called *field reporters*, *general-assignment reporters*, or *special-assignment reporters*. Reporters who are stationed at some distance are called *correspondents*. As a special-assignment reporter, you might cover a regular beat, such as crime, politics, or a particular section of a large city. Few stations can afford such specialists and prefer to put field reporters on special assignment from time to time.

As a field or general-assignment reporter, you will be given your daily schedule by an assignment editor. Some assignments will involve *hard news* events—fires, explosions, chemical contamination, tornadoes, and similar unanticipated events—while other assignments will be *soft news*. News departments maintain a *future file*, thirty-one folders (for the days of the month) into which is placed information about meetings, trials, briefings, hearings, news conferences, and

FIGURE 12.1
Field reporter Randy
Shandobil reporting live
from the scene of a fire.
(Courtesy KTVU, Oak-
land)

IN SAN FRANCISCO:
Randy Shandobil

other scheduled events. As notices of these events reach the station,
they are placed in the folder bearing the appropriate date. Each day,
the assignment editor searches the file for the most promising news
stories and schedules reporters and camera operators to cover them.
Scheduled meetings are often dropped at the last minute in favor of
late-breaking hard news events.

As a field reporter, you will work with an ENG (*electronic news gathering*) operator. When working with tape, you will have an opportunity
to plan your coverage, engage in on-site investigation, think through
and write your opening and closing *stand-ups,* and record a second or
third take if the first effort falls apart.[1] With live reporting by way of
microwave or satellite transmission, however, you will report events as
they are happening, and this precludes scriptwriting and reshooting.
The ability to ad-lib an unfolding news event in an accurate, effective
manner is the key to success with live ENG.

---

[1] A *stand-up* is an on-camera commentary from the reporter. Stand-ups may come at any
point in the story, but one always comes at the end as a tag.

Taped field reports, as well as live ENG stories, are often longer than similar stories prepared for radio newscasts. Television coverage is much more expensive than radio coverage, and technical complexities are greater. Hence you are expected to cover only one to three stories in a given workday. You must not assume that your field reports will dominate a newscast, however, for most stories from the field run only between thirty seconds and three minutes in length. To create a usable sixty-second report, you may have to spend several hours, both in the field and back at your station. Aside from travel time, time must be devoted to investigation of the story, lining up witnesses or others you may want to interview, conducting the interviews, making notes for your stand-up, and then taping the story.

Your job is usually not over when you have completed the field coverage. Although a messenger can return the tape to the station to be edited by an assistant producer, the customary practice is to have the reporter complete a package—a report that will need only a lead-in by a news anchor.

Preparing a Package on Tape[2]

Let's follow you, as the reporter, through the steps involved in making a news package. At the station, the assignment editor (the *desk*) gives you your day's assignment. If it is a slow news day, you may be given a soft news story to cover, and in this event you may be asked for ideas. On the other hand, if a lot of hard news is breaking, you can expect to be told what you are to cover. After receiving the assignment, you leave the station with an ENG operator. You may travel in a station wagon with sparse equipment, in a van that has equipment for viewing tapes on the return to the station, or a microwave or *uplink* truck that can send picture and sound back to the station. The *uplink* equipment bounces the program material off a satellite.

On arriving at the scene of the story, you undertake relevant research to learn what has happened, who is involved, what is going on at the moment, why the event is happening—in other words, the traditional *who, what, when, where,* and *why* of journalism. As you investigate, your ENG operator is setting up to tape whatever is pertinent to the story. In some instances, you ask the ENG operator to tape this or that person or object; in other instances, you rely on the professionalism of the operator to make sound judgments. As you gather

[2]This discussion is based on the practices of Wayne Freedman, feature reporter for KRON-TV.

FIGURE 12.6
Wayne Freedman makes notes prior to the recording of his stand-up. (Courtesy KRON-TV, San Francisco)

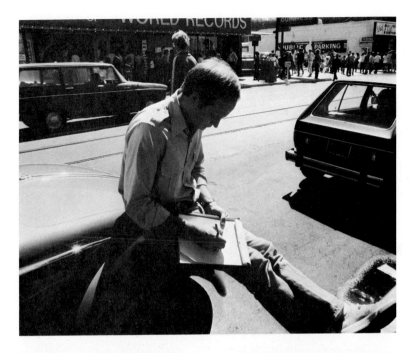

FIGURE 12.7
Wayne Freedman records his stand-up next to a statue of an old-time sea captain. (Courtesy KRON-TV, San Francisco)

SLUG	VIDEO	WRITER	TRT
DEMOLITION		FREEDMAN	2:47

WF CUT

It is the urban American way. Every

day we commute to the city, find our

little niche of office space . . .

and do something constructive.

SOT (#1; 11:18)

(SMASH INSIDE)

SOT (#1; 16:16)

IN: WELL, IT'S CONSTRUCTIVE

OUT: IN ANOTHER . . .

WF CUT

This is the Kodak Building . . . At

least, it used to be.

SOT (#1; 14:51)

(CRASH FROM EXTERIOR)

As you can see, the total running time of the package is two minutes and forty-seven seconds. The slug line is "demolition." This portion of the script shows two cuts featuring the reporter, and three sound-on-tape excerpts, two of a wrecker's ball smashing into the building, and one a sound bite, with in- and out-cues given. This is the kind of script you are to prepare for each package you produce.

Before leaving the scene of your report, ask your ENG operator to tape material to be used as *cutaway shots*. Cutaways are used to avoid a jump cut, as when editing an interview. During editing, you may want

FIGURE 12.8
News anchor Barbara
Simpson shares the
screen with a box graphic
that symbolizes the story
she is reporting. (Courtesy
KTVU, Oakland)

to cut some comments out of an interview in which the camera has been focussed on the speaker. By inserting a brief shot of yourself apparently listening to the speaker, when we return to the speaker for the remainder of the interview, your viewers will not be aware of a change in position of the speaker. To prepare for the anticipated need of cutaways, ask your ENG operator to tape you as you look into the camera lens and give slight nonverbal acknowledgement to the speaker's remarks. Cutaways are a form of insurance.

You work with the tape editor in the sound bay until the entire package is completed, with sound bites, cutaways, visuals and graphics prepared at the station, your on-camera stand-up closing comments, and your voice-over intros and transitions, dubbed to a single tape. When properly labeled, it is ready to be sent to the videotape room for later playing during the newscast.

A variation of the foregoing procedures is to perform all the steps taken to produce the package except for the stand-ups. After the package has been edited, you return to the scene of the story, where, during the newscast, you do a live introduction and close.

At a small television station, you may do your own camera work. You go to the scene of a story, conduct your investigation, and record sound bites, including interviews; before leaving the scene, you place the camera on a tripod, start the recorder, walk to a position in front of the camera lens, and do your stand-up. When you return to the station, you write the script and edit and assemble your package.

Reporting Live from the Field   Most television news operations make use of one or more remote vans equipped with ENG equipment: minicams (miniaturized cameras), portable tape recorders, microwave transmitters, and, at some stations, an uplink to a satellite. These vans are sometimes used for conventional coverage of a news story (covering and taping a report in the field), but their chief purpose is to enable reporters to cover and transmit their stories directly to the station, often live during a newscast. Only those reporters who are excellent journalists, have widespread knowledge of many subjects, and can ad-lib fluently and informatively are successful at live reporting.

First let's look at journalistic background. A study of journalism will prepare you to quickly size up a story, make judgments about its potential news value, identify the most salient points of the event, and organize the information for ready comprehension by the public. When you are covering slow-breaking stories (in fact, whenever time permits), a background in journalism will enable you to engage in investigative or depth reporting. Knowing how and where to look for hidden information is essential for depth reporting. Finally, journalism courses will teach you the laws regarding libel, contempt, constitutional guarantees, access to public records, the invasion of privacy, and copyrights. All reporters should be competent journalists, of course, but those who report the news live must be especially well prepared. If a defamatory statement is made on a live broadcast, there is simply no way to undo it.

A widespread knowledge of many subjects is also a prerequisite for reporters and, again, especially for those who report live. It is customary for anchors to end a live report with a question-and-answer session with the reporter. Your reports may vary from a demonstration at a nuclear power plant to the birth of a rare animal at the zoo. In a Q&A session, it is often necessary to speak knowledgeably about facts beyond the range of the story being reported. Blank looks, incorrect information, and the response "I don't know" are equally unacceptable. Reporters should have a broad liberal arts and sciences education

FIGURE 12.9
A miniaturized earphone, called an interrupted fold-back, or IFB. News anchors and reporters, as well as sports play-by-play announcers, receive cues and instructions over the IFB from a producer or a director. (Courtesy WBZ-TV, Boston. Photo by Sarah Hood.)

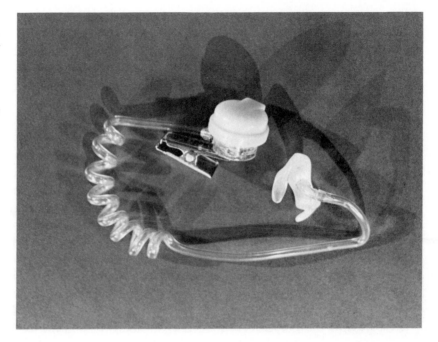

and should consider themselves life-long students. The reading of selected new books, several appropriate news magazines, and two or more daily papers should be routine preparation for your work as a reporter.

As a reporter going on live during a newscast, you must concentrate under pressure and sometimes confusion, and you must develop your ability to speak smoothly, coherently, and in an organized fashion. When reporting some stories, you will address the camera amidst high levels of ambient noise, you may be distracted by onlookers, and you may be in a position of danger. You will work without a script or a prompter, but you will hear the words of the director and anchor on an earpiece, an *IFB* (interrupted foldback).[4] You can expect to face an additional problem when your communication with the anchor is by way of a satellite. A delay of about one and one-half seconds occurs between the time the anchor speaks and the time you hear the anchor's voice. It is necessary to pick up cues as rapidly as possible to make the delay less noticeable. Unless special provisions are made, you can also

---

[4] *Foldback* is the term for an earphone system; *interrupted* indicates that with this system a producer or director can interrupt you with questions or instructions.

expect to hear your own voice coming back to your ear a second and a half after you have spoken. Engineers can *minus out* your voice, so that the anchor and the viewers hear your voice, but you do not. If no technical adjustment has been made to minus out your voice, you must develop the ability to give your reports despite the distraction of hearing your words on delay.

THE NEWS ANCHOR

To a news anchor, performance abilities are as important as journalistic skills. News directors look for anchors who are physically appealing (which need not be construed as handsome in the conventional sense), have pleasing voices, are skilled in interpreting copy, can work equally well with or without a prompting device, and can ad-lib smoothly and intelligently—as when questioning a reporter who has just delivered a report live. The chapters that discuss interviewing, voice and diction, principles of communication, and foreign pronunciation, together with the chapter on language, provide suggestions and exercises that will help you perform well as an anchor. The discussion of radio news, and especially the section on news writing, can be applied to the work of the television anchor. This chapter will not repeat those discussions but will concentrate, instead, on aspects of preparation and performance that are unique to television news anchors.

Working conditions vary from station to station, but at a typical medium-sized or large television station, you might find yourself (1) writing between 25% and 50% of the copy you read on the air, (2) covering some stories in the field, (3) preparing occasional feature reports, (4) working with a co-anchor as well as sports and weather reporters, (5) preparing and delivering two newscasts daily, five days a week, and (6) sitting with newsroom management as the final make-up and the running order of the newscasts are determined. As a novice anchor, you might combine some weekday field reporting or news writing with anchoring weekend newscasts.

Preparing the Newscast   As anchor, you will work with materials from a variety of sources: field reporters, news writers, wire-service agencies, a parent network, and even local newspapers. Final decisions on the content of newscasts rest with the news director—or, when delegated, with the news producer—but you are involved in nearly every step in the preparation of the newscast. You have been hired partly because of your journalistic judgment, so you keep abreast of developing stories. You check with reporters as they leave on assignment and as they

FIGURE 12.10
News anchor Bob Jiminez checks his script for words or names that may need to be transcribed into phonetics, and to mark the script for emphasis. (Courtesy KRON-TV, San Francisco)

return; you scan wire reports and a number of newspapers; you confer at regular intervals with your producer; and you view taped reports, both to determine their usability and to write lead-ins for those selected.

Your preparation is, in general, similar to that of a radio news anchor. Your script writing consists of writing lead-ins for packages, writing voice-over narration, writing straight news stories to be delivered without pictorial embellishment, and writing teases. A *tease* comes just before a commercial break and is designed to hold viewer interest by headlining a news item to be delivered after the break. A *toss* is a brief introduction to the weather or sports reporter, consumer affairs consultant, or other member of the news team. Tosses are indicated on your script, but they are delivered ad-lib. You toss the program to someone else merely by turning to that person and, in about five seconds, making a transition to the next program segment.

To give you an idea of what is expected of a television anchor, we will examine a typical day's preparation for a thirty-minute newscast. The composite picture reflects what you might expect if you

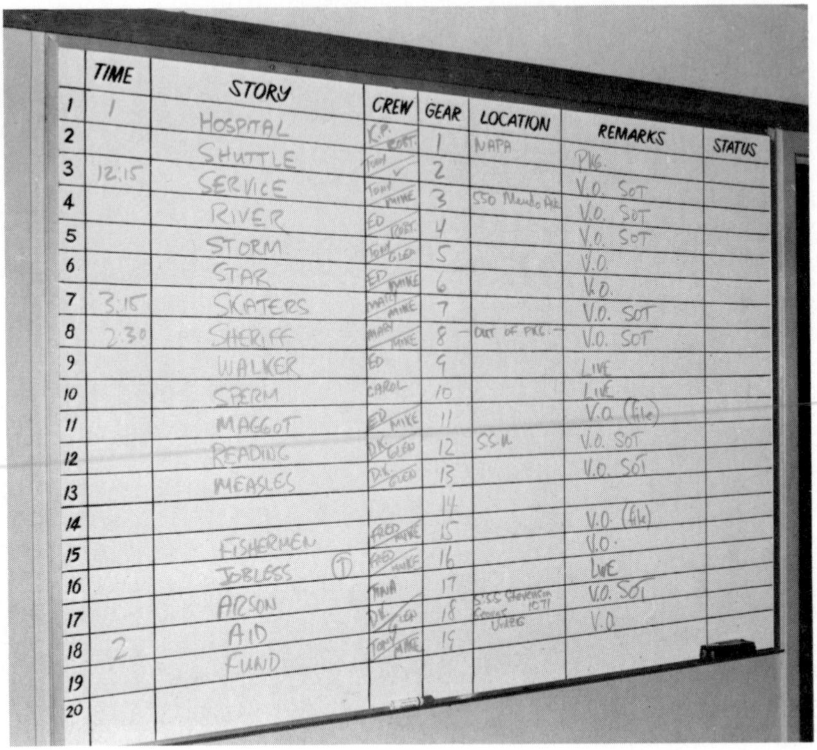

FIGURE 12.11
A typical "board" used in television newsrooms to outline and arrange the elements of the nightly newscast. (Courtesy KFTY, Santa Rosa)

work at a medium-sized or large station with a well-supported news department.

During the day you talk by phone three or four times with the news producer. When you arrive at the station, you will have about two hours to prepare for the newscast; it is imperative that you have an accurate idea throughout the day of the developments in news stories you will later be reporting. On the phone, the producer discusses with you the latest developments in a threatened strike by city bus drivers, a large drug arrest, a new police tactic in dealing with panhandlers, an escape from the women's jail, and an appeal for large quantities of blood for a child hemophiliac who will soon need an operation. As time goes by, it becomes obvious that the threatened bus drivers' strike will be the lead story. You place several calls from your home to union leaders, the city manager, the president of the board of supervisors, and a few bus drivers.

When you arrive at the station (at 3:00 P.M. to prepare for the 5:00 P.M. news), you already have a good idea of what will make up the newscast. The news producer gives you a run-down of the program, which is subject to change if late-breaking news demands it. The rundown sheet gives the running order of the show, item by item. It indicates which anchor is responsible for each report (where there are co-anchors); the running time of each segment; the visual source of each story, whether live, ENG on tape, or VTR (videotaped); the slug lines for each story; the initials of field reporters responsible for each story; and the placement of commercial breaks. As you write your copy, you may decide you need art work. As anchor, you sometimes have the responsibility of determining when a graphic aid is appropriate.

The ingredients for your newscast may originate from any of a number of sources: videotape from your ENG unit, live ENG, network videotape, UPI Unifax, live phoned-in beeper reports, or the in-studio report of a field reporter who has just returned from the scene of a developing news event. As anchor, you need to work effectively with all program inputs. At a few stations, to be sure, you are expected only to show up in time to apply your pancake make-up, insert your contact lenses, pick up your script, and spend the next half-hour playing the part of a broadcast journalist. But if you want something better for yourself and your viewers, preparation for a newscast demands that you be a journalist; that you know the technological possibilities and demands of your medium; that you be a strong writer; that you learn to cope with confusion and last-minute changes; that you learn to work with reporters, producers, assignment editors, directors, graphic artists, and members of the production staff; and that you develop your own style of performance.

In writing your share of the news script, you begin with the standard opening used by your station on all newscasts—for example, "These are the top stories this hour." The opening is followed by headlines of the major stories of the day.

In typing, you may use a special typewriter that features a *bulletin font*—oversized letters—or you may use a word processor with a video display terminal. Such computers are very flexible, and they make adding or dropping stories quite simple. They are equipped with a device for moving a wire-service story to the side or to the top of the screen, with room left for you to paraphrase the story in your own style. *Hard copy*—a printed script—is made by both electronic and nonelectronic machines. The script is printed on *copy sets*, prepared script forms of six or more sheets of paper, each of a different color. Later, when the entire script has been written, the sheets will be separated, and complete scripts will be given to you, your co-anchor, the

FIGURE 12.12
Meteorologist Mark Thompson stands before a blank chroma key screen. He points out temperatures and weather features by watching the weather map and himself on a hidden monitor. (Courtesy KRON-TV, San Francisco)

director, the prompter operator, the producer, and anyone else who needs to work from a script. Your script will feature pages in two colors: yellow for the words you will read and blue for the words read by your co-anchor. Most news scripts are typed in capital letters only, and the left side of the script is used for video information, the right side for audio. The video column is seldom marked by anyone other than the director, so you do not have to indicate the shots to be taken.

When writing teases, be sure to review the news item or feature being teased; viewers are resentful of teases that keep them watching yet do not live up to their advance billing. Viewers also resent teases if they feel that the *information,* rather than the *tease,* should have been given. Wouldn't anyone object to hearing "Another world leader was assassinated today—details at eleven"?

THE WEATHER REPORTER

Television has three primary ways of handling weather information in regularly scheduled newscasts. In one, most often used on small or low-budget stations, the anchor delivers the report. Larger stations retain a professional meteorologist who not only reports the weather

FIGURE 12.13
Home viewers see both
meteorologist Mark
Thompson and the
matted-in weather map.
(Courtesy KRON-TV, San
Francisco)

FIGURE 12.13
Home viewers see both meteorologist Mark Thompson and the matted-in weather map. (Courtesy KRON-TV, San Francisco)

but explains the causes of meteorological phenomena, subtly and continually educating the audience. Many meteorologists engage in television reporting as only one part of their professional careers. At some stations, a professional announcer who is not a trained meteorologist may become a specialist in weather reporting.

Nearly all television stations use chroma-keyed maps and satellite photos for weather information. The weather reporter stands before a large blank screen, usually of a medium shade of blue, and points out salient features of the day's weather by looking at an air monitor that carries a picture of the reporter and the weather map. In Figures 12.12 and 12.13, meteorologist Mark Thompson shows how this looks both in the studio and on the air.

Weather maps are stored in the station's computer. After determining weather patterns from the complex information sent by the U.S. Weather Bureau, the meteorologist goes to the art department and tells the operator where to place graphics showing weather fronts, storms, high and low temperatures, and similar information. The satellite photos are received directly from the U.S. satellite service and are stored in the computer until used.

FIGURE 12.14

Newsroom anchor Evan White interviews a representative of the Salvation Army about relief operations during a flood. (Courtesy KRON-TV, San Francisco)

As a weather reporter you may be asked to do special features from time to time. If there is a snowstorm of unusual proportions, if snow falls at a time of year when it is not expected, or if there is prolonged rain or drought, you may be asked to do street interviews to assess public opinion. In doing so, you follow essentially the same techniques as for any other interview of random passers-by, but unless the weather news is serious or tragic, you look for humorous or offbeat interviews.

When reporting the national weather, remember that most people do not really care about the weather other than where they are, where they may be traveling, or where they may have come from. Unless a weather report from two thousand miles away is unusual, it is not news at all. The people of Georgia may care nothing about the weather in Kansas, but they do care about the price of wheat and pork. Therefore, where it is possible, tie weather reports to something people care about. In other words, when reporting the weather from distant places, try to arouse interest by interpreting its significance.

It is obvious that weather is newsworthy when it is violent. Tornadoes, hurricanes, exceptional snowfalls, and floods need only be accurately reported to serve the interest of viewers and listeners. At the same time, slow-developing conditions brought on by weather, such as a two-year drought, must also be reported, and they cannot be adequately covered by a mere recitation of statistics. To serve your public, you must go beyond the kind of weather news traditionally offered by wire services. In a drought, for example, periodically record telephone interviews with a variety of experts on a range of drought-related problems. Ask a representative of the Audubon Society about the effects of the drought on birds in your area. Ask a fish and wildlife expert about the prospects for survival of fish and wild mammals. Ask the farm bureau about the effects on farming. Get drought information from professional gardeners and share plant-saving tips with your listeners. In short, use your imagination and constantly ask yourself these questions: Why should my listeners be interested in today's weather report? What am I telling them that will be of use? Too often, weather reports become routine recitations of fronts, temperatures, inches of precipitation, and predictions of things to come. Most viewers and listeners find this of some interest but, aside from frost, flood, or storm warnings, there is really nothing useful about the information. Always strive to make your weather reports *useful* to your audience.

PHILOSOPHIES OF BROADCAST JOURNALISM

To conclude these two chapters on radio and television news it is appropriate to include a few words about the special responsibilities of broadcast journalists.

As a broadcast journalist, you will make important decisions daily. Your means of reporting stories will influence the attitudes and actions of your listeners and viewers. For this reason, it is imperative that you develop a working philosophy of broadcast journalism.

In a free world, there really are only two theories of the press worthy of consideration. The first, the *libertarian theory,* is based on the belief that, aside from defamation, obscenity, or wartime sedition, there should be no censorship or suppression of news whatsoever. The second, called the *social responsibility theory* by Wilbur Schramm, maintains that journalists must exercise judgment as to whether a particular story should be covered or ignored and, if covered, how it will be covered.[5]

The libertarian theory grew out of democratic movements toward the end of the seventeenth century in England, and received renewed impetus a hundred years later through the writings and speeches of

[5] Wilbur Schramm, *Responsibility in Mass Communication,* Harper & Row, New York, 1957.

Thomas Paine, Thomas Jefferson, and other American revolutionaries. Essentially, the libertarian theory of the press was a response to centuries of suppression and censorship by church and state. Jefferson believed that the only security that a democratic people had is grounded in a fully informed electorate. "If a nation expects to be ignorant and free, in a state of civilization, it expects what never was and never will be," wrote Jefferson in 1816. The implications of this statement are clear: allow full and free publication of all shades of opinion and all items of information. The basic premise of the libertarians was (and is) that a free people in full possession of the facts will act responsibly.

The social responsibility theory of the press was a response to what many saw as shortcomings in the idealistic libertarian theory. In practice, the public simply was not receiving all of the facts necessary to make responsible judgments. In the wake of the civil disorders of the late 1960s, a Presidential commission called attention to what is perceived to be the failure of the press in adequately informing the public: "Disorders are only one aspect of the dilemmas and difficulties of race relations in America. In defining, explaining, and reporting this broader, more complex and ultimately far more fundamental subject, the communications media, ironically, have failed to communicate."[6] A libertarian defense of riot coverage was unacceptable to the Commission for several reasons: reported facts may have been exceptional rather than typical; disclosing some facts may have caused even more serious incidents; and, although the reported fact indeed may have happened, it may have occurred only because the news media were encouraging certain actions by their very presence. The social responsibility theory of the press asks that journalists report not only "the facts," but also the truth behind the facts.

The concerns expressed over a libertarian approach to journalism are understandable when one thinks of serious news events such as riots, wars, or insurrections. But the social responsibility theory demands that journalists apply their best judgment and weigh their conduct, on a daily basis, and regardless of the nature or scope of the story being covered. To practice journalism as a socially responsible person, good intentions are a starting point, but they are not enough. Only a solid education in broadcast and journalistic law, ethics, and investigative reporting can lead to your success as a responsible broadcast journalist.

[6] *Report of the National Advisory Commission on Civil Disorders,* Bantam, New York, 1968, pp. 382–383.

13
MUSIC ANNOUNCING

American radio is heavily oriented toward recorded popular music. There are more than 9,600 AM and FM radio stations in the United States, and approximately 7,000 of these are all-music or nearly all-music stations. The person who identifies the music and provides pertinent "chatter" on a popular music station is called a *disc jockey*, a *jock*, or a *DJ*. The term is not well chosen, and some who perform this function prefer to be called *personalities* or *on-air talent*, even though these terms refer to qualities and not to people. *Personage* is the correct term for which *personality* has been substituted, but it is unlikely that any announcer would want to be referred to as a *personage*. For better or for worse , the term *disc jockey* has been with us for many years, and it is sure to be around even when carted tapes have completely replaced discs. The term is used for a great range of announcing styles, from frenetic to casual, or laid back, but it is associated only with popular music. Announcers on classical music stations are not included under this term, even though their work has much in common with that of a disc jockey. This chapter discusses the work of both the radio disc jockey and the classical music announcer.

THE DISC JOCKEY

As a disc jockey, you can expect working conditions to vary widely from station to station. If you are talented and lucky enough to become a popular disc jockey on a prosperous major market station, your on-air hours will be few, and your salary will be in five or even six figures. If, on the other hand, you end up or begin at a small-market station or at a marginal station in a medium or large market, you can expect to be on the air four hours or more a day and to perform other duties for an additional four hours each day. In either situation your work will be demanding, because many hours a week of off-duty preparation are required for continued success.

At a small station, you may find yourself with an air shift of four

hours, with an additional four hours spent in selling time, writing commercials, producing commercials for local retailers, auditioning and selecting music, or reporting news and weather. You will work in a combination announce booth and control room, and you will perform the combined functions of announcer and engineer. This is called working *combo*. You will be responsible for preparing and delivering hourly five-minute newscasts; for selecting, pulling, playing, and refiling musical numbers; for finding and reading commercials and public-service announcements; for playing carted commercials and station IDs; for keeping both the program and engineering logs;[1] and, in some operations—especially on weekends and holidays—for answering the telephone. While doing all this, you are expected to be wise, witty, personable, and, at most stations, brimming with vitality.

If you watch a disc jockey at work as a combo operator, you will be immediately impressed with the skill that is required. Should you work combo at a station that plays records rather than carted music, a few minutes of your workday might be spent as follows:[2]

[1] The FCC no longer requires radio stations to keep program logs, but nearly all stations continue to log their offerings for billing purposes.
[2] Working with carted music greatly simplifies the work of the disc jockey.

FIGURE 13.2
This well-equipped and comfortable on-air studio features a BMX-III audio console and Tomcat cart machines. (Courtesy WYAY, Atlanta, and Pacific Recorders and Engineering Corporation)

3:00 P.M.   You read a five-minute newscast, complete with one live and one carted commercial. News is from a wire service and was selected, edited, and timed by you before the start of your shift at 3:00 P.M.

3:05:00   You introduce your first record cut. This, too, was chosen by you and cued up before the start of your shift. Start record.

3:08:50   You sight-read a thirty-second commercial for a local tire-recapping company.

3:09:20   You read several ten-second PSAs from file cards prepared by your public affairs director.

3:09:50   You introduce the next record, starting the disc so as to finish the intro just as the vocal comes in. Now, having run out of material prepared prior to your shift, you have approximately three and a half minutes (playing time of the record being broadcast) to find and cue up the next record. Check the copy book and the log to see which live and carted commercials are coming up. Make a reading and an entry in the engineering log, check the emergency broadcast system to make sure it is working, and make entries in the program log.

3:13:20   You play a carted commercial for a drug store and then
           headline some of the musical numbers coming up. You
           give the control room phone number so that requests
           may be phoned in, and you then read a commercial for
           a pizza parlor and start the next record. While this rec-
           ord is playing, you select and cue up the next one, look
           over copy for the next commercial to be delivered live,
           take two phone calls, and make a note of the selections
           requested.

3:16:00   You read the next commercial, play a carted commercial,
           and start the cued-up record. Now you have time to make
           several record selections, pulling from the record library
           those requested by callers, as well as choices of your own.
           You refile tape carts and records played so far and check
           the latest weather forecast so that you can give an ad-lib
           report when the record ends.

There are many variations of this demanding schedule. At some
stations, you would play two to four selections without interruption,
back announcing at the end of each *set*.[3] You might also spend relatively
more time reading and playing commercials, giving weather reports,
making announcements of concerts, and making brief humorous or
informational comments between numbers. Although the preceding
sixteen-minute work sequence had the disc jockey selecting records,
music directors, not DJs, at most major and secondary market stations
choose and schedule all music.[4]

Regardless of variations, the skills involved in the mechanical part of
disc jockey work can be acquired in a few weeks. The challenge is to
perform all of the collateral and routine duties well and to be energized
and articulate during the few minutes each hour when you are in direct
communication with your listeners.

As a disc jockey on a larger station, you will have some of the same
problems and challenges as your counterpart on a small station but,
generally speaking, you will have more help. Even though you are
very likely to work combo, all music selections will have been carted so
that turntable work will be unnecessary; a traffic department will have

---

[3] A *set* is two or more selections played back-to-back without interruption. Identifying
them at their conclusion is *back announcing*.

[4] A *major market* is one with a potential audience of over 1,000,000; a *secondary market* is
one of between 200,000 and 1,000,000 potential viewers; a *smaller market* has fewer than
200,000 potential listeners.

arranged your program log and your commercial copy in the most readily retrievable manner; and the days of six-hour shifts will be behind you. You are likely to have collateral duties with your daily two-hour or three-hour shift, and these may add up to a solid eight-hour workday.

Music stations range in music policy from those that play one narrowly defined type of music to those that play a broader spectrum of musical genres. Single-sound stations predominate. The style of music featured by a station is called its *format*. Single-sound music stations describe their formats in a number of ways. A country music station may call itself *bluegrass*, while a Black-oriented station may refer to its format as *urban contemporary*. A few stations have music policies that do not fit any standard format. These include *contemporary religious, gospel-inspirational*, and the even more unusual *country-Spanish*.

Formats of Popular Music Stations

Despite the many ways in which popular music stations describe their formats, most fit into one of eleven general categories, the twelfth being classical. The categories listed below are neither rigid nor unchanging. Nearly any type may be automated and may be in a market of any size; most types are heard on AM, AM stereo, and FM.

1. *Adult contemporary* or *A/C*. This type of station plays soft to moderate rock, ballads, and current hits by artists and groups such as Stevie Wonder, Sade, Sting, Lionel Ritchie, and Phil Collins. It typically provides hourly news reports, traffic information during peak drive times, sports reports, live play-by-play coverage of baseball and football, and business reports. Adult contemporary stations are tightly formatted; that is, all music is selected and programmed by a music director, but disc jockeys are allowed to chatter with few restrictions on time or topics. Success at an A/C station is tied to the DJ's ability to develop a personal following.

2. *Middle-of-the-Road* or *MOR*. Stations featuring middle-of-the-road music may call their formats *bright, uptempo, good listening, easy listening, standards*, or *entertainment*. MOR stations are almost indistinguishable from A/C stations, but they tend to be more conservative in their musical selections. In addition to soft rock, MOR stations play the music of Barry Manilow, Frank Sinatra, and Barbra Streisand. MOR stations often provide the same collateral services as those of A/C stations.

3. *Country*, also known as *bluegrass, contemporary country*, or *modern country*. Stations featuring country music tend to be moderately paced,

even though they are as tightly formatted as adult contemporary stations.[5] Country music seems at odds with the frenetic pace maintained by most top-40 stations. Country stations feature ballads of drifters and of love affairs gone bad, and they occasionally offer novelty songs.

4. *Top 40*, also known as *contemporary hit radio (CHR)*. Top-40 stations may call their format *contemporary, rock, request, popular music,* or *hit parade*. A typical top-40 station rotates the top 12 to 20 hits of the day with some golden oldies interspersed according to a formula. Station policies vary, but most repeat all current hits within 90 to 150 minutes of broadcast time.

5. *Album-oriented rock* or *AOR*. AOR stations may also be called *progressive, progressive rock, underground, alternative, hard rock,* or *free form*. AOR stations play all types of rock, including heavy metal and punk, plus some reggae and folk music. Most progressive stations permit DJs to play nearly anything they like, but what they play is expected to add up to an overall identifiable station sound. Some AOR stations are tightly formatted, with all music chosen by a music director.

6. *Black*, also called *urban contemporary, rhythm and blues,* or *soul*. Black-oriented stations play contemporary hits by Black artists—vocal and instrumental—and groups. Many Black stations are programmed much like a top-40 station (rotation of current hits, with inclusion by formula of hits of the past) and are fast-paced, with little chatter from the DJs. Because of the universal appeal of much Black music, stations that formerly claimed a predominantly Black audience now reach an audience of fans from all ethnic groups. Because of this, many Black-oriented stations list themselves as *urban contemporary* or *adult contemporary*.

7. *Golden oldies*, also known as *nostalgia, old gold, solid gold, rock,* or *classic gold*. These stations play hits from the early 1960s to the recent past. Songs by the Honeycombs, the Byrds, Blood, Sweat and Tears, the Beatles, the Supremes, the Ronettes, Sonny and Cher, and the Righteous Brothers are typical offerings of these stations.

8. *Beautiful music*, also called *easy listening, good music,* or *instrumental music*. These stations feature music (usually instrumental) that is in-

---

[5] *Format* is used in several ways in the broadcasting field. A television talk show outline is called a *format*. In radio, *format* refers to the type of programming provided by a station (all-news format, country music format, etc.). A *tight format* or a *loose format* refers not to a type of music but to the degree of restrictions placed on DJs as to choice of music and the sequence in which the numbers are played.

tended to provide background to some other activity. Its detractors call it "supermarket" or "wall-flower" music, but it does have its fans. The format calls for low-key arrangements of recent hits, musical comedy songs, standards, and some light classics. Many of these stations are automated, and even hourly news summaries are recorded just before being broadcast. The term *good music,* once used only to describe stations playing classical music, has been taken over by stations of the beautiful music type.

9. *Jazz.* There actually is more than one type of all-jazz station. The first plays only classic jazz from the past, focusing on the 1920s through the 1950s. The second type plays these hits as occasional reference points but features contemporary jazz by artists such as Steve Rawlins, Grover Washington, Sonny Rollins, Ramsey Lewis, Herbie Mann, and Anita Gravine. Both Dixieland jazz and the music of greats such as Louis Armstrong, Django Reinhardt, Billie Holiday, and Oscar Peterson may be heard on both types of stations.

10. *Big-band* stations feature the music of Artie Shaw, Benny Goodman, Glenn Miller, Tommy Dorsey, and Stan Kenton. Also known as *nostalgia* stations, they can be heard in most parts of the United States, though their numbers are few. Big-band stations, like jazz stations, encourage their DJs to talk about the music and the artists.

11. *Spanish,* including stations in Puerto Rico. Spanish-language stations play music appropriate to the origin of their listeners. Stations in Florida favor Cuban music; stations in the Southwest generally feature music from Mexico; and stations in areas with sizable populations of Central Americans—Guatamalans, Costa Ricans, Salvadorans, Hondurans, Nicaraguans, or Panamanians—feature music of these countries. Spanish music stations generally provide more nonmusic programming than do English-language music stations, and they may carry baseball games from Latin America, U.S. games broadcast in Spanish, and interview and religious programs.

A breakdown of music stations by format should be of interest to anyone who is thinking of a career as a disc jockey. As you look at the following percentages, keep the following points in mind. First, radio is a dynamic field, and changes in musical taste are quickly reflected by changes in programming and station format. Second, the information has been supplied by broadcasters, and some are known to subtly misrepresent their formats to make their air time more attractive to time buyers. All percentages are approximate. (These figures do not add up to 100% because they do not include all-news, all-talk, and so-called variety stations.)

Country	24 percent
Adult contemporary	16 percent
Middle-of-the-road	14.5 percent
Top 40	10 percent
Album-oriented rock	5.7 percent
Beautiful music	4 percent
Black/urban contemporary	3 percent
Golden oldies	3 percent
Jazz	2.5 percent
Spanish	1.5 percent
Big band	1 percent

Though approximate and subject to change, the percentages are clear in their implications. While country is the single most prevalent format, adult contemporary and middle-of-the-road stations—which are nearly identical in music played and style of announcing—add up to over 30 percent. Big band, jazz, golden oldies, and Black/urban contemporary account for only 8½ percent of all U.S. radio stations. If there is a correlation between numbers of station types and numbers of DJs employed, these percentages should give you a rough guide to employment opportunities.

Some Representative Popular Music Stations

Just as there is no typical radio station, there is no typical popular music station. At the same time, one can speak meaningfully about *types* of music radio stations and about the responsibilities and require- ments of disc jockeys. The following profiles represent a range of radio station types. Each is described to give you an idea of the working conditions you might encounter there.

1. *WKKK-AM and FM.* These MOR stations are located thirty-five miles from a major market, and they are the only stations serving the south- ern county in which they are located. The daytime-only AM station operates with a 1,000-watt signal, and the FM station, licensed to oper- ate twenty-four hours a day, broadcasts with 1,900 watts. When both stations are on the air, they simulcast; the FM station continues alone from sunset to sunrise. At this station, you are a member of a staff of six regular announcers, each of whom works four-hour board shifts five days a week. An additional seven part-time disc jockeys fill in between midnight and 6:00 A.M. seven days of the week and are the

only announcers on board during the weekends. These part-timers also fill in for regulars when they are absent for vacation or illness. The six full-time announcers have collateral duties: one is the program director, one is the music director, one specializes in weather, two more do the news during the prime hours when they are not working the board, the remaining two sell time and write and produce commercials. The part-timers work six-hour board shifts.

2. *KMMM*. This country station is located in a community of 25,000, about sixty miles from a major market. Although it receives some competition from stations in the large city, the sometimes poor reception of city stations gives it an advantage in its own area. This station is not automated. It has a power of 1,000 watts and is licensed for full operation, though it must beam its signal in only one direction after sundown. As an announcer on this station, you work a three-hour board shift six days a week. You spend another three hours daily in one of several ways: as a writer of commercial copy for local retailers, as a producer of commercials, or as a newscaster. At this station you work from a play list developed by the music director. You operate your own board and play music and commercials on turntables and cart machines. To serve the interests of its listeners, KMMM features camping news, fishing and boating information, and commodity reports. To succeed on this station, you must know and enjoy country music.

3. *KQQQ*. This metropolitan top-40 station is in a large western city. It operates with a 5,000-watt nondirectional signal and broadcasts twenty-four hours a day. KQQQ has a tight format featuring current hits from the record charts, plus regularly scheduled golden hits of the past. The station categorizes music as "current," "power gold," "regular gold," "recurrent," "image," and "stash." *Recurrent* refers to songs just off the play list; *image* refers to songs chosen to provide a change of pace and enhance the station's image, songs by Mick Jagger or the Beatles, for example; *stash* refers to songs not on the playlist, but which are occasionally played.

Some music on this station is *dayparted*, which means that a few of the songs on the play list are to be played only during a specified *daypart*—a term referring to segments of the broadcast day, typically morning drive time, midday, and nighttime. A novelty song, for example, may be *dayparted* to morning drive time, and a teen hit may be dayparted to nighttime only.

As a jock on KQQQ, you are expected to maintain a loud, frenetic pace between carted music selections. You ad-lib between songs or sets of songs, but you are expected to keep your remarks brief; you also are expected to demonstrate a good sense of humor. Once each quarter hour you work from *liner notes,* prepared by your program or music director, from which you promote upcoming station features, such as a weekend of 1960s British hits, a contest, or a crossplug for another jock.

You work combo at KQQQ, operating an elaborate console and banks of cart machines. To generate energy, you stand throughout your shift. All selections are dubbed to carts, and your days of cuing records are over. At KQQQ, you work a three-hour shift, five days a week. The pay is excellent, working conditions are good, and the competition is keen.

4. *WSSS-AM and FM.* The AM station operates at 5,000 watts with a directional antenna, and the FM station operates at 100,000 watts. Both are on the air twenty-four hours a day, and they simulcast from 4:00 A.M. to 10:00 A.M. daily. They are located in a large Midwestern city. Both stations are automated and have tight formats. They feature gentle or beautiful music—soundtracks from movies, instrumental arrangements of old standards, and music from operettas and musicals. As an announcer on WSSS, you are given explicit instructions on every detail of your work—for example, you are told to say "Lake Island has 74 degrees," not "the temperature at Lake Island is 74 degrees." All music intros, commercials, and PSAs are taped by you and other announcers, and only the weather summaries and the hourly news capsules are delivered live. As an announcer for WSSS, you are not known by name to your audience. You were hired because you sounded like others already employed by the station, and the desired sound is low, mellifluous, and resonant—just like the music.

5. *KMZ.* KMZ is a Black-oriented music station in a large western metropolitan area. It operates twenty-four hours a day, with a power of 5,000 watts. It plays 90 percent rhythm and blues and 10 percent gospel music. KMZ is a powerful force in the Black community because it is one of only two Black-oriented stations in an area with a large Black population. Public-service announcements and community issues of importance to Blacks must be adequately broadcast by KMZ or chances are they will not reach their intended audience at all.

KMZ features eight air personalities who have collateral duties. In addition to a four-hour board shift five days a week, announcers must spend an additional four hours in production: writing and producing on carts some of the hundreds of PSAs produced by KMZ each year, working on the production of local commercials, and carting the musical selections played by KMZ.

All announcers on KMZ are Black. As a disc jockey for KMZ, you are expected to know rhythm and blues, soul, jazz, and Black rock music. You are also expected to volunteer your time to youth, social, and civic community organizations.

6. *KPPP.* This 5,000-watt AOR station is located in a major Eastern market. It has solid *cumes* (an abbreviation of cumulative ratings, an indication of the number of listeners at a given time), and its prosperity allows considerable specialization. KPPP maintains a news staff of two, a full-time sales staff, and programming, engineering, and traffic departments. You work combo, with both taped carts and discs.

The music director selects all music, but you are allowed to play the selections in any order you choose. Your ideas about music are solicited and given objective consideration, but final decisions are not yours to make. As an announcer (or personality) on this station, you are known to your listeners by name, and you are expected to build and maintain a personal following. You have no *official* duties beyond your three-hour air shift, but maintaining name and voice recognition virtually requires unpaid service at a variety of events—softball games to raise funds for recreational programs, charity auctions, telethons, and opening-day ceremonies at county fairs and the Little League baseball season.

Your abilities and your popularity create an opportunity for extra income. When your station sales staff sells a commercial package to a local merchant, the spots are written and produced by station personnel, with you as talent. You receive a weekly fee for your voice work on commercials. If you bring in new clients who buy air time, you are given a finder's fee.

7. *WDDD-AM and FM.* The AM station is a daytime-only, 5,000-watt station; the FM station has an effective radiated power of 3,000 watts, both horizontal and vertical. The FM station broadcasts from 6:00 A.M. to midnight. Located in a farming area and having no local competition, your station attempts to meet a great range of interests: MOR music, featuring hits from 1958 to the present; local news at the top of the hour and national news at the bottom, with expanded newscasts four times daily; weather summaries every fifteen minutes, with expanded weather reports three times daily; a twice-weekly telephone

call-in show; a daily fifteen-minute call-in swap show; local seasonal sports events presented live. As a disc jockey for WDDD, you are expected to handle a number of these features in addition to your music chores. Specialization in weather, sports, farming, and news would help any announcer's chances of employment at this station. As in all but the largest and wealthiest of stations, you work a heavy forty-hour week.

8. *KHHH-FM.* This station broadcasts sixteen hours a day in Spanish but makes additional blocks of time available for broadcasts in any foreign language. It is located in a large cosmopolis, and KHHH-FM is the only station on which homesick Serbs, Bohemians, Swedes, or Germans can hear their native tongues and the music of their cultures. All announcers on KHHH-FM must be fluent in Spanish (those sponsoring programs in other languages bring their announcers with them), and they must be able to perform as remote announcers for parades, sports contests, and live broadcasts of Mexican and Central American music. As an announcer on this station, you also perform as a time seller and as writer and producer of local commercials. You are expected to have a sound knowledge of both contemporary and standard Latin American music.

9. *WZZZ.* This MOR station, located in a small resort community in the eastern part of the country, is a daytime-only station. It operates with 500 watts of power and is automated. The station is run by three employees. As an announcer at this station, you sell time, write and produce commercials, program and service the automation equipment, voice recorded intros to the music, keep the various station logs, and perform as a newscaster on live hourly news summaries.

These, then, are examples of some of the popular music station types to be found in the United States and Canada. In practicing for a career as a disc jockey, work to develop the obvious skills—the ability to operate audio consoles of varying degrees of complexity, turntables, tape cartridge machines, compact disc players, and reel-to-reel tape recorders—and become an authority on the type of music you intend to announce. Beyond this, work to develop an engaging air personality. Concentrate on the chapters in this book that discuss performance, interpreting copy, ad-lib announcing, commercial interpretation and delivery, news writing, news delivery, and interviewing.

Preparation for
Disc Jockey Work

Although your chances of success as a disc jockey will be greatest if you develop a unique air personality, it is helpful for beginners to listen to a wide range of successful announcers. This can be done by listening to all popular music stations in your reception area, instead of concentrating only on the one or two stations you prefer. For a serious study of music announcing types, you can buy airchecks from companies that specialize in this service.[6] Both current and classic airchecks may be obtained for a modest price, and even videotapes of popular disc jockeys at work are available.

Successful disc jockeys have a well-developed sense of humor, usually of the "off-the-wall" variety. It is unlikely that a person without a sense of humor can develop one after reaching adulthood, but it is possible to improve skills in almost anything, including the area of comedy. An analysis of puns, jokes, and one-liners that you find funny can tell you much about the nature of your sense of humor. Even professional disc jockeys need help now and then, and companies have arisen that sell jokes for use by DJs. Gags must be very brief, as in these two examples: "People tell me I have a great face for radio," and "This day in history! In 1776, George Washington crossed the Delaware, not to attack the British, as we were taught in school, but because he was a cheapskate and wanted to find the dollar he'd thrown across the river a few weeks earlier."[7] These jokes are typical of the kind expected of disc jockeys on fast-paced popular music stations. As you practice DJ work, see what kinds of gags you can invent and test their effectiveness on your friends.

In addition to this sort of chatter, you will need to gain considerable knowledge of music and musicians, including historical facts, trivia, and current developments. This is best accomplished by reading on a regular basis several trade magazines and newspapers. Among the most useful are *Billboard, R&R, The Gavin Report,* and a variety of tip sheets.

If you do not have an opportunity to do on-air disc jockey work, you still can practice introductions to recorded music and the kind of

[6] An *aircheck* is a sample of an announcer's on-air work. Information about available airchecks may be found in *R&R, Radio and Records,* a weekly newspaper about the popular music field.

[7] These examples of DJ humor are from a subscription comedy service, CHEEP LAFFS, located in Sunnyvale, California. Del Gundlach is the writer and publisher of the service.

FIGURE 13.3
Disc jockey Bill Monihan
reads public-service an-
nouncements from 3-by-
5-inch file cards. (Cour-
tesy KTIM, San Rafael,
California)

humorous chatter required of DJs. To practice ad-lib music announcing, you need only a record player or cassette deck for playing music,
and a second machine (cassette or reel-to-reel) for recording your performance. A stopwatch is also essential. First, select and time your
records. Time not only the entire selection, but also the instrumental
introduction from its start to the time the vocal begins. If the instrumental intro lasts eleven seconds, then you have just short of eleven
seconds to make appropriate comments about the song. As you gain
experience in this, make your timing more detailed. If the intro is
eleven seconds but a horn or a drum roll is heard at six seconds, make
note of that, for you will want to pause in your comments at that
precise moment. End your comments a split second before the vocal
begins. At some stations, announcers speak during a *set* (two or more
songs played back to back), speaking from the moment the vocal ends
on selection one until just before the vocal begins on selection two.
Practice doing this with dubs made to an audiotape unless you have
two turntables at your disposal.

Practice announcing for both fast-paced and more relaxed music
station formats. Some stations want a relaxed, intimate, and informative performance. This is especially true of jazz, big-band, country, and
golden-oldie stations. Do some research on the music you play—when
a recording was made, who some of the key artists are, and anything of

FIGURE 13.4
Disc jockey Pete Kelly operates a BMX 14 audio console and speaks into an AKG 414EB microphone. All musical selections are on tape cartridges. (Courtesy KZST, Santa Rosa, California)

significance about the recording techniques used or the occasion at which a live recording was made. Refer to a news service, such as *R&R*, for information such as important anniversary dates (Altamont, the breakup of Led Zeppelin, the death of John Lennon, for example), and for important music happenings of one, five, and ten years ago. Publications such as *R&R* are expensive, but you may be able to examine a back issue at a local radio station; once you are on a station's payroll, you will have regular access to a number of trade publications.

When you are ready to apply for a job as a disc jockey, you will need a résumé and an audition tape. Your school placement office or career guidance center can help you develop a résumé. Once developed, it should be typed by a professional typing service and duplicated on good bond paper by a high-quality duplicating company.

The best audition tape often is an aircheck made during an on-air shift at a college radio station. Being on the air gives you a higher level of energy than can be simulated in a nonbroadcast circumstance, such as at a professional recording studio. If you are unable to produce an audition tape from an actual broadcast, the next best thing will be to turn to a professional who works with a recording studio. There are certain to be qualified persons in your area who will offer any or all of these services: providing records or carts; furnishing written chatter and gags; coaching you in delivery; scheduling you into a professional recording studio; engineering and recording your performance; and making several copies of the finished audition tape. Before agreeing to work with anyone on such a project, check with music station personnel to make sure the person you select is qualified and dependable.

To apply for a job as a disc jockey, first find the name of the program directors of those radio stations for which you would like to work. Names are listed in *Broadcasting Yearbook*, which can be found at some libraries and at nearly every radio and television station. Send a brief letter, a résumé, and your audition tape to these program directors. In your letter, state that you will call in a week to see if an interview can be arranged. Follow through with the telephone call, but don't be discouraged if all or nearly all the station managers express a lack of interest in you. Perseverance is the most important quality a prospective disc jockey can possess.

If you live in a major or secondary market, it is unlikely that you will be hired without years of on-air experience. Therefore, be prepared to look for work in a smaller market. *Broadcasting Yearbook* can be of real help in locating stations to which you may apply. It lists every radio station in the United States, indicates its signal strength (a clue as to its audience size, and therefore its economic standing), gives names of chief administrative personnel, and tells you the music format featured

FIGURE 13.5
Disc jockey Bobby Ocean stands during his shift to help maintain alertness and high energy. (Courtesy Bobby Ocean, Inc., and KFRC, San Francisco)

on each station. Above all, remember that there *are* jobs *if* you are well trained, have native talent, are willing to begin at a modest salary, are hardworking, and continue to grow with experience.

Here are a few suggestions for practicing DJ work.

1. In selecting music to introduce and play, *choose music you know and like.* Look especially for music you can talk about. You will not have the opportunity to select your own music on most radio stations, but it is good practice to begin with the easiest possible challenge.

2. When practicing, *actually play your records,* and play them all the way through. Correct pacing and mood demand that you and your music work together for a total impression.

3. *Practice headlining songs you will play later.* This is a realistic practice used to hold listeners who otherwise might switch to another station.

4. *Give the name of the song and the performers at the start or the conclusion of each selection.* Most stations have policies on music identification and you will have to conform to them, but as you practice, aim for the communication of a maximum amount of information. Regardless of station policy, listeners appreciate the information.

5. *Practice commercials and public-service announcements.* It is unrealistic not to do so.

6. *Practice cuing records.* You may later work only with carts or compact discs, which are cued automatically, but you must be prepared to work with conventional discs.

7. *Practice working with an audio console where possible.* You almost certainly will be expected to operate your own console as a professional disc jockey.

8. Practice musical intros by first timing the music between the start of the record and the start of the vocal; then *work to introduce the number so that your voice ceases just as the vocal begins.* Although you may not appreciate DJs who talk over music, many stations require it.

9. *Practice ad-libbing about the music, the day's events, or ideas that intrigue you.* You may have little chance to ad-lib on a station with a tight format, but other stations will consider you for a job only if you are able to entertain in a spontaneous, ad-lib manner.

10. *Introduce your records ad-lib.* Scripts (other than for commercials, PSAs, and newscasts) are unknown to the disc jockey.

11. *Avoid corny clichés.* Try to develop your own oral style. The positive idiosyncrasies of popular disc jockeys' expressions become the clichés of unimaginative and unoriginal announcers.

12. Before engaging in practice sessions, *remember that all music stations work to achieve a particular sound.* A station's sound is the end result of a number of factors: the type of music played, the voices and personalities of the announcers, the energy level of the DJs, the kinds of things that announcers say, whether announcers speak over instrumental introductions or endings of songs, and the general pace of music and speech. Useful approaches to practice should include initial determination of the specific sound you are attempting to achieve and selection of music appropriate to that sound.

THE CLASSICAL MUSIC ANNOUNCER

There are classical music stations in nearly all parts of the United States, even though they add up to only 2 percent of radio stations that feature music. With fewer than two hundred classical music stations on the air, it should be apparent that job opportunities in this demanding specialization are limited. You should not single-mindedly prepare yourself only for a career as an announcer on a classical music station unless your love of both classical music and radio is so strong that you are willing to put practical considerations aside. On the other hand, preparing for classical music announcing as part of your study of the entire field of broadcast announcing can be of considerable benefit. Learning about a great treasure of music, learning musical terms, and practicing the foreign pronunciation that is required of all announcers on classical music stations will enrich your life and make you more competent in any announcing specialization.

Classical is not really a good title for stations featuring concert and operatic music. An important period in music history, roughly the last half of the eighteenth century, is known as the classical period, and the music of that time—represented by Haydn and Mozart—is, strictly speaking, classical music. *Classic,* which means "of the highest or best order," is a better choice of name for stations of this type. One such station calls itself "your classic music station," but most stations that feature operatic and concert music refer to themselves as classical music stations. Because the tradition is widespread, we will follow this usage.

As an announcer on a classical music station, you will have some duties in common with the disc jockey. At most stations you will cue up and play your own records; follow and sign the program log; operate an audio console; ad-lib your musical introductions, usually from information contained on the dust jackets of the albums; and read public-service announcements and commercials or play them on tape cart machines. A high percentage of classical music stations are noncommercial, and you will not, of course, deliver commercials as part of your work at such stations. You will have collateral duties—carting music from records, preparing newscasts and summaries, and maintaining the operating log, to name but three.

Unlike a disc jockey, you will not be concerned with hit records. You will, however, be expected to keep abreast of new recordings of standards, releases of music not previously recorded, and a small output of new works. You will be required to have an extensive knowledge of classical music and to be accurate in pronouncing names in French, Italian, German, Spanish, and Russian.

On a classical music station, your name might be known to your listeners, but it is unlikely that you will be expected to build a personal following. If you were assigned to or if you developed a specialty program—a music quiz, a telephone talk show centering on classical music, or a program featuring the best of the new releases—you might become well known to your listeners, but such prominence is rare. Most classical music fans turn to stations because of the music, not because of the announcers.

No ladder extends from the small classical music station to the big time. Most classical music stations are noncommercial FM stations, and working conditions and salaries tend to be uniform. There are highly profitable AM and FM classical music stations in major metropolises and salaries there are quite good, but they account for an extremely small percentage of professional radio announcers.

Your announcing job at a classical music station will be more relaxed than that of a disc jockey on a popular music station. Musical selections are longer than most popular songs, many running from thirty minutes to as long as two and a half hours. And you will not be expected to keep up the rapid delivery that is characteristic of many popular music stations. Aside from a small number of specialized classical music programs, such as a music quiz, you will spend most of your time announcing general music programs: a Bach fugue, followed by a Strauss tone poem, a Vivaldi concerto, and a Mozart symphony, rounded off by ballet music by Tchaikovsky.

Seldom will you select the music or even the specific recordings. This is done by a music director, who is responsible for the total sound of the station. There is usually a coherent plan to a day of broadcast classical music: brisk and lively short works during morning commute hours (especially true of commercial classical music stations), concert programs and programs featuring operatic excerpts during midday, shorter works again during evening commute time, and longer works throughout the evening, including complete operas, masses, and oratorios. Music directors keep a list of all musical selections played, complete with date and time of each playing. Most stations have a policy requiring the lapse of a certain number of weeks or months between playings.

The most important requirements for employment as a classical music announcer are impeccable foreign pronunciation and a thorough knowledge and appreciation of classical music. If you choose to specialize in this type of announcing, you should enroll in as many general courses in music as are offered to nonmajors. Of course, if you are a musician, more specialized courses will be available to you. Listen to classical music broadcasts, collect records and tapes, practice aloud the introductions to musical selections, and learn to use at least some of the source books mentioned under Chapter 13 in Appendix E.

The *Schwann Record and Tape Guide,* published monthly, provides up-to-date information on new listings and albums, tapes, and compact discs that are currently available. Schwann lists birth and death dates of composers and, where known, the date of composition of each selection listed.

Practice: Announcing Classical Music

The last section of this chapter presents scripts for the introduction of music featuring Spanish, Italian, French, and German names and words. Begin your practice with these scripts, and then move on to scripts of your own creation and to ad-lib introductions. Concert music usually is introduced only with names of the composer, the selection, the orchestra (or other musical group), the conductor, and, if appropriate, the soloist (as in a concerto or an aria). On some stations, you will be asked to add the name of the record company. When introducing opera, you will most likely give a résumé of each act or scene and identify the leading singers. As you practice classical music announcing, keep these suggestions in mind.

1. Perfect your foreign pronunciation.
2. Perfect your use of phonetic transcription. While wire-service phonetics may be adequate for most announcers, as a classical music announcer you should master the IPA.
3. Practice with commercials and PSAs.
4. Practice cuing up and playing the records or tapes you introduce.
5. Create music programs. Invent titles, write openings and closings, select theme music, and make sample program offerings.
6. Practice ad-libbing with only album liners as your source of information.
7. Practice reading news headlines and five-minute news summaries because this is a typical part of a classical music announcer's broadcast day.

Practice: Reading Classical Music Copy

SPANISH MUSIC COPY

Manuel de Falla inherited the role of Spain's first composer with the death of Granados in 1916. De Falla, who died in 1946, fulfilled his mission well, and even outshone his mentor in popularity outside of Spain. We hear next seven "Canciones populares Españolas"--'El paño moruno,' 'Seguidilla murciana,' 'Austuriana,' 'Jota,' 'Nana,' 'Canción, and 'Polo.' Victoria de Los Angeles now sings seven "Canciones populares Españolas" by Manuel de Falla.

Our featured work tonight is an out-of-print recording of the Spanish operetta "La boda de Luís Alonso," by Giménez. Soloists are Carlos Munguia as Luís Alonso, Inés Rivandeneira as María Jesús, Gregorio Gil singing the part of

Paco, Raphael Maldonado as Miguelito, and Ana María Fernández as Picúa. The Gran Orquesta Sinfónica of Madrid and the Coros Cantores de Madrid are directed by Ataúlfo Argenta. We hear now "La boda de Luís Alonso" by Giménez.

Now for music of the bull ring. We will hear the "Banda Taurina" of the Plaza de Toros of Mexico City. The music is a typical group of selections played at appropriate points during a "corrida." The musical selections we will hear today are "Las toreras," a dedication to lady bull fighters; "Canero"; "Toque cuadrillas," a signal for the assistants to capture the attention of the bull; "Purificación," played at the moment of the killing; "Toque Banderillas," a signal for the placing of the darts; "El imponente," a sign of respect for a very big bull; "Canitas," played for a bull that has earned much respect; "Gualvidal," a musical selection played for a famous matador; "Toque de muerte," the signal of death; "Dianas," musical "applause," played after a successful encounter; and "Porque te quiero," played whenever the company enters or leaves the arena. And now, music of the bull ring.

ITALIAN MUSIC COPY

Gaetano Donizetti's "L'elisir d'amore," "The Elixir of Love," begins in the fields of Adina's farm. It is harvest time, and the chorus of farm workers sings "Bel conforto

al mietitore"--"What comfort to the harvester." Nemorino,
who is secretly in love with Adina, then sings the aria
"Quanto è bella, quanto è cara!"--"How beautiful she is!
How dear!" Adina, who has been reading the story of Tris-
tan and Isolde, laughs aloud, and is asked by the workers
to share the source of her good humor. As she tells the
story of the love potion, all present--but especially
Nemorino--wish for a similar potion. Our cast features
Rosanna Carteri as Adina, Luigi Alva as Nemorino, Rolando
Panerai as Belcore, Giuseppe Taddei as Il Dottor Dulcam-
ara, and Angela Vercelli as Giannetta. The chorus and orchestra of Teatro alla Scala of Milan are conducted by
Tullio Serafin. And now, Act One of Donizetti's "L'elisir
d'amore."

On tonight's program, we will hear three overtures by
Gioacchino Rossini. The first is the overture to
"L'Italiana in Algeri," first performed in 1813. Following
that, we will hear the overture to "La Cambiale di Matrimonio," written in 1810. The third of Rossini's overtures is that written for the opera "La Cenerentola,"
first presented in 1817. Fernando Previtali conducts the
Orchestra Dell'Accademia de Santa Cecilia in three overtures by Gioacchino Rossini.

This afternoon on "Musical Echoes" we will hear nine arias
sung by the legendary Enrico Caruso. During the first por-

tion of the program, we will hear the aria "Chi mi frena
in tal momento," from "Lucia di Lammermoor," by Gaetano
Donizetti; "Siciliana," from "Cavalleria rusticana," by
Pietro Mascagni; "La donna è mobile," from "Rigoletto," by
Giuseppi Verdi; and "Invano Alvaro," from "La forza del
destino," also by Verdi.

Following the news, we will hear the Great Caruso singing
the traditional song "Santa Lucia." The four arias in this
part of the program are: "Cielo e mar," from "La Gioconda," by Amilcare Ponchielli; "Vesti la giubba," from
"I pagliacci," by Ruggero Leoncavallo; "Recondita ar-
monia," from "Tosca," by Giacomo Puccini; and "Brindisi,"
from "Cavalleria rusticana," by Pietro Mascagni. And now,
Enrico Caruso sings "Chi mi frena in tal momento," from
"Lucia di Lammermoor," by Gaetano Donizetti.

FRENCH MUSIC COPY

Maurice Ravel, one of the giants of modern French music,
died in 1937. He left behind him such masterpieces as
"Pavanne pour une infante défunte," "La valse," and "Daph-
nis et Chloë." Tonight we will hear one of Ravel's lesser
known works, "L'enfant et les sortilèges." Suzanne Danco,
soprano, and Hugues Cuénod, tenor, are accompanied by the
Orchestre de la Suisse Romande, conducted by Ernest
Ansermet.

Georges Bizet wrote his opera "Les pêcheurs de perles"--
"The Pearl Fishers"--in 1863. Since that time it has had
its ups and downs, but it never has become a staple with
opera companies around the world. Despite this, "Les
pêcheurs de perles" contains some of Bizet's most inspired
music. This afternoon we will hear the opera in its en-
tirety. The cast includes Janine Michaeu, Nicolai Gedda,
and Ernest Blanc. The chorus and orchestra of the Opéra-
Comique de Paris are conducted by Pierre Dervaux. "The
Pearl Fishers," by Georges Bizet.

Next we will hear some delightful ballet music by the
French composer André Grétry. The compositions are
"Céphale et Procris," "La caravane du Caire," and
"Lépreuve villageoise." Raymond Leppard conducts the
English Chamber Orchestra.

Marc-Antoine Charpentier's seldom heard "Messe pour
plusieurs instruments au lieu des orgues" is our next
selection on "Musical Masterpieces." Jean-Claude Malgoire
conducts the Grand Ecurie et la Chambre du Roy.

GERMAN MUSIC COPY

"Die Dreigroschenoper" was first presented to the public
in 1928. The success of this work, which is neither opera
nor musical comedy, established a new genre of musical
theater. Its authors, Kurt Weill and Bertolt Brecht, took

the two-hundred-year-old "Beggar's Opera," by John Gay, as
their model, and fashioned a biting satire on the Germany
of the 1920s. Tonight we will hear three selections from
"Die Dreigroschenoper," as performed by Lotte Lenya, Wolfgang Neuss, Willy Trenk-Trebitsch, and Inge Wolffberg.
First will be "Die Moritat von Mackie Messer," followed by
"Die Unsicherheit Menschlicher Verhältnisse." The concluding selection is "Die Ballade vom Angenehmen Leben." The
orchestra and chorus are conducted by Wilhelm Brückner-
Rüggeberg. Three selections from "Die Dreigroschenoper."

Wolfgang Amadeus Mozart wrote "Die Entführung aus dem
Serail"--"The Abduction from the Seraglio"--in 1782, when
the composer was twenty-six years of age. Often considered
Mozart's happiest comedy, the opera contains some of his
most beautiful arias. Today we will hear excerpts from the
third act. First, Gerhard Unger, in the role of Pedrillo,
sings the romantic "Im Mohrenland gefangen war," followed
by Gottlob Frick in the role of Osmin singing "O, wie will
ich triumphieren." Finally, Anneliese Rothenberger as Con-
stanze, and Nicolai Gedda as Belmonte, sing the duet,
"Welche ein Geschik! O Qual der Seele!" The Vienna
Philharmonic Orchestra is conducted by Josef Krips. Three
excerpts from Mozart's "Die Entführung aus dem Serail."

Next on the "Musical Stage" we will hear the complete
"Merry Widow." "Die lustige Witwe," as it is called in

German, was written by Franz Lehar in 1905, and has been
popular with audiences all over the world since that time.
In tonight's performance, the part of Hanna Glawari is
sung by Hilde Güden, the Graf Danilo Danilowitsch is sung
by Per Gruden, Waldemar Kmentt sings the part of Camille
de Rosillon, and Emmy Loose is Valencienne. The Vienna
State Opera Chorus and Orchestra are conducted by Robert
Stolz. We hear now, without interruption, the complete
"Merry Widow," by Franz Lehar.

MIXED LANGUAGES MUSIC COPY

Welcome to "Music 'til Dawn." During the next five hours
we will hear works from opera and the concert stage. This
morning's program features works from Italian, Spanish,
German, and Italian masters.

Our program begins with excerpts from Wolfgang Amadeus
Mozart's opera "The Marriage of Figaro." Featured are
Hilde Güden as the Countess, Hermann Prey as the Count,
Anneliese Rothenberger as Susanna, Walter Berry as Figaro,
and Edith Mathis as Cherubino. The Dresden State Orchestra
and Chorus are directed by Otmar Suitner.

We then will hear excerpts from Handel's seldom performed oratorio "Belshazzar." Featured are Sylvia Stahl-
man, soprano, and Helen Raab, contralto, with Helmuth Rill-
ing conducting the Stuttgart Kirchenmusiktage Orchestra.

Andrés Segovia will then perform as soloist in the "Concierto del Sur," by Manuel Ponce. André Previn conducts the London Symphony Orchestra.

During the third hour, we will hear George Bizet's "Jeux d'enfants," with Jean Martinon conducting the Orchestre de la Société des Concerts du Conservatoire de Paris.

Following will be Gabriel Fauré's "Masques et bergamasques." The Orchestra de la Suisse Romande is conducted by Ernest Ansermet.

Vincent D'Indy's "Symphony on a French Mountain Air" will bring us to our intermission, during which we will present a news summary.

In the fourth hour, we will hear "Lieder und Gesänge aus der Jugendzeit," by Gustav Mahler. This is sung by Dietrich Fischer-Dieskau, baritone.

Gioacchino Rossini's overtures to "L'Italiana in Algeri" and "Il Signor Bruschino" will hail the final hour of our concert, which features music from the Italian opera. Our first operatic excerpts will be from Gaetano Donizetti's "L'elisir d'amore." Featured in the cast are Rosanna Carteri, soprano, Giuseppe Taddei, baritone, and Luigi Alva, tenor. Tullio Serafin conducts La Scala Orchestra.

The last selection on "Music 'til Dawn" will be excerpts from the opera "La Favorita," by Gaetano Donizetti. The cast includes Giuletta Simionato, mezzosoprano, Gianni Poggi, tenor, and Ettore Bastianini, baritone. The Maggio Musicale Fiorentino is conducted by Alberto Erede.

14
SPORTS ANNOUNCING

Sports announcing is very competitive, and years of dedicated effort must be invested before there is a likelihood of significant reward. Despite this, the attraction of spending a career in close association with the world of sports motivates scores of young people to undertake the struggle. Sports announcing includes sports reporting, play-by-play coverage, and play analysis. Some sports announcers become expert in one or two of these specialties; nearly all beginning sports announcers must learn to perform all three. Interviewing and delivering commercials are additional tasks that you must manage well in order to succeed in sports announcing.

As a sports announcer, you will work for a radio or television station (perhaps both), a network, or an athletic team. Your working conditions, responsibilities, and income will be determined by your relationship with your employer. Network sports announcers, whether play-by-play, analysts, or reporters, are generally at the top of the salary range and have the least strenuous schedules. Network sportscasters seldom broadcast more than one game a week, and even those who add reporting chores to their schedules are responsible for only a few minutes of sports news a day.

Sports reporters who work for radio stations are usually responsible for hourly reports during their shifts, with additional taped reports to prepare for broadcast after working hours. Television sports reporters produce several minutes of visually informative sports news each day and also produce taped sports features to be used on weekends.

Sports announcers who work for athletic teams have the most strenuous work of all, though, in the opinion of many, it is the most exciting and rewarding. As an employee of a professional baseball, basketball, football, or hockey team, you will travel with your club or team, owe your loyalty to your employer, and sometimes find it difficult to reconcile your judgment with that of your boss. Some team

FIGURE 14.1
Play-by-play announcer
Don Klein and color
commentator Don Hein-
rich broadcasting a pro-
fessional football game.
(Courtesy *49ers Report*)

owners demand that their play-by-play sportscasters root for the team and promote ticket sales; some ask their announcers to favor their team but to do so with discretion; other owners make no demands on the play-by-play staff but expect announcers as well as all other members of the organization to maintain loyalty to the team, especially during adversity. Even when working for the most benign and aloof owner, you will not have the freedom of the reporter who works for a newspaper or a radio or television station.

Most sports announcers have a variety of professional roles. The simplest combination is doing play-by-play baseball during its long season and basketball, football, or hockey during the winter. Other sports announcers combine five-day-a-week sports reporting for a station with weekend play-by-play reporting of college sports. If you become a sports announcer, your professional life might well conform to one of the following models.

1. Your primary job is as a sports reporter for an all-news network-affiliated radio station in a major market. You are responsible for six live reports each day and three carted reports to be played during the evening after you have left the station. In addition to this steady and welcome job, your popularity has opened up supplemental jobs that

do not conflict with your station work: You do football play-by-play for a major university; you do play-by-play during the football preseason for a professional team in your area; you prepare periodic reports for your network's sports programs, which are broadcast nationally; and you do recorded commercials for a variety of clients, including a chain of sporting goods stores. Your work schedule is extremely demanding. Aside from the obvious demands of a six- to seven-day week, you must constantly keep up with developments in all major sports at amateur and professional levels, and this means hours of reading each week—several newspapers, *Sporting News, Sports Illustrated,* and a number of other specialized sports publications. Beyond this are the team receptions and banquets, news conferences, and civic functions at which you have been asked to speak. Finally, you schedule yourself to cover as many sports events as possible; you do postgame interviews for use on your daily sports reports, and you make notes as you watch the game from the press box so that you can give a firsthand review the following day.

2. As sports director for a popular MOR station, you prepare and perform a daily ten-minute sports show, which is followed by a two-hour telephone talk program on sports. You prepare and send one to three weekly feeds to the network, each of which centers on local teams or athletes. Your station carries play-by-play broadcasts of local college and professional football games as well as professional basketball and hockey contests. You do not do play-by-play regularly, but you do produce locker room and dugout features before and after these games. You work free-lance to increase your income and your exposure, and this brings you jobs such as preseason play-by-play, post-season tournament and bowl play-by-play, and vacation relief sports reporting for a local television station. Because you cannot predict the kinds of questions and comments that will arise on your telephone talk show, you read constantly to develop an encyclopedic knowledge of sports.

3. As sports director for a network-owned and -operated (O&O) television station, you prepare sports news for the daily 6:00 and 11:00 P.M. newscasts. This necessitates viewing and editing tapes of sports action, selecting sports photos sent by wire services, and writing two three- to five-minute news segments each day. You spend much of your time attending sports events with an ENG operator. Pre- and postgame interviews with players and coaches make up a good portion of your

nightly sportscast. On a number of weekends, you spend hours at your station watching games on network television. With the help of a station engineer, you select and have dubbed off certain key plays that you may want to use later on the air. A three-hour game may provide you with as much as thirty minutes of dubbed action, from which you will choose a maximum of three minutes for use on your two sports segments.

Your day's work leaves little time for moonlighting. You attend from three to five sports events each week to see the nontelevised events firsthand and to tape interviews. You ordinarily spend your early afternoons covering a sports story, again accompanied by an ENG operator. You arrive at the station at 3:00 P.M. This leaves you three hours in which to view or review all available tape, make your selections, review sports news from the wire services, write your script, and prepare for on-air performance during the six o'clock news. Between the 6:00 and 11:00 P.M. newscasts, you eat dinner, prepare for the 11:00 P.M. news, and review sports scores as they come in on the teletype machines. Your workday ends after the 11:00 P.M. news, but it will begin the next day long before you tape your sports news story of the day. Mornings are spent arranging interviews, reading several sports magazines and the sports sections of newspapers, and answering requests for information about the life of a sports reporter sent your way by high school and college students who would like to have your job.

4. As sports director for a medium-market radio station, you focus on high school, college, and minor-league sports events. You work for the station and for the AAA baseball team whose games are broadcast over a three-station network. When not on the road with the team, you do play-by-play descriptions of the most important high school football and basketball games. You work with a group of students you have recruited and trained to phone in ongoing scores of the games not being broadcast. You do play-by-play of home football games for the university. You provide several brief sports reports each day for the hourly five-minute newscasts. You act as spotter for play-by-play sportscasters when university sports events are regionally telecast. And as time allows, you do play-by-play of newsworthy sports events such as tennis and golf tournaments, hockey and soccer championship play-offs, Little League, Babe Ruth, and Pop Warner championships, and the most important track and field meets in your area.

5. As a sportscaster for a television network, you owe no allegiance to owners, managers, teams, or players; your responsibility is to your

viewers, and they expect accurate, balanced, and entertaining reports of the games they watch. Because your continued success depends on perfection, you avoid moonlighting and other commitments that might cut down on the hours of careful preparation necessary for a first-rate sportscast. Your schedule requires play-by-play work one day a week, which translates into a minimum of twenty-five baseball games during the season plus preseason and postseason games and sixteen professional football games plus divisional play-off games and the Super Bowl.

This schedule adds up to nearly a game a week for the calendar year, depending on the duration of play-offs, but it is possible to succeed at this because you are able to spend a minimum of five days a week memorizing players by appearance, number, and position and to rely on a professional support staff that includes a play and game analyst, a statistician, and (in the case of football) spotters. The travel schedule is demanding, but you are able to return home for at least a portion of each week. Your salary is very high, yet this increases the numbers of aspiring sportscasters who seek your job. Competition for your job is ample reason—if none other was apparent—for you to apply yourself constantly to the perfection of your skills.

6. As the regular play-by-play announcer for a professional major-league baseball team, you lead a life similar to that of the athletes in many respects. You travel with your team, so you do not have to make separate arrangements for transportation or lodging; a traveling secretary handles all details, and this eases the rigors of travel considerably. You spend early spring in a training camp and, if your team is one of two ultimate survivors, you spend early October as a guest announcer for the radio or television coverage of the World Series. Including spring practice games and games that are rained out before the sixth inning and must be replayed, but not including divisional play-offs or World Series games, you call more than one hundred and seventy games during the season. You work with a partner, who regularly calls three innings of games broadcast on radio only, and you move to the television announce booth for twenty televised games during the season, while your partner covers all innings of these games for radio.

You make nine or ten road trips a season, each lasting two to seventeen days. The longer trips find you visiting as many as five cities and spending two to four days in each one. By the time you have settled into your hotel room, sent out your laundry, spent time brushing up on the names, numbers, and positions of your team's opponents, and reviewed the press information kit furnished by the publicity director of the home team, you have little time for sight-seeing or for visiting friends in the area.

7. You are the play-by-play announcer for a minor-league professional baseball team. You call fewer games each season than your major-league counterpart, but both travel and play-by-play announcing are more rigorous. One of the ways underfunded minor-league teams manage to survive is by economizing on travel. Buses are used for travel wherever possible, your team remains in each town for five to six days, and you must call six games during a five-day visit. This schedule includes weekly double-headers, made slightly easier for you (and the players) because double-header games are scheduled for seven innings each. Your only assistance comes from an engineer, and this means that you must call every inning of every game and serve as statistician and play analyst as well as play-by-play announcer.

You stay in motels and your per diem allowance barely covers your expenses on the road. Broadcast booths are, without exception, substandard, and your broadcast equipment is quite primitive. The cheapest (and thus the poorest quality) phone lines are used to send your sportscast back home. Despite poor audio quality, you have many listeners and are in demand as a banquet speaker and as an auctioneer at various sports-related fund-raising events.

8. As a play-by-play announcer for a professional football team, your life is unlike that of a baseball, basketball, or hockey announcer. Aside from preseason and postseason games, your team plays sixteen games a season, a week apart. You broadcast almost exclusively on radio. Even when your team is featured on a network telecast, you remain in your radio booth while the announce and production teams of ABC, CBS, NBC, or a cable network produce the telecast.

Obviously, eight away games spread over a sixteen-week season demand little in travel stamina. You stay in excellent hotels, your per diem allowance is generous, and all travel arrangements are made for you by the traveling secretary. However, your work is extremely demanding in other ways. You spend a minimum of twenty hours each week memorizing names, numbers, positions, and basic statistical data and studying the kinds of offensive and defensive strategies your team's opponents have relied on during the season.

9. As team play-by-play announcer for a university football team, you call approximately eleven games each season, assuming funds are

available for you to make road trips with the team. Most universities offer free transportation to away games on charter flights but do not furnish per diem money to announcers covering their games. If your station, your university, and one or more advertisers put together a commercial package for broadcasting an entire season, then your full travel expenses are met. Both home and away games are radio-only broadcasts, except the big game that concludes your regular season. This game is shown on videotape delay, and it gives you your one experience each year to do television play-by-play.

10. You are play-by-play announcer for a professional basketball team and part of a four-person announcing staff.[1] You and a partner do television play-by-play, while radio coverage is provided by the two other members of the team's broadcasting staff. The radio broadcasts are regular and uncomplicated—all eighty games, both home and away, are broadcast live over a small regional network. Telecasts are furnished to fans in a less regular and more complicated manner. All home games are carried over cable television, whereas thirty-five away games are telecast over a local commercial station. As is true of announcing employees of all major professional sports, you and your colleagues travel with the team. A typical road trip sees you and your team involved in five matches in as many cities over twelve days.

11. As sports announcer for a professional hockey team, you follow a travel and broadcast schedule nearly identical to that of your basketball counterpart. Your team plays eighty games, aside from preseason and play-off games. As with basketball, a typical road trip sees you and the team engaged in five matches in five cities spread over twelve days. Your friends who do play-by-play for minor-league hockey teams call fewer games each season, but they also have demanding travel schedules.

INTERVIEWING ATHLETES

Interviews are an important resource for nearly all sports reporters. The chapter on interviewing will help you develop a general approach to interviewing, but additional comments, directed at sports reporting, are in order.

For the most part you will be interviewing players, coaches, man-

---

[1] Professional basketball announcing staffs range from four members to one. Typical is a team of two who work together during radio-only broadcasts and separately when a game is covered by both radio and television.

agers, trainers, and owners. Your interviews will usually be conducted on one of two occasions: at a sports event or at a news conference. Pre- and postgame interviews are common to all sports. As you approach such interviews, keeping several considerations in mind will increase your chances of obtaining worthwhile actuality or *sound bite* material.[2] What is the overriding significance of the game to be played or just concluded? Is there news in a one-on-one player match-up? Is there something unique in the playing ability or game strategy of the person you interview? Has your athlete been on a hot streak? A cold streak? Is there an unusually important or interesting game coming up? If you are interviewing a manager or an owner, is there trade or free-agent information that might be newsworthy?

When interviewing for later editing into several individual ac- tualities, clearly determine in advance whether your questions will remain on tape. This will be important because your questions and the answers you receive must be guided by the use you will later make of the tape. Here are a question and an answer that would be difficult to use if your question were not to be included in the actuality as it eventually was broadcast.

> Q: You were in foul trouble early tonight. Do you think the refs were blowing a quick whistle?
> A: Well, I guess we had a little difference of opinion on that. I thought they were overeager. Talk of the possibility of some revenge for the last game probably had them uptight.

Without your question, the answer makes little sense. Of course, you can cut your question and write a lead-in that serves the same purpose:

> LEAD-IN: I asked Ricky if he thought his early fouls came because the refs were blowing a quick whistle.

This works, but it would have been better if you and Ricky had under- stood from the beginning of the interview that you wanted complete statements that included the question as well as the answer. In that event, Ricky might have responded to your question as follows:

> RICKY: I got into foul trouble early, and I think the reason might have been . . . .

---

[2] A *sound bite* is the television equivalent of a radio actuality.

Interviews with athletes can be somewhat frustrating. The code of the locker room seems to demand that athletes, other than professional tennis players, wrestlers, and boxers, be modest about their own accomplishments and praise their teammates or opponents regardless of the facts. Moreover, athletes are preoccupied before a game and exhausted afterward. Finally, the noise and confusion in dugouts and locker rooms and on the playing field can make sensible, coherent conversation difficult. When interviewing sports stars, keep the following points in mind.

1. *Assume that your audience is interested in and capable of understanding complex, precise discussions about training and technique.* Avoid asking superficial, predictable questions. Your audience probably knows a lot about the sport and the athlete and wants to find out more, not the same old things. Followers of tennis and golf are less tolerant of superficial interviews than most other sports fans. They have come to expect precise analytical comments, and they feel cheated if interviews with participants do not add to their understanding of strategies. Basketball and football have developed increasingly complex offenses and defenses, and fans have been educated to understand and appreciate detailed information about them. Baseball, one of the most subtly complex of all major sports, seldom enjoys enlightened explanation or discussion through interviews, but this should not deter you from seeking the answers to complex questions.

2. *Work up to controversial or critical questions with care.* If you ask a big question without preparation, you are likely to get a routine statement "for the record" from athletes and coaches. Sports figures are interviewed so often that most of them can supply the questions as well as the answers. They tend to rely on safe explanations for most common questions. If you want more than this, lead up to big questions with a sequence of less controversial ones. If you begin an interview with a football coach by asking whether the coach approves of a trade recently made by the club's owners, the coach is naturally going to say yes and avoid elaborating. Begin instead by talking about the team and its strengths and weaknesses. Move to a question about the playing abilities of the traded player. Ask specific questions about the player's strong and weak points. Finally, ask the coach to explain how the loss of this player will affect the team. A coach will seldom criticize the capricious decisions of the club's owners, but if you want more than a vague response, do not ask the big question straight out. Give your guest a chance to comment informatively as well as loyally.

3. *Get to know the athletes who are likely to appear on your interview show.* This will help you have some idea of the kinds of questions they can and cannot handle. Some sportscasters travel with teams, visit locker rooms, and are invited to opening-day parties, victory celebrations, and promotional luncheons. If you have such opportunities, use them to become acquainted with the athletes who attend.

4. *Listen to conversations among athletes and coaches.* A good way to discover what they think is timely and important is by simply listening to their conversations. Though time pressures sometimes require you to enter into conversation yourself in order to come up with a story or anecdote for your program, you can often learn more by just listening. If you are lucky enough to have meals with athletes and are accepted in clubhouses or locker rooms, try to be a silent observer. You will be amazed at the spontaneous insights that will emerge.

SPORTS REPORTING

At many radio and television stations, the title *sports reporter* is synonymous with *sports director*, because only the most prosperous stations can afford the services of more than one sports specialist. Radio station sports directors are usually responsible for both live and carted reports. An additional responsibility is preparation of a set of instructions to be followed by nonspecialist announcers who must at times report sport news and who regularly give in-progress scores and the results of games played.

A television sports reporter is less likely to see double duty as reporter and director. It is common to find three or more sports specialists at television stations: a sports director who may or may not appear before cameras and two or more reporters who prepare and deliver sports reports during regular newscasts. Typically one sports reporter works the Monday-through-Friday newscasts and the second does the weekend sports report. Both cover sports news events with camera crews and prepare taped material for the sports segment of the station's newscasts.

The Television Sports Reporter

As sports reporter for a local television station, you might find yourself preparing and delivering three sports features daily—for the 5:00, 6:00, and 11:00 P.M. newscasts—plus a taped feature for weekend broadcast. Another common arrangement has one sports reporter perform for the 5:00 P.M. news with the second reporter featured on the 6:00 and 11:00 P.M. newscasts. The first reporter does weekend sports.

As a sports reporter for a medium- or major-market television station, you can expect to have these resources available to you: (1) an ENG operator for taping sports action and pre- and postgame interviews; (2) videotaped sports action from a parent network; (3) tapes and slides from professional and university athletic organizations; (4) sports news from the AP and UPI; (5) slides from AP's PhotoColor slide service; (6) sports magazines and the sports section of newspapers; (7) press information kits and media guides from all major professional and university athletic organizations; and (8) a telephone-audio recorder setup that allows you to make audio recordings of telephone interviews.

Your job consists mainly of collecting, selecting, editing, and organizing the materials available to you into a cohesive, action-oriented package for each of the evening's newscasts and of writing an entertaining and informative script. Using essentially the same visual materials and sports news items, you must prepare as many as three different sports reports, and the trick is to organize and write your reports to avoid redundancy. Many of your viewers will see two of your nightly reports, and a few will see all three, so *all* reports must provide fresh information for addicted fans.

You will be under constant pressure from your sports director to make your reports more visual. Because you are on television, it is obviously impossible for your reports to be anything *but* visual; what is actually wanted is a great deal of illustrative material (videotaped inserts, even still photos) to avoid what many directors and producers call *talking heads*. Your judgment may tell you that a plethora of such shots may be more confusing than enlightening or that some important stories should be narrated directly into a taking camera, but it is doubtful that your judgment will prevail. You can minimize this problem by working to tie words and pictures cohesively. On television, when words and pictures do not reinforce one another, the sound tends to fade from the viewer's awareness. Confine your remarks to the few essential comments needed to enhance understanding of what your viewers are seeing.

The Radio Sports Director

As sports director for a medium-market or major-market radio station, you will have many of the same responsibilities as your television counterpart. You will be expected to produce several fast-moving sports reports each day, you will produce material for later broadcast, and you will establish and supervise station policy about sports. This last responsibility will see you preparing an instruction sheet or manual for use by general or staff announcers. In the manual you will indicate how sports bulletins are to be handled, how the sports news section of general newscasts is to be structured, and the order and manner of reporting scores and outcomes of games. Depending on your geographical region, you might ask that any of a number of sports be given priority in reporting. In the Northeast, hockey often comes before basketball; in Indiana, basketball usually comes before baseball; in Chicago, baseball almost always comes before tennis; and in Florida, tennis inevitably comes before hockey. If your town has a minor-league baseball team, you might ask that it be given priority over major-league results.

As a radio sports director, you will have available the following resources: a cassette audio recorder on which you can record (without the services of an engineer) interviews and news conferences for later editing and broadcasting; the services of a studio engineer for the final carting of tapes; sports news and scores from the news wire services; audio feeds from the wire services and perhaps from a parent network; a telephone beeper for recording phone interviews; press books and other sources of factual information from professional and university sports organizations; and a variety of newspapers and magazines to which your station subscribes.

AP and UPI provide extensive material for sports reporters. Here is a summary of the service provided by UPI.

1. *All year*. "Speaking of Sports," "Sports Previews," and "Great Moments in Sports"
2. *March*. "Sizing Up the Majors"
3. *April*. "Sizing Up the Masters"
4. *May*. "Sizing Up the Derby"
5. *May*. "Sizing Up the Indy 500"
6. *June*. "Sizing Up the U.S. Open"
7. *August*. "Sizing Up the PGA"
8. *August*. "Sizing Up College Football" and "Sizing Up Pro Football"
9. *Football season*. "Football Prophet," "Pro Prophet," and "Football Periscope"
10. *October*. "Sizing Up the World Series"
11. *November–April*. "Ski World"
12. *December*. "The Year in Sports" and "Athlete of the Year"
13. *Every four years*. "Sizing Up the Olympics"

These services are in addition to regional and national reporting of both sports news items and up-to-the-minute score reporting.

One of your most time-consuming jobs will be to prepare the tape carts for your broadcasts. This includes gathering the recorded material, determining the portions you will use, writing a script to accompany the recorded inserts, supervising the editing of the excerpts, and providing the on-air engineer the information needed to reduce the chances of error. Because modern radio practice demands extensive use of carted inserts, the procedures followed by one outstanding sports director, Don Klein of KCBS Radio, San Francisco, are outlined here.

Don Klein records most of his taped material. He attends many sports events and news conferences, accompanied at all times by a high-quality cassette tape recorder and a first-class microphone. He obtains additional recorded material from telephone interviews. Arriving at the station a few hours before his first report is scheduled, he listens to his tapes and writes a script to accompany the portions he wants to use. From the script, he prepares a cut sheet for the station engineer. The *cut sheet* tells the engineer how to edit the tapes from reel-to-reel to cart for broadcast. A typical cut sheet looks like this:

Raider Quarterback
1. why New England tougher
    ST: they've gotten players in there
    OUT: :16 "stands for itself"
2. added pressure even for 13–1 team
    ST: we've gone into play-offs before
    OUT: :32 "team that's going to win"
3. overcame early inj and adjusted
    ST: early in the year, our defense (double in)
    OUT: :33 "sign of a good team"
4. effect of the NE victory
    ST: I don't think there's any carry-over
    OUT: :27 "the third down plays"
5. what impressed you with NE defense
    ST: they don't give you anything cheap
    OUT: :13 "think they are"
6. what went wrong at Foxboro
    ST: Well, we had three called back
    OUT: :22 "happened to us"

7. key to victory against NE
    ST: pass protection's going to be
    OUT: :24 "pass protection" (double out)

This cut sheet tells the engineer to prepare seven carts for broadcast. All are brief, ranging from thirteen to thirty-three seconds. The cut sheet gives the in-cue of each excerpt (marked ST for start) and the out-cue for each (marked OUT). The first notation ("why New England tougher") summarizes the point to be made in the comment that follows. The words following ST are the first words of the excerpt; "double in" (in cut 3) warns the engineer that the person interviewed repeated the words "early in the year." This precaution is taken so that the engineer will record from the first rather than the second utterance of the phrase. "Double out" (in cut 7) warns the recording and on-air engineers that the speaker repeats the words "pass protection" in the statement and that the second time the words are used will end the excerpt. A "triple out" is not uncommon.

In carting the excerpts, the engineer will dub from reel-to-reel to seven individual carts, each labeled with the cart number and the information on the cut sheet. The tape carts are stacked in order and turned over to Don Klein, who hands them and his script to the on-air engineer just before his broadcast. Split-second timing and perfect coordination between Don and his engineer are required to avoid the twin sins of letting dead air stand between live and recorded portions of the sportscast and having Don and a cart talking over one another.

Don Klein prepares six live sports reports daily and records three more for later use. Each report lasts two and a half to three minutes. His personal formula calls for a minute and a half of hard sports news or important sports results plus two features or actualities, each lasting forty-five seconds. He is responsible for between twenty-two and twenty-seven minutes of broadcast material a day. For this, he spends a minimum of eight hours in preparation.

PLAY-BY-PLAY AND GAME ANALYSIS

Play-by-play coverage of football, basketball, hockey, and baseball accounts for most of the many hours of sports reporting on radio and television. Added to this are important golf and tennis tournaments, several popular horse racing events each year, auto racing, quadrennial summer and winter Olympic Games, soccer matches, and a number of nonstandard sports such as wrist wrestling, "hot dog" ski-

ing, and lumberjack championships. The person who *calls* the game, race, match, or event is known as the *play-by-play announcer*, even though in sports such as track and field there are no actual plays. In many types of sports events, the play-by-play announcer works with a play and game *analyst*. This person used to provide *color* (describing on radio such things as card stunts, marching formations, and band uniforms) and now is most often used to analyze individual plays and overall strategies and developments as they unfold. Analysts are, without significant exception, former athletes of the sports they describe. Auto racers, skiers, baseball and football players, swimmers, gymnasts, golfers, tennis players, and others who have gained fame in sports can now be heard giving in-depth analysis during sportscasts. Because play and game analysis is so highly specialized, and because proper preparation requires devoting oneself fully to the sport itself, little will be said about this specialization. The emphasis will be on play-by-play announcing.

Covering the Major Sports

If you are a sportscaster for a team playing many games during a long season, you will easily accumulate the kind of information you need for intelligent ad-lib commentary. Your association with league players will make player identification routine, and your exclusive involvement with a single sport should give you plenty of material for illuminating analyses of tactics and game trends. At the highest levels of amateur and professional sports broadcasting, you will have help from your broadcast staff and the team management. Each day of broadcast, you will be given a press information kit updating all relevant statistics. During the game, a wire leased from Western Union will give you the scores of other games. Perhaps a full-time statistician will work with you, unearthing and bringing to your attention significant records, dates, or events you can incorporate into your running commentary. An engineer will continuously balance your voice with crowd sounds to add drama to your narrative. If you telecast a game, you will have instant replay to enrich the coverage. A famous athlete may be at your side from whom evaluations and predictions will add another dimension to the broadcast. It is still difficult and demanding work, but at least you have budget, personnel, and working conditions in your favor.

If you work for a smaller station and must announce a wide variety of games—ranging from high school to small colleges to semipro and so on—your job will be much more difficult. Rules of play may not be standardized, players may be unknown to you, press information kits may not exist, and you can expect little help and a low budget. If you begin, as most do, at a small station, you can expect to cover all major sports. In the big leagues, however, overlapping and ever-expanding seasons as well as the competition of single-sport specialists will require you to focus on no more than two or three major sports.

As a novice, you should practice play-by-play at every opportunity, even though your voice may be going nowhere but onto an audio cassette. Attend every sports event you can, including Babe Ruth, Pop Warner, and high school games. Practice calling these games into the mic of a battery-operated cassette recorder. Set your tapes aside until your memory of the game has faded; then listen to the tapes and see whether they paint a clear picture of the game. If you find your reporting incomplete, inaccurate, marred by numerous corrections, or tedious, then you will have a guide to the work ahead of you. Notice improvement. Improvement builds confidence, and confidence guarantees further improvement. Aside from the major sports, cover tennis, track and field, gymnastics, and skiing—anything, in short, that is recognized as a sport and is the subject of radio or television broadcasts.

It is difficult for a student of sports announcing to practice play-by-play for television. Your first telecast will probably be broadcast to an audience. Your apprenticeship for this challenge must, in most instances, be served by observing others as they call games for television. If you can, obtain permission to be a silent and unobtrusive witness in announce booths during the telecasts of games in your area. If this is not possible, begin to view games on television with a critical eye and ear. Make notes of your observations. Analyze moments of exceptionally competent and exceptionally incompetent play-by-play narrative. Decide for yourself how much description is illuminating, and learn to sense the moment at which announce booth chatter begins to take away from your enjoyment of the game. Play-by-play practice with an audio recorder will help prepare you for television, but there are important differences in style, quantity of information given, nature of information provided, and use of resources available to you, including instant replay.

Preparation for Play-by-Play Announcing

Preparation is the key to successful sportscasting. As Don Klein says, "The two to three hours spent in calling a game is the easiest part of a play-by-play announcer's work. Preparation for most sportscasts requires up to twenty hours of study." This, of course, refers to covering contests between teams that are unknown or only slightly known to you; less preparation of a different kind is appropriate for play-by-play announcers who work for a team, and whose team plays the same opponent as many as eighteen times a season—as in major league baseball and basketball. Here the problem of player recognition is minimized, so preparation focuses on making each sportscast unique. Before even entering the booth, you should ask yourself a number of questions. Is there anything unusual about this game? Is either team or is a player on a streak of any sort? Are there any interesting rivalries in this match-up? How might the weather affect the game? Is there a home-team advantage? How have these teams fared during the season and over the past few years? Pondering the answers to these and similar questions should make you ready to call an interesting game.[3]

In preparing for the coverage of a game wherein at least one of the teams is unknown to you, you must begin your preparation as far in advance as possible. Your resources are team media guides, press in-

[3]The foregoing questions are based on the suggestions of play-by-play sports announcer Denny Matthews.

formation kits, official yearbooks, newspaper stories and columns, wire-service reports, and specialized sports magazines. Professional teams will provide you with their yearbooks, and these are your most complete sources of information. Each player's sports career is outlined in detail; statistics are given for individuals, the team, and the team's opponents; each major player's photograph is included to make recognition easier. Along with statistics, interesting, significant, and curious facts are provided to help you bring to your narrative a sense of authority and familiarity.

Preparation includes memorizing all players by name, number, position, and, if possible, appearance. It includes making notes, usually on file cards, of information you feel might be useful during the game. Preparation also requires spotting charts, scoring sheets, and any similar materials appropriate to the sport being called.

Plan to arrive early on the day of the game. Check starting line-ups. If in doubt, check on the pronunciation of players' names with assistant managers or team captains. If possible, spend time with the players before the game; your effectiveness in describing the game will be enhanced by understanding how the players feel. Enter the booth long before game time. Set up your spotting charts and lay out your scoring sheets, cards of statistical and anecdotal information, and whatever notebooks or other materials you plan to use during the game. Check out your broadcast equipment. Whether yours is a radio or a television sportscast, chances are that commercials, if any, will be recorded just before game time. This adds to the burden of distraction from the upcoming event, but it will reduce pressure during the game.

Plan ahead. Think about everything you will need and make sure you have it all with you when you arrive at the booth. Aside from the spotting charts, scoring sheets, and information cards, you will need pencils, erasers, pins for the chart, water or some other beverage, binoculars, and perhaps even an electric heater to keep your teeth from chattering!

Calling the Game   Your booth set-up will vary with the sport. Football usually demands the services of a team of four: a play-by-play announcer, a play analyst, and two spotters. If you are doing play-by-play, you will sit between the two spotters, and your analyst partner will sit next to the spotter whose team is the less familiar of the two. In high school, college, or other professional games, chances are the analyst will be quite familiar with the home team, so his or her proper position is next to the spotter who points for the visiting team. The spotting charts are two-sided. One side lists the offensive players, the other the defensive unit. Pins are usually used to indicate the players in the game at any given moment. Playing positions are arranged in ranks that relate to the positioning of the players. The offense chart shows one straight line of six players: left tackle, left guard, center, right guard, right tackle, and tight end. Two wide receivers are shown outboard of this line of six. Behind the center of the line is a space for the quarterback and, behind the quarterback, two spaces for the running backs. The defensive chart shows a front line of five players—two tackles, two ends, and a linebacker—two spaces behind and outboard of the front line for two more linebackers, and four additional spaces directly behind the front line for defensive players such as cornerbacks and strong and free safety. Because football, especially at the professional level, is an extremely complex game, the spotting chart does not provide adequate flexibility to cover offensive and defensive re-alignments. Because you, as the play-by-play announcer, are concentrating on the handling of the football, your spotters are responsible for showing changes in the lineups—the defense spotter will hold up five fingers to indicate a nickel defense; the offensive spotter will hold up three fingers to indicate three wide receivers in the game, to give two examples.

The spotting chart also has three words written on it: *rush, beat,* and *tackle.* As appropriate, the spotters will point to one or another of these words and then point to a player's name. *Rush* indicates the key players on a rush; *beat* tells you who beat whom in a one-on-one situation; and *tackle* indicates players who made or missed key tackles.

In general, use your spotters for the things you cannot see for yourself. It is your job to follow the football, so leave other details of each play up to your spotters.

In calling a football game, you might benefit from standing rather than sitting. Walt Brown, sports director and play-by-play announcer for KTVK-TV, Phoenix, stands to broadcast any sport where standing is possible. Not only does he feel much more energy—which is communicated to his listeners—but he cites practical reasons as well. When standing, he finds it is easier to move, as needed, to relate to the field, the television monitor, spotter's charts, and the play analyst.

The booth set-up for baseball can be as simple as one play-by-play announcer sitting with a microphone and the kinds of information sheets and scoring charts needed to call the game. Radio and television coverage often is enhanced by adding two others to the announcing

team—a play and game analyst and a statistician. The normal three-
person team is arranged with the statistician on the left, play-by-play in
the center, and analyst on the right. Before them are at least three cards
or sheets of paper: a diagram of the baseball field with the names of the
defensive players written in and two score sheets, one for each team.

Basketball and hockey move so fast and have so few players that
play-by-play announcers have neither time nor need for spotters. A
name and position chart with pins indicating the players in the game at
any given moment may be helpful at times, but in general there is little
time to refer to them. The booth set-ups for basketball and hockey are
simple and quite similar. Where two-person announcing teams are
used, the second announcer provides analysis and, on radio, color.
Water polo coverage is in most respects similar to coverage of hockey
and basketball.

Boxing, golf, tennis, speed and figure skating, skiing and ski jump-
ing, and gymnastics present no problems of competitor recognition.
Spotting is unnecessary, and many of the complexities that make football and hockey difficult to call are not present. But most of these sports
require in-depth knowledge, and fans have come to expect reporters to
have superior comprehension and judgment. It has become common

for sports generalists to introduce, talk around, and summarize gymnastics and figure skating, with the actual play-by-play covered by a former practitioner of the sport. Boxing, golf, and tennis are covered by announcers who may not have competed in those sports but who have made long and intense study of them. Announce booths may be lacking altogether at the sites of these sports; at the opposite extreme, a highly sophisticated electronic center may have been created for their coverage.

In covering any sport as a member of a two-person team, it is necessary to develop and use simple nonverbal signals to avoid confusion. A sportscast can be deadly for your listeners if you and your partner are constantly interrupting one another or if you start speaking at the same time. The general rule is that the play-by-play announcer is the booth director. As play-by-play announcer, you will do all the talking unless you invite your play analyst or statistician to contribute. Play analysts indicate that they have a comment to make by raising their hand; if you decide to allow the comment, come to the end of your own remarks and then throw a cue by pointing an index finger. Analysts must always complete their remarks well ahead of time when you must again pick up the play-by-play.

When calling the game, you must keep many important principles in mind. First of all, you must truly believe that your chief responsibility is to your listeners. This will be difficult to hold to at times. Unreasonable owners, outraged players, and others who have a stake in your broadcasts may make irrational demands. In the long run, though, you will prosper best if you have a loyal following of viewers or listeners who have developed faith in your ability and your integrity and who know that you are not merely a shill for a profit-hungry sports organization.

Second, remember that it is your responsibility to report, entertain, and sell. Your reports must be accurate and fair. As an entertainer, you must attract and hold the fans' attention for up to three hours at a time. Selling means selling the sport more than the team. It means selling yourself as a credible reporter; it means communicating the natural enthusiasm you feel; it means avoiding hypocrisy, condescension, forced enthusiasm, and any other trait that will cause listeners to question your values.

Finally, avoid home-team bias. *Homers* are not unknown to sportscasting, and some have managed to retain their jobs and maintain popularity. Among the many practical reasons for avoiding a home-team bias, one stands out as of supreme importance: your bias will blind you to the actual events taking place before you. Regardless of affiliation or loyalties, it is your responsibility to provide fans with a clear, accurate, and fair account of the game. This responsibility is somewhat more pertinent to your work if you do play-by-play for radio. Television fans can compare your work with what they see, and this operates as a governor on what otherwise might be unchecked subjectivity. But as the eyes of your radio listeners, you have a considerable obligation to report with objectivity; your account is nearly their total experience of the event.

Further Tips on Sportscasting

Some of these suggestions are appropriate to all sports; others apply to one or two. They are given in no special order.

1. *Communicate the important events in a game and provide interpretation where appropriate.* A game is more than a series of individual plays or events. Plays are part of a process that adds up to an overall pattern. If you are perceptive and deeply into the event, you will be able to point out crucial plays and turning points immediately after they occur. It is your responsibility first to comprehend the significance of a play or an incident and then to communicate your awareness to your viewers or listeners. The importance will be transmitted not only by what you say but also by how you say it. At times, critical situations will be apparent to any reasonably sophisticated fan, but at other times it will be necessary for you to be so tuned in to the game that your interpretation transcends common knowledge.

2. *When doing play-by-play on radio, you must provide listeners with relatively more information than is necessary for a telecast.* Listeners need to know what the weather is like, how the stadium or court looks, how the fans are behaving, the right- or left-handedness of players, the wind direction, what the score is, who is on first, how many yards for a first down, how many outs or minutes left in the game, and whether a particular play was routine or outstanding. These are only a few obvious items of essential information.

3. *Never make events in a game seem more important than they are.* In a dull game, there is a natural temptation to entertain by exaggerating. Avoid this.

4. *Do not overuse sports clichés.* "Pigskin," "horsehide," "ducks on the pond," and "he got all of it" are some of the clichés of sports announcing. It is not entirely possible to avoid sports clichés, because there are a limited number of ways of describing things that happen over and over in a game. But you should be conscious of clichés and try to avoid them. (There are some very popular sportscasters, particularly in baseball, whose intrinsic style demands one cliché after another. The point here is that, if you are going to use clichés, at least become proficient in their use.)

5. *Have statistics in front of you or firmly in mind before you start to talk about them.* If you make an error, you can correct it, of course: "That's the fourth walk allowed by Rollins—hold it, it's the *third* walk." Taken alone, there is nothing wrong with this. The problem becomes annoying, however, if you find yourself repeatedly making corrections.

6. *On television, concentrate on interpreting the events and adding comments about things not clearly shown by the camera.* The television viewer does not necessarily see everything that a trained observer sees. With your help and the help of instant replay, viewers can be given a myriad of specific details that will illuminate, instruct, and entertain.

7. *When doing play-by-play on television, avoid the extremes of too much and too little commentary.* Avoid extraneous chatter that confuses and distracts viewers. At the opposite extreme, do not assume that your viewers or listeners have been with you throughout the entire game and therefore know everything important that has occurred. From time to time, review key plays, injuries, and other pertinent facts.

8. *When a player is injured, never guess about the nature or severity of the injury.* If you consider it important to report on the details of the injury, send an assistant to the team trainer or physician. Inaccurate information about an injury can cause unnecessary worry for friends and family.

9. *Do not ignore fights or injuries, but do not sensationalize them.*

10. *If you are not sure about your information, do not guess.* Wait as long as necessary to give official verdicts on whether a ball was fair or foul, whether a goal was scored, and whether a first down was made. Constant corrections of such errors are annoying to the fans.

11. *Repeat the score of the game at frequent intervals.* Tell a baseball audience what inning it is as you give the score. Tell football, basketball, and hockey audiences which period it is and how much time is left. Football audiences need to be reminded frequently of who has the ball, where the ball is, and what down is coming up. It is all but impossible to give such information too often.

12. *Give scores of other games, but never allow this to interfere with the game at hand.* When telecasting, remember that your viewers are being bombarded with information not only from you and your play analyst and the camera coverage of the game, but also from supers called up by the director for providing statistical information, identifying the game, promoting a program or another sportscast coming up, and so on. Because of this overload, you must be careful not to further distract viewers from the game they are watching. Give scores of other games but be discreet.

13. *Take care of first things first.* Before going to an analysis of a play, make sure that you have told your audience what it most wants to know. In baseball, do not describe the double play until you have told the fans whether or not the player on third scored. In football, do not start talking about key blocks or sensational catches until you have indicated whether or not a first down was made on the play.

14. *Do not keep telling your audience how great the game is.* If it is a great game, the events and the way you report them will speak for themselves. If it is not a great game, no amount of wishful thinking will make it exciting.

15. *If you cannot immediately identify a player, cover the play without mentioning names and give the name when you have it.* Here is a poor example of identifying players:

> ANNCR: The ball is taken by Richards . . . He's back in the pocket to pass . . . He's being rushed . . . He barely gets it away and it's intercepted by Pappas . . . no, I think it's Harrison . . . He has it on the twenty-five, the thirty, the thirty-five . . . and he's brought down on the thirty-seven. Yes, that *was* Pappas, the All-American defensive back.

Here is a better example:

ANNCR: The ball is taken by Richards . . . He's back in the pocket to pass . . . He's being rushed . . . He barely gets it away and it's intercepted on the twenty . . . back to the thirty, the thirty-five, and all the way to the thirty-seven. A beautiful interception by Charley Pappas, the All-American defensive back.

16. *Learn where to look for the information you need.* In baseball, watch the outfielders instead of a fly ball to see whether the ball will be caught, fielded, or lost over the fence. Watch line umpires to see whether a ball is fair or foul. In football, watch the quarterback unless you clearly see a handoff or a pass, then watch the ball. Let your spotters or analyst watch the defense and the offensive ends.

17. *Do not rely on scoreboard information.* Keep your own notebook and record the data appropriate to the sport you are covering. For football, note the time when possession begins, the location of the ball after each play, the nature of each play, and the manner in which the drive ends. This will help you summarize each drive and will single out the most important plays. For baseball, keep a regular scoring chart and learn to read it quickly and accurately. For basketball and hockey, rely on a statistician for data such as goals attempted and fouls and penalties assessed.

FIGURE 14.4
Bill King and Lon Simmons in a baseball stadium announce booth. Note the hanging microphone, used to pick up the sounds of the crowd. (Courtesy Oakland Athletics)

18. *Give statistics and records.* Baseball fans are always interested in batting and earned-run averages, fielding percentages, strike-out records, and comparative statistics. Track and field followers are obsessed with distance and speed records. Statistics are of only slightly less importance to followers of football, basketball, hockey, and golf.

19. *Avoid adopting meaningless catch phrases.* Perhaps the most prevalent and annoying habit of many sports announcers is the interjection of "of course" into statements in which the information being given is not necessarily known by all who are listening: "Wilson, of course, has run for over one hundred yards in each of his last seven games." Even when the information is widely known, "of course" adds nothing to most statements: "Whitey Ford, of course, was a Yankee pitcher."

20. *Eliminate or control the use of the word "situation."* With some sports announcers, nearly everything is a "situation"—"It's a passing situation," "It's a bunting situation," "It's a third-and-three situation"—and the constant repetition of the term can become very tiresome.

21. *Use background sounds to your advantage.* In most sports, there are moments of action that precipitate an enthusiastic response from the crowd. The sounds of cheering fans can enhance your game coverage. Do not be afraid to remain silent while the fans convey the excitement of the game for you.

22. *When working with a play analyst, as in the coverage of a football game, make sure you and your partner agree on the pronunciation of names that could be pronounced in different ways.* During a recent professional football telecast, play-by-play announcer and play analyst pronounced the names of three players in very different ways:

NAME	FIRST PRONUNCIATION	SECOND PRONUNCIATION
McMahon	(MUK-MAN') [mək'mæn]	(MUK-MAY'-UN) [mək'meən].
Lippett	(LIP'-UHT) ['lɪpət]	(LIH-PET') [lɪ'pet].
Clayborn	(KLAY'-BORN) ['kle,bɔrn]	(KLY'-BERN) ['klaɪ,bɚn].

These differences may have gone unnoticed by most listeners, but you always should aim for the acceptance of your most attentive listeners and viewers.

Play Analysis   A play analyst provides information and interpretation that comple-
ments rather than duplicates that offered by the play-by-play an-
nouncer. The analyst must have clear instructions about what to look
for and how to report it. In football, the analyst looks for key blocks,
tackles, and similar events of importance. In baseball, hockey, and
basketball, the analyst (when one is used) usually performs as a statistician and as an analyst of the game rather than of individual plays. In
these sports, the analyst sees little or nothing that is not seen by the
play-by-play announcer, so information such as "that was Ponce's
twenty-first inning without giving up a walk" or "Garrett's forty-one
points are a season high for him, but they're a long way from the
record set by Wilt Chamberlain—he scored one hundred points in one
game in 1962" is the kind of contribution expected of a play analyst.
Hockey and basketball move so fast that opportunities for play analysis
are limited, and when they are discussed at all, it is the play-by-play
announcer who discusses them.

Gymnastics, figure skating, and similar sports of an artistic nature
are usually described by experts in the event. Analysis is the primary
responsibility of people who cover sports in which points are assigned
by judges and the vast majority of the viewers have little precise
knowledge of the pluses and minuses of individual performances.

Here are a few tips on play and game analysis.

1. Never repeat either exactly or by paraphrase that which has just
   been said by the play-by-play announcer.
2. Do not feel called on to comment after every play of a football game
   or after every pitch of a baseball game. If you have nothing
   significant to report, remain silent.
3. If your agreement with the play-by-play announcer requires it, be
   prepared to make intelligent comments during time-outs and inter-
   missions in basketball and hockey contests.
4. Be precise in the comments you make. "What a great catch" is
   neither useful nor welcome. "Frick has just gone over the hun-
   dred-yard mark for the eighth time this season" is precise and
   useful.
5. Do your homework on both teams. The play-by-play announcer
   will also have prepared, but in the heat of the game it may fall to
   you to remember facts or statistics forgotten by your partner.
6. Your major contribution is to see the game with an objectivity not

always possible for a play-by-play announcer. Look for the dramatic structure of the contest and report it when appropriate. Make notes of key moments of the game. Look for the drama of the event but do not overdramatize it.

7. Never correct your partner on the air. If an important mistake has been made, write and pass a note. Listeners and viewers become uncomfortable when they sense conflict between members of the announcing team.

8. A discussion between play-by-play announcer and analyst in which different points of view are expressed can be useful to fans. As long as the discussion is friendly, there should be no reason to avoid or prematurely terminate it.

9. Be careful what questions you ask of your partner. Even the most seasoned veteran can draw a blank when concentrating on a game.

10. Follow the rules set down by your play-by-play partner. You will probably be required to ask for an opportunity to speak and will do so only when your partner gives you your cue.

11. Always be sure to end your comments before the next play begins.

It may be difficult to maintain harmonious relations with your partner, but it is imperative. Fans appreciate listening to announcing teams that complement each other and work together to present the sports experience competently and completely.

If you hope to become a professional sports announcer of any kind—reporter, play-by-play, analyst—you should build your own sports library and become an expert in as many sports as possible. And remember that there is no substitute for practice.

APPENDIX A
COMMERCIALS AND
PSA EXERCISES

A series of fact sheets begins the exercise appendix. Fact sheets contain only the essentials of a particular product, service, or special occasion, such as a sale. They are sometimes sent to stations by advertising agencies, but most often they are prepared by time sellers working for a station. Fact sheets can be used in two ways: they can be the basis of an ad-lib delivery, or they can provide the information you need to write and perform scripts. You might even want to produce some of these scripts, mixing music, sound effects, and voice to make a complete commercial package.

Following the fact sheets, scripts for radio and television commercials and public-service announcements are provided. Some call for music or sound effects; it would be good practice to work with these audio elements whenever you can.

Note that the pronunciation of uncommon or difficult words is given within each commercial or public-service announcement in wire-service phonetics and in the symbols of the International Phonetic Alphabet.

COMMERCIALS

FACT SHEET 1

     AGENCY: Gappa Communications

     CLIENT: The Home Improvement Center

   OCCASION: Pre-Inventory clearance of carpets and rugs

MERCHANDISE: Roll stock--Hi-Lo Long Wear Nylon--$4.95/yard

              Herculon (HER'-KYOO-LAHN) ['hɜˈkjulɑn] Rubberback, com-

              mercial grade--$4.49/yard

              Summerdale by Barwick, polyester--$6.00/yard

              Area rug sale--

              Sarouk (SAH-REWK') [sɑˈruk]

              Kirman (KIHR'-MAHN) ['kɪrmɑn]

              Bachtiar (BAHK-TEE-AHR') [bɑktiˈɑr]

              Heriz (HAIR-EEZ') [hɛrˈiz]

              from $69.95 to $399.95

 SALE DATES: Saturday and Sunday, Mar. 10-11, 9:00-9:00

FACT SHEET 2

     AGENCY: Mills Advertising

     CLIENT: S & F Drive-In

MERCHANDISE: Hot pastrami, chiliburgers, fishy-burgers, corny-dogs,

              fries, onion rings, shakes

              NOTHING OVER 88¢

    ADDRESS: Just outside of town on Highway 44

       NOTE: CLIENT WANTS A HUMOROUS COMMERCIAL.

FACT SHEET 3

CLIENT: Cafe International

OCCASION: Weekend features

MERCHANDISE: From Italy, stufato di manzo alla Genovese (STEW–FAH'-TOE

DEE MAHN'-TSOH AH'-LAH JEN–OH–VAY'-SAY) [stuˈfatˌo di ˈmantʃˌo

ˈalˌaˌdʒenoˈveˌse]

From Germany, gewürztes Rindfleisch (GEH–VIRTS'-ESS RIHND'-

FLYSCH) [geˈvɪrtsˌɛs ˈrɪndˌflaɪʃ]

From Mexico, carne in salza negra (KAR'-NAY EEN SAHL'-SAH

NAY'-GRAH) [ˈkɑrˌne in ˈsɑlsə ˈneˌgrə]

From France, ratatouille (RAT–UH–TOO'-EE) [rætəˈtuˌi]

Wines of the week: Cabernet Sauvignon 1949 (KAB'-AIR–NAY

SO–VEEN–YAWN') [ˈkæbɛrne sovinˈjɔn]

Gewürztraminer (GAY–VIRTS'-TRAH–MEEN'-ER) [geˈvɪrts trɑˈminɚ]

DATES: This Fri and Sat eve, Sun noon to 11:00 P.M.

ADDRESS: 118 Central, between Jefferson and Adams

NOTE: CLIENT EXPECTS YOU TO AWAKEN CURIOSITY ABOUT THESE DISHES.

CHECK OUT WHAT THEY ARE, SO THAT YOU CAN DESCRIBE AT LEAST

ONE OR TWO OF THEM. CORRECT PRONUNCIATION A MUST!

FACT SHEET 4

CLIENT: Chapman's Drugs

OCCASION: Department Managers' Summer Sale

MERCHANDISE: Cascade automatic dishwashing detergent--35 oz. size, 93¢

Puritan Jam--18 oz. jar, 99¢

Fire extinguisher--$5.99

Picnic jug, one gallon--$2.66

Save on all garden needs

Sunglasses, 25% off

Low prices on cosmetics, vitamins, and bathroom needs

DATES: 9 big sale days, June 12 thru June 20

ADDRESS: 3 locations--in Downtown Novato, Red Hill Shopping Center, and North Gate Shopping Center

---

FACT SHEET 5

CLIENT: Red Boy Pizza

MERCHANDISE: Red Boy Pizza features a thick, delicious crust, prepared at time of ordering. Six different types of grated cheese. Homemade tomato paste. Sixteen pizzas to choose from, including vegetarian, Devil's Delight, pepperoni, plus many combinations.

NOTE: CLIENT WANTS A RELAXED AND FRIENDLY COMMERCIAL. USE ONLY AS MUCH COPY AS CAN BE DONE COMFORTABLY IN 60 SECONDS.

ADDRESS: Kenosha and Clark Streets, across from Murray Park

FACT SHEET 6

AGENCY: John Christian Services, Inc.

CLIENT: Allison's Pet Center

OCCASION: Christmas Sale

MERCHANDISE: Guppies and goldfish, 39¢ each

Aquariums, 10-gal., with filter, $19.95

White mice, $1.00 a pair

Squirrel monkeys, $95.00 each

DATES: Dec. 15th 'til Christmas Eve

ADDRESS: Corner Fulton and North Streets, Petaluma

NOTE: CLIENT WANTS HUMOROUS COMMERCIAL.

FACT SHEET 7

AGENCY: Paul C. Smith Communications, Inc.

CLIENT: Harmony Music

OCCASION: Semi-annual clearance sale, June 10-30

MERCHANDISE: Seventy-five new and reconditioned pianos to choose from.
High trade-ins. 35% to 50% off.
All world famous piano and organ makes--Hammond, Kawai
(KUH-WY') [kə'waɪ], Farfisa (FAR-FEE'-SUH) [far'fisə], Ibach
(EE'-BACH) ['ibax], Steinway, Chickering, and Sheidmeyer
(SCHYD'-MY-ER) ['ʃaɪd,maɪɚ].

ADDRESS: Cherry Hill Shopping Center

FACT SHEET 8

AGENCY: Barsotti Associates

CLIENT: The Drapery House

MERCHANDISE: Drapery consultant will bring samples to your home--no

obligation, no charge.

Prices from $4.49 to $18.99 a yard.

Drapes feature 4" permanent buckram, blind-stitched side

hems, and weighted corners. Tie-backs and valances

(VAL'-UNS-UHZ) ['vælənsəz].

FACT SHEET 9

AGENCY: Meyers Muldoon & Ketchum

CLIENT: Safeway Stores

FEATURES: Valchris or Armour Star Broth Basted Hen Turkeys, only 69¢

a lb.

Red or Golden Delicious Apples--crisp and sweet--4 lbs.

for just a dollar.

Mrs. Wright's Supersoft Bread--3 one-pound loaves for only

a dollar.

Nu Made Peanut Butter--the big 18 oz. jar--just $1.69.

When it comes to helping you save, Safeway does a little

more!

Safeway. Everything you want from a store, and a little

bit more.

```
       CREATION AND
        PRODUCTION:  Chuck Blore & Don Richman, Inc.
            CLIENT:  AT&T
            LENGTH:  60 seconds

         CATHIANNE:  Hello.
             DANNY:  Uh, hi. You probably still remember me, Edward introduced
                     us at the seminar . . .
         CATHIANNE:  Oh, the guy with the nice beard.
             DANNY:  I don't know whether it's nice . . .
         CATHIANNE:  It's a gorgeous beard.
             DANNY:  Well, thank you, uh, listen, I'm gonna, uh, be in the city
                     next Tuesday and I was, y'know, wondering if we could
                     sorta, y'know, get together for lunch?
         CATHIANNE:  How 'bout dinner?
             DANNY:  Dinner? Dinner! Dinner's a better idea. You could pick
                     your favorite restaurant and . . .
         CATHIANNE:  How 'bout my place? I'm my favorite cook.
             DANNY:  Uh, your place. Right. Sure. That's great to me.
         CATHIANNE:  Me too. It'll be fun.
             DANNY:  Yeah . . . listen, I'll bring the wine.
         CATHIANNE:  Perfect. I'll drink it.
              BOTH:  (LAUGH)
             DANNY:  Well, OK, then, I guess it's a date. I'll see you Tuesday.
         CATHIANNE:  Tuesday. Great.
             DANNY:  Actually, I just, uh, I called to see how you were and
                     y'know, Tuesday sounds fine!
             SOUND:  PHONE HANGS UP
             DANNY:  (YELLING) Tuesday . . . AHHHH . . . she's gonna see me
                     Tuesday. (FADE)
              SUNG:  REACH OUT, REACH OUT AND TOUCH SOMEONE
```

```
CREATION AND
PRODUCTION:   Chuck Blore & Don Richman, Inc.
    CLIENT:   Hallmark Cards
    LENGTH:   60 seconds

     JOSH:   My dad says we'll only be gone 4 to 5 weeks, tops.
    NANCY:   You're going to call me, aren't you?
     JOSH:   You know I'm gonna call you.
    NANCY:   I have a surprise for ya.
     JOSH:   Oh . . .
    NANCY:   Pick a hand
     JOSH:   Right hand
    NANCY:   Okay, see this?
     JOSH:   What is it?
    NANCY:   It's a charm. All you do is rub his stomach and you'll
             have luck for the rest of the day.
     JOSH:   Thanks, I have something for you also.
    NANCY:   You got me something?
     JOSH:   Here, it's a card.
    NANCY:   Ohhhh!
     JOSH:   It's a Hallmark card.
    NANCY:   (LAUGHS)
     JOSH:   You're gonna read it, aren't ya?
    NANCY:   Of course.
             Ohhh! I love you too. (LAUGHS)
     JOSH:   You don't have to get all choked up about it.
    NANCY:   Gimme a hug, man.
   UNISON:   (LAUGHING)
     REGE:   Sharing caring feelings, one-to-one, heart-to-heart. How
             could you give anything less than a Hallmark Card?
             Hallmark Cards. When you care enough.
```

AGENCY: Ketchum Communications

CLIENT: CIBA-GEIGY Corp.

LENGTH: 60 seconds

MUSIC: UP AND UNDER THROUGHOUT

ANNCR: Harvest time in sorghum country. The air is dry and
          dusty--thick with the smell of diesel. A combine pauses in
          a field of deep red sorghum, having gathered its first
          load of the day.

          This is the finest sorghum grown, kept clean and free of
          weeds and grasses with Bicep herbicide and Concep II
          safened seed--the most cost-effective weed control program
          available.

          Concep II provides the protective shield for young
          sorghum. Bicep provides the tough control of weeds and
          grasses--like pigweed, crabgrass, signalgrass and
          barnyardgrass. Nothing works better. Nothing lasts longer.
          So you get nothing but sorghum--with no danger to crops,
          no tank mixing, and no broadleaf weeds or grasses--a
          clean, healthy harvest. With Bicep and Concep II, sorghum
          growers' first choice for cleaner, more profitable
          sorghum.

AGENCY: Ketchum Communications

CLIENT: Lyon's Restaurants

LENGTH: 50 seconds (+ 10-second tag)

ANNCR: There are lots of ways to start your day. But the most
          delicious is with breakfast at Lyon's Restaurant. And the
          only thing better than a hearty Lyon's breakfast is a deal
          on a hearty Lyon's breakfast! Well, that's exactly what
          Lyon's offers every weekday--from midnight until eleven
          AM. Just order any three of Lyon's special breakfast
          favorites for just one-ninety-five. That's right! Any
          three for one-ninety-five. You could choose Lyon's fresh
          ranch eggs, fluffy pancakes, and crisp bacon strips. Then,
          Lyon's lets you add other special breakfast items for only
          sixty-five cents each. Like savory sausage links . . .
          Lyon's famous French toast . . . hash browns . . . juices
          . . . and other breakfast eye-openers. All just sixty-five
          cents each . . . as part of Lyon's one-ninety-five
          breakfast special. So for a delicious deal on the best way
          to start your day . . . head for Lyon's . . . (ROAR) . . .
          and eat like a king!

LIVE: INSERT LIVE TAG HERE.

AGENCY: Ketchum Communications

CLIENT: Lyon's Restaurants

LENGTH: 50 seconds (+ 10-second tag)

ANNCR: Everyone knows Lyon's Restaurants create some of the best roast beef sandwiches around--like Lyon's famous French Dip; tender, flavorful beef--roasted to juicy perfection and sliced to order. It's served up on a big French roll with plenty of rich Au Jus. And Lyon's Beef Dip with Barbecue Sauce--nothing beats that tangy, hickory-smoked flavor. Well, right now, Lyon's invites you to enjoy these delights even more--with a delicious deal on Lyon's entire family of roast beef sandwiches, including Lyon's Hot Roast Beef sandwich with mashed potatoes . . . and their French Beef 'n Cheese sandwich. Choose your favorite for just three-forty-nine for any Lyon's roast beef sandwich. Every one includes your choice of fries or salad, plus fresh fruit. But hurry into Lyon's--this delicious three-forty-nine deal won't last forever. Only at Lyon's (ROAR) where you can eat like a king!

LIVE: INSERT LIVE TAG HERE

AGENCY: Millar Advertising, Inc.

CLIENT: Andre's International Bakery

LENGTH: 60 seconds

ANNCR: Hot fresh breakfast rolls, glistening with melting butter!
          Croissants and cafe au lait (KRAH-SAHNTS' KAHF'-AY-OH-LAY')
          [kraˈsɑnts, ˈkæfeˌoˈle]. Raisin bran muffins to go with your
          poached eggs. Andre's has these delicacies, and they're
          waiting for you now. For afternoon tea, Andre suggests
          English biscuits, served with lemon marmalade. Or scones
          and plum jam. For after dinner desserts, what about
          baklava (BAHK-LAH-VAH') [bɑklɑˈvɑ] the Persian delicacy made
          with dozens of layers of paper-thin pastry, honey, and
          chopped walnuts? Or, if your taste runs to chocolate, a
          German torte (TOR'-TUH) [ˈtɔrtə]? These and many other
          international delicacies are created daily by Andre and
          his staff. Made of pure and natural ingredients--grade A
          cream and butter, natural unrefined sugar, pure chocolate
          and cocoa, and pure spices. For mouth-watering pastries
          from around the world, it's Andre's International Bakery.
          We bring you the best from the gourmet capitals of the
          world. Visit Andre's today! In the Corte Madera Shopping
          Center. Andre's!

CREATION AND

PRODUCTION: Chuck Blore & Don Richman, Inc.

    CLIENT: Campbell Soup

    LENGTH: 30 seconds

DON: You're eating chunky chicken soup with a fork?

JOHN: Well, you've got to spear the chicken to get it into your mouth. Look at that. Look at the size of that. You gotta use a spoon for the noodles.

DON: You got some noodles on your fork.

JOHN: Yeah, but they slide through.

DON: Well, you use the spoon, you use the fork.

JOHN: That's right.

DON: Is chunky chicken a soup or a meal?

JOHN: I leave that up to the experts, but I personally . . .

DON: (OVER LAUGH) Why'd you say that?

JOHN: I know, but I mean, you know, I'm not a connoisseur on the food department but I would say it's a meal.

DON: But it's a soup.

JOHN: It's a meal within a soup can. Let's put it that way.

DON: Campbell's Chunky Chicken . . . it's the soup that eats like a meal.

CREATION AND

PRODUCTION: Chuck Blore & Don Richman, Inc.
   CLIENT: Michigan Travel
   LENGTH: 45 seconds

(Note: This humorous commercial requires precise timing.
Pauses must sound like natural hesitancies as the typed
words catch up with the spoken words.)

   EFFECT: TYPING BEHIND
     BILL: Dear Mom . . .

Skiing in Michigan is even cheaper than you . . .
said it would be. I just hate the thought of you . . .
missing all the fun, so I hit Mary Ruth . . .
with the idea that you join us midweek. She said, "No, . . .
time like the present to tell her about Michigan's low
mid . . .
week rates. Mom, when you get here, you'll see your son
going downhill . . .
Your daughter-in-law going cross-country and you'll
smell . . .
the clean, pine-scented air. And the ski instructors . . .
can spend more time with you midweek, which gives us more
time to soak . . .
up all the winter wonders of skiing Michigan with
love . . .
Your son, Hot Dog Billy.

     SUNG: WINTER SPORTS OF ALL SORTS
NEAR YOU

AGENCY: Grey Advertising, Inc.

CLIENT: Bank of America

LENGTH: 60 seconds

SFX: OFFICE AMBIENCE. THEN UNDER THROUGHOUT

MAN #1:   Hey partner of mine. Come over here and check out this ad.

MAN #2:   Don't tell me. Another prospectus. For this you interrupt my calls?

MAN #1:   Don't start, just read.

MAN #2:   Alright. Alright. Says: Bank of America offers more of what small business needs to succeed. Hmmm . . . Can they do that?

MAN #1:   They can do that. Keep reading—you impress me.

MAN #2:   Says Bank of America offers every banking service to help your small business make it in the marketplace. Gee . . . Can they do that?

MAN #1:   They can do that. (HE CONTINUES READING) Everything from business checking to unmatched worldwide capabilities. (HE STOPS READING) And what does our banker (your brother) do that's extra besides take us up skiing and tell corny jokes for two days?

MAN #2:   And look at this: Says Bank of America has over 1,000 Business Bankers all over the state committed exclusively to small business? Can they do that?

MAN #1:   They can do that! In fact, I'm gonna call B of A right now. I bet someone will see us straight away.

MAN #2:   Can they do that?

MAN #1:   Let me put it this way . . . They can do that!

TAG: Bank on the leader. Bank of America.

AGENCY: Grey Advertising, Inc.
CLIENT: Bank of America
LENGTH: 60 seconds

SFX: FOOTSTEPS WALKING ACROSS HARD SURFACE
ANNCR: Bank of America would like to show you the way to get into
a car. (FOOTSTEPS STOP) The key (KEYS JINGLE) is
affordability. Bank of America has so many different auto
loan options, one's bound to let you afford the car you
want. Let's try (KEYS JINGLE AGAIN) this key. 100%
financing--no down payment if you qualify. (KEY GOES INTO
LOCK AND UNLOCKS CAR DOOR) Well that was good for openers.
The next key gives you good rates on fixed rate loans.
(CAR DOOR OPENS) Now this key (KEYS JINGLE) gives you $\frac{1}{4}$%
off for automatic payment from a B of A checking or
savings account. While this key . . . (KEY GOES INTO
IGNITION & CAR STARTS) . . . makes it easier to start with
lower initial monthly (CAR DRIVES OFF UNDER) payments on
variable rate loans. Or the "Almost-Like-A-Lease Loan."
Now let's see if we can fuel the affordability with a
variable rate loan that has fixed monthly payments and a
rate cap.
ATTENDANT: Key please.
ANNCR: This should do. (BELL ON GAS PUMP RINGS AS TANK IS BEING
FILLED) Come to California's lending leader. We'll show
you the affordable way to get into a car.
SINGERS: Bank on the Leader.

Bank of America.

CLIENT: Houston Hearing Aid Center[1]

LENGTH: 60 seconds

ANNCR: Good evening, this is _____. Listen to me whisper this
          sentence. (WHISPERING) Do you have difficulty hearing
          someone speaking in a low voice? (NORMAL VOLUME) If you
          couldn't hear the previous statement because I was
          whispering, then you might need hearing assistance. Al
          Sawyers and associates at the Houston Hearing Aid Center
          is a licensed hearing aid dispenser, and offers a complete
          audiometric service. The Houston Hearing Aid Center on
          Starr Lane has been helping the hearing impaired since
          1947 with sales, service, and repairs on all brands of
          hearing aids. Offering a senior citizens' discount, 30-day
          free trial, and credit terms, Al Sawyers of Houston
          Hearing Aid Center can assist you in creating a brighter
          outlook on life with the correct hearing aid. Call Al
          Sawyers at the Houston Hearing Aid Center, 787-3333, for an
          appointment, or for their free in-home service. This is
          _____ for the Houston Hearing Aid Center.

[1] Courtesy Gerry Sher, Accounts Executive, KABL Radio.

CLIENT: Eyes Have It[2]

LENGTH: 60 seconds

ANNCR: Where do you go when your eye doctor gives you a new
          prescription? If you live in the Willamette Valley, you
          should check out Eyes Have It in Eugene and Salem. As
          dispensing opticians for fifteen years, Eyes Have It has
          brought style to the necessity of wearing eyeglasses. You
          should look good if you wear glasses, and we'll see to it
          that you do. At Eyes Have It, you'll feel the family-owned
          warmth as you try on quality high-fashion eye wear. With
          our own lab, and custom tinting, Eyes Have It is the
          complete dispensing optician for the entire family. Open
          weekdays from nine-thirty to five-thirty, and Saturday ten
          to one. Eyes Have It makes it easy for you who live away
          from Eugene or Salem. Look over the new look you'll get
          with sensational new high-fashion eye wear, from people
          who are homey, sensitive, pressureless, and fully knowl-
          edgeable to what's going on in the world of eye wear. We
          have Eyes Have It—you'll love the look!

[2]Courtesy Gerry Sher, Accounts Executive, KABL Radio.

CLIENT: Norwegian Designs[3]

LENGTH: 60 seconds

ANNCR: If I told you I have a hang-up for you, would that be misleading? I'm _____ of Norwegian Designs. We're the new and exclusive working wall system store in the Financial District. At Norwegian Designs, our hang-ups are leasable. It's probably the first time anyone has offered your walls a new look with suspended furniture. I could describe the file systems, or the hidden bar, or many of the other features that space-saving wall units offer your office, but I'd much prefer if you'd walk in on me, and look at them in all their displayed beauty. I'm at the corner of State and Michigan. Norwegian Designs. Oh, I wasn't fooling about the leasing part—we really do lease this office furniture. We carry major systems of suspended furniture, with great varieties of wood, tones, and colors. Your office may need just an inexpensive face lift that's totally utilitarian. Stop by and see them at Norwegian Designs. What a hang-up!

[3]Courtesy of Gerry Sher, Accounts Executive, KABL Radio.

AGENCY: Ammirati & Puris, Inc.

CLIENT: Schweppes—Mixers

LENGTH: 60 seconds

SFX: WINTER SOUNDS (RAIN, SLUSH, ETC.)

BRITISH VO: Leave it to American ingenuity to take a rather bleak time
of year and transform it into a season full of quaint but
cheerful holiday traditions.

SFX: HOLIDAY MUSIC

And leave it to British ingenuity to impart a rare sparkle
to these festivities——Schweppes.

For example, when feasting until immobilized on an oversized bird, Schweppes Club Soda, bursting with Schweppervescence, makes a lively dinner companion.

Your ritual of cramming as many people as possible into a
department store elevator, meanwhile, inspires a thirst
only Schweppes Ginger Ale with real Jamaican ginger can
quench.

And while transfixed to the telly watching a group of
massive, helmeted chaps smash into one another, what could
be more civilized than Schweppes Tonic Water with essence
of lime and Seville oranges?

And while many of your holiday traditions seem quite curious to us, we certainly toast their spirit. And suggest
you do the same, with the purchase of Schweppes. The Great
British Bubbly.

AGENCY: Ammirati & Puris, Inc.

CLIENT: Schweppes Ginger Ale

LENGTH: 60 seconds

BRITISH VOICE,   (GUITAR MUSIC AND TUNING UP UNDER VOICE)

EARLY 20s TO

EARLY 30s: Years ago, if a fellow gargled with floor sweepings, he'd be called crazy. But today, it's just one of the things we've got to do to be heavy metal stars here in England. In fact, we scream our flippin' lungs out. Makes us awfully parched and thirsty. Which is why me and the boys, the Sleeze-Hunks, keep a lot of Schweppes Ginger Ale on stage. You see, for all our obscene wealth, there's still nothing like Schweppes Ginger Ale's cheeky little bubbles and thirst-quenching Schweppervescence to make sure our voices don't crack and the windows do. (LAUGH) Here, take this little ditty we whipped up, for instance:
(MUSIC, HE SINGS)

     "Coat-check woman--You make me sore!

     When I got back, I found my coat on the floor!"
See what I mean? Totally taxing to the old vocal cords. Not to mention thirst-building. So it's no wonder this Schweppes Ginger Ale, made with real Jamaican ginger, is so popular with us Brits. I like it so much, I had my hair dyed that lovely green on the label. (LAUGH)

ANNCR: Schweppes Ginger Ale. The great British bubbly.

AGENCY: Ammirati & Puris, Inc.

CLIENT: Schweppes

LENGTH: 60 seconds

(BRITISH MARCHING MUSIC UNDER)

BRITISH

ANNOUNCER: For many years it seemed, if there were a place in the
world far too hot and altogether too sunny, then we
British would inevitably make it a part of our empire. In
fact, we practically cornered the market on deserts.
Making us, if not enormously wealthy, enormously thirsty.
Thus creating a brisk demand for Schweppes Tonic Water,
the great British bubbly. From the parched outback of
Australia, where thirst-crazed Kiwi hunters virtually
subsisted on Schweppes Tonic Water. To the Saharan
Tungsten Mines, where we British would gratefully relish
its cheeky little bubbles. To the Manchurian Gobi Desert,
where plucky yak traders would linger over its savory
taste of lemons and Seville oranges. Schweppes Tonic Water
turned out to be just the thing. So refreshing and
Schweppervescent. So thirst-quenching, that even after we
gave back all those blasted deserts, we British still
thoroughly enjoy Schweppes Tonic Water. The great British
bubbly.

This commercial was written to give you practice in reading an over-long commercial in sixty seconds. It is hack copy, but sooner or later you will have to meet the challenge of reading commercials like this one.

AGENCY: Client's copy

CLIENT: Compesi's Meat Locker

LENGTH: 60 seconds

ANNCR: How would you like to save <u>dollars</u>, while serving your
         family the best in beef, pork, chicken, and lamb? Sounds
         impossible? Well, it isn't, <u>if</u> you own a home freezer and
         buy your meats wholesale at Compesi's Meat Locker.
         Hundreds of families have discovered that it actually
         costs less to serve prime rib, steaks, and chops than it
         does to scrimp along on bargain hamburger and tough cuts.
         The secret? Buy your meat in quantity from Compesi's.
         Imagine––one hundred pounds of prime beef steaks and
         roasts for less than $2.00 a pound! Save even more by
         purchasing a quarter or a side. With every side of beef,
         Compesi's throws in twenty pounds of chicken, ten pounds
         of bacon, and a leg of spring lamb––absolutely free! If
         you don't own a freezer, Compesi's will get you started in
         style. Buy any of their 300-pound freezers, and Compesi's
         will give you a <u>freezer full</u> of <u>frozen food free</u>! Meat,
         vegetables, even frozen gourmet casseroles, all free with
         the purchase of a new freezer. Prices for freezers start
         at $299, and terms can be arranged. Beat the high cost of
         living! Come into Compesi's and see which plan is best for
         your family. Compesi's has two locations––in the Lakeport
         Shopping Center, and downtown at 1338 Fifth Street.

RADIO PROMOTION

IN—HOUSE: CHANNEL 7

   TITLE: 3:30 Movie, Creepy Creatures Tease[4]

AUDIO EFFECTS	COPY
(MUSIC: "THE DAY TIME ENDED")	Hello. Afraid of those creepy things
(STING ON "NIGHT")	that go bump in the night? Well, I
	wouldn't watch Channel 7's "3:30
	Movie" because we've got a whole week of
	creepy creatures. Monday, it's Ray
(SFX: LOUD FROG)	Milland and his giant (SFX) "Frogs."
	(SLIGHT PAUSE)
	Tuesday, Hank Fonda is all wrapped up
(SFX: MALE SCREAM)	in "Tentacles." (SFX)
	Wednesday, it's back to those good old
(SFX: ELEPHANT TRUMPET, BACKWARDS)	days, with prehistoric creatures (SFX)
	in "The People Time Forgot."
	Thursday, little gnomes (GUH—NOMES)
	are after a luscious young wife in
	"Don't Be Afraid of the Dark." Fi-
	nally, Friday——if you haven't had
	enough——it's a submarine full of
	snakes in "Fer—de—lance."
	Creepy Creatures starts Monday on
	Channel 7's "3:30 Movie."
(SFX: WOLF HOWL)	

[4]Courtesy of KGO-TV, San Francisco.

AGENCY: Ketchum Advertising

CLIENT: Safeway Stores

LENGTH: 30 seconds

ANNCR: Now's the time to fill your kitchen shelves with canned goods because this week Safeway's having a big Del Monte Round Up Days Sale with special prices on some of their most popular items!! You'll find savings on Del Monte Fruit Cocktail, peaches, pears, and big 46 oz. cans of fruit drinks. Look for inflation fighter prices on Del Monte vegetables, too. Safeway's even reduced the price of Del Monte Tomato Sauce and Ketchup. Don't miss Del Monte Round Up Days at Safeway!!! Safeway. Everything you want from a store and a little bit more!!!

LOCUTOR: Ahora es el momento de almacenar en su cocina productos enlatados, porque esta semana Safeway tiene la Gran Venta "Del Monte Round Up Days", ¡¡¡con precios especiales en varios de sus productos más populares!!! Ahorre al comprar Coctel de Frutas marca Del Monte, así como también sus duraznos, peras, y las grandes latas de 46 onzas de las bebidas de frutas. También encontrará vegetales marca Del Monte a precios que combaten la inflación. Además, Safeway ha reducido el precio del Ketchup y la Salsa de Tomate marca Del Monte. ¡¡¡No se pierda la venta "Del Monte Round Up Days" en Safeway!!! Safeway. Todo lo que usted desea de una tienda ¡¡¡y un poquito más!!!

AGENCY: Miller and Stein, Advertising

CLIENT: Su Casa (SOO KAH'-SAH) [su'kasa]

LENGTH: 60 seconds

MUSIC: MEXICAN HARP, UPBEAT TEMPO, IN AND UNDER TO CLOSE.

ANNCR: Ole, Amigos! (OH-LAY' AH-MEE'-GOS) [o'le a'migos] Su Casa means
          "your home," and that's what Ramona wants you to feel when
          you visit her at San Antonio's most elegant Mexican
          restaurant. Su Casa. Ramona features the most popular
          dishes from Mexico, including enchiladas verde or
          rancheros (EN-CHIL-AH'-DAS VEHR'-DAY or RAHN-CHER'-OHS)
          [entʃɪ'ladas 'vɛrde or ran'tʃer,os], chile con queso (CHEE'-LAY KAHN
          KAY'-SO) ['tʃi,le kan 'ke,so], and chimichangos (CHEE'-
          MEE-CHANG'-GOS) ['tʃimi'tʃaŋgos]. But, Ramona also has
          special family recipes that you won't find anywhere else.
          Try Pescado en Concha (PES-KAH'-DO EN COHN'-CHAH) [pɛs'ka,do
          ɛn 'kontʃa], chunks of sole in a rich cream and cheddar
          cheese sauce, served in scallop shells. Or Scallops La
          Jolla (LAH-HOY'-UH) [la 'hɔɪə] prepared with wine, lemon
          juice, and three kinds of cheeses. Or Baked Swordfish
          Manzanillo (MAHN-ZAH-NEE'-OH) [manza'ni,o]. See
          Ramona today, where her home is your home. Su Casa!

CLIENT: Hymie's[5]

LENGTH: 60 seconds

MUSIC: INSTRUMENTAL FROM "FIDDLER ON THE ROOF"

ANNCR: Ah ha, it's a New York flavor in music . . . and at Hymie's
          you'll get the true New York flavor in deli. How can the
          true taste be transferred to Omaha? It's simple. You just
          serve true Eastern beef, cured and pickled to Hymie's
          unmatched palate, and sliced to your order. Of course,
          there's hot New York corned beef . . . hot pastrami . . .
          Hebrew National salami and baloney . . . lox . . . bagels
          . . . and much much more--all with Hymie's taste buds
          controlling the taste that has not been in Omaha until
          now. At Hymie's when you taste the Kosher pickles and the
          sour tomatoes you'll remember those days. How about a
          knish--potato, kasha, or beef? If you've never had a
          Hymie's knish, then you're in for a gourmet's delight.
          Actually, Hymie's wife makes them, but where would Hymie
          be without her anyway . . . Mrs. Hymie also makes the
          matzo ball soup, the borscht, and the change. Hymie's
          isn't easy to find . . . but it's worth the look. To find
          Hymie's, first find the Flatiron Building, and there,
          practically in its shadow on Oak Street, is Hymie's . . .
          actually, it's next to Logan's Irish Pub. Hymie's--777 Oak
          Street . . . A New York tradition in Omaha.

[5]Courtesy of Gerry Sher, Accounts Executive, KABL Radio.

CLIENT: Peaches & Cream
SUBJECT: Boutiques
LENGTH: 60 seconds

ANNCR: This is _____ from Peaches & Cream with some highly
          significant facts about shopping in our boutiques; first
          of all you'll find an extraordinary selection of jeans,
          tops, sweaters, and dresses. We buy from 138 different
          manufacturers, so you can find just what you want . . .
          and you don't have to pay a lot of money. Of the 138
          different lines we carry, 137 of them are inexpensive and
          the other one, we keep in the back room. Furthermore at
          Peaches & Cream you don't have to deal with uppity
          salesladies who are snotty to you because you aren't
          flashing a large wad of bills. All of our salesladies are
          especially selected for their easy-going, personable
          dispositions . . . and besides none of them are on com-
          mission, this is a very important fact. Lastly nobody at
          Peaches & Cream has a perfect body, to make you feel fat.
          There is a Peaches & Cream in Sausalito and in Mill Val-
          ley. If you haven't heard about Peaches & Cream, you had
          better hurry down before we get famous and lose our hum-
          ble charm . . . .

AGENCY: Ketchum Advertising

CLIENT: The Potato Board

LENGTH: 60 seconds

ANNCR: The Potato Board wants to ask you a question: have you
          ever thought of the potato as a <u>vegetable</u>? The potato
          . . . as a vegetable? Most people only think of the potato
          as a starch--a filler food. They couldn't be more wrong,
          because The Potato Board reminds us the potato is a
          <u>vegetable</u> that contains lots of good things like vitamins,
          minerals, complex carbohydrates, and, of course, fiber.
          But the potato is <u>not</u> full of calories. Only 100 in a
          medium-sized baked potato--and just 40 more with some
          butter. That 140 calories is less than a cup of green
          salad with two tablespoons of dressing. As a vegetable,
          the potato is the crown prince of versatility. And The
          Potato Board says you can serve potatoes in dozens of
          delicious ways, both as a side dish and an entree, for any
          meal of the day. So next time you think of the humble
          potato--please, please think of it first as a nutritious
          vegetable. Because that's exactly what the potato is.

AGENCY: Ketchum Advertising

CLIENT: Lindsay Olives

LENGTH: 60 seconds

MUSIC IN BACKGROUND.

YOUNG MAN
(MID-20s):   I was a homely looking olive when I was born. Not ugly,
but homeliness is next to nothingness if you're trying to
be a handsome Lindsay Olive. So, I tried to change . . . to
become one of the Beautiful Olives. I wore contact lenses.
I had my pimiento styled by Mr. Joe. Nothing helped. So I
turned to olive surgery. I mean, I was desperate to become
a quality Lindsay Olive. Now, some surgeons wouldn't touch
an olive that looked like me--said it was too risky. But
you can always find someone who'll take out a wrinkle here
and inject an imitation of that great Lindsay Flavor
there--if the price is right. What did I have to lose? So
I tried it. The Lindsay People gave me a second look, and
I almost got in. But, one inspector saw a scar, and I was
through. I guess the Lindsay People were right after all
. . . beauty is only skin deep, but ugliness goes all the
way to the pit.

WOMAN ANNCR: An olive is just an olive, unless it's a Lindsay.

YOUNG MAN: Well, maybe another olive company will give me a break.
MUSIC OUT.

AGENCY: Post-U-Chair, Inc.

CLIENT: Post-U-Chair

LENGTH: 60 seconds

ANNCR: Orthopedic specialists will tell you that backaches are often the result of poor posture. Standing or sitting with the spine in a curved position can weaken muscles and cartilage and make you susceptible to backache and spinal injury. The POST-U-CHAIR has been designed to help avoid an unnatural curvature of your sacroiliac (SAK-RO-ILL'-EE-AK) [sækro'ɪliæk]. POST-U-CHAIR and regular exercise can help prevent lumbago (LUM-BAY'-GO) [ləm'be‚go], sciatica (SY-AT'-IK-UH) [saɪ'ætɪkə], and other aches and pains associated with back trouble. Of course, POST-U-CHAIR can't do the job alone--knowing the correct way to stand, walk, and lift is important, too--but, POST-U-CHAIR can keep your back in a straight line while resting, reading, or watching television. Send for our free booklet, "Caring for your Back," and see how the POST-U-CHAIR can combine with exercise and common sense to give you a strong, trouble-free back. Send a card to P.O. Box 333, Ames, Iowa, and POST-U-CHAIR will send the booklet by return mail.

AGENCY: Allen and Dorward

CLIENT: New Century Beverage Company

LENGTH: 60 seconds

ANNCR: Here is your one-minute gnu (NEW) [nju] training lesson for
         today. Gnu is spelled G-N-U. The first question most new
         trainers ask is, "What's gnu?" The gnu is part ox, part
         antelope, and part horse. This gives him a slight identity
         complex and makes him mean. He may charge, hook you with
         his horns, throw you down, and stomp on you. That's when
         you start the lesson. Remember, you can't teach an old gnu
         new tricks. Give the command, "Pay attention." If he hooks
         you and throws you and stomps you again . . . you have his
         attention. So stop the lesson and pour yourself a frosty,
         ice-cold Mug Old Fashioned Root Beer. Mug Root Beer is the
         ideal drink for gnu trainers and old gnu trainers. Mug Old
         Fashioned Root Beer. Regular or Diet. You haven't tasted
         root beer like this in years.

AGENCY: Cunningham & Walsh, Inc.

CLIENT: Schieffelin & Co.

LENGTH: 60 seconds

ANNCR: Once again, Stiller and Meara for Blue Nun.

ANNE: Hello, I'm Frieda Beidermyer, your interior decorator.

JERRY: Oh, yes, come in. This is my apartment.

ANNE: Don't apologize.

JERRY: Huh?

ANNE: They didn't tell me you were color blind. Plaid windows?

JERRY: I want decor that makes a statement about me, that exudes confidence, savoya fair. Where do we begin?

ANNE: The Last Chance Thrift Shop. Everything's gotta go.

JERRY: Everything?

ANNE: Everything.

JERRY: These are mementos my parents brought back from their honeymoon.

ANNE: They honeymooned in Tijuana?

JERRY: You noticed the terra-cotta donkey?

ANNE: I noticed. Out.

JERRY: So, where do we start?

ANNE: We start with a little Blue Nun.

JERRY: I want my apartment converted, not me.

ANNE: No, Blue Nun white wine. It'll lend you some style.

JERRY: I never tried Blue Nun.

ANNE: You have so much to learn, my naive nudnick. Blue Nun tastes terrific.

JERRY: I <u>want</u> good taste.

ANNE: That's why you can get Blue Nun by the glass or by the bottle at swank bars and restaurants.

JERRY: Gee, style, confidence, and taste. Will Blue Nun do all that for me?

ANNE: It's a bottle of wine, honey, not a miracle worker.

ANNCR: By the glass or by the bottle, there's a lot of good taste in Blue Nun. Imported by Schieffelin (SHIFF'-UH-LIN) & Co., New York.

PUBLIC SERVICE ANNOUNCEMENTS

CLIENT: U.S. Customs Service, Department of the Treasury
LENGTH: 30 seconds

ANNCR: If there's a foreign port in your future, there should be
         a U.S. Customs Travel Pack in your present. Before you go
         anywhere overseas, get a free Travel Pack from your local
         travel agent or the U.S. Customs Service, Washington,
         D.C., 20229. This helpful kit of useful facts and a dec-
         laration form helps travelers smooth their return to the
         states.

CLIENT: U.S. Customs Service, Department of the Treasury
LENGTH: 20 seconds

ANNCR: There's a law that says you've got to report what you
         bought overseas. If you have a Travel Pack, you can keep a
         written record on a declaration form. This and lots more
         is in a free Travel Pack ready for you, and it's loaded
         with helpful information. To get yours, write Travel Pack,
         U.S. Customs, Washington, D.C., 20229, or ask any travel
         agent.

CLIENT: U.S. Customs Service, Department of the Treasury
LENGTH: 10 seconds

ANNCR: Planning an overseas trip? Get a free U.S. Customs Travel
         Pack before you go. Write U.S. Customs, Washington, D.C.,
         20229, or ask any travel agent.

CLIENT: Amigos de las Americas

LENGTH: 60 seconds

ANNCR: Are you a teenager, sixteen years or older? Are you
          looking for the adventure of a lifetime? Why not check
          out Amigos de las Americas? Amigos is a non-profit
          organization, with chapters in cities all over America.
          Amigos spend the school year studying Spanish and
          paramedic work, and spend the summer working in a Latin
          American country. What do Amigos do? Well, last year
          Amigos administered over 230,000 dental treatments to
          60,000 children. They gave over 90,000 immunizations for
          polio and other diseases. And, they tested over 22,000
          people for tuberculosis. Amigos work in rural areas and
          big city slums. They are <u>not</u> on <u>vacation</u>. Assignments in
          Panama, Ecuador, Paraguay, and the Dominican Republic,
          among others, call for dedicated, caring young people. If
          you think Amigos is for you, write for information. The
          address is: 5618 Star Lane, Houston, Texas, 77057. Or, use
          the toll-free number: 1-800-231-7796. Amigos!

PSA FACT SHEET

WHO: The Westside Community Club

WHAT: Annual Spring Flower Show

WHERE: Westside Community Club Clubhouse

WHEN: Thursday, April 28th, Friday, April 29th, 9:00 A.M.–7:00
        P.M.

WHY: This is one of two major fund-raising events held each
        year to support our public parks. Funds are used to help
        maintain gardens in three Westside parks.
        Admission is free. Handmade novelties and plants will be
        on sale. Evening barbecue starts at 5:00 P.M.

CLIENT: Volunteer Center of Clark County

ANNCR: It took 3½ years to build, and is on the market for 3.75
        million dollars! It's the Clark County Designer Showcase
        house on Mount Hilary. Proceeds from tours go to the
        Volunteer Center of Clark County. Visit your dream house.
        Call 461–1986 for ticket information.

CLIENT: Project Family

ANNCR: Interested in adoption? Call Project Family at 775-1313.
          Project Family provides recruitment and preliminary
          screening of families interested in adopting. The Project
          seeks homes for children in need of permanent or temporary
          living situations. Make a difference in a child's life--
          and in yours--by adopting a child in need. Call 775-1313
          today.

CLIENT: Ashland Chapter of American Diabetes Association

ANNCR: The Ashland Chapter of the American Diabetes Associa-
          tion proudly presents Dr. William M. Sloane, one of the
          nation's foremost diabetologists (DY-UH-BEET-AHL'-
          O-GISTS), as their guest speaker, Thursday,
          September 5, at 7:30 in the High School auditorium. There
          is no charge for this event.

CLIENT: U.S. Navy

ANNCR: Chances are you know someone who is in the Navy. Maybe a
          brother, or just a guy you went to school with. Maybe a
          son or daughter. Then you've heard first hand about the
          experience and top technical training today's Navy pro-
          vides. Whether they're electronic technicians or diesel
          mechanics, pilots or shipboard officers whose management
          skills would be welcome in any industry, some of the top
          people in their fields are working in the Navy. They're
          highly skilled men and women with the experience to work
          anywhere, but who chose a Navy career. Serving with a
          commitment that benefits us all. People who not only
          believe in being the best at what they do, but also
          believe it means a little bit more when it's done for
          their country. Navy know-how. It's working for America.

CLIENT: U.S. Navy

ANNCR: Chances are you know someone who is in the Navy. Then
          you've heard first hand about the top technical training
          today's Navy provides. Men and women who believe being the
          best means more when it's done for their country. Navy
          know-how. It's working for America.

TELEVISION COMMERCIAL SCRIPTS

Only a few television commercial scripts are provided here for your practice. Nearly all television commercial productions require elaborate sets, complex graphics, or animation, none of which is available to most students. We suggest that you adapt some of the radio scripts and public-service announcements for straight on-camera presentation.

AGENCY: Ketchum Advertising

CLIENT: Safeway Stores, Inc.

LENGTH: 30 seconds

——— VIDEO ———	——— AUDIO ———
	SFX: MUSIC UNDER.
OPEN ON SAFEWAY LOGO. MOVE IN UNTIL ENTIRE SCREEN IS RED.	MALE VO: Safeway's international cheese experts invite your taste buds
DISS. TO WHEEL OF WISCONSIN CHEDDAR WITH CRACKERS ON TOP AND PIECE OF BUNTING ON SIDE.	
DISS. TO LARGE SLICE OF DUTCH GOUDA WITH DUTCH FLAG.	and your taste budget to enjoy some of the world's finest cheeses.
DISS. TO SLICES OF HAVARTI AND CRACK-ERS WITH HAVARTI ON THEM. DANISH FLAG IS STUCK IN ONE SLICE OF CHEESE.	So we feature them at low Safeway prices.
DISS. TO SLICE OF JARLSBERG ON CUT-TING BOARD, WHEEL OF JARLSBERG IS IN BACKGROUND. WOMAN'S HAND PLACES NORWEGIAN FLAG ON SLICE OF JARLSBERG.	A deliciously economical world taste tour that you can enjoy <u>now</u>.
DISS. TO SQUARE OF SWISS CHEESE WITH SWISS FLAG. SMALL PIECES OF CHEESE ARE ON CUTTING BOARD. WOMAN'S HAND LIFTS PIECE OF CHEESE.	Quality world cheeses, low Safeway prices. No passport required; just an appetite. SFX: MUSIC ENDS.

DISS. TO CU MAN BEING FED SWISS   MAN: Mmmmmm.
CHEESE BY WOMAN'S HAND.
DISS. TO SAFEWAY LOGO.   LOGO: Safeway. Everything you want
                                        from a store and a little bit more.

AGENCY: Backer & Spielvogel, Inc.
CLIENT: Quaker
PRODUCT: Celeste Pizza
LENGTH: 30 seconds

SUPER: Giuseppe Celeste
          Fictitious Little Brother

GIUSEPPE: I need your help. My big sister, Mama Celeste, she make a
          great crust for her pizza. But was Giuseppe's idea. I say,
          "Mama, you make perfect sauce, perfect toppings, make a
          perfect crust." She do it. But I think it. So my picture
          should be on the box, too, no? Which you like? (HOLDS UP
          PICTURES) Happy--"Hey, I think of great crust!"? Or
          serious--"Yes, I think of great crust."? Or it could be
          bigger? (HOLDS UP HUGE PICTURE)

ANNCR VO: Celeste Pizza. Delicious crust makes it great from top to
          bottom.

CLIENT: Herald Sewing Machines
TITLE: Pre-holiday Sale
LENGTH: 60 seconds

---------------- VIDEO ----------------   --------------- AUDIO ---------------
OPEN ON SHOT OF ANNCR SEATED BEHIND   ANNCR: This is the famous Herald sew-
SEWING MACHINE CONSOLE. ZOOM IN ON   ing machine.

MACHINE, AND FOLLOW SEQUENCE OF SHOTS INDICATED BY ANNCR.	Notice the free arm, perfectly designed to allow you to sew sleeves, cuffs, and hems. Note, too, the stitch regulator dial. You move easily and instantly to stretch stitch, embroider, or zig-zag stitches.
ANNCR DEMONSTRATES THE REGULATOR DIAL.	
	The Herald has a drop feed for darning, appliquéing, and monogramming.
ANNCR DEMONSTRATES.	This advanced machine has a self-stop bobbin winder. Other standard features include a built-in light, a thread tension dial, and a snap-on extension dial for flat bed sewing.
ZOOM BACK TO MEDIUM SHOT OF ANNCR AND MACHINE.	Yes, there isn't a better or more versatile sewing machine available today.
ANNCR STANDS, AND WALKS AROUND MACHINE AND TOWARD CAMERA.	But, I've saved the best for last. The Herald Star model sewing machine is now on sale at dealers everywhere. The Star, the most advanced model Herald makes, is regularly priced at two hundred and forty-nine dollars.
ANNCR HOLDS UP SALE SIGN, WITH $249 CROSSED OUT AND $199 WRITTEN IN.	During this month, you can buy the Star for only one hundred ninety-nine dollars—a saving of fifty dollars.
	You can't beat a deal like this, so visit your Herald dealer soon, while you still have your choice of color. Check the yellow pages for the dealers in your area.

AGENCY: In-house
CLIENT: Madera Foods
LENGTH: 60 seconds

———————————— VIDEO ————————————   ———————————— AUDIO ————————————

OPEN ON ANNCR STANDING BEFORE   ANNCR: I'm here at Madera Foods,
CHECKOUT STAND.   checking up on the specials you'll
                                        find here this weekend.

CUT TO PRODUCE SECTION. ANNCR WALKS   There are excellent buys this weekend
INTO FRAME.   in fresh fruits and vegetables. Like
ANNCR PICKS UP A GRAPEFRUIT.   extra fancy Indian River ruby red
                                        grapefruit, three for ninety-nine
ANNCR POINTS TO LETTUCE.   cents. Or iceberg lettuce, three
                                        heads for seventy-nine cents. And,
                                        don't overlook the relishes--green
                                        onions or radishes, two bunches for
                                        twenty-nine cents.

CUT TO MEAT DEPARTMENT. ANNCR WALKS   Meat specials include rib roast at
INTO FRAME.   two sixty-nine a pound, all lean
                                        center cut pork chops at one seventy-
                                        nine a pound, and lean ground chuck
                                        at only one thirty-nine a pound.

CUT BACK TO CHECKOUT STAND.   And, here I am, back at the checkout
                                        stand. Here's where you'll really
                                        come to appreciate Madera Foods.
                                        Their low, low prices add up to a
                                        total bill that winds down the cost
CUT TO ANNCR OUTSIDE FRONT ENTRANCE.   of living. So, pay a visit to Madera
                                        Foods this weekend. Specials are of-
                                        fered from Friday opening, to closing

on Sunday night. Madera Foods is located in the Madera Plaza Shopping
Center. Hours are from 9:00 A.M. 'til
10:00 P.M., seven days a week.

DISSOLVE TO MADERA FOODS LOGO SLIDE.   See you at Madera Foods.
HOLD UNTIL CLOSE.

AGENCY: Sherman Associates, Inc.
CLIENT: Bayview Health Club
LENGTH: 60 seconds

VIDEO	AUDIO
OPEN ON MCU OF TALENT.	Get ready, ladies! Bikini season is almost here! Now is the time to shed those excess pounds and achieve the body you know is hidden somewhere within you.
ZOOM OUT TO MEDIUM SHOT.	The Bayview Health Club will help you find the possible you. Bayview is a complete fitness club. We offer day
CUT TO STILL PHOTOS OF EACH FEATURE AS IT IS MENTIONED.	and evening classes in weight train-ing, aerobic and jazzercise dance, full Nautilus equipment, tanning, Jacuzzi and sauna facilities.
CUT TO MCU OF TALENT.	In addition, we sponsor weight reduc-tion clinics, jogging and running programs, and health and beauty semi-nars, with a supportive staff to coach you in every facet of personal health care. Bayview is tailored

CUT TO INFO CARD.	for you—the modern woman— and, for this month only, we're offering new members an intro- ductory price to join: Just half price! That's right, a 50 percent reduction during the month of April.
CUT TO MCU OF TALENT.	So, call now for a tour of our facilities. Meet the staff, and chat with satisfied members. Bayview Health Club, in downtown Portland. Join now. Don't lose time—instead, lose that waist, with a 50 percent reduction in membership costs.
MATTE IN ADDRESS AND PHONE NUMBER.	Find the hidden you, and be ready for Bikini time! Bayview Health Club: we're ready when you are!

AGENCY: Scott Singer
CLIENT: Partytime Novelties
LENGTH: 30 seconds

—————————— VIDEO ——————————	—————————— AUDIO ——————————
OPEN ON EMPTY STUDIO. DRACULA SWEEPS IN.	(SCARY MUSIC) (BELA LUGOSI IMITATION) Good evening. You are probably expecting me to say that my name is Count Dracula, and that I am a Vampire. Do you know what makes a Vampire? Do you . . . really? It's
DRACULA STROKES HAIR.	not the hair—bah! greasy kid's stuff! It's not the cape, made from

CU OF DRACULA'S FANGS.

CUT TO MS.

SUPER PHONE AND MAIL INFO.

CUT TO ECU OF DRACULA.

your sister's satin bed sheets. No! It is the fangs that make the Vampire. SEE? Now, you too can have the fangs. Dress up for parties-- frighten the trick-or-treaters on Halloween. These plastic marvels fit over your regular teeth, but once there--you'll be the hit of the party. Amaze and delight your ghoul friend. It is so much fun! I know. So, send for your fangs today. Send $2.98 to "FANG," Box 1001, Central City, Tennessee. Or dial toll-free:

800-DRA-CULA. Order before midnight tonight. That's an order!

APPENDIX B
PRONUNCIATION

This appendix consists of about 300 words, selected for one or more of the following reasons. The word is often mispronounced. The word is unusual or new but might well appear in broadcast copy. Or the word is of foreign origin but is widely used in the English-speaking world. Some of the words are common in commercial copy for fabrics, foods, or fashions.

Whereas standard dictionaries provide more than one pronunciation for a word, that which sees greatest use in broadcasting is given here. Pronunciation is for General American speech.

All words are transcribed into the International Phonetic Alphabet (IPA), diacritics, and wire-service phonetics. The source of diacritical transcriptions is *The American Heritage Dictionary*.[1]

Because this is a pronouncing dictionary, definitions are given only where necessary. Users should note that brief definitions given for words such as *gestalt* and *nihilism* are inadequate to explain these concepts fully. This appendix is not a substitute for a good dictionary.

It should be noted that many common words are omitted from this appendix because either of two common ways of pronouncing them is correct. In this category are words such as *economic*, *program*, and *pianist*.

accessory [æk'sɛsəri] (ăk-sĕs'ər-ē) (AK-SESS'-UH-REE)
Something supplementary; one who incites.
accompanist [ə'kʌmpənɪst] (ə-kŭm'pə-nĭst) (UH-KUM'-PUH-NIHST)
aegis ['idʒɪs] (ē'jĭs) (EE'-JIHS)
Protection; sponsorship; patronage.
almond ['ɑmənd] (ä'mənd) (AH'-MUND)
Note: The *l* is not sounded, and the first syllable is like the *a* in *father*.

---

[1] William Morris, ed., *The American Heritage Dictionary of the English Language* (Boston: Houghton Mifflin, 1980).

amateur [ˈæməˌtʃʊr] (ămˈəcho͞or) (AM'-UH-CHOOR)
An athlete, artist, or the like who participates without pay.

amoral [eˈmɔrəl] (ā-môrˈəl) (AY-MOR'-UL)
Not admitting of moral distinctions or judgments; neither moral nor immoral.

a priori [ɑ priˈɔri] (ä prē-ôrˈē) (AH PREE-OR'-EE)
Made before or without examination; deductive; not based on an experiment or experience.

apropos [ˌæprəˈpo] (ăpˈrə-pōˈ) (A-PRUH-PO')
Appropriate.

archetype [ˈɑrkəˌtaɪp] (ärˈkə-tīpˈ) (AR'-KUH-TYPE)
An original model or type after which other similar things are patterned; a prototype.

Arctic [ˈɑrkˌtɪk] (ärkˈtĭk) (ARK'-TICK)
Note: Both *c*s must be sounded; the same is true for *Antarctic.*

argot [ˈɑrgo] (ärˈgō) (AR'-GO)
A specialized vocabulary or set of idioms used by a particular class or group.

art deco [ɑr deˈko] (är dā-koˈ) (AR DAY-KO')
A highly decorative style of artistic design that was popular between the two world wars.

assuage [əˈswedʒ] (ə-swájˈ) (UH-SWAYJ')
To make less burdensome or less severe.

au gratin [o ˈgrɑtn̩] (ō grätˈn) (OH GRAHT'-UN)
Covered with bread crumbs or cheese and browned in an oven.

basalt [bəˈsɔlt] (bə-sôltˈ) (BUH-SALT')
A hard, dense, volcanic rock.

baud [bɔd] (bôd) (BAWD)
A unit of speed in data processing, equal to one binary digit per second.

bestial [ˈbɛstʃəl] (bĕsˈchəl) (BESS'-CHUL)
Behaving in the manner of a brute; savage.

Bethesda [bɪˈθɛzdə] (bĭ-thĕzˈdə) (BIH-THEZ'-DUH)
An urban center in Maryland; the name of a famous government hospital.

bijou [ˈbiˌʒu] (beˈzho͞oˈ) (BEE'-ZHOO)
A small, exquisitely wrought trinket; the name of many American movie houses.

bivouac [ˈbɪvuˌæk] (bĭvˈo͞o-ăk) (BIHV'-OO-ACK)
A temporary encampment made by soldiers in the field.

blasé [blɑˈze] (blä-zā') (BLAH-ZAY')
A jewish international fraternal society, perhaps best known for its
Having no more capacity or appetite for enjoyment.

B'nai B'rith [ˈbne ˈbrɪθ] (bnäˈbrīth') (BNAY' BRITH')
A jewish international fraternal society, perhaps best known for its
sponsorship of the Anti-Defamation League.

boatswain [ˈbosən] (bōˈsən) (BO'-SUN)
A warrant officer or petty officer in charge of a ship's deck crew.

bouclé [buˈkle] (bōō-klā') (BOO-KLAY')
A type of yarn or a fabric knitted from this yarn.

bouquet [boˈke] (bō-kā') (BO-KAY')

bourgeois [bʊrˈʒwɑ] (bōōr-zhwä') (BOOR-ZHWAH')
One belonging to the middle class.

boutique [buˈtik] (bōō-tēk') (BOO-TEEK')
A small retail shop that specializes in gifts, fashionable clothes, and
accessories.

brooch [brotʃ] (brōch) (BROTCH)

buoy [ˈbuˌi] (bōō'ē) (BOO'-EE)

cache [kæʃ] (kăsh) (KASH)
A place for concealment and safekeeping, as of valuables; a store of
goods hidden in a cache.

caisson [ˈkesɑn] (kā'sŏn') (KAY'-SAHN)
A watertight structure within which construction work is carried on;
a large box used to hold ammunition.

calm [kam] (käm) (KAHM)
The *l* is not sounded.

camembert [ˈkæməmˌbɛr] (kăm'əm-bâr) (KAM'-UM-BEAR)
A creamy, mold-ripened French cheese.

canapé [ˈkænəpe] (kän'ə-pā) (KAN'-UH-PAY)
An appetizer. (In broadcast copy, it is likely not to have the acute
accent mark over the *e*.)

caramel [ˈkærəməl] (kăr'əməl) (KARE'-UH-MUHL)

carcinogen [kɑrˈsɪnədʒən] (kär-sĭn'ə-jən) (KAR-SIN'-UH-JUN)
A cancer-causing substance.

Cassiopeia [ˌkæsiəˈpiə] (kăs'-ē-əpē'ə) (KASS-EE-UH-PEE'-UH)
A constellation of the Northern hemisphere.

cataclysm [ˈkætəˌklɪzm̩] (kăt'ə-klĭz'əm) (KAT'-UH-KLIZ-UM)
A violent upheaval.

catarrh [kə'tɑr] (kə-tär') (KUH-TAHR')
Inflammation of mucous membranes, especially of the nose and throat.

caulk [kɔk] (kôk) (KAWK)

chaise longue [ˌʃez' lɔŋ] (shāz'lông') (SHAYZ LONG')

chamois ['ʃæmi] (shăm'ē) (SHAM'-EE)

chartreuse [ʃɑr'truz] (shär-trooz') (SHAHR-TROOZ')
A liqueur; a greenish yellow color.

Charybdis [kə'rɪbˌdɪs] (kə-rĭb'dĭs) (KUH-RIB'-DISS)
A whirlpool off the Sicilian coast, opposite the rock of Scylla. (To be ''between Scylla and Charybdis'' implies that one is between two serious dangers.)

Chianti [ki'ɑnti] (kē-än'tē) (KEE-AHN'-TEE)
A dry, red Italian wine.

chiaroscuro [kiˌɑrə'skjuro] (kē-är'əskyōōr'o) (KEE-AR-UH-SKYUR'-O)
The arrangement of light and dark elements in a pictorial work of art.

chic [ʃik] (shēk) (SHEEK)

chiropodist [kə'rɑpədɪst] (kə-rŏp'ə-dĭst) (KUH-RAHP'-UH-DIST)

ciao [tʃaʊ] (chou) (CHOW)
An Italian greeting, meaning both hello and goodbye.

Cinzano [tʃɪn'zɑno] (chĭn-zän'-o) (CHIN-ZAHN'-O)
An Italian liqueur.

circa ['sɜˑkə] (sûr'kə) (SUR-KUH)
About. Used before approximate dates or figures.

claque [klæk] (klăk) (KLACK)
A group of persons hired to applaud at a performance. Any group of adulating or fawning admirers.

cliché [kli'ʃe] (klē-shā') (KLEE-SHAY')
Note: In broadcast copy, this word may appear without the accent mark.

cloche [kloʃ] (klōsh) (KLOSH)
A close-fitting woman's hat.

cognac ['konjæk] (kōn'yăk') (KOHN'-YAK)
A French brandy.

coiffure [kwɑ'fjur] (kwä-fyoor') (KWAH-FYUR')

colloquial [kə'lokwiəl] (kə-lō'kwē-əl) (KUH-LO'-KWEE-UHL)

coma ['komə] (kō'mə) (KO'-MUH)

comatose ['koməˌtos] (kō'mə-tōs') (KO'-MUH-TOESS)

comparable ['kɑmpərəbl̩] (kom'pər-ə-bəl) (KAHM'-PUHR-UH-BUL)

comptroller [kən'trolə˞] (kən-trō'lər) (KUN-TRO'-LER)
An officer who audits accounts and supervises the financial affairs of
a corporation or governmental body. (The *p* is not sounded, and the
m has the *n* sound.)

conch [kaŋk] (kŏngk) (KAHNK)
Any of various large marine mollusks.

concierge ['kɑnsiə˞ʒ] (kŏn'sē-ûrzh) (KAHN-SEE-URZH')
A person who attends the entrance of a building.

conglomerate (verb) [kən'glɑmə,ret] (kən-glŏm'ərāt')
                     (KUN-GLAHM'-UH-RAYT)
                     (noun) [kən'glɑmərɪt] (kən-glŏm'ərĭt)
                     (KUN-GLAHM'-UH-RIHT)
Verb: to collect into an adhering or rounded mass.
Noun: a collected heterogeneous mass; a cluster. The noun frequently is used to denote a large corporation made up of several
different types of businesses.

conjugal ['kɑndʒugl̩] (kŏn'jo͞o-gəl) (KAHN'-JYU-GUL)
Of marriage or the marital relationship.

consortium [kən'sɔrʃiəm] (kən-sôr'-shē-əm) (KUN-SAWR'-SHEE-UM)
Any association or partnership.

corps [kɔr] (kôr) (KAWR)

cortege [kɔr'tɛʒ] (kôr-tĕzh') (KAWR-TEHZH')
A train of attendants. Usually refers to a funeral procession.

coup [ku] (ko͞o) (KOO)

coxswain ['kɑksn̩] (kŏk'sən) (KAHK'-SUN)

crepe [krep] (krāp) (KRAYP)
A light, soft, thin fabric. Also a type of crinkled tissue paper.

crêpe [krɛp] (krĕp) (KREHP)
In its French usages—crêpe de Chine, a type of cloth, and as a thin
pancake—this word is pronounced as indicated. This word will
probably not have the circumflex over the *e* in broadcast copy, so you
must remember to use the French pronunciation when the context so
indicates.

crescendo [krə'ʃɛndo] (krə-shĕn'dō) (KRUH-SHEHN'-DOH)

crevasse [krə'væs] (krə-văs') (KRUH-VASS')
A deep fissure, as in a glacier.

crevice ['krɛvɪs] (krĕv'ĭs) (KREHV'-ISS)

crinoline ['krɪn'əlɪn] (krĭn'ə-lĭn) (KRIN'-UH-LIHN)
A coarse, stiff cotton fabric.

cryogenics [ˌkraɪo'dʒɛnɪks] (krī'o-jĕn'iks) (KRY-OH-JEN'-IKS)
The science of low-temperature phenomena.

cuisine [kwɪˈzin] (kwĭ-zēn') (KWIH-ZEEN')
A characteristic manner or style of preparing food.

culottes [kuˈlɑts] (ko͞o-lŏts') (KOO-LOTS')
A divided skirt.

cupola [ˈkjupələ] (kyo͞o'-pə-lə) (KYOO'-PUH-LUH)

cybernetics [ˌsaɪbɚˈnɛtɪks] (sī'bər-nĕt'ĭks) (SY-BER-NET'-IKS)

cynosure [ˈsaɪnəˌʃʊr] (sī'nə-sho͞or') (SY'-NUH-SHOOR)
A center of interest or attraction.

dachshund [ˈdɑksˌhʊnt] (däk̦s'ho͝ont') (DAHKS'-HUHNT)
Note: The word ends with a *t* sound, and the vowel sound in the second syllable is as in *took*.

Dacron [ˈdekrɑn] (dā'krŏn) (DAY'-KRAHN)

dais [ˈdeɪs] (dā'ĭs) (DAY'-ISS)
A raised platform.

demise [dɪˈmaɪz] (dĭ-mīz') (DIH-MYZ')
Death.

demur [dɪˈmɝ] (dĭ-mûr') (DIH-MUHR')
To take exception.

denier [dəˈnje] (də-nyā') (DUH-NYAY')
A unit of fineness for rayon, nylon, and silk yarns. (This word is spelled the same as that which means *one who denies*; the context should make clear which of its meanings is intended.)

despot [ˈdɛspət] (dĕs'pət) (DES'-PUHT)

détente [deˈtɑnt] (dā-tänt') (DAY-TAHNT')

dialysis [daɪˈæləsɪs] (dī-ăl'ə-sĭs) (DY-AL'-UH-SIS)

dichotomy [daɪˈkɑtəmi] (dī-kŏt'ə-mē) (DY-KAHT'-UH-MEE)
Division into two (usually contradictory) parts or opinions.

diminution [ˌdɪməˈnjuʃən] (dim'ə-nyo͞o'shən) (DIM-UH-NYOO'-SHUN)
The act or process of diminishing.

diocese [ˈdaɪəsɪs] (dī'əsĭs) (DY'-UH-SIHS)

diphtheria [dɪfˈθɪriə] (dĭf-thîr'ē-ə) (DIFF-THIR'-EE-UH)
Note: The *ph* is pronounced *f*.

diphthong [ˈdɪfθɔŋ] (dĭf'thông') (DIFF'-THONG)
A combination of two vowel sounds; a glide.

diva [ˈdivə] (dē'və) (DEE'-VUH)
An operatic prima donna, or leading singer.

dossier [ˈdɑsiˌe] (dŏs'ē-ā') (DAHS'-EE-AY)

dour [dʊr] (do͝or) (DUHR) (rhymes with *poor*)
Silently ill-humored; gloomy.

drought [draʊt] (drout) (DRAWĦT) (rhymes with *snout*)

dysentery ['dɪsənteri] (dĭs'ən-tĕr'-ē) (DISS'-UN-TARE-EE)

dyspepsia [dɪs'pɛpʃə] (dĭs-pĕp'shə) (DISS-PEP'-SHUH)
Indigestion.

eczema ['ɛksəmə] (ĕk'sə-mə) (EK'-SUH-MUH)
An inflammation of the skin.

Eire ['ɛrə] (âr'ə) (AIR'-UH)
The Gaelic name for the Republic of Ireland.

emollient [ɪ'mɑljənt] (ĭ-mŏl'yənt) (IH-MAHL'-YUNT)
An agent that softens or soothes the skin.

Empire [ɑm'pɪr] (ŏm-pîr') (AHM-PEER')
Note: Pronounced as indicated when referring to the dress or the
artistic style of the first Empire of France, 1804–1815.

encephalitis [ɛn,sɛfə'laɪtɪs] (ĕn-sef'ə-lī'tĭs) (EN-SEFF-UH-LY'-TISS)
Inflammation of the brain.

endocrine [ɛndə'krɪn] (ĕn'də-krĭn) (EN'-DUH-KRIHN)
Glandular; a gland.

ennui ['ɑn'wi] (än'wē') (AHN'-WEE')
Listlessness and dissatisfaction resulting from lack of interest;
boredom.

en route [ɑn 'rut] (än rōōt') (AHN ROOT')

ensemble [ɑn'sɑmbl̩] (än-säm'bəl) (AHN-SAHM'-BUHL)

ensign—Two pronunciations:
        a flag—['ɛn,saɪn] (ĕn'sīn) (EN'-SYN)
        a naval officer—['ɛnsən] (ĕn'sən) (EN'-SUN)

entourage [,ɑntu'rɑʒ] (än'tōō-räzh') (AHN-TOO-RAZH')

entrée ['ɑntre] (än'trā) (AHN'-TRAY)

envoy ['ɛnvɔɪ] (ĕn'voi) (EN'-VOY)
Note: Do not make the first syllable "AHN," unless you are going to
give the word its correct French pronunciation.

Epiphany [ɪ'pɪfəni] (ĭ-pĭf'ə-nē) (IH-PIFF'-UH-NEE)
A Christian festival held on January 6.

epitaph ['ɛpə,tæf] (ĕp'ə-tăf') (EP'-UH-TAFF)
An inscription on a tombstone; a tribute to a deceased person.

epitome [ɪ'pɪtəmi] (ĭ-pĭt'ə-mē) (IH-PIT'-UH-MEE)
One that is representative of an entire class or type; embodiment.

era ['ɪrə] (îr'ə) (IHR'-UH)

err [ɝ] (ûr) (ER)
Note: Do not pronounce this as the word *air*.

erudite ['ɛrjuˌdaɪt] (ĕr'yoo-dīt') (AIR'-YOU-DYT)
Deeply learned.

euphemism ['jufəˌmɪzm̩] (yoo'fə-mĭz'əm) (YOU'-FUH-MIZ-UM)
A term substituted for one considered offensively explicit.

exacerbate [ɛg'zæsɚˌbe] (ĕg-zăs'ər-bāt') (EGG-ZASS'-ER-BAYT)
To increase the severity of.

exquisite ['ɛkskwɪzɪt] (ĕks'kwĭ-zĭt) (EKS'-KWIH-ZIT)
Note: Do not place the stress on the second syllable.

extraordinary [ɛk'strɔrdəˌnɛri] (ĕk-strôr'də-nĕr'ē) (EK-STROR'-DUH-NARE-EE)

façade [fə'sɑd] (fəsäd') (FUH-SAHD')
Note: In broadcast copy, the cedilla on the *c* is usually lacking.

faux pas [fo 'pɑ] (fō pä') (FOH PAH')
A social blunder; a breach of etiquette.

fiduciary [fɪ'duʃiˌɛri] (fĭ-doo'shē-ĕr'ē) (FIH-DOO'-SHEE-AIR-EE)
Of, pertaining to, or involving one who holds something in trust for another.

finite ['faɪˌnaɪt] (fī'nīt) (FY'-NYT)
Having boundaries; limited.

foible ['fɔɪbl̩] (foi'bəl) (FOY'-BUL)
A minor weakness or failing of character.

forecastle ['foksl̩] (fōk'səl) (FOKE'-SUL)
The section of the upper deck of a ship located at the bow.

forehead ['fɔrɪd] (fôr'ĭd) (FOR'-IHD)
(The *h* is not sounded.)

forte—Two words, spelled the same, but pronounced differently:
A person's strong point—[fɔrt] (fôrt) (FORT)
Music direction, meaning "loudly"—['fɔrte] (fôr'tā) (FOR'-TAY)
(Do not say, "This is my FOR'-TAY.")

frijoles [fri'holes] (frē-hō'lās) (FREE-HO'-LAYS)
Beans prepared as in parts of Latin America.

fungi ['fʌndʒaɪ] (fŭn'jī) (FUN'-JY)
Plural of *fungus*, but note that the letter *g* is sounded differently in the two words.

garage [gə'rɑʒ] (gə-razh') (GUH-RAHZH')

gauche [goʃ] (gōsh) (GOOSH)
Note: This word rhymes with the first syllable of *lotion*.

geisha [ˈgeʃə] (gā'shə) (GAY-SHUH)
A Japanese woman trained to provide entertainment, especially for men.

genre [ˈʒɑnrə] (zhän'rə) (ZHAHN'-RUH)
Type; class.

gestalt [gəˈʃtɑlt] (gə-shtält') (GUH-SHTAHLT')
A unified configuration that cannot be explained merely as the sum of its parts.

Gethsemane [gɛθˈsɛməni] (gĕth-sĕm'ə-nē) (GETH-SEM'-UH-NEE)
The garden outside Jerusalem where Christ was arrested.

gherkin [ˈgɝkɪn] (gûr'kĭn) (GUHR'-KIHN)
A small pickle.

Gila (monster; national park; and river) [ˈhilə] (hē'lə) (HEE'-LUH)

gist [dʒɪst] (jĭst) (JIST)
The central idea of some matter.

googol [ˈgu,gɑl] (gōō'gŏl') (GOO'-GAHL)
The number 10 raised to the power 100; the number 1 followed by 100 zeros (from the new math).

grosgrain [ˈgro,gren] (grō'grān') (GROW'-GRAIN)
A heavy silk or rayon fabric with narrow horizontal ribs.

gunwale [ˈgʌnl̩] (gŭn'əl) (GUN'-UL)
The upper edge of a ship's side.

habeas corpus [ˈhebiəs ˈkɔrpəs] (hā'bĕ-əs kôr'pəs) (HAY'-BEE-US KAWR'-PUHS)
A writ that may be issued to bring a party before a court or judge, having as its purpose the release of a party from unlawful restraint.

hasten [ˈhesn̩] (hās'ən) (HAYS'-UN)
Note: The *t* is not sounded.

hearth [hɑrθ] (härth) (HAHRTH)

hegemony [hɪˈdʒɛməni] (hĭ-jĕm'ə-nē) (HIH-JEM'-UH-NEE)
Predominant influence of one state over others.

Hegira [hɪˈdʒaɪrə] (hĭ-jī'rə) (HIH-JY'-RUH)
The flight of Mohammed from Mecca to Medina; any flight, as from danger.

height [haɪt] (hīt) (HYT)

heinous [ˈhenəs] (hā'nəs) (HAY'-NUS)
Grossly wicked or reprehensible.

hiatus [haɪˈetəs] (hī-ā'-təs) (HY-AY'-TUS)
A gap or missing section.

hierarchy   ['haɪə‚rɑrki]   (hī'ə-rär'-kē)   (HY'-UH-RAR-KEE)

hors d'oeuvre   [ɔr 'dɝv]   (ôr dûrv')   (OR DURV')

hyperbole   [haɪ'pɝbə‚li]   (hī-pûr'bə-lē)   (HY-PER'-BUH-LEE)
An exaggeration or extravagant statement used as a figure of speech.
(Do not confuse this word with the geometric term *hyperbola*.)

impotent   ['ɪmpətənt]   (ĭm'pə-tənt)   (IHM'-PUH-TUNT)
(Do *not* place stress on the second syllable.)

imprimatur   [‚ɪmprə'metɝ]   (ĭm'-prə-mā'tər)   (IHM-PRUH-MAY'-TUR)
Official approval or license to print or publish.

impugn   [ɪm'pjun]   (ĭm-pyōōn')   (IHM-PYOON')
To oppose or attack as false; criticize; refute.

integer   ['ɪntədʒɝ]   (ĭn'tə-jər)   (IN'-TUH-JUHR)
Any member of the set of positive whole numbers (1, 2, 3, . . .),
negative whole numbers (−1, −2, −3, . . .), and zero (0).

integral   ['ɪntəgrəl]   (ĭn'tə-grəl)   (IN'-TUH-GRUHL)
Note: Do not place stress on the second syllable.

Io   ['aɪo]   (ī'o)   (EYE'-OH)
A satellite of Jupiter, named for a maiden in Greek mythology who
was loved by Zeus.

irony   ['aɪrəni]   (ī'rə-nē)   (EYE'-RUH-NEE)
(Avoid "EYE'-ER-NEE.")

jeroboam   [dʒɛrə'boəm]   (jĕr-ə-bō'əm)   (JEHR-UH-BO'-UM)
A wine bottle holding about ⅘ of a gallon.

juvenile   ['dʒuvənl̩]   (jōō'və-nəl)   (JOO'-VUH-NUHL)
Note: "JOO'-VUH-NYL" is acceptable, but the word is seldom given
that pronunciation by professional announcers.

kibbutz   [kɪ'buts]   (kĭ-bōōts')   (KIH-BOOTS')
A collective farm or settlement in modern Israel.

lamé   [læ'me]   (lă-mā')   (LA-MAY')
A fabric having metallic threads in the warp or in the filling. (In
broadcast copy, the accent mark may be missing—the context
should tell you whether the copy refers to a cloth or to the condition
of being lame.)

liaison   [‚li‚e'zɑn]   (lē'ā-zŏn')   (LEE-AY-ZAHN')

libation   [laɪ'beʃən]   (lī-bā'shən)   (LY-BAY'-SHUN)
The pouring of a liquid offering as a religious ritual. *Informal:* An
intoxicating beverage.

llama ['jɑmə] (yä'mə) (YAH'-MUH)
Note: In broadcast speech, it is helpful to use the Spanish pronunciation, as given here, to avoid confusion with *lama*, a Buddhist monk of Tibet or Mongolia.

lozenge ['lɑzɪndʒ] (lŏz'ĭnj) (LAHZ'-INJ)

macabre [mə'kɑbrə] (mə-kä'brə) (MUH-KAH'-BRUH)
Gruesome; ghastly.

Magi ['medʒaɪ] (mā'jī) (MAY'-JY)
The "wise men from the East" who traveled to Bethlehem to pay homage to the infant Jesus.

mandamus [mæn'deməs] (măn-dā'məs) (MAN-DAY'-MUS)
A writ used by a superior court ordering a public official or body or a lower court to perform a specified duty.

Maya ['mɑjə] (mä'yə) (MAH'-YUH)
A member of a race of Indians in southern Mexico and Central America.

measure ['mɛʒɚ] (mĕzh'ər) (MEHZH'-UR)
(Avoid "MAYZH'-UR.")

melee ['mele] or [me'le] (mā'lā) or (mālā') (MAY'-LAY) or (MAY-LAY')

meringue [mə'ræŋ] (mə-răng') (MUH-RANG')

mien [min] (mēn) (MEEN)
One's bearing or manner.

mnemonic [nɪ'mɑnɪk] (nĭ-mŏn'ĭk) (NIH-MAHN'-IK)
Relating to, assisting, or designed to assist the memory. *Note.* The *m* is not sounded.

moisten ['mɔɪsn̩] (mois'ən) (MOYS'-UN)
Note: The *t* is not sounded.

Moog [mog] (mōg) (MOHG)
A music synthesizer. *Note:* It is *not* pronounced "MOOG."

mores ['mɔrez] (môr'āz) (MAWR'-AYZ)
The accepted traditional customs and usages of a particular social group; moral attitudes.

mot [mo] (mō) (MO)
A witticism or short, clever saying.

mousse [mus] (moos) (MOOS)
Any of various chilled desserts.

myopia [maɪ'opiə] (mī-ō'pē-ə) (MY-O'-PEE-UH)
A visual defect; nearsightedness.

naivete [nɑˌivˈte] (näˈēv-täˈ) (NAH-EEV-TAY')

naphtha [ˈnæfθə] (năfˈthə) (NAF'-THUH)
Note: The *ph* is sounded as an *f*.

née [ne] (nā) (NAY)
Born. Used when identifying a married woman by her maiden name.

niche [nɪtʃ] (nĭch) (NITSCH)
Note: Rhymes with *rich*.

nihilism [ˈnaɪəlˌɪzm̩] (nīˈəl-ĭzˈəm) (NY'-UHL-IZ-UM)
In ethics, the rejection of all distinctions in moral value. Also, the belief that destruction of existing political or social institutions is necessary to ensure future improvement; extreme radicalism.

Nisei [ˈnise] (nēˈsā) (NEE'-SAY)
One born in America of immigrant Japanese parents.

nonpareil [ˌnɑnpəˈrɛl] (nŏnˈpə-rĕlˈ) (NAHN-PUH-RELL')
Without rival; matchless; peerless; unequaled.

non sequitur [nɑn ˈsɛkwɪtɚ] (nŏn sĕkˈwĭ-tōŏrˈ) (NAHN-SEK'-WIH-TOOR)
An inference or conclusion that does not follow from established premises or evidence.

nouveau riche [nuvo ˈriʃ] (nōō-vō rēshˈ) (NOO-VOH REESH')
One who has recently become rich.

nuclear [ˈnukliɚ] (nōōˈklē-ər) (NOO'-KLEE-UHR)

nuptial [ˈnʌpʃəl] (nŭpˈshəl) (NUHP'-SHUL)

objet d'art [ɑbʒe ˈdɑr] (ôb-zhĕ därˈ) (AHB-ZHAY DAR')
An object valued for its artistry.

obsequies [ˈɑbsəkwiz] (ŏbˈsə-kwēz) (AHB'-SUH-KWEEZ)
A funeral rite or ceremony.

often [ˈɔfən] (ôˈfən) (AWF'-UN)
Note: The *t* is not sounded.

oregano [əˈrɛgəno] (ə-rĕgˈənōˈ) (UH-REG'-UH-NO)
An herb. (The first syllable may be sounded as "O.")

paean [ˈpiən] (pēˈən) (PEE'-UN)
A song of joyful praise or exultation.

Pago Pago [ˈpæŋgo ˈpæŋgo] (päng'gō päng'gō) (PANG'-GO PANG'-GO)
The capital of American Samoa.

Pall Mall ['pɛl 'mɛl] (pĕl'mĕl') (PELL'-MELL')
A street in London.

palm [pɑm] (päm) (PAHM)
Note: This word alone, or in combinations such as Palm Beach or palm oil, does not sound the *l*. The *l is* sounded in *palmetto,* a small tropical palm.

papier-mâché ['pepɚ məˈʃe] (pāˈpər mə-shāˈ) (PAY'-PER MUH-SHAY')
Note: This word is almost universally Anglicized in broadcast speech.

papyrus [pəˈpaɪrəs] (pə-pīˈrəs) (PUH-PY'-RUSS)

paradigm ['pærədaɪm] (părˈə-dīmˈ) (PARE'-UH-DYM)
Any example or model. The first *a* is sounded as in *pat.*

paroxysm ['pærəkˌsɪzm̩] (părˈək-sīzˈəm) (PAR'-UK-SIZ-UM)
A sudden outburst of emotion or action; a spasm or fit.

passé [pæˈse] (pă-sāˈ) (PA-SAY')
Note: This word may appear without the accent mark in broadcast copy.

pâté [pɑˈte] (pä-tāˈ) (PAH-TAY')
A meat paste (may appear without the accent marks).

patent—Two pronunciations:
Obvious—['petn̩t] (pātˈənt) (PAYT'-UNT)
Right or title—['pætn̩t] (pătˈənt) (PAT'-UNT)

pejorative [pɪˈdʒɔrətɪv] (pĭ-jôrˈə-tĭv) (PIH-JOR'-UH-TIV)
Disparaging; downgrading.

per se ['pɝ 'se] (pûr' sāˈ) (PER' SAY')
In or by itself.

perseverance [ˌpɝsəˈvɪrəns] (pûrˈsə-vîrˈəns) (PER-SUH-VEER'-UNS)

pestle ['pɛsl̩] (pĕsˈəl) (PES'-UHL)

petit ['pɛti] (pĕtˈē) (PET'-EE)
Note: This word, meaning "small" or "minor," is pronounced as shown in combinations such as *petit larceny, petit four,* and *petit mal.*

phlegm [flɛm] (flĕm) (FLEM)
Thick mucus.

picot ['piko] (pēˈkō) (PEE'-KO)
An ornamental edging on ribbon or lace.

pieta [pjeˈtɑ] (pyā-täˈ) (PYAY-TAH')
A depiction of Mary with the Dead Christ.

piety ['paɪəti] (pīˈə-tē) (PY'-UH-TEE)
Religious devotion.

pincers ['pɪnsɚz] (pĭnˈsərz) (PIN'-SERZ)

piqué [pɪ'ke] (pĭ-kā') (PIH-KAY')
A fabric. (This word may appear without accent mark in scripts, so do not confuse it with *pique*, which is pronounced PEEK.)

placebo [plə'sibo] (plə-sē'bō) (PLUH-SEE'-BO)
A substance containing no medication, administered to humor a patient.

potable ['potəbḷ] (pō'tə-bəl) (PO'-TUH-BUL)
Fit to drink; drinkable.

potpourri [popʊ'ri] (pō'pōō-rē') (PO-POO-REE')

primer—Two pronunciations:
   A textbook—['prɪmɚ] (prĭm'ər) (PRIM'-ER)
   An undercoat of paint; an explosive—['prɑɪmɚ]
   (prīm'ər) (PRYM'-ER)

pseudo ['sudo] (sōō'dō) (SOO'-DO)

purée [pjʊ're] (pyōō-rā') (PYOO-RAY')

Purim ['pʊrɪm] (pōōr'ĭm) (POOR'-IHM)
A Jewish holiday celebrating the deliverance of the Jews from massacre by Haman.

Qiana [ki'ɑnə] (kē-än'ə) (KEE-AHN'-UH)
A particular synthetic fabric.

quay [ki] (kē) (KEE)
A wharf.

ragout [ræ'gu] (ră-gōō') (RA-GOO')
A meat and vegetable stew.

recoup [rɪ'kup] (rĭ-kōōp') (RIH-KOOP')

regime [re'ʒim] (rā-zhēm') (RAY-ZHEEM')

reprise [rə'priz] (rə-prēz') (RUH-PREEZ')
Repetition of a phrase, verse, or song.

respite ['rɛspɪt] (rĕs'pĭt) (RES'-PIT)
A temporary cessation or postponement.

ribald ['rɪbḷd] (rĭb'əld) (RIB'-ULD)
Pertaining to or indulging in vulgar, lewd humor.

riboflavin ['rɑɪboflevɪn] (rī'bō-flā'vĭn) (RY'-BO-FLAYV-IHN)
The principal ingredient in vitamin B$_2$.

rodeo ['rodiˌo] (rō'dē-o') (RO'-DEE-O)
Note: The Spanish pronunciation, "RO-DAY'-O," is heard less and less in the United States.

roof [ruf] (ro͞of) (cannot be accurately indicated with wire-service phonetics)
Note: Roof, like *room* and *root,* uses the same vowel sound as the word *boot.*

roué [ru'e] (ro͞o-ā') (ROO-AY')
A lecherous and dissipated man. (The accent mark may be missing in broadcast copy.)

rouge [ruʒ] (ro͞ozh) (ROOZH)

sachet [sæ'ʃe] (să-shā') (SA-SHAY')
A small bag containing perfumed powder.

sake ['sɑki] (sä'kē) (SAH'-KEE)
A Japanese rice wine.

salve [sæv] (săv) (SAV)
(The *l* is not sounded.)

sauté [so'te] (sō-tā') (SO-TAY')
Note: The accent mark may be omitted in broadcast copy.

schism ['sɪzm̩] (sĭz'əm) (SIHZ'-UM)

schizoid ['skɪt,sɔɪd] (skĭt'soid') (SKIT'-SOYD)

sciatica [saɪ'ætɪkə] (sī-ăt'ĭ-kə) (SY-AT'-IK-UH)
Neuralgia of the sciatic nerve; a pain in the area of the hip or thigh.

scion ['saɪən] (sī'ən) (SY'-UN)
A descendant or heir.

Scylla ['sɪlə] (sĭl'ə) (SILL'-UH)
A rock on the Italian side of the Straight of Messina, opposite Charybdis.

segue ['sɛg,we] (sĕg'wā) (SEG'-WAY)
A transition from one program element to another (usually music) without overlap or pause.

skein [sken] (skān) (SKAYN)
A loose coil of thread or yarn.

slough [slu] (slo͞o) (SLEW)
A marsh. (To cast off or shed is to *sluff.*)

soften ['sɔfən] (sôf'ən) (SAWF'-UN)
Note: The *t* is not sounded.

sophomore ['sɑfə,mɔr] (sŏf'ə-môr') (SAHF'-UH-MOR)
Note: Sound all three syllables.

soufflé [su'fle] (so͞o-flā') (SOO-FLAY')

succinct [sək'sɪŋkt] (sək-sĭngkt') (SUK-SINGKT')

Succoth ['sʊkot] (so͞ok'ōt) (SOOK'-OT)
A Jewish harvest festival.

sukiyaki [ski'ɑki] (skē-äk'ē) (SKEE-AHK'-EE)
A Japanese dish of meat and vegetables.

superfluous [su'pɝfluəs] (soō-pûr'floō-əs) (SU-PER'-FLU-US)

synod ['sɪnəd] (sĭn'əd) (SIN'-UD)
A church council.

taffeta ['tæfətə] (tăf'ə-tə) (TAF'-UH-TUH)
A glossy fabric.

Tagalog [tə'gɑlɔg] (tə-gä'lôg) (TUH-GAH'-LOG)
A people native to the Philippines; their language.

Terpsichore [tɝp'sɪkəri] (tûrp-sĭk'ə-rē) (TERP-SIK'-UH-REE)
The Muse of dancing.

tertiary ['tɝʃiˌɛri] (tûr'shē-ĕr-ē) (TER'-SHEE-AIR-EE)
Third in place, order, degree, or rank.

testosterone [tɛs'tɑstəron] (tĕs-tŏs'tə-rōn') (TES-TAHS'-TUH-ROHN)
A male sex hormone.

Thames [tɛmz] (tĕmz) (TEMZ)
A river of England.

thyme [taɪm] (tīm) (TYM)
An herb.

tiara [ti'ɑrə] (tē-är'ə) (TEE-AHR'-UH)
A crownlike headpiece.

tortilla [tɔr'tijə] (tôr-tē'yə) (TAWR-TEE'-YUH)
A thin, unleavened Mexican pancake.

touché [tu'ʃe] (toō-shā') (TOO-SHAY')
Note: The accent mark may be missing in broadcast copy.

toward [tɔrd] (tôrd) (TAWRD)
Note: This is a one-syllable word.

treacle ['trikḷ] (trē'kəl) (TREE'-KUL)
Molasses.

trestle ['trɛsḷ] (trĕs'əl) (TRESS'-UL)

tricot ['triko] (trē'kō) (TREE'-KO)
A soft cloth.

troche ['troki] (trō'kē) (TRO'-KEE)
A small lozenge.

trough [trɔf] (trôf) (TRAWF)

tulle [tul] (toōl) (TOOL)
A fine starched net of silk, rayon, or nylon.

tzar [zɑr] (zär) (ZAHR)
Former ruler of Russia. The word is sometimes spelled *czar,* but both are pronounced the same.

unguent ['ʌŋgwənt] (ŭng'gwənt) (UNG'-GWUNT)
A salve.

urethane ['jurəθen] (yōōr'ə-thān') (YOUR'-UH-THANE)

valance ['væləns] (văl'əns) (VAL'-UNS)
A short, ornamental drapery hung across the top of a window or along a bed, shelf, canopy, or the like. (Do not confuse this word with the term from chemistry, *valence,* which is pronounced "VAY'-LUNS.")

venal ['vinl̩] (vē'nəl) (VEE'-NUL)
Open or susceptible to bribery.

venire [vɪ'naɪri] (vĭ-nī'rē) (VIH-NY'-REE)
A panel of prospective jurors from which a jury is selected.

vicar ['vɪkɚ] (vĭk'ər) (VIK'-ER)

victual ['vɪtl̩] (vĭt'l) (VIT'-UL)
Food.

vicuña [və'kunjə] (və-kōōn'yə) (VUH-KOON'-YUH)
A mammal of the Andes; the fleece of this animal. (The tilde may be missing in broadcast copy.)

vigilante [ˌvɪdʒə'lænti] (vĭj'ə-lăn'tē) (VIDG-UH-LAN'-TEE)
A member of an informal council exercising police power.

vin ordinaire [vẽ ɔrdi'nɛr] (văn ôr-dē-nâr') (VAN AWR-DEE'-NARE)
Note: The first *n* should be nasalized.

virulent ['vɪrjələnt] (vîr'yə-lənt) (VIHR'-YUH-LUNT)
Extremely poisonous.

vis-à-vis [ˌvizə'vi] (vē'zə-vē') (VEEZ-UH-VEE)
Face-to-face.

viscount ['vaɪˌkɑunt] (vī'kount') (VY'-KOUNT)
A British peer.

viscous ['vɪskəs] (vĭs'kəs) (VISS'-KUSS)

voile [vɔɪl] (voil) (VOYL)
A sheer fabric.

waistcoat ['wɛskɪt] (wĕs'kĭt) (WESS'-KIHT)

worsted ['wustɪd] (wŏōs'tĭd) (WUHSS'-TIHD)

yeoman ['jomən] (yō'mən) (YO'-MUN)

Yom Kippur [ˌjom kɪ'pur] (yōm' kĭ-pōōr') (YOOM KI-POOR')
The holiest Jewish holiday.

Yosemite [jo'sɛməti] (yō-sĕm'ə-tē) (YO-SEHM'-UH-TEE)

APPENDIX C
U.S. DEPARTMENT
OF LABOR REVISED
JOB TITLES

For generations, users of English and American English have tacitly assumed that certain jobs were appropriate only for persons of a particular group. Thus one who held a low position in management was a *junior executive,* one who held a certain position in a police department was a *head matron,* and a person who delivered letters was a *mailman.* Recognizing that occupational titles are often discriminatory, the U.S. Department of Labor has published a handbook titled *Job Title Revisions to Eliminate Sex- and Age-Referent Language from the Dictionary of Occupational Titles.* This publication preceded a thorough overhaul of the *Dictionary of Occupational Titles,* 4th ed. (U.S. Department of Labor, Washington, D.C., 1977).

In revising the *Dictionary,* the Labor Department reviewed all recognized job categories and made changes in nearly 3,500 job titles. It is important for broadcast announcers to become familiar with the new terminology. For perhaps the first time in human history, we are attempting to precipitate social change, in part, by making changes in language.

The new titles do not please everyone, and it is likely that some titles will undergo further change as people react to them. A *bellman* will not object to the new title *bell hop,* inasmuch as bell hops have used the "new" title for many years. *Farm boys* will undoubtedly be pleased to learn that they now are *farm hands,* just as *city hostesses* may be pleased with their new title, *goodwill ambassadors.* But some practitioners of ancient and honorable professions will take their new titles as an affront. An *animal husbandman* is now an *animal scientist,* a *bat boy* is now a *bat keeper*, a *brewmaster* is now a *brewery director*, and a *ring master* is now a *ring conductor*.

Some of the new job titles will undoubtedly be easy to live with once we get used to them. Among these are many different kinds of *repairmen*, who have become *repairers*. This last term makes grammatical sense, though it is somewhat difficult to articulate in a clear and unaffected manner. It is to the credit of the people who prepared the revised list that they avoided almost completely the temptation to replace *man* with *person*. Thus we do not have to contemplate titles such as *repairperson*, *longshoreperson*, or *fireperson*. In avoiding *person*, however, they came up with some titles that are either awkward or subject to misinterpretation, such as *servicer* for *serviceman* and *braker* for *brakeman*.

A few titles that reflect sexual identification were left unchanged. *Leading man* and *leading woman* remain as they always have been; here "sex is a bona fide occupational requirement." Similarly, *juvenile* has been left untouched, because age in the dramatic arts is a valid criterion. Some jobs were exempted from name change because they are fixed by legislation, international treaties, or other binding legal agreements; these include *ship master*, *able seaman*, and *masseur* and *masseuse*. In a few instances dual male-female job titles were retained, although both male and female titles are to be used by governmental agencies whenever the titles are used. Examples are *host-hostess* and *waiter-waitress*. It is unlikely that such double titles will find their way into common usage.

The effort of the Department of Labor to remove sex and age referents from job titles is to be commended. Considering the fact that the effort was without precedent, it was inevitable that some mistakes would be made. It is unlikely that anyone in television will accept the term *property handler* for *floorman*. *Floor director*, *floor manager*, and *stage manager* are the terms most commonly used today. Also, it would have been simpler (and more logical) to remove unnecessary "ettes" and "esses" from such terms as *drum majorette*, *sculptress*, and *stewardess* than to change the terms to something altogether different. *Drum major* and *sculptor* may be used for people of either sex.

There follows a selected list of the job titles approved by the U.S. Department of Labor. For the complete list, see *Job Title Revisions to Eliminate Sex- and Age-Referent Language from the Dictionary of Occupational Titles*, U.S. Department of Labor, Washington, D.C., 1977. Occupations marked with an asterisk (*) were changed by the Department of Labor at an earlier date.

OLD OCCUPATIONAL TITLE	NEW OCCUPATIONAL TITLE
Advance man	Advance agent
Advertising lay-out man	Advertising lay-out planner
Airplane steward	(title deleted)
Airplane stewardess	Airplane flight attendant
Alteration woman	Alterer
Animal husbandman	Animal scientist
Animal man	Animal keeper
Appliance repairman	Appliance repairer
Art lay-out man	Art lay-out planner
Audio man*	Audio operator
Audio-video repairman	Audio-video repairer
Automobile-body repairman	Automobile-body repairer
Automobile radiator man	Automobile radiator mechanic
Automobile radio man	Automobile radio repairer
Automotive-parts man	Automotive-parts stock clerk
Bakery girl	Bakery clerk
Ballet master	Ballet master-mistress
Bar boy	Bartender helper
Barmaid	Waiter-waitress, tavern
Barman	Bar attendant
Bat boy	Bat keeper
Bellman	Bell hop
Bomb disposal man	Bomb disposal specialist
Bondsman	Bonding agent
Boom man	Log sorter
Border patrolman	Border guard
Brakeman (any industry)	Brake holder
Brakeman, automobile	Brake repairer
Brakeman, passenger train	Braker, passenger train
Brakeman, road freight	Brake coupler, road freight
Brakeman, yard	Yard coupler
Brewmaster	Brewing director
Bridal consultant	Wedding consultant
Bus boy	Dining room attendant

OLD OCCUPATIONAL TITLE	NEW OCCUPATIONAL TITLE
Bus boy, dishes	Dish carrier
Bus boy, room service	Room service assistant
Bus girl	(title deleted)
Cable man (tel. and tel.)	Cable installer
Cable repairman (tel. and tel.)	Cable repairer
Camera girl	Photographer
Camera repairman	Camera repairer
Cameraman (television)	Camera operator
Cameraman, animation (mo. pict.)	Camera operator, animation
Cameraman, assistant (television)	Dolly pusher
Cameraman, first (mo. pict.)	Camera operator, first
Cameraman, second (mo. pict.)	Camera operator, second
Cameraman, special effects (mo. pict.)	Camera operator, special effects
Cameraman, title (mo. pict.)	Camera operator, title
Camp watchman	Camp guard
Carburetor man	Carburetor mechanic
Carpenter foreman, stage (mo. pict.)	Carpenter supervisor, stage
Cart boy (medical services)	Cart attendant
Cattle-ranch foreman	Supervisor, cattle ranch
Cellarman (hotel and rest.)	Cellar clerk
Chambermaid	Room cleaner
Charwoman	Charworker
Checkroom girl	Checkroom attendant
Cigarette girl	Cigarette vendor
Circus foreman	Circus supervisor
City hostess	Goodwill ambassador
Clean-up man (agriculture)	Clean-up hand
Clergyman	Clergy
Club boy (hotel and rest.)	Club attendant
Clubhouse boy (amusement and rec.)	Clubhouse attendant
Coachman	Coach driver
Coffee girl	Coffee maker
Comedian	Comedian-comedienne

OLD OCCUPATIONAL TITLE	NEW OCCUPATIONAL TITLE
Contact man	Song plugger
Control-room man (radio and TV)	Control operator
Control supervisor, junior (radio and TV)	Control supervisor I
Control supervisor, senior (radio and TV)	Control supervisor II
Copy boy	Messenger, copy
Copy cameraman	Copy-camera operator
Correction man (print. and pub.)	Proofsheet corrector
Counter bus boy	Counter dish carrier
Countergirl	Counter attendant
Counterman (retail trades)	Salesperson
Credit man	Credit-mail clerk
Dairy husbandman	Dairy scientist
Day watchman	Day guard
Delivery boy	Deliverer, merchandise
Deliveryman II	Delivery driver
Depot master	Depot supervisor
Display man (any trade)	Sign painter, display
Display man (retail trades)	Merchandise displayer
Dock watchman	Dock guard
Dockman I	Stevedore, dock
Doorman	Doorkeeper
Draftsman	Drafter
Dredgemaster	Dredge operator
Electrical appliance repairman	Electrical appliance repairer
Electrical appliance serviceman	Electrical appliance servicer
Electrical propman (mo. pict.)	Electrical prop handler
Electrical repairman	Electrical repairer
Engineman	Engine operator
Exploitation man (amuse. and rec.)	Exploitation writer
Farm boy	Farm hand, general I
Farm foreman	Farm supervisor
Farm housemaid	Houseworker, farm

OLD OCCUPATIONAL TITLE	NEW OCCUPATIONAL TITLE
Fire patrolman (govt. serv.)	Fire ranger
Fireman*	Fire fighter
Fireman, diesel locomotive	Firer, diesel locomotive
Fireman, electric locomotive	Firer, electric locomotive
Fireman, locomotive	Firer, locomotive
Fireman, marine	Firer, marine
Fireman, stage	Fire inspector, stage
Fireworks man	Fireworks display artist
Fisherman	Fisher
Flagman	Flagger
Flight stewardess	(title deleted)
Floorlady	Floor supervisor
Floorman* (TV)	Property handler
Flyman (amuse. and rec.)	Flyer
Footman	Butler, second
Forelady	Supervisor (followed by specialty)
Foreman	Supervisor (followed by specialty)
Foster mother	Foster parent
Fountain girl	Fountain server
Fountain man	Fountain server
Furnaceman	Furnace installer
Garbageman*	Garbage collector
Gateman (any industry)	Gate tender
Gateman (amuse. and rec.)	Gate attendant
General foreman	General supervisor
Governess	Child mentor
Groceryman, journeyman	Grocer
Hand propman (mo. pict.)	Hand prop handler
Hat-check girl	Hat-check attendant
Headmaster	Principal, private school
Headwaiter	Headwaiter-headwaitress
Herdsman, dairy	Cattle herder, dairy
Herdsman, swine	Herder, swine
High-rigging man (amuse. and rec.)	High-rigging installer

OLD OCCUPATIONAL TITLE	NEW OCCUPATIONAL TITLE
Highway-maintenance man	Highway-maintenance worker
Homicide-squad patrolman	Homicide-squad police officer
Horseman, show	Horse breeder, show
Host	Host-hostess
Hostess, hotel	Social director, hotel
House repairman	House repairer
Houseman (dom. serv.)	Caretaker, house
Housemother	Cottage parent
Iceman	Driver, ice route
Inkman	Inker
Installment man	Installment collector
Interior-display man	Merchandise displayer, interior
Junior executive	Executive trainee
Knock-up man (woodworking)	Knock-up assembler
Laundress (dom. serv.)	Launderer I
Laundry routeman	Driver, laundry route
Laundryman (dom. serv.)	Launderer II
Lay-out man (print. and pub.)	Lay-out planner
Lineman (amuse. and rec.)	Line umpire
Lineman (tel. and tel.)	Line installer-repairer
Longshoreman	Stevedore
Maid, general	Houseworker, general
Maid, hospital	Cleaner, hospital
Mail boy	Messenger, mail
Mailman*	Mail carrier
Maintenance man, building	Maintenance repairer, building
Make-up man (amuse. and rec.; mo. pict.)	Make-up artist
Master of ceremonies	Master-mistress of ceremonies
Matron, head (govt. serv.)	Police sergeant
Messman	Mess attendant
Midwife	Birth attendant
Milkman	Driver, milk route
Motel maid	Motel cleaner
Motion-picture-equipment foreman	Motion-picture-equipment supervisor
Motorcycle patrolman	Motorcycle police officer

OLD OCCUPATIONAL TITLE	NEW OCCUPATIONAL TITLE
Motorman II (r.r. trans.)	Streetcar operator
Mounted policeman	Mounted police officer
New car salesman	New car sales associate
Newsboy	Newspaper vendor
Night watchman	Night guard
Nursemaid	Child monitor
Nursery governess	Child mentor, nursery
Nurseryman	Manager, nursery
Office boy	Office helper
Office girl	Office helper
Ordnanceman	Ordnance artificer
Outside-property man (mo. pict.)	Outside-property agent
Page boy	Page
Park foreman	Park maintenance supervisor
Park watchman	Park patroller
Parlor matron	Parlor chaperon
Patrolman (govt. serv.)	Police officer I
Paymaster	Pay agent
Personal maid	Lady's attendant
Pin boy	Pin setter
Policeman*	Police officer
Policewoman	Police officer
Produce man	Produce seller
Product-development man	Product-development worker
Production man (radio and TV)	Production coordinator
Property man (amuse. and rec.)	Property coordinator
Property man (mo. pict.)	Property handler
Property master (mo. pict.)	Property supervisor
Public-address serviceman	Public-address servicer
Public relations man	Public-relations practitioner
Public-relations woman	Public-relations practitioner
Radio patrolman	Radio police officer
Radio repairman	Radio repairer
Repairman	Repairer
Rest-room maid	Rest-room attendant
Rewrite man	Rewriter
Ring master	Ring conductor

OLD OCCUPATIONAL TITLE	NEW OCCUPATIONAL TITLE
Salad girl	Salad maker
Salad man	Salad maker
Salesman	Sales associate (sales agent, sales representative, soliciter, driver)
Sandwich girl	Sandwich maker
Sandwich man	Sandwich maker
Sculptress	(title deleted)
Seamstress	Sewer, custom (mender, alterer)
Shoe repairman	Shoe repairer
Shop foreman	Shop supervisor
Song and dance man	Song and dance person
Sound-effects man	Sound-effects technician
Special-effects man (mo. pict.)	Special-effects specialist
Special-events man (radio and TV)	Special-events coordinator
Stage-door man	Stage-door attendant
Stage man	Stage hand
State-highway patrolman	State-highway police officer
Station master	Station manager
Steward	Steward-stewardess
Stewardess	Steward-stewardess
Television-installation man	Television installer
Television service and repair-man	Television-and-radio repairer
Traffic patrolman	Traffic police officer
Used car salesman	Used car sales associate
Valet	Gentleman's attendant
Video man	Video installer
Waiter	Waiter-waitress
Waitress	Waiter-waitress
Wardrobe mistress	Wardrobe supervisor
Watchman, crossing	Crossing tender
Watchman I (any industry)	Guard II
Wine steward	Wine steward-stewardess

APPENDIX D NATIONS AND CITIZENS OF THE WORLD

Prior to the Second World War, much of Africa and Oceania and some of Asia were colonies or possessions of European nations. As such, they were given names convenient to their occupiers: Tanganyika, Palau, and New Hebrides, to name three. Upon achieving independence, many of these nations immediately changed their names, and Tanganyika became Tanzania, Palau became Belau, and New Hebrides became Vanuatu. Other nations, long independent, have changed their names in recent years, including Kampuchea (Cambodia), Burkino Faso (Upper Volta), and Benin (Dahomey). Because of such changes, announcers—and especially news reporters and anchors—must have available an up-to-date source of correct terminology for every nation of the world.

Additionally, as stated at the end of Chapter 8, it is important for announcers to know how to refer to citizens of all nations of the world. It may come as a surprise to learn that a citizen of the Ivory Coast is an Ivorian, a citizen of Lesotho is a Masotho (plural Basotho), and a citizen of the Seychelles a Seychellois. Appendix D presents the Americanized name of every nation of the world and gives both usage and pronunciation for these nations and their citizens. Where they differ, both nouns and adjectives are given for a nation's inhabitants.

NATION	PRONUNCIATION	PERSON FROM THAT NATION	PRONUNCIATION
Afghanistan	[æfˈɡænəstən] (AF-GANʹ-UH-STAN)	Afghan	[ˈæfɡæn] (AFʹ-GAN)
Albania	[ælˈbeniə] (AL-BAYʹ-NEE-UH)	Albanian	[ælˈbeniən] (AL-BAYʹ-NEE-UN)
Algeria	[ælˈdʒɪriə] (AL-JEER-EE-UH)	Algerian	[ælˈdʒɪriən] (AL-JEER-EE-UN)
Andorra	[ænˈdɔrə] (AN-DOORʹ-UH)	Andorran	[ænˈdɔrən] (AN-DOORʹ-UN)
Angola	[ænˈɡolə] (AN-GOʹ-LUH)	Angolan	[ænˈɡolən] (AN-GOʹ-LUN)
Antigua	[ænˈtigwə] (AN-TEEG-WUH)	Antiguan	[ænˈtigwən] (AN-TEEGʹ-WUN)
Argentina	[ɑrdʒənˈtinə] (AR-JUN-TEEʹ-NUH)	Argentine	[ˈɑrdʒənˌtin] (ˈAR-JUN-TEEN) or [ˈɑrdʒənˌtaɪn] (ˈAR-JUN-TYNE)
Australia	[ɔˈstreljə] (AW-STRAYLʹ-YUH)	Australian (Aussie is slang but not bad taste)	[ɔˈstreljən] (AW-STRAYLʹYUHN)
Austria	[ˈɔstriə] (AWSʹ-TREE-UH)	Austrian	[ˈɔstriən] (AWʹ-STREE-UN)
Bahamas	[bəˈheməz] (BUH-HAYʹ-MUZ)	Bahamian	[bəˈhemiən] (BUH-HAYʹ-MEE-UN)
	[bəˈhaməz] (BUH-HAHʹ-MUZ)		[bəˈhɑmiən] (BUH-HAHʹ-MEE-UN)
Bahrain	[bɑˈren] (BAH-RAINʹ)	Bahraini	[bɑˈreni] (BAH-RAYʹ-NEE)
Bangladesh	[ˈbɑŋɡlədeʃ] (BAHNGʹ-GLUH-DESH)	n. Bangladeshi	[bɑŋɡləˈdɛʃi] (BAHNG-GLUH-DESHʹ-EE)
		a. Bangladesh	(same as name of nation)
Barbados	[bɑrˈbedoz] (BAR-BAYʹ-DOZ)	Barbadian	[bɑrˈbediən] (BAR-BAYʹ-DEE-UN)
Belau	[beˈlaʊ] (BAY-LAUʹ)	Belauan	[beˈlaʊn] (BAY-LAU-UN)
(The Republic of Belau was formerly known as Palau)			
Belgium	[ˈbɛldʒəm] (BELʹ-JUM)	Belgian	[ˈbɛldʒən] (BELʹ-JUN)
Belize	[bɛˈliz] (BEH-ʹLEEZ)	Belizean	[bɛˈliziən] (BEH-ʹLEEZ-EE-UN)
Benin	[bɛˈnin] (BEH-NEENʹ)	Beninese	[bɛnəˈniz] (BEN-UH-NEEZʹ)
Bermuda	[bəˈmjudə] (BER-MYOOʹ-DUH)	Bermudian	[bəˈmjudien] (BER-MYOOʹ-DEE-UN)
Bhutan	[buˈtɑn] (BOO-TAHNʹ)	Bhutanese	[butɑˈniz] (BOO-TAH-NEEZʹ)
Bolivia	[boˈliviə] (BO-LIVʹ-EE-UH)	Bolivian	[boˈliviən] (BO-LIVʹ-EE-UN)
Botswana	[bɑtˈswɑnə] (BAHT-SWANʹ-UH)	n. Motswana (sing.), Batswana (pl.)	[mɑtˈswɑnə] (MAHT-ʹSWAN-UH) [bɑtˈswɑnə] (BAHT-SWANʹ-UH)

(Note: Batswana and Botswana receive the same pronunciation.)

NATION	PRONUNCIATION	PERSON FROM THAT NATION	PRONUNCIATION
Brazil	[brəˈzɪl] (BRUH-ZIL')	Brazilian	[brəˈzɪljən] (BRUH-ZIL'-YUN)
Brunei	[bruˈnaɪ] (BRUH-NY')	Bruneian	[bruˈnaɪən] (BRUH-NY'-UN)
Bulgaria	[bʌlˈɡɛriə] (BUHL-GARE'-EE-UH)	Bulgarian	[bʌlˈɡɛriən] (BUHL-GARE'-EE-UN)
Burkina Faso	[burˈkinəˈfasˌo] (BOOR-KEEN'-UH FAH'-SO)	Burkinan	[burˈkinɑn] (BOOR-KEEN'-UN)
(Formerly Upper Volta)			
Burma	[bɜˈmə] (BER'-MUH)	*n.* Burman	[bɜˈmən] (BER'-MUN)
		a. Burmese	[bəˈmiz] (BER-MEEZ')
Burundi	[buˈrundi] (BUH-RUHN'-DEE)	*n.* Burundian	[burundiən] (BUH-RUHN'-DEE-UN)
		a. Burundi	(same as name of nation)
Cameroon	[kæməˈun] (KAM-ER-OON')	Cameroonian	[kæməˈuniən] (KAM-ER-OON'-EE-UN)
Canada	[ˈkænədə] (KAN'-UH-DUH)	Canadian	[kəˈnediən] (KUH-NAY'-DEE-UN)
(French Canadians pronounce it [ˌkɑˌnɑˈdɑ] (KAH-NAH-DAH'), with a slight stress on the last syllable. Females are Canadienne [ˌkɑˌnɑˈdjɛn] (KAH-NAH-DYEHN'), and males are Canadien [ˌkɑˌnɑˈdjɛ̃] (KAH-NAH-DYEH')			
Cape Verdi	[ˈkepˈvɛrdi] (KAYP'-VEHR'-DEE)	*n.* Cape Verdean;	both pronounced [ˈvɛrdiən] (VEHR'-DEE-UN)
		a. Cape Verdian	
Central African Republic		Central African	
Chad	[tʃæd] (TCHAD)	Chadian	[ˈtʃædiən] (TCHAD'-EE-UN)
Chile	[ˈtʃili] (TCHIL'-EE)	Chilean	[ˈtʃiliən] (TCHIL'-EE-UN) or [tʃɪˈlɛən] (TCHI-LAY'-UN)
China	[ˈtʃaɪnə] (TCHY'-NUH)	Chinese	[tʃaɪˈniz] (TCHY-NEEZ')
(Mainland China is the People's Republic of China; the Republic of China is on Taiwan and nearby islands.)			
Colombia	[koˈlʌmbiə] (KO-LUM'-BEE-UH)	Colombian	[koˈlʌmbiən] (KO-LUM'-BEE-UN)
(Most dictionaries give KUH-LUM'-BEE-UH, but current radio and television usage favors the more nearly Spanish pronunciation.)			
Comoros	[kəˈmɔrˌoz] (KUH-MOR'-OHZ)	Comoran	[kəˈmɔrˌən] (KUH-MOR'-UN)
Congo	[ˈkɑŋɡo] (KAHNG'-GO)	Congolese	[kɑŋɡəˈliz] (KAHNG-GUH-LEEZ')
(The Republic of Congo is not the former Belgian Congo, but a part of what was once French Equatorial Africa.)			

Nation		Citizen	
Cook Islands	[kʊk] (KOOK)	Cook Islander	
Costa Rica	['kɔstə'rikə] (KOST'-UH REE'-KUH)	Costa Rican	['kɔstə'rikən] (KOST'-UH REEK'-UN)
Cuba	['kjubə] (KYOO'-BUH)	Cuban	['kjubən] (KYOO'-BUN)
Cyprus	['saɪˌprəs] (SY'-PRUSS)	Cypriot	['sɪpˌriət] (SIP'-REE-UT)
Czechoslovakia	[ˌtʃɛkoslo'vɑkiə] (CHECK-OH-SLO-VAHK'-EE-UH)	Czechoslovakian	[ˌtʃɛkoslo'vɑkiən] (CHECK-OH-SLO-VAHK'-EE-UN)
Denmark	['denˌmɑrk] (DEN'-MARK)	n. Dane; a. Danish	[den] (DAYN); ['denʃ] (DAYN'-ISH)
Djibouti	[dʒɪ'buti] (JIH-BOOT'-EE)	Citizen of Djibouti	
Dominica	[də'mɪnkə] (DUH-MIN'-IK-UH)	Dominican	[də'mɪnkən] (DUH-MIN'-IK-UN)
Dominican Republic	[də'mɪnkən]· (DUH-MIN'-IK-UN)	Dominican	[də'mɪnkən]· (DUH-MIN'-IK-UN)
Ecuador	['ɛkwəˌdɔr] (EK'WUH-DOOR)	Ecuadorean	[ˌɛkwə'dɔriən] (EK-WUH-DOOR'-EE-UN)
Egypt	['idʒɪpt] (EE'-JIPT)	Egyptian	[i'dʒɪpʃən] (EE-JIP'-SHUN)
El Salvador	[ɛl'sælvəˌdɔr] (EL SAL'-VUH-DOOR)	Salvadoran	[ˌsælvə'dɔrən] (SAL-VUH-DOOR'-UN)
Equatorial Guinea	[ɛkwə'tɔriəl'gɪni] (EK-WAH-TOR'-EE-UL GIN'-EE)	Equatorial Guinean	[ɛkwə'tɔriəl'gɪniən] (EK-WAH-TOR'-EE-UL GIN'-EE-UN)

(There are three Guineas in Africa: Equatorial Guinea, once known as Spanish Guinea, Guinea, and Guinea-Bissau. GIN should be pronounced like the last syllable of *begin*.)

Nation		Citizen	
Eritrea	[ˌɛrɪ'treə] (AIR-IH-TRAY'-UH)	Eritrean	[ˌɛrɪ'treən] (AIR-IH-TRAY'-UN)
Ethiopia	[ˌiθi'opiə] (EE-THEE-O'-PEE-UH)	Ethiopian	[ˌiθi'opiən] (EE-THEE-O'-PEE-UN)
Falkland Islands	['fɔk,lənd] (FAWK'-LUND)	Falkland Islander	
Faroe Islands	['fæˌro] (FA'-RO)	Faroese	[ˌfæro'iz] (FA-RO-EEZ')
Fiji	['fidʒi] (FEE'-JEE)	Fijian	['fidʒiən] (FEE'-JEE-UN)
Finland	['fɪnlənd] (FIN'-LUND)	n. Finn; a. Finnish	[fɪn] (FIN); ['fɪn,ɪʃ] (FIN'-ISH)
France	[fræns] (FRANS)	n. Frenchman or Frenchwoman; a. French	['frɛntʃmən], ['frɛntʃwumən] (FRENTSH'-MUN), (FRENTSH'-WUH-MUN)
French Guiana	[gi'ænə] (GEE-AN'-UH)	n. French Guianese; a. French Guiana	[giə'niz] (GEE-UH-NEEZ') (same as name of nation)
French Polynesia	[pɑlə'niʒə] (PAHL-UH-NEEZH'-UH)	French Polynesian	[pɑlə'niʒən] (PAHL-UH-NEEZH'-UN)

NATION	PRONUNCIATION	PERSON FROM THAT NATION	PRONUNCIATION
Gabon	[gɑˈbɔn] (GAH-BAWN')	Gabonese	[ˌgɑbəˈniz] (GAH-BUH-NEEZ')
(Gabon Republic was once part of French Equatorial Africa.)			
Gambia	[ˈgæmbiə] (GAM'-BEE-UH)	Gambian	[ˈgæmbiən] (GAM'-BEE-UN)
Germany	[ˈdʒɜˈməni] (JER'-MUH-NEE)	German	[ˈdʒɜˈmən] (JER'-MUN)
(East Germany is the German Democratic Republic; West Germany is the German Federal Republic.)			
Ghana	[ˈgɑnə] (GAH'-NUH)	Ghanaian	[gɑˈneən] (GAH-NAY'-UN)
(Some dictionaries list *Ghanian* (GAH'-NEE-UN) as an alternative to *Ghanaian*, but the Documentation and Terminology Service of the United Nations does not suggest this usage.)			
Gibraltar	[dʒɪˈbrɔltəˈ] (JIH-BRAHLT'-ER)	*n.* Gibraltarian	[dʒɪbrɔlˈteriən] (JIH-BRAHL-TARE'-EE-UN)
		a. Gibraltar	(same as name of nation)
Greece	[gris] (GREES)	Greek	[grik] (GREEK)
Greenland	[ˈgrinˌlənd] (GREEN'-LUND)	*n.* Greenlander	[ˈgrinˌləndəˈ] (GREEN'-LUND-ER)
		a. Greenland	(same as name of nation)
Grenada	[grəˈnedə] (GRUH-NAY'-DUH)	Grenadian	[ˌgrəˈnediən] (GRUH-NAY'-DEE-UN)
Guadeloupe	[gwɑdəˈlup] (GWAH-DUH-LOOP')	*n.* Guadeloupian	[gwɑdəˈlupiən] (GWAH-DUH-LOO'-PEE-UN)
		a. Guadeloupe	(same as name of nation)
Guatemala	[gwɑtəmɑlə] (GWAH-TUH-MAHL'-UH)	Guatemalan	[gwɑtəˈmɑlən] (GWAH-TUH-MAHL'-UN)
Guinea	[ˈgɪnˌi] (GIN'-EE)	Guinean	[ˈgɪnˌiən] (GIN'-EE-UN)
Guinea-Bissau	[bɪsˈaʊ] (BISS-OW')	Guinean	[ˈgɪnˌiən] (GIN'-EE-UN)
Guyana	[gaɪˈænə] (GUY-AN'-UH)	Guyanese	[gaɪəˈniz] (GUY-UN-EEZ')
Haiti	[ˈheˌti] (HAY'-TEE)	Haitian	[ˈheʃən] (HAY'-SHUN)
Honduras	[hɑnˈdurəs] (HAHN-DUHR'-US)	Honduran	[hɑnˈdurən] (HAHN-DUHR'-UN)
Hong Kong	[hɔŋ ˈkɔŋ] (HAWNG'-KAWNG')	Citizen of Hong Kong	
Hungary	[ˈhʌŋgəri] (HUNG'-GUH-REE)	Hungarian	[hʌŋˈgɛriən] (HUNG-GARE'-EE-UN)
Iceland	[ˈəɪslənd] (EYES'-LUND)	*n.* Icelander	[ˈəɪslændəˈ] (EYES'-LUND-ER)
		a. Icelandic	[aɪsˈlændɪk] (EYES-LAN'-DIK)

Term	IPA	Pronunciation
India	[ˈɪndiə]	(IN'-DEE-UH)
Indian	[ˈɪndiən]	(IN'-DEE-UN)
Indonesia	[ˌɪndoˈniʒə]	(IN-DO-NEEZH'-UH)
Indonesian	[ˌɪndoˈniʒən]	(IN-DO-NEEZH'-UN)
Iran	[ɪˈrɑn]	(IH-RAHN')
Iranian	[ɪˈrɑn,iən]	(IH-RAHN'-EE-UN)
Iraq	[ɪˈrɑk]	(IH-RACK')
Iraqi	[ɪˈrɑki]	(IH-RACK'-EE)
Ireland	[ˈaɪɚlənd]	(EYE'-ER-LUND)
n. Irishman; Irishwoman	[ˈaɪrɪʃ]	(EYE'-RISCH)
a. Irish	[ˈaɪrɪʃ]	(EYE'-RISCH)
Israel	[ˈɪzriəl]	(IZ'-REE-UL)
Israeli	[ɪzˈreli]	(IZ-RAY'-LEE)

(Dictionaries and announcers prefer IZ'-REE-UL and IZ-RAY'-LEE, but more nearly correct IZ'-RY-EL' and IZ-RY-AY'-LEE are heard more and more often. Use *Israelite* when referring to Biblical times.)

Term	IPA	Pronunciation
Italy	[ˈɪtəli]	(IT'-UH-LEE)
Italian	[ɪˈtæljən]	(IH-TAL'-YUN)
Ivory Coast	[ˈaɪvri ˈkost]	(EYE'-VRY KOST)
Ivorian	[aɪˈvɔriən]	(EYE-VOR'-EE-UN)
Ivoirien	[ɪvwɑrjɛ̃]	(IH-VWAR'-YEN)

(République du Côte d'Ivoire; French *Ivoirien* is interchangeable with Anglicized *Ivorian*.)

Term	IPA	Pronunciation
Jamaica	[dʒəˈmekə]	(JUH-MAKE'-UH)
Jamaican	[dʒəˈmekən]	(JUH-MAKE'-UN)
Japan	[dʒəˈpæn]	(JUH-PAN')
Japanese	[ˌdʒæpəˈniz]	(JAP-UH-NEEZ')
Jordan	[ˈdʒɔrdən]	(JAWR'-DUN)
Jordanian	[dʒɔrˈdeniən]	(JAWR-DAYNE'-EE-UN)
Kampuchea	[ˌkɑmpuˈtʃiə]	(KAHM-POO-CHEE'-UH)
Kampuchean	[ˌkɑmpuˈtʃiən]	(KAHM-POO-CHEE'-UN)

(Kampuchea was formerly known as Cambodia.)

Term	IPA	Pronunciation
Kenya	[ˈkɛnjə]	(KEN'-YUH)
Kenyan	[ˈkɛnjən]	(KEN'-YUN)

(The pronunciation KEEN'-YUH is of British colonial origin, and Kenyans dislike that pronunciation.)

Term	IPA	Pronunciation
Kiribati	[kɪrɪˈbɑti]	(KEER-IH-BAHT'-EE)
n. Kiribatian	[kɪrɪˈbɑtiən]	(KEER-IH-BAHT'-EE-UN)
a. Kiribati		(same as name of nation)
Korea	[kɔˈriə]	(KAW-REE'-UH)
Korean	[kɔˈriən]	(KAW-REE'-UN)

(South Korea is the Republic of Korea; North Korea is the People's Democratic Republic of Korea.)

Term	IPA	Pronunciation
Kuwait	[kuˈet]	(KOO-WAYT')
Kuwaiti	[kuˈeti]	(KOO-WAYT'-EE)
Laos	[ˈlɑˌos]	(LAH'-OSS)
n. Lao	[ˈlɑ,o]	(LAH'-O)
a. Laotian	[leˈoˌʃən]	(LAY-OH'-SHUN)
Lebanon	[ˈlɛbəˌnɑn]	(LEB'-UH-NAHN)
Lebanese	[ˌlɛbəˈniz]	(LEB-UH-NEEZ')

NATION	PRONUNCIATION	PERSON FROM THAT NATION	PRONUNCIATION
Lesotho	[lɛˈsoto] (LEH-SOˈ-TOE)	n. Mosotho (sing.), Basotho (pl.), a. Basotho	[moˈsoto] (MO-SOˈ-TOE) [bɑˈsoto] (BAH-SOˈ-TOE)
Liberia	[laɪˈbɪriə] (LY-BEERˈ-EE-UH)	Liberian	[laɪˈbɪriən] (LY-BEERˈ-EE-UN)
Libya	[ˈlɪbiə] (LIBˈ-EE-UH)	Libyan	[ˈlɪbiən] (LIBˈ-EE-UN)
Liechtenstein	[ˈlɪktənˌstaɪn] (LIKˈ-TUN-STYN)	n. Liechtensteiner	[ˈlɪktənˌstaɪnə] (LIKˈ-TUN-STYN-ER)
		a. Liechtenstein	
Luxembourg	[ˈlʌksəmburg] (LUKSˈ-UM-BOORG)	n. Luxembourger	[ˈlʌksəmburgə] (LUKSˈ-UM-BOORG-ER)
		a. Luxembourg	(same as name of nation)
Macau	[məˈkaʊ] (MAH-KOWˈ)	n. Macanese	[mɑkɑnˈiz] (MAH-KAHN-EEZˈ)
		a. Macau	(same as name of nation)
Madagascar	[mædəˈgæskɑr] (MAD-UH-GASˈ-KAHR)	Malagasy	[mɑləˈgɑsi] (MAHL-UH-GAHSˈ-EE)
Malawi	[məˈlɑˌwi] (MAH-LAHˈ-WEE)	Malawian	[məˈlɑˌwiən] (MAH-LAHˈ-WEE-UN)
Malaysia	[məˈleʒə] (MUH-LAYˈ-ZHUH)	Malaysian	[məˈleʒən] (MAH-LAHˈ-ZHUN)
Maldives	[ˈmældaɪvz] (MALˈ-DYVEZ)	Maldivian	[mælˈdiviən] (MAL-DIVˈ-EE-UN)
Mali	[ˈmɑli] (MAHˈ-LEE)	Malian	[ˈmɑˌliən] (MAHˈ-LEE-UN)
Malta	[ˈmɔltə] (MAWLˈ-TUH)	Maltese	[mɔlˈtiz] (MAWL-TEEZˈ)
Martinique	[mɑrtənˈik] (MAHR-TAN-EEKˈ)	Martiniquais	[mɑrtæniˈke] (MAHR-TAN-EE-KAYˈ)
Mauritania	[mɔrɪˈteniə] (MAWR-IH-TAYNˈ-EE-UH)	Mauritanian	[mɔrɪˈteniən] (MAWR-IH-TAYNˈ-EE-UN)
Mauritius	[mɔˈrɪtˌiəs] (MAW-RIHTˈ-EE-US)	Mauritian	[mɔˈrɪtˌiən] (MAW-RIHTˈ-EE-UN)
Mexico	[ˈmɛksɪˌko] (MEHXˈ-IH-KO)	Mexican	[ˈmɛksɪkən] (MEHXˈ-IH-KUN)
Monaco	[ˈmɑnɪˌko] (MAHNˈ-IH-KO)	Monacan or Monegasque	[ˈmɑnɪkən] or [mɑnˈgɑsk] (MAHNˈ-IH-KUN) or (MAHN-IH-GAHSKˈ)
Mongolia	[mɑnˈgoliə] (MAHN-GO-LEE-UH)	Mongolian	[mɑnˈgoliən] (MAHN-GOˈ-LEE-UN)
Morocco	[məˈrɑkˌo] (MUH-RAHKˈ-O)	Moroccan	[məˈrɑkən] (MUH-RAHKˈ-UN)

Nation	Pronunciation	Citizen / Adjective	Pronunciation
Mozambique	[mozæm'bik] (MO-ZAM-BEEK')	Mozambican	[mozæm'bikən] (MO-ZAM-BEEK'-UN)
Namibia	[nə'mɪbiə] (NUH-MIB'-EE-UH)	Namibian	[nə'mɪbiən] (NUH-MIB'-EE-UN)
Nauru	[nɑ'u‚ru] (NAH-OO'-ROO)	Nauruan	[nɑ‚u'ruən] (NAH-OO-ROO'-UN)
Nepal	[nɛ'pɑl] (NEH-PAHL')	Nepalese	[nɛpə'liz] (NEH-PUH-LEEZ')
Netherlands	['nɛðɚ‚ləndz] (NETH'-ER-LUNDZ)	Netherlander	[nɛðɚ'lændɚ] (NETH-ER-LAND'-ER)
Netherlands Antilles	[æn'tɪl‚iz] (AN-TIL'-EEZ)	Netherlands Antillean	[æn'tɪliən] (AN-TIL'-EE-UN)
New Caledonia	[kælə'doniə] (KAL-UH-DON'-EE-UH)	New Caledonian	[kælə'doniən] (KAL-UH-DON'-EE-UN)
New Zealand	['zilənd] (ZEE'-LUND)	n. New Zealander	['zilændɚ] (ZEE'-LUND-ER)
		a. New Zealand	(same as name of nation)
Nicaragua	[nikə'rɑg'wɑ] (NIK-UH-RAHG'-WAH)	Nicaraguan	[nikə'rɑgwən] (NIK-UH-RAHG'-WUN)
Niger	['naidʒɚ] (NY'-JER)	n. Nigerien	[nɪʒɪr'jɛ̃] (NIH-ZHIHR-YEHN')
		a. Niger	(same as name of nation)

(*Nigerien* applies only to citizens of Nigeria. Use the French *Nigerien* and the anglicized *Niger* for citizens of the Republic of Niger.)

Nation	Pronunciation	Citizen / Adjective	Pronunciation
Nigeria	[nai'dʒɪriə] (NY-JEER'-EE-UH)	Nigerian	[nai'dʒɪriən] (NY-JEER'-EE-UN)
Norway	['nɔrwe] (NAWR'-WAY)	Norwegian	[nɔr'widʒən] (NAWR-WEEJ'-UN)
Oman	[o'mɑn] (OH-MAHN')	Omani	[o'mɑni] (OH-MAHN'-EE)
Pakistan	['pɑki‚stɑn] (PAHK'-IH-STAHN)	Pakistani	[‚pɑki'stɑni] (PAHK-IS-TAHN'-EE)
Panama	['pænə‚mɑ] (PAN'-UH-MAH)	Panamanian	[‚pænə'meniən] (PAN-UH-MAYNE'-EE-UN)
Papua New Guinea	['pæpjuə] (PAP'-YOU-UH)	Papua New Guinean	['gɪniən] (GIN'-EE-UN)
Paraguay	['pɑrəgwai] (PAHR'-UH-GWY)	Paraguayan	[pɑrə'gwyən] (PAHR-UH-GWY'-UN)
Peru	[pə'ru] (PUH-ROO')	Peruvian	[pə'ruviən] (PUH-ROO'-VEE-UN)
Philippines	['filəpinz] (FIL'-UH-PEENZ)	n. Filipino	[filə'pino] (FIL-UH-PEEN'-O)
		a. Philippine	
Poland	['polənd] (PO'-LUND)	n. Pole	[pol] (POL)
		a. Polish	['polɪʃ] (PO'-LISH)

NATION	PRONUNCIATION	PERSON FROM THAT NATION	PRONUNCIATION
Portugal	[ˈpɔrtʃəgəl] (PAWR'-CHUH-GUL)	Portuguese	[pɔrtʃəˈgiz] (PAWR-CHUH-GEEZ')
Qatar	[kɑˈtɑr] (KAH-TAHR')	Qatari	[kɑˈtɑri] (KAH-TAHR'-EE)
Reunion	[riˈjunjən] (REE-YOON'-YUN)	Reunionese	[rijunjənˈiz] (REE-YOON-YUN-EEZ')
Romania	[roˈmenjə] (RO-MAYNE'-YUH)	Romanian	[roˈmenjən] (RO-MAYNE'-YUN)
	[roˈmenɪə] (RO-MAY'-NEE-UH)		[roˈmenɪən] (RO-MAY'-NEE-UN)

(Romania is also Rumania and may be pronounced with initial ROO.)

NATION	PRONUNCIATION	PERSON FROM THAT NATION	PRONUNCIATION
Rwanda	[ruˈɑndə] (ROO-AHN'-DUH)	Rwandan	[ruˈɑndən] (ROO-AHN'-DUN)
	[ˈrwɑndə] (RWAN'-DUH)		[ˈrwɑndən] (RWAN'-DUN)
St. Christopher-Nevis-Anguilla	[ˈsent ˈkrɪstəfə-ˈnevis-æŋˈgwilə] (SAYNT KRIS'-TUH-FER-NEHV'-ISS-ANG-GWEE'-LUH)	Kittsian, Nevisian, Anguillan	[ˈkɪtsiən], [nɛˈvisiən], [æŋˈgwilən] (KITS'-EE-UN), (NEHV-ISS'-EE-UN), (ANG-GWEE'-LUN)
St. Lucia	[ˈluʃə] (LOOSH'-UH)	St. Lucian	[ˈluʃən] (LOOSH'-UN)
St. Vincent and the Grenadines	[ˈvinsənt-grɛnəˈdinz] (VIN'-SUNT, GREN-UH-DEENZ')	St. Vincentian	[vinˈsɛntiən] (VIN-SENT'-EE-UN)
San Marino	[ˈsæn məˈrino] (SAN MUH-REEN'-O)	Sanmarinese	[san marinˈese] (SAN MAHR-EEN-AY'-SAY)
São Tomé and Príncipe	[sãuˈtome, ˈprinsiˌpe] (SAUNG-TOE'-MEH, PREEN'-SEE-PEH)	São Toméan	[sãu ˈtomɛən] (SAUNG-TOE'-MEH-UN)
Saudi Arabia	[sɑˈuˈdi] (SAH-OO'-DEE)	n. Saudi a. Saudi Arabian	(same as name of nation)
Senegal	[senəˈgɑl] (SEHN-UH-GAHL')	Senegalese	[senəgəˈliz] (SEHN-UH-GUH-LEEZ')
Seychelles	[seˈʃɛlz] (SAY-SHELZ')	n. Seychellois a. Seychelles	[seˈʃɛlˈwɑ] (SAY-SHEL-WAH') (same as name of nation)
Sierra Leone	[siˈɛrə liˈon] (SEE-AIR'-UH LEE-OWN')	Sierra Leonean	[liˈoniən] (LEE-OWN'-EE-UN)

Nation		n. / a. Citizen
Singapore	['sɪŋgəpɔr] (SING'-GUH-PAWR)	n. Singaporean [sɪŋgə'pɔriən] (SING-GUH-PAWR'-EE-UN) a. Singapore (same as name of nation)
Solomon Islands	['sɑləmən] (SAHL'-UH-MUN)	Solomon Islander
Somalia	[so'maljə] (SO-MAHL'-YUH)	Somali [so'mali] (SO-MAHL'-EE)
South Africa		South African
Soviet Union	[sovi'ɛt] (SO-VEE-ET') [sovjɛt] (SOV'-YET)	Russian ['rʌʃən] (RUSH'-UN)

(Union of Soviet Socialist Republics, USSR, like the U.S., presents a problem. *Russian* is correct for only about half the nation. *Soviet* means *council*, even though it often is used to mean "Citizen of the USSR." Formal usage calls for "Citizen of the Soviet Union" or "Citizen of the USSR"; less formal usage, *Soviet citizen;* informal, *Russian.*)

Spain	[spen] (SPAYN)	n. Spaniard ['spænjəd] (SPAN'-YERD) a. Spanish ['spænʃ] (SPAN'-ISH)
Sri Lanka	[sri 'lɑŋkə] (SREE LAHNGK'-UH)	Sri Lankan [sri 'lɑŋkən] (SREE LAHNGK'-UN)
Sudan	[su'dæn] (SOO-DAN')	Sudanese [sudə'niz] (SOO-DUH-NEEZ')
Surinam	['sʊrɪˌnɑm] (SOOR'-IH-NAHM)	n. Surinamer [sʊrɪ'nɑmɚ] (SOOR-IH-NAHM'-ER) a. Surinamese [sʊrɪnɑ'miz] (SOOR-IH-NAH-MEEZ')
Swaziland	['swɑziˌlænd] (SWAZI'-LAND)	Swazi ['swɑzi] (SWAH'-ZEE)
Sweden	['swidən] (SWEED'-UN)	n. Swede [swid] (SWEED) a. Swedish ['swidɪʃ] (SWEED'-ISH)
Switzerland	['swɪtsɚlənd] (SWITZ'-ER-LUND)	Swiss [swɪs] (SWISS)
Syria	['sɪriə] (SIHR'-EE-UH)	Syrian ['sɪriən] (SIHR'-EE-UN)
Taiwan	[taɪ'wɑn] (TY-WAHN')	Taiwanese [taɪwɑn'iz] (TY-WAHN-EEZ') Chinese [tʃaɪ'niz] (CHY-NEEZ')

(*Note:* 14% of the population of Taiwan is from mainland China; 84% is native Taiwanese.)

Tanzania	[tænzə'niə] (TAN-ZUH-NEE'-UH)	Tanzanian [tænzə'niən] (TAN-ZUH-NEE'-UN)
Thailand	['taɪˌlænd] (TY'-LAND)	Thai [taɪ] (TY)
Togo	['toˌgo] (TOE'-GO)	Togolese [ˌtoˌgo'liz] (TOE-GO-LEEZ')
Tonga	['tɔŋgə] (TAWNG'-GUH)	Tongan ['tɔŋgən] (TAWNG'-GUN)

NATION	PRONUNCIATION	PERSON FROM THAT NATION	PRONUNCIATION
Trinidad and Tobago	[ˈtrɪnɪdæd, təˈbego] (TRIN'-UH-DAD, TUH-BAY'-GO)	Trinidadian	[trɪnəˈdædiən] (TRIN-UH-DAD'-EE-UN)
		Tobagonian	[təbəˈgoniən] (TUH-BUH-GOHN'-EE-UN)
Tunisia	[tuˈniʒə] (TOO-NEEZH'-UH)	Tunisian	[tuˈniʒən] (TOO-NEEZH'-UN)
Turkey	[ˈtɜˑki] (TERK'-EE)	n. Turk	[tɜˑk] (TERK)
		a. Turkish	[ˈtɜˑkɪʃ] (TERK'-ISH)
Tuvalu	[tuˈvɑlu] (TOO-VAHL'-OO)	Tuvaluan	[tuvəˈluən] (TOO-VUH-LOO'-UN)
Uganda	[juˈgændə] (YOU-GAND'-UH)	Ugandan	[juˈgændən] (YOU-GAND'-UN)
United Arab Emirates	[emˈmɪrɪts] (EH-MIHR'-ITS)	Emirian	[ɛˈmɪriən] (EH-MIHR'-EE-UN)
United Kingdom		n. Briton	[ˈbrɪtən] (BRIHT'-UN)
		collective plural, British	
		a. British	[ˈbrɪtɪʃ] (BRIHT'-ISH)
United States (American for a U.S. citizen is resented by a few North and South Americans because they are Americans, too. Despite this, the term is widely used and is understood to mean a person who lives in or is a citizen of the United States.)			
Upper Volta	[ˈvoltə] (VOLT'-UH)	Upper Voltan	[ˈvoltən] (VOLT'-UN)
Uruguay	[ˈʊrəgwaɪ] (OOR'-UH-GWY)	Uruguayan	[ʊrəˈgwaɪən] (OOR-UH-GWY'-UN)

Vanuatu	[ˌvɑnˌuˈɑˌtu] (VAHN-OO-AH'-TOO)	Vanuatuan	[ˌvɑnˌuɑˈtuən] (VAHN-OO-AH-TOO'-UN)
(formerly New Hebrides, in South Pacific)			
Vatican City State	[ˈvætəkən] (VAT'-UH-KUN)	Citizen of	
Venezuela	[ˈvenəˈzwelə] (VEN-UH-ZWAY'-LUH)	Venezuelan	[ˈvenəˈzwelən] (VEN-UH-ZWAY'-LUN)
Vietnam	[ˌviˈɛtˌnɑm] (VEE-ET'-NAHM)	Vietnamese	[ˌviˈɛtnəˈmiz] (VEE-ET'-NUH-MEEZ')
Wallis and Futuna	[ˈwɑlɪs, fuˈtunə] (WALL'-US, FOO-TOON'-UH)	Wallisian	[wɑˈlisiən] (WAH-LEES'-EE-UN)
		Futunan	[fuˈtunən] (FOO-TOON'-UN)
		or Wallis and Futuna Islander	
Western Sahara	[səˈhɛrə] (SUH-HARE'-UH)	Saharan	[səˈhɛrən] (SUH-HARE'-UN)
Western Samoa	[sæˈmoə] (SA-MO'-UH)	Western Samoan	[sæˈmoən] (SA-MO'-UN)
Yemen	[ˈjɛmən] (YEHM'-UN)	Yemeni	[jɛˈmɛni] (YEH-MEN'-EE)
(*Note:* There are two Yemens—the Yemen Arab Republic [Sanaa], and the People's Democratic Republic of Yemen [Aden].)			
Yugoslavia	[jugoˈslɑviə] (YOO-GO-SLAV'-EE-UH)	Yugoslav	[ˈjugoslɑv] (YOU'-GO-SLAV)
Zaire	[zɑˈir] (ZA-EAR')	Zairian	[ˌzɑˈiriən] (ZAH-EAR'-EE-UN)
Zambia	[ˈzæmbiə] (ZAM'-BEE-UH)	Zambian	[ˈzæmbiən] (ZAM'-BEE-UN)
Zimbabwe	[zɪmˈbɑbwe] (ZIM-BOB'-WAY)	Zimbabwean	[zɪmˈbɑbwiən] (ZIM-BOB'-WEE-UN)

APPENDIX E
SUGGESTED READINGS

**CHAPTER 1:
BROADCAST
ANNOUNCING**

Rivers, William L., Schramm, Wilbur, and Christian, Clifford G. *Responsibility in Mass Communication*. 3d ed. New York: Harper & Row, Publishers, 1980.

U.S. Department of Labor. *Occupational Outlook Handbook*. Published periodically, and available at U.S. Government Bookstores.

**CHAPTER 2:
THE ANNOUNCER
AS
COMMUNICATOR**

Ecroyd, Donald, and Wagner, Hilda S. *Communicating Through Oral Reading*. New York: McGraw-Hill Book Company, 1979.

Tedlock, Dennis. *The Spoken Word and the Work of Interpretation*. Philadelphia: University of Pennsylvania Press, 1983.

**CHAPTER 3:
PERFORMANCE**

Duerr, Edwin. *Radio and Television Acting: Criticism, Theory and Practice*. Westport, Connecticut: Greenwood Press, 1972.

Hawes, William. *The Performer in Mass Media*. New York: Hastings House, 1978.

Malandro, Loretta A., and Barker, Larry. *Nonverbal Communication*. New York: Random House, 1983.

Pearson, Julia Cornelia, and Nelson, Paul Edward. *Understanding and Sharing*. Dubuque, Iowa: William C. Brown Company Publishers, 1985.

Zannes, Estelle, and Goldhaber, Gerald. *Stand Up, Speak Out*. 3d ed. Reading, Massachusetts: Addison-Wesley Publishing Company, 1983.

**CHAPTER 4:
RADIO
EQUIPMENT**

Alten, Stanley R. *Audio in Media*. Belmont, California: Wadsworth Publishing Company, 1981.

Nisbett, Alec. *The Use of Microphones*. New York: Hastings House, 1975.

Oringel, Robert S. *Audio Control Handbook.* 5th ed. New York: Hastings House, 1983.

Woram, John M. *The Recording Studio Handbook.* Plainview, New York: ELAR Publishing Company, 1982.

CHAPTER 5: PHONETIC TRANSCRIPTION

Bender, James F., ed. *NBC Handbook of Pronunciation.* 3d ed. New York: Thomas Y. Crowell Company, 1964.

Kenyon, John S., and Knott, Thomas A. *A Pronouncing Dictionary of American English.* Springfield, Massachusetts: G. & C. Merriam Company, Publishers, 1953.

McKay, Ian R. A. *Introducing Practical Phonetics.* Boston: Little, Brown and Company, 1978.

CHAPTER 6: VOICE AND DICTION

Anderson, Virgil. *Training the Speaking Voice.* 3d ed. New York: Oxford University Press, 1977.

Eisenson, Jon. *Voice and Diction.* New York: Macmillan Publishing Company, 1985.

Fisher, Hilda B. *Improving Voice and Articulation.* 2d ed. Boston: Houghton Mifflin Company, 1975.

Rizzo, Raymond. *The Voice as an Instrument.* New York: Odyssey Press, 1969.

Sprague, Jo, and Stuart, Douglas. *The Speaker's Handbook.* San Diego: Harcourt Brace Jovanovich, Publishers, 1984.

Uris, Dorothy. *Everybody's Book of Better Speaking.* New York: David McKay Company, Incorporated, 1960.

CHAPTER 7: FOREIGN PRONUNCIATION

Bender, James F., ed. *NBC Handbook of Pronunciation.* 3d ed. New York: Thomas Y. Crowell Company, 1964.

Bras, Monique. *Your Guide to French Pronunciation.* New York: Larousse and Company, Incorporated, 1975.

Bratus, B. V. *Russian Intonation.* Elmsford, New York: Pergamon Press, Inc., 1972.

Cox, Richard G. *The Singer's Manual of French and German Diction.* New York: Schirmer Books, 1970.

Fox, Anthony. *German Intonation: An Outline.* New York: Oxford University Press, 1984.

Jackson, Eugene, and Geiger, Adolph. *German Made Simple.* New York: Doubleday & Company, Inc., 1985.

Jackson, Eugene, and LoPreato, Joseph. *Italian Made Simple.* New York: Doubleday & Company, Inc.

Jackson, Eugene, and Rubio, Antonio. *French Made Simple.* New York: Doubleday & Company, Inc., 1984.

Kantner, Claude E., and West, Robert. *Phonetics,* rev. ed. New York: Harper and Row, 1960.

Kenyon, John, and Knott, Thomas. *A Pronouncing Dictionary of American English.* Springfield, Massachusetts: G. & C. Merriam, 1953.

Pei, Mario A. *World's Chief Languages.* New York: S. F. Vanni, 1960.

CHAPTER 8: AMERICAN ENGLISH USAGE

Follett, Wilson. *Modern American Usage: A Guide.* Edited by Jacques Barzun. New York: Hill & Wang, Inc., 1966.

Newman, Edwin. *Strictly Speaking.* New York: Warner Books, Inc., 1975.

Safire, William. *I Stand Corrected.* New York: Avon Books, 1984.

CHAPTER 9: COMMERCIALS AND PUBLIC-SERVICE ANNOUNCEMENTS

Cary, Norman D. *The Television Commercial: Creativity and Craftsmanship.* New York: Decker, 1971.

Heighton, Elizabeth J., and Cunningham, Don R. *Advertising in the Broadcast Media.* 2d ed. Belmont, California: Wadsworth Publishing Company, 1984.

CHAPTER 10: INTERVIEW AND TALK PROGRAMS

Cavett, Dick, and Porterfield, Christopher. *Cavett.* New York: Harcourt Brace Jovanovich, 1974.

CHAPTERS 11 AND 12: RADIO NEWS AND TELEVISION NEWS

Compesi, Ronald J., and Sherriffs, Ronald E. *Small Format Television Production.* Boston: Allyn and Bacon Inc., 1985.

Fang, Irving E. *Television News.* 3d ed. St. Paul: Rada Press, 1981.

Gans, Herbert J. *Deciding What's News.* New York: Vintage Books, 1979.

Graber, Doris A. *Processing the News.* New York: Longman Inc., 1984.

Green, Maury. *Television News: Anatomy and Process.* Belmont, California: Wadsworth Publishing Company, 1969.

Stephens, Mitchell. *Broadcast News*. New York: Holt, Rinehart and Winston, 1980.

Tuchman, Gaye. *Making News*. New York: The Free Press, 1978.

CHAPTER 13
MUSIC
ANNOUNCING

Apel, Willi. *Harvard Dictionary of Music*. 2d ed. Cambridge: Harvard University Press, 1969.

Baker, Theodore, ed. *Schirmer Pronouncing Pocket Manual of Musical Terms*. Rev. by Nicholas Slonimsky. New York: Schirmer Books, 1975.

Crofton, Ian, and Fraser, Donald. *A Dictionary of Musical Quotations*. New York: Schirmer Books, 1985.

Cross, Milton. *New Milton Cross' Complete Stories of the Great Operas*. New York: Doubleday & Company, Inc., 1955.

Cross, Milton, and Kohrs, Karl. *The New Milton Cross More Stories of the Great Operas*. New York: Doubleday & Company, Inc., 1980.

Ramsey, Dan. *How to Be a Disc Jockey*. Blue Ridge Summit, Pennsylvania: Tab Books, Inc., 1981.

Sadie, Stanley, ed. *The New Grove Dictionary of Music and Musicians*. 20 vols. London: Macmillan Publishers Ltd., 1980.

Smith, W. J. *A Dictionary of Musical Terms in Four Languages*. London: Hutchinson, 1961. This fine book is out of print, but it may be found in libraries.

CHAPTER 14:
SPORTS
ANNOUNCING

Harwell, Ernie. *Tuned to Baseball*. Notre Dame: Diamond Communications, Inc., 1985.

VanderZwaag, Harold J., and Sheehan, Thomas J. *Introduction to Sports Studies*. Dubuque, Iowa: William C. Brown Company Publishers, 1978.

GLOSSARY

A/C Abbreviation of *adult contemporary*, used to describe a type of popular music played by a radio station.

actuality A loosely defined term in radio, referring to a report featuring someone other than broadcast personnel (politicians, police inspectors, athletes, eyewitnesses) who provide an "actual" statement rather than one paraphrased and spoken by a reporter.

adult contemporary Descriptive of the type of music played on a particular radio station. Adult contemporary music is soft to moderate rock, ballads, and current hits.

affricates Speech sounds that combine a plosive (release of air as in saying the letter *p*) with a fricative (friction of air through a restricted air passage as in saying the letter *s*). Example: the "ch" sound in *choose*.

aircheck An audition tape, usually a portion of an actual broadcast.

album oriented rock A music radio station format featuring all styles of rock.

AOR *Album oriented rock,* a radio station format featuring all styles of rock music.

alveolus The upper gum ridge.

ambient noise or sound Unwanted sounds in an acoustical environment (air conditioners, traffic noises, airplanes) are *ambient noise*. Normal background sounds that

do not detract from the recording or the program—and that may add to the excitement of the broadcast, as do crowd sounds at a sports event—are *ambient sounds.*

amplitude The strength of a radio wave.

analyst, play An announcer, usually someone who was once a star athlete, who works with a play-by-play sportscaster to provide insights and analyses of games in progress.

anchor The chief newscaster on a radio or television news broadcast. When two announcers share the role, they are *co-anchors.*

announcer Anyone who speaks to an audience through a medium using one of these electronic devices: radio or television transmission over the public airways; cable or other closed-circuit audio or video distribution; electronic amplification, as in an auditorium or a theater. Announcers include newscasters, reporters, commentators, sportscasters, narrators, "personalities," disc jockeys, and program hosts and hostesses. People who deliver commercial messages (as contrasted with others who act in dramatized commercials) are also announcers.

articulation The physical formation of spoken words. Teeth, tongue, and lips, working together with the soft palate, gum ridges, and each other, break up the phonated sounds into articulate (or even inarticulate) speech sounds.

Note: Glossary terms are defined only as they are used in this book; many of the terms have additional uses and meanings not explained in this Glossary.

aspirate To release a puff of breath, as in sounding the word *unhitch*. Overaspiration results in a popping sound when sitting or standing close to a microphone.

attenuator A volume control on an audio console.

back announcing Identifying songs and artists after the playing of a *set*, two or more songs played back to back without intervening comment.

BB Script symbol for *billboard*, used to indicate to an announcer that an upcoming feature or event should be promoted.

beat check The *beat check* or *phone beat* refers to use of a telephone to search for news stories from a list of agencies—the FBI, police and fire departments, local hospitals, the weather bureau, airport control towers—provided to the person working the beat check. Stories of interest are taped from the telephone.

beautiful music Describes radio stations that feature gentle or restful music from motion picture soundtracks, instrumental arrangements of old standards, and some stage musicals and operettas.

beeper reports A news report, either recorded or live, telephoned to a station, in which an electronic beep is sounded to let the person speaking know that a recording is being made. The beep is not used when station personnel are recorded and need not be used for others if they are told that they are being recorded or being broadcast.

bending the needle An audio console features a meter, called a *VU* or *VI meter*, that gives the operator a visual impression of the degree of sound being sent through the console. The VU meter has a swinging needle that registers volume on a calibrated scale. When the sound is too loud, the needle hits the extreme right side of the scale, and this is called *bending the needle*.

BG Script symbol for *background*, referring most often to background music.

bilabial Sounds articulated primarily by both lips; they are also called *labial* sounds. Examples: *p* and *w*.

billing log A radio station's program log that lists, in sequence, each element of the program day, including commercials; it is called *billing log* by the sales and business departments.

blocking In television, a production is *blocked* when performers are shown where to stand, walk, and so on.

board (1) In radio, a board is an audio console. (2) In television news operations, the board is a large Plexiglas sheet on which the elements of a newscast are entered throughout the day.

board fade Turning down volume on an audio board or console, usually to the point of losing the sound altogether.

boom Short for *audio boom*, a device for moving a microphone without either its operator or the mic being seen on the television screen. Most booms are mounted on movable dollies and have controls to move the microphone in or out, up or down, or sideways. Television camera cranes are sometimes called booms.

brain The computer used to program an automated radio station, also called a *controller*.

bumper The device normally used as a slide to move a television program from one element to another. This may be a transition from the program to a commercial or from one segment of the program to another.

call, calling In sports announcing, the person who gives a play-by-play description of a game is said to be *calling* the game.

cart Short for *audiotape* or *videotape cartridge*. Carts are loops of tape encased in plug-in cartridges that do not have to be threaded and that automatically recue.

carted commercials Commercials dubbed to audiotape or videotape cartridges.

carting The act of dubbing, or recording on, an audiotape or videotape cartridge.

cart machine An electronic device that records and plays back material for broadcast. Some cart machines have only a playback capability.

cart with live tag A commercial that begins with a recorded announcement, often with musical background, and that provides time at the end for a closing tag by a local announcer.

chain A chain is a group of broadcast stations owned by one company or by a network.

channel selector switch A switch on an audio console that enables the operator to select from two or more inputs.

cheat In television to *cheat* is to assume a position that is not normal yet looks normal to the viewer. It is a positive term.

CHR *Contemporary hit radio,* also known as *Top-40 radio.* A station that plays the top rock hits of the day, interspersed with golden oldies.

chroma key An electronic device that makes it possible for one television scene to be *matted in* behind another. Chroma key is used to show a slide or some other graphic aid behind a news anchor, for instance. Blue is generally used for chroma key matting.

combo operator A radio disc jockey who does his or her own engineering, hence a *combination* or *combo operator.*

communicaster Used by some radio stations to identify a telephone call-in host or hostess.

condenser microphone A type of microphone that features a diaphragm and an electrode as a backplate.

console An audio control board.

continuity book Sometimes called *copy book,* it is a loose-leaf compilation of radio commercials in the order they are to be read or introduced (if on tape) by the announcer on duty.

controller The *brain* or *computer control* for an automated radio system.

cooperative commercials Commercials for both radio and television; the cost of broadcasting is divided between a national and a local advertiser.

copy book See *continuity book.*

copy sets A set of script forms, complete with one-use carbon papers, used widely in television newsrooms to provide as many as six scripts of a program.

cover shot A television shot that gives us a picture of a medium-to-large area. On an interview set, the cover shot would include both interviewer and guest(s).

crank up To *crank up the gain* is to increase the volume of sound going through an audio console.

cross fade One program sound fades out while another simultaneously fades in. This is done by manipulating the volume controls of an audio console.

crossplug A term used to identify a pitch made by one disc jockey or talk program host or hostess to promote another person's program on the same station.

CU Television script symbol for *close-up.*

cue box or **cue speaker** The small speaker in an audio control room or on-air studio that allows an audio operator to hear program elements as they are being cued up or previewed.

cumes Abbreviation of *cumulative ratings.* Cumes indicate the number of people listening to or viewing a particular station at a given time.

cutaway shots   In covering an event like a news story with one camera, *cutaway shots*—usually shots of background or action without dialogue—are recorded to be edited in later. They provide transitions between on-camera interviewees.

cut sheet   In radio, a *cut sheet* tells an engineer how to edit one or more cuts from an audiotape to a tape cartridge. In television, videotape engineers in news operations work with an *ENG cut sheet*, a form on which information about taped material is entered during the editing process.

daypart   A term used by music radio stations to identify portions of the broadcast day. The day may be *dayparted* into morning drive time, afternoon, and evening.

debriefing log   A log kept by radio and television stations, providing information about the performance of guests and the degree of audience interest in them.

demographics   The profile of an actual or intended audience; demographic information includes age, sex, ethnic background, income, and other factors that might help a broadcaster attract or hold a particular audience.

desk   The assignment editor is referred to as the *desk* in broadcast news operations.

donut commercial   A commercial with a recorded beginning and end, separated by material read by a local announcer.

double out   A cautionary term in radio production, indicating to an engineer that the speaker repeats the out-cue in a particular tape. A sports coach, for example, may say "early in the year" both in the body of his comments and at the end of the cut; the *double-out* warning is given so that the engineer will not stop the cart prematurely.

DVE   Abbreviation of *digital video effects*. A DVE machine can turn a picture into a mosaic, can swing a picture through space, can make a picture shrink or grow in size, and can achieve many other visually interesting effects.

dynamic microphone   The *dynamic* or *pressure* mic is a rugged, high-quality microphone that works well as an outdoor or hand-held mic.

EFP   *Electronic field production*. Any kind of videotape production using minicams and portable recorders and taking place on location.

ELF   Abbreviation of *easy listening formula*, a test of the clarity of scripts written for oral delivery.

ENG   *Electronic news gathering*. News reports for television, whether live or taped, produced in the field using the same kind of portable equipment employed in electronic field production.

ET   A script symbol for *electrical transcription*, an early term for a certain type of phonograph record, used now for any kind of disc recording.

fact sheet   An outline of the facts relevant to a product or an event, from which a script or continuity writer prepares a commercial or public-service announcement script.

fader   A control on an audio console enabling an operator to increase or decrease the volume of sound going through the board.

field, depth of   Depth of field is the area in front of a camera lens within which everything is in focus. The smaller the aperture of the lens, the greater the depth of field.

format   (1) A type of script used in television, usually a bare script outline. (2) The type of programming provided by a radio station (for example, an MOR format). (3) The layout of a radio or television script, or the manner in which dialogue, sound effects, music, and other program elements are set forth on the page.

freeze In television, to freeze is to remain motionless, usually at the end of a scene.

fricatives Sounds created by the friction of air through a restricted air passage. The letter *f* is a fricative sound.

future file A file of thirty-one folders (one for each day of the month) holding information about coming events that may be considered for news coverage by an assignment editor.

gaffer, gaffer's tape A *gaffer* is the chief electrician on a motion picture set. The tape used to hold cables in place, called *gaffer's tape,* is widely used in television.

gain The degree of sound volume going through an audio console. To *turn up the gain* is to increase the volume by means of a *gain control*—a sliding vertical fader or a rotating knob.

general assignment reporter A radio or television reporter who does not have a regular beat or assignment.

glottal The letter *h,* when uttered without the vibration of the vocal folds, is a glottal sound.

happy talk Usually used in a derogatory way to describe a newscast featuring news personnel who ad-lib, make jokes, and banter with one another.

HFR cabinet A storage area for film or tape to be *held for release.*

I&I Script symbol for *introduce and interview.*

IDs Also called *sounders* or *logos,* IDs are brief musical passages used to identify an upcoming sports report, business report, or other feature.

IFB Abbreviation of *interrupted foldback,* a term for the miniaturized earphone worn by news reporters and anchors, and by sportscasters. Instructions and cues are given over the IFB by producers and directors.

inflection The alteration of the pitch or tone of the voice.

input selector switch Part of an audio console that allows more than one program input (several microphones, for example) to be fed selectively into the same preamp.

interdental A speech sound made with the tongue between the upper and lower teeth. The "th" sound in *thin* is interdental.

in the mud When the volume of sound going through an audio console is so weak that it barely moves the needle of the VU meter, the needle is said to be *in the mud.*

labial A labial speech sound makes primary use of the lips. The sound of the letter *p* is a labial sound.

labiodental A speech sound requiring the lower lip to be in proximity to the upper teeth. Labiodental sounds are associated with the letters *f* and *v.*

larynx The larynx connects the trachea (or windpipe) and the pharynx (the area between the mouth and the nasal passages) and contains the vocal folds.

lavaliere microphone A small microphone worn around the neck as a pendant or clipped to the dress, tie, or lapel of a performer.

lead-in, lead-out Terms that identify the opening and closing phrases of a taped or live report or that indicate the words used by a reporter to introduce and add a conclusion to a taped actuality or voicer.

LED Abbreviation of *light-emitting diode*, a means of indicating volume level through the activation of a series of lights.

liner notes Notes prepared by a radio station executive, from which a disc jockey will promote a contest, an upcoming feature, or another disc jockey.

lingua-alveolar The lingua-alveolar speech sounds are made with the tip of the tongue (or lingua) placed against the upper gum ridge (or alveolus). The sound of the letter *t* is lingua-alveolar.

linguadental A speech sound consisting of an interdental consonant.

linguapalatal A speech sound made with the tip of the tongue nearly touching the upper gum ridge. The sound made by the letter *r* is linguapalatal.

linguavelar The rear of the tongue is raised against the soft palate (or velum), and the tip of the tongue is lowered to the bottom of the mouth, as in sounding the letter *k*.

lip synch The synchronization of the movement of lips with the speech sounds of the performer. This is achieved automatically with video equipment and with single-system film.

logo An aural or visual symbol used to identify a program, product, company, or similar entity. The famous CBS "eye" is the logo for that network.

market The reception area of a radio or television station. Markets are classified as major, secondary, and smaller.

marks Television performers often are asked to *hit marks* as they move from one part of the studio or exterior location to another. The *marks* usually are indicated by small pieces of gaffer's tape on the floor or the ground.

master pot The *potentiometer* on an audio console, capable of raising and lowering simultaneously all sounds going through the board.

matte in To combine electronically two pictures on the same television screen without superimposing one over the other. See *chroma key.*

middle of the road A type of popular music characterized by songs and orchestrations of moderate volume, tempo, and performance style.

minicam A small, lightweight, portable television camera and its associated equipment.

minidoc A short documentary, usually produced as a series for radio and television news programs.

minus out When reporting live by way of a satellite, your voice can be eliminated (*minused out*) from your IFB (miniaturized earphone), so that you will not hear your voice on a one-and-one-half-second delay.

mixer An audio console.

moiré effect A wavering, shimmering effect on a television screen, caused by small checks or narrow stripes.

monitor pot Audio control rooms are equipped with monitor speakers that enable the audio operator to hear the material being broadcast or recorded; a monitor pot is provided on the audio console so that the operator can adjust the volume of sound coming from the monitor speaker without affecting the volume of sound being broadcast or recorded.

monitor speaker See *monitor pot.*

MOR Standard abbreviation for *middle-of-the-road* music. A station featuring such music is said to have an MOR format.

morgue A collection of magazine and newspaper clippings, organized by topic and used for background information for news stories and interviews.

MOS Script abbreviation for a *man-on-the-street* interview. Broadcasters continue to use this abbreviation, despite efforts to avoid gender references in most broadcast terminology.

music bed The musical background of a radio commercial, usually "laid down" before voices are added to it.

musical IDs Musical logos that identify a program or a program segment.

muting relays Devices that automatically cut off the sound from a control room monitor speaker when an announce mic in the room is opened.

nasals Sounds that employ nasal resonance, such as *m, n,* and *ng.*

O&O *Owned and operated.* Referring to radio or television stations owned and operated by a parent network.

out-cue The words that conclude a recorded and carted statement. The out-cue tells the engineer and the announcer when the carted segment has come to its conclusion.

package (1) A complete news report prepared by a field or special assignment reporter that needs only a lead-in by an anchor. (2) A series of programs marketed to television stations as a *package.*

pan pot *Panoramic potentiometer.* A rotating knob on a stereo audio console that allows the operator to shift the sound from one channel to another.

peripheral vision The ability to see out of the corner of the eyes—to see a cue, for example, without looking at the person throwing the cue.

personality An improperly used term for a

disc jockey, program hostess or host, or other popular entertainer. A *personage* is a person of notability; a *personality* is a pattern of behavior.

pharynx The area between the mouth and the nasal passages.

phonation The utterance of speech sounds; articulation breaks up these sounds into recognizable speech.

phone beat See *beat check.*

phoneme The smallest unit of speech sound by which we can distinguish one sound from another.

phone screener Usually a producer or assistant producer who receives telephone calls from listeners or viewers who want to talk with a program host or hostess. A screener attempts to eliminate calls from people who are obvious cranks, drunks, or frequent callers.

pickup pattern The three-dimensional area around a microphone within which sound is most faithfully picked up.

pitch The property of a tone that is determined by the frequency of vibration of the sound waves. In the human voice, the slower the vocal folds vibrate, the lower the pitch.

pitchman A type of announcer whose style is reminiscent of sideshow barkers and old-time medicine men.

play-by-play announcer The sports announcer who describes the action of a game.

plosive A speech sound manufactured by the sudden release of blocked-off air. In English, the plosives are *p, b, t, d, k,* and *g.*

polar pattern Same as *pickup pattern.*

popping The sound made when a plosive is spoken too close to a sensitive mic.

pot Abbreviation of *potentiometer,* the volume control knob on an audio console.

preamplifier An amplifier that boosts the

strength of an audio signal and sends it to the program amplifier.

pressure microphone A rugged professional microphone that features a molded diaphragm and wire coil, suspended in a magnetic field. Also called a *dynamic* microphone.

program amplifier An amplifier that collects, boosts, and sends sounds to a transmitter or tape recorder.

program log The log that lists all commercials, public-service announcements, and program material broadcast by a station.

promo Abbreviation for *promotion*. A station promo is any prepared spot that promotes viewing or listening to a station or a program broadcast by the station.

prompting device Any of several machines that unfold a script before a broadcast performer.

pronouncer A term used by news services to indicate the phoneticized pronunciation of a word or name. A pronouncer is sent to broadcast stations in this manner: "VANUATU (VAHN-OO-AH'-TOO)."

prop Abbreviation for *property*. Any article other than sets or costumes used in a television production.

PSA *Public-service announcement*. A radio or television announcement that promotes a charitable or other nonprofit cause.

rebeep Electronic beeping tones are placed on the audio track of a videotape for cuing. Eight beeps are laid down, one second apart. The last two seconds of the electronic leader are silent, and the director, responding to the rhythm of the eight beeps, allows two more seconds to elapse before giving the next instruction to the technical director. In recording sessions, mistakes are followed by rewinding the tape and rebeeping the leader that precedes the next take.

reslate In rewinding and rebeeping the start of a videotape, the take is also reslated; information about the material being taped—its title, the date of recording, the date of its intended showing, and the number of the take—is recorded visually on the videotape, either by using a plastic "blackboard" or electronically by means of a character generator.

ribbon microphone A sensitive, professional microphone that features a metallic ribbon between the poles of a magnet. Also referred to as a *velocity* mic.

rotating potentiometers The volume controls on an audio console. Many boards feature sliding vertical faders instead of rotating pots.

rotating spots Commercial announcements rotated to vary time of broadcast throughout the week.

running log In radio, the running log lists the times at which every program element will be broadcast.

SAT PIC Abbreviation for *satellite picture*. A view of the Earth's weather taken from a satellite.

segue In radio, playing two program elements back-to-back without overlap or pause. The first sound is faded out, and the second is immediately faded in.

semivowels Speech sounds similar to true vowel sounds in their resonance patterns. The consonants *w*, *r*, and *l* are the semivowels.

set In music announcing, the playing of two or more songs back to back without intervening commentary.

SFX Script symbol for *sound effects*.

sibilance The sound made by the fricatives *s*, *sh*, and sometimes *z*. Sibilance is a part of our spoken language; excessive sibilance is exaggerated by sensitive microphones.

simulcast The simultaneous broadcasting of the same program over an AM and an FM station, or over a radio and a television station.

slip start A method of starting a cued-up phonograph record; the turntable is rotating while the operator's hand holds the disc motionless. Releasing the disc constitutes a slip start.

slug commercial A hard-hitting commercial, usually characterized by high volume, rapid reading, and a frenetic delivery.

slug line The shortened or abbreviated title given to a news event for identification purposes.

SOT Script symbol for *sound on tape*.

sound In radio news, any recorded statement introduced as part of a news story. Sounds include actualities, wraps, sceners, and voicers.

sound bite A term used in broadcast journalism. It refers to a brief statement made on camera by someone other than station personnel. It is the equivalent of radio's *actuality*.

sounder In radio, a *sounder* is a short, recorded musical identification of a particular program element, such as a traffic or sports report, or weather news. Sounders are also referred to as *IDs* and *logos*.

spilling over Another expression for *bending the needle*.

stand-up A direct address made to a camera by a television reporter. *Stand-ups* may come at any time within a news package, and they are almost always used for the closing comments.

station ID *Station identification*

station logo A symbol, either aural or visual, by which a station identifies itself.

stylus Part of a tone arm pickup cartridge, the *needle*.

sweetening Electronically treating music, during recording and in postproduction, to improve the sound quality.

tag To tag is to make closing comments at the end of a scene or program segment.

take a level To speak into a microphone prior to broadcast or recording, enabling an audio engineer to adjust the volume control.

taking camera In a multiple-camera television production, the *taking camera* is that which, at a specific moment, is on the air.

tally light A red light mounted atop a television camera. When the light is on, it indicates the *taking camera*.

talk-back microphone The mic located in a control room that allows the audio operator to speak to people in other production areas, such as studios or newsrooms.

tape cart A cartridge of one-quarter-inch audiotape. It rewinds and recues itself.

tease A brief promotion of a program or of an upcoming segment of a program.

telegraphing movement The subtle indication by a television performer who is about to move, stand, or sit. Directors and camera operators need such warnings to follow movements effectively.

TelePrompTer The brand name of a particular television prompting device.

tight shot A close-up shot.

time-delay system An audiotape recorder used to delay that which is being broadcast on radio by approximately seven seconds; its purpose is to allow a program producer sufficient time to cut off the speaker in the event that profane or defamatory statements are made.

top 40 Descriptive of a radio station that rotates the top hits of the day, usually interspersed with golden oldies. Also called CHR, *contemporary hit radio.*

trachea The windpipe.

UPI Unifax A system that provides television stations with still photos for news broadcasts.

uplink A transmitter that sends a signal to a satellite. The *uplink* is often part of a mobile van.

urban contemporary A radio station music format that features music by Black artists.

variable equalizer A filter that enables an audio console operator to eliminate undesirable frequencies, such as those associated with a scratchy record.

velocity microphone Same as *ribbon microphone.*

velum The soft palate.

vertical fader The sliding lever on certain audio consoles that is moved up or down to raise or lower the volume of sound.

voicer A carted report from a radio news reporter.

VTR Abbreviation for *videotape recorder.*

VTR SOT Abbreviation for *videotape, sound on tape.*

VU meter A *volume unit meter,* part of an audio console that shows, by means of a swinging needle, the volume of sound going through the board.

wild spots A radio commercial guaranteed by the station to be played at some point within a designated block of time.

woodshedding The careful study, marking, and rehearsing of broadcast copy before performance.

wrap A recorded report from the field in which a radio news reporter provides a lead-in and a lead-out, *wrapped around* an actuality.

WX Script symbol for *weather report.*

INDEX

503

Diagnostic readings
 "Battle of Atterbury," 156–
  157, 162
 for medial *l*, 172
 for medial *t*, 165
 for sibilant *s*, 168
 for vowel distortion, 149–
  151
 "William and His Friends,"
  156, 162
Diction. *See* Articulation
Dictionary of Occupational Titles,
  245, 463–464
Diphthongs
 in American English, 114,
  124, 146, 153–155
 distortion of, 153
 French, 193–194
 German, 200
 Italian, 185
 phonetic transcription of,
  124–125, 153
 Spanish, 179–180
Director, sports, 377–378, 384,
  385–386, 387
Disc jockey (DJ)
 alternate terms for, 347
 practice as, 363–364
 working conditions of, 349–
  350, 354–358
Documentaries. *See* Feature
  reports
Donner, Stanley T., 22
Donut commercials, 83–84, 251,
  265
Double in, as editing instruction, 387–388
Double out, as editing instruction, 388
Drill material. *See* Practice
Dynamic (pressure) mi-
  crophone, 89–90, 91, 93
  (fig.), 94 (fig.), 95 (fig.)

Easy listening formula (ELF),
  308–309
Editing, of interviews, 305–306,
  315–318, 323–324
Education
 for announcing, 11–13
 areas recommended, 11–13
 as background, 11–12
 for classical music announcing, 364, 366
 for journalists, 11
 by trade schools, 13
 by universities and colleges,
  13
Electronic field production
  (EFP), 270
Electronic news gathering
  (ENG), 327, 328, 329, 336,
  341
Ellipses, in copy punctuation,
  31, 35
Emergency notification, 16–17
Employment, as announcer, 6–
  9, 362–363
Equipment, and announcer's
  job, 88–109. *See also* Audio
  console; Compact disc
  player; Microphones; Turntables
Ethnicity
 designations of, 241–244
 and pronouncing variations,
  149
Europa Yearbook, 279
Exercises
 for articulation of consonants,
  164–174
 for diphthongs, 153–155
 for excessive sibilance, 167–
  168
 for inflection, 140
 for nasality, 157–159
 for pitch, 139

 for resonance, 160–161
 for tempo, 142–143
 for vowel distortion, 149–153
 for weak medial *l*, 171–172
 for weak medial *t*, 165
Eyestrain, 38–39

Fact sheets, 251, 265–266, 268
Facts on File, 319
Fader, on audio console, 101,
  103–104, 105, 107
Familiar Quotations (Bartlett),
  230
Fang, Irving, 308–309
Feature reports, radio, 318–324
Federal Communications Com-
  mission, PSA definition by,
  266
Feedback, in sound system, 104
Field, depth of, 56
Field reporters, 300, 314–318
Field sceners, 315
Field voicers, 315–317
Foreign pronunciation, 175–219.
  See also Phonetic tran-
  scription
 Americanization of, 112, 175–
  178
 Chinese, 205–208
 and classical music announc-
  ing, 364–367
 in commerical copy, 214–219
 French, 189–197
 German, 197–204
 guidelines for, 176–178
 Italian, 183–189
 of non-Western languages,
  204–208
 practice copy, 208–219, 367–
  374
 references for, 118, 177
 Spanish, 178–183
 variations in, 178